The Crossroads
of
Liberalism

Croly, Weyl, Lippmann, and the Progressive Era

1900-1925

Charles Forcey

OXFORD   UNIVERSITY   PRESS

LONDON   OXFORD   NEW YORK

The author wishes to thank the Macmillan Company for permission to quote from Herbert Croly, *The Promise of American Life,* Herbert Croly, *Progressive Democracy,* Walter Weyl, *The New Democracy,* and Granville Hicks, *John Reed.* The *New Republic* has generously authorized extensive quotation from its columns. Parts of Chapters I, II, III, and VIII have previously been published in different form as "Croly and Nationalism," New Republic, CXXXI (November 22, 1954), "Leadership and 'Misrule by the People,'" *New Republic,* CXXXII (February 21, 1955), and "Walter Weyl and the Class War" in Harvey Goldberg (ed.), *American Radicals* (Monthly Review Press, 1957). The author is grateful for permission to reuse these materials.

To the memory of

HOWARD KENNEDY BEALE

PREFACE

This book grew out of my strong sense during World War II that the world we live in had become the plaything of madmen. While finishing my undergraduate work after the war, I began to learn something of the recent history of the world. The United States seemed to have played a central role in that history, particularly in those periods when it had Presidents of liberal persuasion. To my undergraduate mind "liberalism" was, of course, a good thing. But that only made it more difficult to explain the fearsome tragedies that had overtaken America and the world when liberals were in power. One war had ended in the bitter frustrations of Versailles, the other in the barbarism of Hiroshima and Nagasaki. Though much of this could be blamed on illiberal forces in America and elsewhere, the excuse merely led to further questions. Why had the liberals had so little control over events? Were there fatal flaws in liberalism itself?

My first impulse, which turned out to be an enduring one, was to seek an answer to such questions in the work of men who had faced them before. This took me back to the early decades of the century when, so it seemed to me, most of our chronic problems were still new enough to invite uninhibited speculation. I wanted men who had been neither too close to affairs to think nor too far from them to care. Soon I settled on three political journalists of the progressive era, Herbert Croly, Walter Weyl, and Walter Lippmann. They had a reputation for being both advanced and influential in their thinking. It was said that they had had more than a little to do with some of the policies of Theodore Roosevelt and Woodrow Wilson. And they had founded in 1914 a progressive journal of opinion called the *New Republic*. The magazine provided them, as it would the later historian, with a convenient medium for exploring some of the dilemmas of liberalism.

What follows is an analysis of the successes and failures of the three intellectuals, working at first separately and then together on their magazine, in adapting American liberalism to modern conditions. Themselves middle class in background and deeply committed to the progressive movement, they tried to prove that both prosperity and freedom in a capitalistic democracy could be preserved by a reformist middle class. The rise and decline of their dreams in an era that mingled sublime progress with bloody carnage has a certain poignancy today.

Much of the interest of Croly, Weyl, and Lippmann arises from their closeness to Roosevelt and Wilson. I have tried in the following pages to weigh the relationship between the "men of ideas" and the "men of power," and to suggest the circumstances under which the relationship remains most fruitful. The experience of various "brain trusters" with Franklin Roosevelt in the 'thirties has kept the problem a hardy perennial. Nor have American intellectuals in recent years been shy about flocking to the standards of at least two liberal leaders.

The careers of the three intellectuals have given me a chance to touch on other matters that need only a brief mention here. Since all three men were pragmatists, their speculations allow some treatment of the viability of pragmatism as a philosophy for democratic government. Led by Croly, they also believed that nationalism might be made the binding force behind middle-class reform. Here they confronted directly that peculiarly twentieth-century dilemma: how nationalism with all its demonstrable power can be made to work for good within the framework of democratic practice and ideals. And since Croly and many of the men around him were also distinctively cultural nationalists, the book touches on the fate of cultural aspirations within a modern mass society. Finally, as supporters first of Roosevelt and then of Wilson during World War I, the three writers worked at the vortex of the great controversy between those who would make power and those who would make democratic persuasion the ruling force in world politics. This question, like the others, is still much with us today, though the replacement of the old "balance of power" with the present "balance of terror" leaves us none of the margin for error that Croly, Weyl, and Lippmann enjoyed.

A brilliant course taught by Professor Eric F. Goldman at Princeton University first put me on the trail of Croly, Weyl, and Lippmann. His own work on the progressive era plus generously given encouragement have helped me greatly. I am similarly indebted to Professor Arthur S. Link, who was then (and is now) also at Princeton. A further acknowledgment of his aid will be found in my essay on sources. Professor Richard Hofstadter of Columbia University saw my study of the *New Republic* men through its initial stages. His teaching and writing about progressivism have provided much of the framework for the story that follows. He also read with great patience and perception a draft of this book that preceded the one here printed. The late Professor Howard K. Beale guided my doctoral work at the University of Wisconsin. It is not too much to say that he gave his life to his students. His standards for the writing of history were severe, but not so the spirit with which he helped his students toward them. Though he read none of the later versions of this book, the spell of his discerning eye has hovered over every page of it.

Several people who play a part in the story that follows helped me greatly. Mrs. Walter E. Weyl gave me complete access to her husband's invaluable diaries and miscellaneous papers. My talks with her about Walter Weyl and his colleagues on the *New Republic* were wonderfully helpful, and her reading of an early draft of the chapter on her husband caught several errors. Justice Felix Frankfurter took time out several years ago from a very busy schedule to grant me an interview. He compounded his generosity by giving a critical reading to the first six chapters of a draft of this book. Judge

Learned Hand also talked to me on two occasions about his friends on the *New Republic,* and my note on sources records a further indebtedness to him. He too read with a sharp but humorously benign eye an earlier account of Croly's career and of Croly's (and his own) relationship to Theodore Roosevelt. Sir Norman Angell has also read one of the drafts of my manuscript. His very shrewd suggestions brought about a definite shift in the focus of the final version.

Several personal friends have read this book in one or another of its earlier incarnations. They will forgive me if, counting the affection I feel toward them the sufficient token of my thanks, I merely list them here: Mr. Hamilton Cottier, Professor Louis Filler, Professor Warren Susman, and Professor Charles Vevier. Since none of the people I have mentioned in this preface have seen the book in its present form, none of them have any responsibility for errors of fact or perversities of interpretation.

In 1957 the William A. Dunning Fund of the History Department of Columbia University helped me with a grant for typing services, for which I am grateful. And I cannot close without a word of thanks to the many students I have had during the past eight years. They have shared and helped more than they know in the writing of each word of this book.

Had my friend Howard Beale lived I intended to dedicate this book jointly to him and my wife, Pamela Cottier Forcey. Neither would have forgiven the exclusion of the other, and both would have been right. But Pam well knows the dimensions of my gratitude.

CHARLES FORCEY

New York, New York
December 1960

CONTENTS

BOOK III. THE DECLINE OF THE NEW LIBERALISM

INTRODUCTION

The United States has ever been a land that loved the "new," never more so than in the twentieth century. Political sloganeers in particular have battened on the charms of novelty. During the progressive era* of the early 1900's, publicists and politicians appealed to voters with a host of novel programs— the "New Nationalism," the "New Freedom," even the "New Federalism" and the "New Individualism." A later reform era called forth, of course, the "New Deal." More recently the search for novelty has reached a delightful climax in that contradiction in terms, the "New Conservatism." And in the presidential campaign of 1960 the country was asked, though not for the first time, to rally to the challenge of a "New Frontier." Astonishingly absent from the array, however, has been anything called the "New Liberalism." But that is what this book is about.

American liberalism in the twentieth century has undergone a significant transformation. At the cost of considerable semantic confusion, the old nineteenth-century liberalism of individual rights and laissez faire has gradually given way to a different pattern of thought that also claims the name of liberalism. The claim gains substance from the fact that the older liberalism has become the ideological bastion of conservative defenders of established privilege, of men without that faith in human mutability and social progress so central to the earlier doctrine. A measure of the success of the new

---

* The word "progressive" where it is used to designate the general reform movement of the time or its members is rendered throughout the book without capitalization. This is necessary to distinguish the general movement from that part of it that emerged in 1912 as Theodore Roosevelt's Progressive party.

creed in usurping the old name appeared in the amazement that once greeted the late Robert A. Taft's description of himself as a liberal. Actually, in the nineteenth-century sense of the term, the Senator spoke with his usual semantic precision.

With the easy alchemy of all ideology the "new liberalism" has reworked the elements of the old faith into modern coinage. The earlier emphasis on individualism has been replaced by a concern for individuality, a desire to resist the conformity exacted by an ever more integrated technological society. Equality has been expanded to mean not merely formal equality before the law but also social, religious, and racial equality insured by considerable legal coercion. Liberty has been redefined through a total social view that comprehends how much one man's liberty may be another's bondage. The new liberalism, in sum, has turned away from a dream of automatic progress by the free-wheeling exercise of individual rights to a conviction that only the conscious, co-operative use of governmental power can bring reform.

The new liberalism had its first real beginnings in the minds of certain publicists and politicians of the progressive era. While some of its aspects had been anticipated earlier by men like Edward Bellamy and Lester Ward, the creed first enjoyed a widespread hearing and partial practice while the progressive era was at its height from 1910 to 1917. As such the era marked the crossroads of liberalism, that turning point where two divergent emphases began to emerge within the common liberal faith. Herbert Croly, Walter Weyl, and Walter Lippmann were leaders among the men who sought to move liberalism in the new direction.

The three publicists were parts and products of the progressive movement, as were their heroes Theodore Roosevelt and Woodrow Wilson. To understand these men and their ideas requires some knowledge of the progressive movement. That movement can best be understood if placed in a certain perspective.

The era in its full sweep from about 1902 to 1917 has been much studied by historians. For the most part, however, the recent ones have looked at it from the perspective of the depression 'thirties. Their approach has been gingerly, even on occasion irritable. They have considered the New Deal era and the Populist uprising of the late nineteenth century to be the norm for American reform movements. In such a light the progressive era has seemed unique and rather baffling.

Both the New Deal and the Populist movements revealed a direct and satisfying correspondence between economic grievance and reformist impulse. The coincidence seemed particularly striking to the dominant school of interpretation among historians of the past generation, that of an economic interpretation as outlined by Charles A. Beard. But the Beardians—I might say, "we Beardians," for I am a bludgeoned but essentially unbending disciple—have had trouble with the progressive movement. How, we have asked again and again, could so vast a reform crusade get underway in a time of great prosperity? Business was booming in the early 1900's. The farmers were happily (if unknowingly) building up fat "base years" for later parity payments. Even the workers and their labor movement were doing about as well as could be expected in a strongly capitalistic society. How then progressivism?

Many historians have answered the question by pretending that the progressive movement didn't really happen, or, if it did, that it didn't accomplish much. More recently they have delved into the mysteries of such things as "Reform Darwinism" and "status revolutions" to search out subtler and often sounder explanations. As a result we fairly well know what the progressive movement was about and why it happened.

Even so, such explanations become more meaningful if placed in the perspective not of Populism and the New Deal but in one familiar to older historians, of the whole history of American reform movements. We then find that the rise and fall of reform sentiment in the United States has followed a recurring pattern. Each wave of reform has run its course at intervals of twenty years or so since the founding of the republic. First came the Jeffersonians in the early 1800's, then the Jacksonians in the late 1820's and early 1830's, the Republicans of the 1850's, the Liberal Republicans of the 1870's, the tariff-civil service-trust reformers around 1890, and so on into the twentieth century. The pattern has had a certain momentum of its own in terms of the shifting moods of the populace. Each reform movement has usually begun with a prolonged period of agitation and protest at the state and local levels; then the new issues have been dramatized nationally by some dominant political figure; then, seemingly inevitably, there comes a slackening of public interest followed by a period of reaction and the undoing, usually by indirection, of most of the reforms.

This broader perspective relieves the progressive movement of much of its mystery. The absence of a major depression to spur on the reforming hosts becomes not an enigma but the essence of the normal pattern. All of the earlier reform movements, with the exception of Populism, began and waxed strong in times of prosperity. In fact, there is good reason to believe that the depressions of the nineteenth century either stifled reform movements or swept them in contrary directions. This explains in part why Populism, which had it origins in the agricultural depression of the late 1880's, lost its momentum after 1893 when depression hit the rest of the country. Though the depression stirred the worst-hit farmers and many workers to further reform efforts, it brought a closing of ranks among other Americans. Without middle-class support in 1896, William Jennings Bryan, the Populist-Democratic candidate, was left to writhe upon his cross of gold.

The same perspective serves to turn the usual interpretations of the New Deal upside down. Instead of the crash of 1929 being a cause of the supposedly radical New Deal, it may well explain the remarkable conservatism of that movement in the face of unprecedented opportunities for reform. Another reform movement, according to our pattern, was due in the

1930's. It had long been brewing in the states and cities, not to mention the (as usual) prematurely impoverished farm belt. Yet Franklin Roosevelt in the election of 1932 outdid Hoover in conservative promises to reduce government spending, get the government out of business, and return the country to well-tried ways. What else but the fears roused in the articulate classes by the depression can explain this remarkable conservatism in so acute a politician? How else can we understand the extreme reluctance of Roosevelt and his advisers after the crisis of 1933 to move from recovery measures to reform? Why, in fact, did Roosevelt feel "betrayed" when the propertied class with its Liberty League turned on him? And why was it not until 1935 that the New Deal began, in response to farm and labor pressures, to move hesitantly leftward?

The progressive movement suffered from no such debility. During the prosperity of the early 1900's middle-class men and women felt they could afford the luxury of protest and reform. Like most earlier American reform movements (including to a great extent even the Jacksonians), the progressive crusade was staunchly middle class. Studies that have been done of the movement's leadership reveal a startling picture. The men who took the first steps toward such far-reaching reforms as government regulation of industry or the taxation of incomes were anything but bushy-bearded radicals plotting the downfall of "free enterprise." Instead the great majority of progressive leaders were members of the American elite. In our equalitarian land this meant that they were white Protestants of North European ancestry, usually of the second or third generation of wealth. Most of them were college graduates and, as members of the professions or owners of businesses, had positions of social and economic independence. It is true, of course, that a considerable number of the Populist leaders were men of the same type, as were almost all of the New Dealers later. But progressive leaders were rarely snubbed and reviled as "traitors to their class." The middle class was with them. Not infrequently it was ahead of them.

The key question about progressivism, therefore, is: what got the American middle class of the early 1900's in such an uproar? The progressive movement, if not unique, was at least unusual. At the national level it waxed strong and stormy for at least fifteen years, and, if its first stirrings and later reverberations are taken into account, it lasted much longer. No other reform wave in American history matches it in longevity, and few exceed it in accomplishments.

Progressivism, nevertheless, shared with other reform movements certain characteristics that may be relevant. There has been a remarkable correspondence between major changes in the economic make-up of American society and the stirrings of the reform impulse. Such changes have brought with them both new evils and new needs, and the success of the reformer largely depends on how well in curing the one he can satisfy the other. Jeffersonianism was a direct response to Hamilton's centralization of the commercial capitalism of his day; Jacksonianism both resisted and hastened the emergence of the factory system; the 1850's saw the widespread application of steam power to industry, the 1870's the organization of country-wide businesses, and the 1890's the consolidations of these businesses into "trusts." Who knows, if I may skip a bit, what may be the response in the 1960's to our most recent wave of corporate mergers and to automation?

The further consolidation around 1900 of the earlier "trusts" by finance capitalists like J. P. Morgan tells much about the origins of progressivism. A few figures will show how swiftly the industrial empires of the great banking houses developed. In 1897 the total capitalization of all corporations individually valued at a million dollars or more came to only 170 millions. Three years later the same figure for total capitalization stood at five *billions*, and in 1904 at over twenty billions. So massive and swift a change in the control and ownership of the country's major industries did not go unnoticed. When Theodore Roosevelt suddenly launched an anti-trust suit in 1902 against the giant new Northern Securities Company, he gave the progressive movement its first national momentum. The "trust" question continued to be the pivotal issue for reformers as long as progressivism lasted.

Inflation has also had some part in bringing on many of our reform eras. But here we need only see how rising prices help explain both the decline of Populism and the rise of progressivism. For various reasons a rapid flow of gold into the economy took place after 1895. As a result, the prices farmers received for their crops rose rapidly, while their interest in Bryan's inflationary free-silver program declined precipitately. Having given Populism its *coup de grâce*, prices continued to rise steadily during the early 1900's, with only brief lulls in 1907 and 1914. Farmers benefited ever more handsomely. Workers, however, found food and other things more costly, while their wages remained remarkably sluggish. It was the great American middle class, nevertheless, that suffered, if not most, at least most loudly. The purchasing power of rents, interest, and dividends declined steadily, driving widows and orphans to their classic martyrdom. Professional men struggled to meet expenses by hiking their tradition-laden fees. Middle-class housewives found their market money running short together with their husbands' tempers. Such people, not yet accustomed to the inflation that two World Wars would bring, began to suspect that something was wrong somewhere.

Labor unions, whose membership total at the turn of the century was barely above the Civil War level, were much too weak to be blamed for such troubles. The unions, of course, *were* blamed by some, but to most progressives the real villains became the "trusts." And rightly so, at least in part, since monopolistic prices had much to do with the greater cost of many consumer goods. Middle-class progressives had many other reasons for fearing and disliking "Big Business," but the pinch on their pocketbooks helps explain the sustained volume of their protest. While disgruntled producers were usually the more effective force when it came to in-fighting in Congress, outraged consumers gave progressivism its wider base. The

persistent agitation of the trust question was in part a response
to the consumers' cry. Even the tariff gradually revived as an
issue, as consumers realized the relationship between its pro-
tective wall and the price level. Other progressive legislation,
such as the Pure Food and Drug Act, specifically reflected consumer pressure. Publicists like Croly, Weyl, and Lippmann
were to find the embattled consumer a promising recruit in
their campaign for a new liberalism.

The progressive movement, like earlier reform waves, may
have acquired some momentum from America's constantly
shifting patterns of social status. The many men of property
and prestige who became progressive leaders may have done
so in part because of their relative loss of importance in a
society dominated by Big Business. Owners of local factories
who had once been men of standing in their communities
found themselves being either absorbed or eliminated by the
"trusts" and replaced by "division managers" with much less
local prestige and power. Clergymen were not only losing the
Sunday faithful to secular distractions but also their positions
on the boards of universities and philanthropic institutions.
Small-town lawyers began to find that they were "*just* small-
town lawyers," as the more talented or aggressive members of
their profession organized huge "law factories" in the cities
to answer the omnivorous legal needs of nationwide corporations. Some groups such as architects, journalists, and university professors were rising in status, however; yet if anything
they were more reformist than their brethren on the down-
grade. Instead of stressing the nebulous and fairly constant
factor of status, it may be more sensible to recognize that all of
these groups, whether on the way up or down, had concrete
grievances against the new corporate plutocrats. The progressive era provided unusual opportunities for such men to make
good their protests.

Whatever its causes, the progressive movement did reflect
a massive shift in the mood of large numbers of middle-class

Americans. Within a few years their complacent satisfaction with McKinley Republicanism gave way to the strange mixture of guilt and moral fervor that was progressivism. This shift in mood had consequences that also became causes of the further growth and spread of the movement.

One of these was the emergence of a new generation of leaders in America. Since men are mortal, the passing of the old leaders and the rise of the new would have taken place anyway, but the shift to a reformist mood markedly accelerated the change-over. In city after city around the turn of the century reform candidates for mayor suddenly found once unbeatable political machines to be beatable. Toledo began to be swept clean by "Golden Rule" Jones, Cleveland by Thomas L. Johnson, St. Louis by Joseph W. Folk, New York City by Seth Low, to mention only the most prominent. In the states, too, reform governors like Robert M. La Follette of Wisconsin, Albert Baird Cummins of Iowa, Jeff Davis of Arkansas, James K. Vardaman of Mississippi, and W. R. Stubbs of Kansas overthrew the stalwart minions of railroads and other corporate interests. In New York the Spanish-American War hero Theodore Roosevelt established a moderately reformist record as governor before his election as Vice-President in 1900.

Roosevelt, when he succeeded to the Presidency after McKinley's assassination in 1901, became another force of great importance behind progressivism. Yet Roosevelt's progressivism was also to a great extent a consequence of the new mood. His record before 1902 was one of almost unrelieved conservatism. State and national bosses like Tom Platt and Mark Hanna who feared him did so not because of his opinions but because there was no telling where his pugnacious energy might lead him. They were reassured when the Rough Rider promised to continue "absolutely unbroken" the policies of President McKinley. But the rising winds of reform soon gave a new set to Roosevelt's political weathervane. In 1902 he started his anti-trust campaign and intervened forcefully in the great coal strike of the same year. For the Old Guard, ac-

customed to using the anti-trust laws against unions, not business, both actions came as a shock. The conservatives required
some time to recognize Roosevelt's genius for posing as a
militant progressive while picking his way cautiously down the
middle of the road.

Though men like Robert M. La Follette soon had cause
enough for questioning Roosevelt's sincerity and effectiveness
as a reformer, no one could question his effectiveness in foster-
ing the progressive spirit. The President loved to speak loudly
while wielding a small stick, to exhort the public to a mountain
top while privately negotiating a mole hill. But his exhorta-
tions helped make progressivism respectable. Whatever the
limitations of his concrete accomplishments, Roosevelt gave
the progressive movement a momentum that would over-
whelm the inflexibly conservative Taft and add much to the
success of Wilson.

Muckraking was another consequence of progressivism that
became a major cause of its further spread. The journalistic
movement got its name from the President himself on one of
those occasions when he was balancing his attacks on "male-
factors of great wealth" by berating the "lunatic fringe" among
the reformers. It became part of progressivism quite by accident, when *McClure's Magazine* in 1903 coincidentally published three articles of exposure in a single issue. The articles,
from the effective pens of Ida Tarbell, Lincoln Steffens, and
Ray Stannard Baker, created a sensation. Soon not only *Mc-
Clure's* but a score of other magazines were happily capital-
izing on the receptive mood of the public with ever more horrendous exposés. Standard Oil, the "Beef Trust," and the
"Money Trust," corruption in the cities and in labor unions,
patent medicines, and the white-slave traffic were but a few of
the subjects that were raked for all their muck before the hor-
rified eyes of the middle class.

Only a few years earlier similar articles had either been
ignored or swamped beneath piles of angry letters to the editor.
Yet the very enthusiasm of the public's response makes some-

thing of a mystery of the early demise of the muckraking movement. By 1909 many of the muckraking magazines were in trouble. Editors began to resign after quarrels with the magazines' owners. The exposés became milder and less numerous. Several of the magazines folded, while others changed hands and stopped muckraking. By 1913 only two or three were left as recognizable instruments of protest. Scholarly post-mortems have differed in weighing the effects of business pressure and of waning public interest in causing the death of the movement. But in any case its demise gave Croly, Weyl, and Lippmann a chance to experiment with a different kind of political journalism by founding the *New Republic* in 1914.

The ever stronger mood of protest stirred up by Roosevelt and the muckrakers had a variety of circumstances to feed upon. America's rise to world power and the growth of its empire in the late 1890's added to the sense of responsibility felt by many progressives. Since the ideals of American democracy were being forced on "little brown brothers" in the Philippines and elsewhere, simple logic required that they be kept as pristine as possible at home. The progressives' middle-class love for "efficiency" was much strengthened by the thought that only a strong, efficient nation could hope to defend such policies as the Monroe Doctrine and the "Open Door." The tying together of progressivism with national power had particular appeal for Roosevelt with his "big-stick" diplomacy. Herbert Croly did much to make it part of progressive ideology.

Progressives were also acutely conscious of the recent passing of the great American frontier. They assumed that the expanding frontier had long provided a "safety valve" for the discontents of more settled regions. Twentieth-century historians have shown this assumption to be largely false, but not soon enough to avert the great trauma the end of the frontier occasioned. Most progressives were sure that the United States was in for a long period of heightened social tension. The bloody strikes and wild agrarian crusades of the late nineteenth century were thought to be only the precursors of real class warfare in the future. Much of the urgency with which progressives fought for social justice sprang from their feeling that if their "constructive" solutions failed it would soon be too late.

The five-fold increase in union membership during the first decade of the twentieth century also had a profound impact on progressive thought. A few progressives saw this growth of the unions for what it was, the most hopeful alternative to the class warfare so many of them feared. But the great majority of progressives viewed the unions with suspicion or hostility. They believed that, once the trusts were broken up and regulated, there would be no need for such menacing aggregations of power. Even the very conservative A. F. L., in which most of the union growth was concentrated, remained on the fringe of progressive councils. Progressives tended to find the very much smaller though obstreperous I. W. W. more indicative of labor's true tendencies. Even men as sophisticated as Croly, Weyl, and Lippmann gave their new liberalism a much more radical cast after 1912 when the revolutionary I. W. W. moved east to lead the Lawrence and Paterson strikes.

The continued large-scale immigration of the early years of the century also twisted progressive thinking in odd directions. Prejudice against the immigrants had been common among middle-class Protestants at least since the 1840's. But the concentration among late nineteenth-century immigrants of Catholics and Jews from southern and central Europe intensified such feelings. Progressive crusades for "clean government" were not a little sullied by rancor against the foreign-born voters upon whom corrupt bosses based their power. Immigrants were also widely feared as revolutionaries, though revolution was the farthest thing from the minds of the peasants who made up most of the migration. Not surprisingly, the first determined efforts to get a general restriction of immigration came during the progressive era.

For all the extraneous forces that molded and pushed it along, progressivism continued to have a life and momentum of its own. Negatively it had been a reaction to Populism, more positively to McKinley Republicanism, and its own growth and success built up the eddies of a later reaction.

Progressivism had stored up great energies during its early stirrings in the murky depths of state and local politics. When Robert M. La Follette campaigned for the direct primary in Wisconsin and won the governorship from the Republican Old Guard, he created a progressive "machine" that continued to give him strong support for the rest of a long career. Though few other local reform organizations were as successful or long-lived as La Follette's, taken all together they had force enough to bridge the rift between state and national politics on which so many American reform movements have foundered.

In this respect it is possible to take a more sympathetic view of Theodore Roosevelt than I have so far or shall in later pages. Roosevelt became President when state and local reform movements were just getting underway. Not until his second term did men like La Follette move from their states to Congress to badger the Old Guard. If Roosevelt's accomplishments were meager in proportion to the noise he made, they were so in part because he had to work with party and congressional leaders inherited from the McKinley era.

Roosevelt's domestic actions were more precedent-setting than concretely productive. Though he had little desire to advance the cause of the unions, his intervention in the Coal Strike of 1902 initiated an era of at least benevolent neutrality on the part of the government in labor-management disputes. While his anti-trust prosecutions did little if anything to inhibit the growing concentration of corporate power and wealth, his Bureau of Corporations began the long process of trying to put the more uninhibited "trusts" under government control. The Elkins and Hepburn Acts were the first effective steps toward regulation of the railroads, though it was the latter law that led Senator La Follette to charge the President with settling willingly for "half a loaf." Roosevelt's acts to save large forest and mineral resources from wasteful exploitation gave new impetus to conservation, which stands, perhaps, as his most solid domestic achievement.

Though Roosevelt in foreign policy had a much freer hand, he was again more the trail-blazer than sound, creative leader. His rape of Panama in 1903, while hastening slightly the building of the isthmus canal, left a legacy of Latin American hostility that the United States has yet to overcome. His extension of the Monroe Doctrine to include America's unilateral policing of the Western Hemisphere reflected more his virile energies than any objective dangers that faced the country. The sending of the great "White Fleet" around the world in 1907 may have demonstrated the willingness of Americans to "fight for peace," but it also encouraged some Japanese to plan accommodating them at the earliest opportunity. Similarly, Roosevelt's interference in the Russo-Japanese War in Asia and the Moroccan crisis in Europe produced results quite contrary to his intentions. Such actions, however, did amount to a precocious effort on the part of an American President to make the weight of the United States felt in the world balance of power. Herbert Croly was to make much of this in elaborating the foreign policy necessary to a new liberalism.

Roosevelt had a genius for seeming the crusading innovator while actually moving with great caution among potentates both at home and abroad. His hand-picked successor, William Howard Taft, was somewhat more conservative and had none of the lusty Colonel's talent for self-dramatization. While Taft wallowed ineptly in the treacherous sands of American politics, progressivism continued to rise to new heights.

So inept was Taft that he managed to alienate the progressives of both parties while actually accumulating a more impressive record as reformer than Roosevelt. Though the Payne-Aldrich Tariff of 1910 failed to bring the reduction in rates Taft had promised, it did include a tax on corporation incomes of far-reaching significance. Taft also deserves much credit for the passage and ratification of the Sixteenth Amendment, which sanctioned an even more important tax on personal incomes. He used his executive powers more fully than Roosevelt to conserve natural resources, instituted about twice as many anti-trust prosecutions, and supported measures that put real teeth into the railroad laws passed earlier under Roosevelt. Even so, he fumbled and retreated enough on other issues to earn the conservative label, while Roosevelt, safely out of power, became ever more the hero of Republican progressives.

Taft's blunders forced on him an alliance with the Old Guard that brought progressivism to a major crossroads. Roosevelt, by desperately trying to keep the Republican insurgents in line, was himself driven steadily to the left and toward a break with Taft. The Democrats in view of Taft's increasing conservatism had little chance to outflank the Republicans from the right. The result was the three-cornered Presidential campaign of 1912, in which Taft held the right, while Roosevelt and his new Progressive party battled Wilson and the Democrats for the center and left.

Progressivism meanwhile had created a market in the magazines and among book publishers for intellectuals like Croly, Weyl, and Lippmann who were bent on rethinking the basic ideas of American democracy. The conjunction of the speculations of the intellectuals with the programmatic needs of the politicians brought forth two progressive philosophies for debate in 1912, Roosevelt's "New Nationalism" and Wilson's "New Freedom."

Of the two philosophies Wilson's had the lesser claim to being "new," since it was at best a modern re-statement of Jeffersonian ideals long central to American liberalism. Roosevelt's "New Nationalism," on the other hand, had definite novelty, for it sought to infuse liberalism with many of the ideas of Jefferson's fiercely conservative rival, Alexander Hamilton. Jefferson rather than Hamilton, of course, was the hero of most progressives in 1912, not only in their rhetoric but also in the guidelines of their chosen programs. While a few reformers, like Theodore Roosevelt and Albert J. Beveridge, had expressed private admiraiton for Hamilton over Jefferson, they had not emphasized the preference in public. Most progressives, men as diverse in origins and intentions as Louis Brandeis, Robert M. La Follette, William Jennings Bryan, or Woodrow Wilson, had clung fast to the equalitarian individualism of Thomas Jefferson. Roosevelt's campaign for the set of ideas that I have called the "new liberalism" amounted to a bold effort to bend progressive thought in a new direction.

William Allen White later dismissed the difference between the "New Nationalism" and the "New Freedom" as merely a matter of Tweedle-Dum and Tweedle-Dee. But for the men of the time, including White himself, the choice seemed real. When Croly, Weyl, Lippmann, and others stood with Roosevelt at Armageddon that year, they believed that the decision between Roosevelt's welfare nationalism and Wilson's individualistic freedom held the country's fate.

Thanks largely to the divided opposition, the Democrats and their refurbished Jeffersonian liberalism triumphed in 1912, but since then most of the victories have gone to the newer nationalistic strain. Even under Wilson, Croly and his friends could soon gleefully note that in effect if not in stated intention the President's domestic policies derived more from the New Nationalism than from the New Freedom. World War I, however, extended the older liberalism abroad in Wilson's peace program of free trade, self-determination of peoples, and a democratic League.

During the 'twenties both varieties of liberalism retreated amidst the reverberations of the debacle at Versailles. The older liberalism was even further weakened by the growing fondness of conservatives for such of its cherished ideals as weak government, decentralized power, and economic laissez faire. The 'thirties, of course, brought a revival and with it the culmination of the factional struggle within liberalism. Many "brain trusters" who turned against the New Deal did so out of loyalty to the older liberal creed, and Franklin Roosevelt himself, nurtured as he was on the prevailing ideology of the progressive era, frequently restrained his reforms out of deference to laissez-faire principles.

Yet in the end the actual needs of the depression 'thirties vanquished, at least for reformers, the remnants of the nineteenth-century creed. The triumphs of the "new liberalism" have been consolidated since by another war and another postwar decade. So complete has been the victory that recently liberal Eisenhower Republicans managed to meld within their "progressive conservative" faith not only most of the old liberalism but also, however reluctantly, much of the new. Many critics, for example, have had difficulty distinguishing so staunch an expositor of the "new conservatism" as Clinton Rossiter from liberals of the New Deal era. A half century later the essential philosophy of Herbert Croly's *The Promise of American Life* of 1909 has become the prevailing political faith of most Americans.

BOOK I

IDEAS IN THE MAKING

ONE

Herbert Croly: Nationalist Liberal

1900-1909

1. THREE INTELLECTUALS AND A POLITICIAN

"There will be just you three and I," wrote Theodore Roosevelt to Herbert Croly in November 1914. The former President was asking Croly, Walter Weyl, and Walter Lippmann for dinner and the night at his Oyster Bay home. On the appointed evening, the conversation between the politician and the three political writers flowed easily. They sat comfortably around the great hearth of the "Trophy Room," where for years Roosevelt had entertained an odd assortment of sportsmen, writers, artists, and politicians.

The Colonel, as always, dominated the talk, for he had the prestige of power, plus erudition and enthusiasm to match any of the others. Croly filled a quieter role, interjecting a diffident remark only where some turn of the discussion particularly stirred him. Weyl played his favorite part as conversational catalyst, now volubly outlining a theme for discussion, now quizzically listening, waiting for some chance to crystallize the argument with a phrase or quip. Lippmann, cherubically brilliant at twenty-five, could hardly have restrained his formidably didactic mind from now and then setting the others straight. Years later he still remembered how well it had all gone, with "Roosevelt fresh as a daisy at two in the morning, Walter Weyl as alert as ever, and Croly dozing in his chair."

The four men had much to talk about. Just two weeks

before, Croly, Weyl, and Lippmann had started publishing a strongly pro-Roosevelt journal of opinion, the *New Republic*. The second issue of the magazine a few days earlier had tried to show how Roosevelt's strong hand in the Presidency would have accomplished far more than had Woodrow Wilson's "timid neutrality" toward the war then raging in Europe. Roosevelt himself had just written a laudatory review of Croly's and Lippmann's most recent books, wherein they had carried further their long search for a coherent progressive philosophy. The *New Republic* and its editors were "in high favor with the Colonel."

The intimacy between the intellectuals and the politician was of long standing, for Roosevelt had been the focus for much of the publicists' thought and work. His ideas and personality had figured prominently in Croly's *The Promise of American Life*, Weyl's *The New Democracy*, and Lippmann's *A Preface to Politics*, books that had established the three as leading progressive theorists. Their closeness to Roosevelt during the Bull Moose campaign of 1912 had been heartening and exciting. Even after the Progressive party's defeat that year, much of their hope for influence on American life had remained bound up in Roosevelt's leadership. Their most recent books had been written and the *New Republic* founded in the confident faith that the Bull Moose "movement was established . . . [and] that Roosevelt would continue to lead it."

Yet, for all the amiability of their 1914 meeting, the publicists and the progressive leader were near a crisis in their relationship. The alarums of the war in Europe, the perils of Roosevelt's own political position, the evident decline of progressive sentiment in the recent congressional election, all were having an effect on the politician. Excited by the war, vitriolically critical of Wilson, fighting desperately to maintain his own influence in American politics, the Colonel had less patience than usual with the theories and distinctions of his philosophical friends.

The crisis came a month after the Oyster Bay gathering,

when the *New Republic* criticized one of Roosevelt's more intemperate attacks on Wilsonian policy. For the politician, the magazine's plea for fairness was too much. Charging the editors bitterly with "disloyalty," Roosevelt ended his cordial relations with the intellectuals.

Such a rupture with a chosen leader was a critical hazard of the role Croly, Weyl, and Lippmann chose to play in the nation's life. Living in a day when intellectuals had more to say in the land than usual, the three publicists hovered like moths on the flaming edges of power. Though writers, theorists, journalists first of all, they also sought a more direct influence than their published words could bring. But more than once they were to come away from the bright light of power both chastened and charred.

2. PORTRAIT OF A PUBLICIST

Herbert Croly's *The Promise of American Life* was widely, if erroneously, held to have had a profound influence on the dynamic Roosevelt. Published in 1909, the book was reputed to be the source of that philosophy of democratic nationalism with which a new Roosevelt blazed forth on the hustings in 1910. By the next year, Croly's close friend, Judge Learned Hand, only half jested when he proclaimed that the publicist was "becoming an authority." "I find that by actual mention of my intimacy with you, I acquire a distinct political significance," wrote Hand to Croly. The *American Magazine* merely reflected common opinion when, at the height of the 1912 campaign, it hailed Croly as "the man from whom Colonel Roosevelt got his 'New Nationalism.'"

Croly's reputation, however, rested on more than his purported impact on Roosevelt. Men whose own thought first took shape during the progressive period have strongly praised the publicist's contribution. Lippmann called his former associate "the first important political philosopher who ap-

peared in America in the twentieth century"; Alvin Johnson
grants Croly "the palm of the leadership in the philosophy of
the progressive movement"; Waldo Frank terms him "the
greatest publicist of his generation," while Felix Frankfurter
credits him with "the most powerful single contribution to
progressive thinking." Though all of these men spoke as onetime friends, still their very closeness to Croly emphasizes his
importance. For Croly stirred not only the minds of his own
generation, but, through men like Frank, Johnson, Lippmann,
and Frankfurter, those of later generations as well.

The mantle of such a renown sits strangely on Croly. He had
little of the public charm of men like William Allen White or
Lincoln Steffens, important political writers of the day among
whom he deserves to be numbered. Of moderate height, slight
of stature, Croly looked out on the world from behind a face
of considerable homeliness. His forehead was high and bulging; a pair of rimless glasses decorated his heavy nose. Soft-
spoken, deliberate, inordinately shy, he seemed incongruous
as the prophet of Roosevelt's virile nationalism.

Croly's shyness approached the pathological. Strangers who
had occasion to visit him often came away much bewildered
by his manner. "If the visitor were himself at all difficult,"
Edmund Wilson relates, "he would be likely to find the conversation subsiding into a discontinuous series of remarks
... to which Croly would utter responses more and more
fragmentary and more and more imperfectly audible." In time
the conversation would stop altogether; the air would become
"taut with panic," while Croly sat "absolutely motionless, his
eyes dropped on his hands, which would be clasped in his lap,
his face ... hostile and morose." After a "terrible silence," the
visitor would try a few more random remarks; then, still meeting no response, he would leave, much perplexed by the
personality of the man who had so important a reputation
among progressives.

Devastating to the stranger, the passivity of Croly's manner
affected all his works. Its reflection in his writing made his

success as a publicist and journalist a triumph of mind over manner. The written word came for Croly as laboriously as the spoken. Constructing sentences long and tortuously involved, he piled phrase upon phrase, clause upon clause, until often he left his reader in a state of bemused exasperation. Words like "regeneration," "fulfillment," "human deliverance" clogged the flow of his sentences and rang strange echoes in the secular air of the twentieth century. A friend, John Chamberlain, confessed that Croly's style was "in its rambling abstractedness—enough to keep a semanticist busier than a bird dog in an aviary."

The *New Republic* inevitably took on something of the aura of Croly's strange impassivity. Editors and visitors to the magazine's staff lunches found themselves talking in low tones in deference to the editor's near-whisper. Francis Hackett, a founding editor, later described Croly as "settling like a stone crab in the middle of a lively company."

Even the pages of the magazine bore the mark of Croly's manner. Never raucous or strident, rarely angry, the *New Republic* weighed the issues of the day with an omniscient calm that impressed some but irritated many others. "They give us sage advice with the air of people who have private information about the constitution of the universe," complained Harold Laski at a time when he was himself working for the magazine. "Their moral hyperbolas grow at times nauseating." Critics less friendly than Laski found comfort in the epigram, "Crolier than thou."

To strangers Croly's dedicated sincerity often seemed sanctimonious; to close friends Croly's shyness and air of consecration, while present and even dominant, were mingled with more beguiling traits. Though such friends were impressed by the publicist's "solemnity," his "anguished seriousness," his "morbid sensitivity," they also knew another man. They knew that away from strangers and large groups Croly could temper his diffidence with friendliness, that he was capable of humor and even a certain loquaciousness. They recognized the quality in the man that made him, when being most solemn about advising a politician like Roosevelt, dismiss his own portentousness with a saving "Me Big Injun."

Croly refused, furthermore, to run from his own unease. Despite the discomfort meeting people caused him, he insisted on entertaining and made his home in New York the center of an active social life. He had none of the asceticism that might have followed from his peculiarly thwarted personality. He liked good wines and food and smoked only the best cigars. He was devoted to the theater, played a strong game of tennis, and was addicted to both poker and bridge. In the twenties he thought it a matter of pleasure as well as of principle to violate the prohibition laws.

While Croly loved the good life and lived it, still there seemed always within him something that made him not quite part of the life around him. Yet the very strangeness of his personality explains part of the marked influence he had over fellow-progressives. His odd sensitivity won their loyalty in a way a more galvanic manner might not have done. When his friends among the reformers set him down as "authentically humble," "an absolutely candid and honest person," they merely made his outward shyness the sign of an inward integrity. Croly's yogi-like bearing became his own peculiar armor for a career that spanned three controversial decades.

3. A Man and a Movement

So outwardly unprepossessing a man as Croly could hardly have gained such a reputation among progressives had he not answered a real need in their movement. Without powerful friends or personal magnetism, without the activist's interest in concrete reform, Croly built his reputation largely upon a single book. When *The Promise of American Life* appeared in November 1909 it helped give a new direction and coherence to a movement already faltering.

The year 1909 marked a break in the progressive movement, a time when many felt American liberalism to be at a crossroads. With Roosevelt out of the presidency and off in Africa shooting lions, much of the fire and quite a bit of the wind of reform were gone. In Washington, Congress, even though called for a special tariff session by President Taft, took a temporary breather, enjoying its freedom from the endless lashing of presidential messages. Though insurgents and conservatives had already begun to joust over the Payne-Aldrich bill, the break between them was still not open. The western Republicans who were following Senator La Follette in the fight for a lower tariff operated informally, not yet the united junta that would split their party.

For the moment, too, the attitude of Roosevelt's heir to the presidency remained in doubt. Not until two weeks before Croly's book came out did Taft, by praising the Republicans' high tariff, make his conservatism clear. Even the first cracklings of the Pinchot-Ballinger controversy later in 1909 hardly foretold the storm of protest that would challenge the power of the arch-conservatives the next year.

Progressives everywhere in 1909 seemed to find themselves at a parting of the ways. With Roosevelt's dramatic leadership temporarily gone, with the political situation in flux, a veritable orgy of soul-searching took place.

The spectacle of the conservatives ramming the Payne tariff bill through the House that year, for instance, made Congressman George Norris ashamed that he was not more of a maverick. "I then and there concluded," he wrote, "that the institutions of democracy needed some reformation, and needed it badly." Out in Kansas, William Allen White decided the accomplishments of progressivism required appraisal. Asking friends throughout the country about the success of various reform laws, White compiled his findings in a breezy book called *The Old Order Changeth*, which tried to show where the progressive movement was tending. At about the same time, the muckraker, Lincoln Steffens, tiring of the sensationalism of the popular press, gave up an investigation he was doing of Congress. He resolved in 1909 to "do more than rake muck all . . . [his] life." Other journalists like Ida Tarbell and Ray Stannard Baker felt a similar revulsion. Miss Tarbell felt a need for something "positive," while Baker began looking "for a leader who could be trusted with the aspirations of an honestly progressive, and truly democratic movement."

Coming at such a time, Croly's book seemed destined for influence. Croly himself, in fact, sensed how the prevailing dissatisfaction might lead to new developments. With remarkable foresight—before Taft's failure as a progressive leader—Croly predicted the three-way split in the reform cause that took place in 1912.

"Reformers," he wrote in *The Promise of American Life*, "who believe reform to be a species of higher conservatism will be forced where they belong, into the ranks of the supporters and beneficiaries of the existing system." Beyond the Taft defection, Croly foresaw a schism among "sincere reformers" exactly like that of the Roosevelt and Wilson factions two years later. One of the reform groups would, like Wilson's in 1912, "stick faithfully . . . to the spirit of the true Jeffersonian faith." The second group, however, would follow Croly's own program. "It may discover," declared the publicist, "that the attempt to unite the Hamiltonian principle of national political responsibility and efficiency with a frank democratic purpose will give . . . a new power to democracy." Croly in 1909 both prophesied Roosevelt's New Nationalism and prepared anathema for Wilson's New Freedom.

How well Croly had called the turn soon became evident. Two months before Roosevelt returned from abroad to formulate his New Nationalism, more than two years before Woodrow Wilson campaigned for the presidency under the banner of the New Freedom, the editors of the *Outlook* hailed Croly and Wilson as the leading spokesmen for rival creeds. In April 1910 the magazine analyzed at length the way Croly's philosophy and that of the Princeton president led "in opposite directions." Two years before the event, the editors foresaw the conflict between the New Nationalism and the New Freedom, between the new liberalism and the old, that was to stir the country in 1912. Recognizing the Democrats as "temperamentally . . . the party of individual liberty," and the Republicans as "the party of social order," the *Outlook* thought it would be good for the United States if one party could present Wilson's "principle of individual liberty under government protection," and the other Croly's "principle of co-operative action for the common welfare." The magazine was sure that a "debate between these two principles of national action would be a great education . . . for America." Well might Learned Hand have concluded that his philosopher friend had become "quite the rage."

4. MIDDLE-CLASS INTELLECTUAL IN THE MAKING

A factor in the game of the president-makers by 1910, Croly had traveled a remarkably tortuous course to such eminence. Though he was forty years old when *The Promise of American Life* was published, his earlier career had not been particularly distinguished. While he had attended Harvard intermittently over a period of eleven years, he received no degree. Not until 1910 did Harvard make him a B.A., and then only in recognition of *The Promise of American Life.* From 1900 to 1906 he had been an editor on an important architectural magazine, the *Architectural Record,* but since his father had been a close associate of the owner of the magazine the position was something of a family sinecure. Neither his two rather prosaic books on architecture nor his writings for the *Architectural Record* gave much promise of the trenchant political critic to come.

Croly was in many ways typical of the progressive reformers of his generation. Born of a newspaper-and-magazine-editing family, he was a member of the upper middle class. As an editor himself, he belonged to the professions, not business. City-born and bred, living most of his life in New York, he, like most eastern progressives, saw national problems from the perspective of the metropolis. By taking a wealthy and "socially prominent" wife, he fulfilled Charles A. Beard's dictum that "a reform leader in the United States ... [had] better have money, or, next best, marry it."

Some things in Croly's background, however, set him off from other reformers. He was not, as were most progressive leaders, of native American stock. While descent from an Irish immigrant father and an English mother kept Croly close enough to the American Anglo-Saxon stereotype to make assimilation easy, still the elder Crolys' belated arrival in the land of promise may have had an effect on the son. Beyond saving the nationalism he preached from any breast-beating celebration of the American past, his family's consciousness of its English and Irish heritage helps explain Croly's own detachment, his peculiar capacity to look at the United States with half an alien's eye.

Both Croly and his parents before him, moreover, were relatively recent arrivals in the upper middle class. Croly had little of that long-established social status that cast a patrician glow over the thoughts of so many progressives. His father, David Goodman Croly, had started life in America as a silversmith's apprentice. Only a grind of debating societies, self-taught shorthand, and night schools won the elder Croly a reporting job, and even then it was a slow climb to posts as managing editor of the New York *World* and ultimately editor-in-chief of the New York *Daily Graphic*. Croly's mother, Jane Cunningham Croly, though born the genteel daughter of an English clergyman, also had had a struggle. Left almost penniless at twenty-five by her father's death, she made for herself a career in journalism that gave her substantial claim to being the first full-time newspaperwoman in America.

Based as it was upon wit and talent rather than inherited position, the Crolys' social status among the New York intellectuals might well have been transient. In the 1890's, for instance, with David Croly dead and the mother's earnings cut by old age, the family fell to a point where Jane Croly was reported by a newspaper as stranded destitute in England. While Harvard and a favorable marriage consolidated upper-middle-class status for the son, neither college nor marriage could give him the real security of deep roots and inherited wealth.

Born to parents of remarkable energy and talent, Croly could hardly avoid absorbing something of their powerful impress. He learned very early that society was something not merely to be lived in but to be reformed. His mother was an ardent feminist and, as editor of *Demorest's Monthly* and *Godey's Lady's Book*, delighted in her role as an English-woman preaching culture to a provincial America. The father's reform efforts ranged from attacks on Boss Tweed's Tammany machine to espousals of such bizarre causes as the eugenics experiments of the then flourishing Oneida Community. Growing up in a household that seemed always mobilized for one cause or another, Croly came naturally by his life-long confidence that the world might be changed by argument and effective exhortation.

The sources of Croly's intensely shy, oddly thwarted personality lie somewhere in the formative years that he spent with his strong-willed, energetic parents. While even a psychologist of the time would have hesitated to explain the mature Croly's peculiarities, the facts are suggestive. There was a certain tension in the relations of mother and son. Croly's friends later found him rather ashamed of the literary labors of the famed "Jenny June." Among her friends Mrs. Croly inspired more awe than affection; in her son it appears there was little of either.

Quite possibly, too, a certain neglect stunted Croly's emotional development. He was born the third of five children in 1869, at the height of his mother's career. During his infancy, three hours of Jane Croly's mornings were reserved for children and household; the rest of her day was spent at the office in work. "I always worked up to midnight and seldom put down my pen until two-o'clock," Mrs. Croly said later of her active years. A friend of the family noted that the intense activity of both parents "prevented them from enjoying the home circle to the extent that each of them desired." "Here, as in so many cases," he observed, "the individual was sacrificed for the benefit of the public."

Even when the Crolys were at home, their time was given less to their children than to a remarkably active social life. Meetings of women's clubs and other groups were often held in the Croly house near Washington Square. Mrs. Croly entertained at regular Sunday evening receptions that, one admirer has testified, were "as near to a salon after the traditional Parisian standards as any that America has known." Yet the mother's social success accentuated rather than relieved the diffidence of the son. Young Herbert's fate at such gatherings, a friend records, was to "suffer from shyness in the presence of the affectionate ladies until he could reach the portieres within which to wrap himself."

The effects of the relative neglect of Croly's early years were probably compounded by the later excessive attentions of an eccentric father. Most of Croly's teens were spent in intimate colloquy with the elder Croly. A man of strong principles and choleric prejudices, David Croly could so little accept the usual compromises of the newspaper world that his active career in journalism came to an end when he was forty-eight and his son only nine. A high-tariff, hard-money, anti-machine Irish Democrat, the father fought constantly with the owners of the various newspapers he edited. In 1872 he resigned as managing editor of the New York *World*, partly because the owners refused to join the then raging fight against Boss Tweed, partly because their support of the weak candidacy of Horace Greeley seemed to have helped re-elect the Republican President Grant. Six years later, similar quarrels with the owners of the New York *Daily Graphic* ended David Croly's last important post as an editor.

The irascible newspaperman turned then from office to home and made his young son a chief outlet for his energies. For eleven years, until the elder Croly's death in 1889, man and boy were as close as father and son could be. Half-bedeviled, half-inspired by a mind both erratic and obscure, the father planted ideas in the son that echoed far beyond the paternal grave. Croly himself acknowledged something of the debt when twenty years later he dedicated *The Promise of American Life* to his father's memory.

For fifteen years before his retirement, David Croly, along with his wife, had been a leading American prophet of Positivism, Auguste Comte's new religion of science. The French philosopher wanted to replace the worship of God by a "religion of humanity"; he hoped to resolve the conflict between Christianity and science by making science the heart of a religion in the Christian mold. Positivism, as its name implied, would end the ancient negative struggle between faith and reason; instead, religion cleansed of superstition would be fused with science to bring to reason a new beauty and a new strength.

So rational a religion appealed strongly to Herbert Croly's parents. Ardent reformers, they found in Comte's "altruistic teaching . . . the only remedy for the wrongs and sufferings of the world." Founding a society to spread the new faith, they became known among their friends in New York as Positivism's "chief promoters." Beginning in 1868 frequent meetings were held in the Croly home, where the initiates went through Positivism's peculiar ritual. When Herbert Croly was born the next year, he became, with symbolic propriety, the first child in the United States to be christened in the new "Religion of Humanity."

The christening was appropriate because the religion of humanity was something Herbert Croly never entirely abandoned; he returned again and again throughout his life to the lost hope of an early faith. Living close to his father for eleven years after the age of nine, the son inevitably absorbed a large

measure of the parental creed. "From my earliest years," wrote
Croly later, "it was his endeavor to teach me to understand and
believe in the religion of Auguste Comte. . . . Under the circumstances it was not strange that in time I dropped instinctively into his mode of thinking."

The father's strong obsession was not so strange, for Positivism played something of the role for late-nineteenth-century
reformers that transcendentalism had for an earlier generation. Later pragmatism would fill the same role for progressives. Herbert Croly, deeply influenced by his father, yet part
of the progressive era, later had constantly at war within him
the skepticism of pragmatism and the affirmation of Positivism. The product of one reform tradition, a prime mover in
another, Croly found himself caught between the inspiration
of his father's near-mysticism and the restraint of his own stern
realism. Out of the clash and conflict of the two creeds there
grew a tension of mind that was never completely resolved.

5. FROM POSITIVISM TO PRAGMATISM

When Herbert Croly went to Harvard in 1886 at the age of
seventeen, he moved from one world to another, almost from
one century to another. He left the Victorian moralism of his
mother and father for a life where new forces and ideas were
stirring. Recently revitalized by President Charles Eliot's new
elective system, Harvard had much to offer a young man so
comfortably middle class and competently intellectual as
Croly. Professors and students alike were feeling the excitement of Eliot's new dispensation. Changing rapidly itself,
Harvard in the 1880's could hardly fail to challenge Croly's
home-grown faith.

A true son of his father, Croly in 1886 had already decided
to major in philosophy, hoping some day to teach it. Philosophy at the time was Harvard's chief glory. William James,
turning away from experimental psychology, had become a

professor in the philosophy department a year before the freshman Croly's arrival. James had brought Josiah Royce to the
university several years earlier and had already begun to sharp-
en his own theory of pragmatism against the whetstone of
Royce's Hegelianism. George Santayana, in Germany in 1886,
soon returned to Harvard to add his particular luster to Croly's
lengthy and much-interrupted studies there. George Palmer,
an older man known more as teacher than scholar, shared with
William James the teaching of the freshman philosophy course
during Croly's first year.

So creative and persuasive a group of men could hardly help
but shake the positivist faith David Croly had planted so dil-
igently in his son. Croly's friends later gathered that at college
he had gone through "a profound spiritual crisis . . . in revolt
against Auguste Comte." Since the crisis involved a revolt
against the authority of the father as well as of the father's
faith, the psychological strains were bound to be severe.

Less than six weeks after his son had left for the university,
David Croly was writing: "My Dear Boy—You said something
about the divergence of my ideas from those of the philosophers whose works you are reading at college. Let me beg you
to form your own judgment on all the higher themes—religion
included—without any reference to what I have said." The
father's own faith was so strong, however, that he could not
resist a plea for at least the spirit of his teaching. "Do cultivate
all the religious emotions," David Croly continued. "Educate,
train every side of your mental and emotional nature."

Men who knew Croly afterwards recognized how deeply he
had taken his father's advice to "cultivate all the religious emotions," but the son soon put the formal creed of Positivism
behind him. "While I was at college," Croly wrote, "I was surrounded by other influences, and while I retained everything
that was positive and constructive in . . . [my father's] teaching,
I dropped the negative cloth in which it was shrouded." Croly
meant that he had stripped from his father's faith the denial of
God and Christ, what the son felt was a sterile dedication to a

purely scientific ideal. He retained throughout his life, however, David Croly's impulse toward altruism and religious
emotion.

Of the twenty-six courses Croly took during his four much-
interrupted years at Harvard from 1886 to 1897, ten were in
philosophy and three in the related field of religion. Significantly for his later work, he had but one course each in history,
politics, and economics. Though not all of his time was spent
in study (he later boasted to friends that he had "partly supported himself by playing poker"), obviously philosophy was
his major passion. In that subject he took his most concentrated
work from Josiah Royce and George Santayana.

Of all his teachers Royce seemed most likely to appeal to a
student of Croly's background and temperament. By the 'nineties the philosopher had become a leading prophet of that
sense of community in an "organic society" that underlay so
much of Croly's later thought. Royce, too, was deeply concerned with the relation between religion and philosophy, a
problem David Croly had driven close to his son's heart.
Royce's strong interest in reform, his marked patriotism, his
postulate of an idealist Absolute, all must have attracted a
young philosopher who sought certitude so fervently as Croly.
Yet for all the probabilities of appeal, Croly's three courses
with Royce produced no overt echoes in *The Promise of
American Life* or in other works. At most, Royce's teaching
seems to have given Croly enough sense of the philosophical
niceties to avoid any inadvertent Hegelianism in his own
writing.

The impact of professors on students is inevitably haphazard and indefinable, but in the case of George Santayana a
measure of direct influence on Croly is evident. Scattered references to the Spanish-American philosopher in Croly's writings and a more than coincidental similarity of thought indicate that Croly forged beyond the classroom to read and
ponder Santayana's works. Santayana was invoked, in fact, in
the last paragraph of *The Promise of American Life*, where

Croly brought to a climax his plea for "constructive individualism" to spark a program of "national regeneration." Quoting Santayana's judgment that "if a noble and civilized democracy is to subsist, the common citizen must be something of a saint and something of a hero," Croly, in the final words of his book, called upon his "exceptional fellow countrymen" to give the common citizen "acceptable examples of heroism and saintliness."

Croly's obligation to Santayana, however, went further than a borrowed phrase. The part of *Reason in Society* from which Croly quoted expressed a theory of politics much like his own. Santayana thought the ideal social order would be "a government of men of merit" bound together by a patriotic ideal. He named his society, rather sardonically, a "socialistic aristocracy." Both Croly and Santayana wanted rule by a non-hereditary elite, an emphasis on motives of virtue and patriotism over those of profit, and a wide and even sharing of wealth. The power of their elite was to rest on excellent example rather than on riches or inherited privilege. While Croly argued that all men in the country would benefit from his nationalized society, Santayana, more candid, conceded that "the glory and perfection of the state ... would not be a benefit to anyone who was not in some degree a philosopher and a poet."

Santayana, poet, philosopher, student of the arts, was part of the rather rarefied atmosphere out of which came *The Promise of American Life*. Croly's closeness to Santayana helps explain why the publicist later often seemed alien to the progressive movement with its (to the aristocrat) grubby passions for politics, sanitation, and pure drugs. Santayana fortified in Croly an inborn distrust of mass culture and politics, a distrust that lingered until the progressive movement itself radically changed Herbert Croly. Croly was always, however, concerned with the welfare of all the people—rich and poor, ignorant and wise alike—a catholicity of taste Santayana would have thought rather sentimental.

Yet neither Royce's idealism nor Santayana's naturalism was the real solvent for Croly's baptismal positivism. Instead, Croly took the pragmatism of William James as his creed. Whether the young student learned pragmatism from James or not remains uncertain, for nowhere in his writing did Croly quote or refer to James or use such phrases as "the will to believe" or "a moral equivalent for war" that were favorites with other publicists of the progressive era. The possibility of direct influence, nevertheless, is strong, for James had been turning the main points of pragmatism over in his mind for at least a decade before Croly enrolled for his "Logic and Psychology" in the spring term of 1887. Croly at the time was probably receptive to new ideas, since only the term before Palmer's "History of Philosophy" had created that strong "divergence" between his father's ideas and those Croly was absorbing at college. Since James's own pragmatism had developed in part from a revolt against positivism, the persuasive teacher and his perplexed student may have enjoyed a meeting of minds.

Pragmatism was Croly's guiding philosophy during his most active years as publicist and editor. Acquired early in life, it was later fortified and refined by the ideas of John Dewey, who became a frequent contributor to the *New Republic*. Croly's friends testified to the impact of pragmatism on him. One described him as "adept in the philosophy of William James and John Dewey"; another saw Croly as "*en rapport* with all the pragmatists . . . had to say about the nature of conduct"; still another spoke of Croly's "apparent dedication to the Pragmatism of John Dewey." "At a time when John Dewey was still struggling with . . . his . . . pragmatic philosophy," wrote John Chamberlain, "Herbert Croly was already a full-fledged instrumentalist."

Pragmatism, in fact, was so much in the air during the years Croly worked out his political philosophy that direct issue from James or Dewey was unnecessary. Dating his own career as reformer from 1890, Croly like other reformers found himself challenging a system that defended itself by ideals ostensibly pure and eternal. Inevitably, reformers like Croly found pragmatism a handy tool for testing American ideals by their results, results the muckrakers soon showed to be far from ideal. "We were all Deweyites before we read Dewey," J. Allen Smith said of himself and fellow-progressives. The admission could as easily have been Croly's.

The fact of Croly's pragmatism needs to be emphasized, for his thinking had so much of the abstract quality of an earlier day that its pragmatic content has occasionally been missed or denied. Yet for a man as well trained in technical philosophy as Croly, the pragmatic tenor of his thought was hardly accidental or unconscious. Again and again when Croly took up critical questions in his political theory he resolved them in pragmatic fashion. He described the state, for instance, not as some abstract entity to be worshipped, but instead as the result of the actions of a strong, active, national democracy. "The state," he wrote, "lives and grows by what it does rather than by what it is." Even Croly's ideal of nationalism, which along with democracy he proposed as a guide for reform, was not an absolute. "There is nothing final about the creed," he said in the closing pages of *The Promise of American Life.* "It must be modified in order to define new experiences and renewed to meet unforeseen emergencies. But . . . [the creed] should grow, just in so far as the enterprise itself makes new conquests and unfolds new aspects of the truth."

Having committed himself to pragmatism at the very start of his publicist career, Croly in time came to see the philosophy as bound up with all his other hopes for progressivism. When in 1915 the American reform movement seemed threatened by the backlash of the First World War, he approved a *New Republic* editorial that made the crisis "the first real test of . . . our whole American pragmatic philosophy." "We can put our ideals behind us and worship them," said Croly's magazine, "or we can put them ahead of us and struggle toward them." Americans had to make their choice "between an old immutable idealism and a new experimental idealism."

6. THE GHOST OF WILBUR LITTLETON

In the first years of the century Croly showed few outward signs of the serious purpose that eventually made him so important a spokesman for the progressive movement. On the surface, he seemed nothing more than an ordinary upper-middle-class man of letters. His work on the monthly *Architectural Record* left him ample leisure. He indulged to the full his passions for tennis, the theater, the novels of Henry James, and poker. During the summers, he broke away from New York for lengthy vacations at his substantial country home in the artists' colony of Cornish, New Hampshire. Remote from the then much-agitated evils of slum, sweatshop, and political corruption, Croly led a model life of cultured, urban insularity. Out of just such a life, however, came one of the strongest and, philosophically, most radical voices of the progressive era.

What drove Croly to move outside his leisured, cultivated circle was a problem that lay at the very center of his work on the *Architectural Record*—the dilemma of the artist or intellectual in an industrial society. The problem was first brought home to him, oddly enough, by the reading of a rather bad novel, Judge Robert Grant's *Unleavened Bread*. Coming upon the book in 1900, Croly was impressed by the way Grant had dramatized an apparent contradiction between ordinary American democratic ideals and those an artist needed to do his best work. This contradiction "struck me as deplorable," wrote Croly some ten years later, when explaining the inspiration of *The Promise of American Life*, "and I began to consider [its] . . . origin and meaning . . . and the best method of overcoming it."

The moral of Grant's tale rested in the fate of its hero, Wilbur Littleton, a stereotype of the dedicated architect caught in the trammels of a business world. Littleton, Judge Grant assured his readers, was a designer of genius "who abhorred claptrap and specious effects and aimed at high standards of artistic expression." He had a wife, however, who thought Wilbur would profit more from designing elegant Fifth Avenue mansions than the schools and churches that were his particular passion. The conflict between husband and wife reached its end only when Littleton, having clung to his ideals through horrendous trials and tribulations, worked himself to death trying to satisfy both his wife's ambition and his own.

To Croly, Wilbur Littleton's saga seemed a symbol for the central tragedy of American life. For Littleton had been destroyed not so much by his scheming wife as by America's most cherished "patriotic formulas." The United States, argued Croly, was a country where empty individualism had run riot, where individual merit was measured only in cash, where the whole meaning of society was defined only negatively in terms of proscriptive rights. Littleton, like other American artists, had had to fight for his art without the aid of a "well-domesticated tradition that would . . . make him build better than he knew."

Ignored though it has been, Croly's vital concern for the intellectual in America goes far toward explaining both the origin and the essential meaning of *The Promise of American Life*. Grant's specter of the disenchanted architect wrenched Croly from his preoccupation with art and made him seek in the progressive movement some expiation of Wilbur Littleton's martyrdom.

Croly's cultural motive, furthermore, gave a particular cast to the new liberalism he hoped to substitute for the prevailing American liberal tradition. Though Croly became an ardent nationalist, though he became the reputed author of Theodore Roosevelt's New Nationalism, still his patriotic faith had rather different origins from that of the blood-and-thunder hero of the Spanish-American War. Croly emphasized the cultural aspects of nationalism, not the military. His plea for nationalism was the call of a disenchanted intellectual, not the battle cry of a frustrated militarist and jingo.

When Croly first roughed out the themes of his nationalistic

philosophy in the *Architectural Record* in 1901, he showed
the rather subtle nature of his cultural concern. Surveying the
problems of contemporary architects, Croly did not complain
that American designers were neglected by the public. Instead
he argued that American architects, grinding out plans from
offices "organized like any other great business concern," were
too much flattered by their public; they were if anything "all
too prosperous." What ruined architecture in the United
States was not neglect or poverty but rather the need constantly
to struggle against a Philistine culture.

In seeking a cure for America's blighted culture Croly re-
sorted to the dangerous device of analogy. He projected a
parallel between the United States and earlier great cultures
where art had flourished. He wondered how America might
capture the glories of "periclean Athens ... [or] the north
Italian cities of the fifteenth century, ... [where] the peoples
themselves were artistically gifted ... [and] spent themselves
in lives of the most violent and exciting social, political and
military activity." "None of ... [these] conditions," said Croly
in 1901, "exist at the present time in the United States."

Croly granted the difficulties of infusing a huge and sprawl-
ing country like the United States with the spirit of a city-state
of ancient Greece or Renaissance Italy. Still he thought the
modern sentiment of nationalism might be made to approximate such a spirit. "The modern democratic community,"
he wrote, "is a new thing under the sun. Its potentialities are
only beginning to be vaguely foreshadowed, ... [but] if such
an enlarged community can ever get fairly underway, if its
members can ever become closely united by some dominant
and guiding tradition, there is no telling what may become of
it." In *The Promise of American Life* democratic nationalism
became that "dominant and guiding tradition" under which
all American art and life might flower.

The problem Croly hoped to resolve through nationalism
was one that remains still much alive in American life. Croly
was protesting against the anonymous standardization and

specialization of an industrial society. With a middle-class sensitivity to questions of status, he felt that intellectuals were becoming mere specialists, mere cogs in the mechanism of an ever-growing industrial machine. "Modern industry is too entirely mechanical," he wrote in 1901, "modern culture too bookish, intellectual and self-conscious." The problem Croly faced, if not the solution he proposed, has had more recent echoes in the books of C. Wright Mills and David Riesman.

"The idea, when it came to me, seemed to have some power," wrote Croly in 1909 of the central theme of his book. He felt that he had been able to develop and express the theme "without tripping over any apparently dangerous obstacles." Yet even in its inception Croly's thought suffered from a serious schism, which lay between the cultural and political aspects of his nationalism. He drew too easy an analogy between the golden ages of Greece and Italy and the renaissance he desired for modern America. Even if the communal spirit of Athens and Florence helped explain their glory, there was no certainty that nationalism would work a similar miracle in a twentieth-century republic. If the analogy is taken seriously, moreover, further problems arise, problems that much be-clouded Croly's future. The patriotic *élan* of the old city-states had moved beyond mere civic pride to a vitriolic chauvinism that ultimately brought their destruction in war. The widening of Croly's own horizons as he worked out his ideas for his book suggests that his patriotic vision may have had a similar expansive tendency. By making nationalism his creed Croly had plunged into the stream of the most violent modern emotion. How well the primly impassive publicist would fare there only his book and the publicist career it led to could tell.

7. "THE PROMISE OF AMERICAN LIFE"

"Your book came today, but, of course, I have not yet had time even to look into it," wrote Judge Learned Hand to Croly early in November 1909. "I look forward to the book as a sort of bromo-seltzer, to help clear the head." A massive, closely reasoned work of more than four hundred and fifty pages, Croly's *The Promise of American Life* was destined to produce more cerebral anguish than relief. Judge Hand praised it mightily a month later, but he could hardly have found it the effervescent tonic he had anticipated.

The uncompromising turgidity of Croly's argument mattered little. Though he hoped to convert a nation to nationalism, his own notion of political dynamics required no popular political tract. Without blush or apology, Croly addressed himself to his "exceptional fellow-countrymen," to the Wilbur Littletons of the land who might both appreciate and practice a philosophy so carefully argued.

As a consistent nationalist, however, Croly opened his book by appealing not to the self-interest of the "superior few," but to their patriotism. Croly put off the plight of America's Wilbur Littletons until the end of the book; he began with a picture of America as unfulfilled promise. Taking the protests of muckrakers, insurgents, and reformers as his index, Croly argued that America's day of optimistic, automatic progress was over; the stern challenges of a new century had to be faced. With its frontier gone and its surrounding oceans no longer guarantees of security, the United States had lost its license for political innocence. If the superior men of the country were to save themselves, they had to save America first.

Though written in a day of rising prosperity when the country still soared on the moral buoyancy of Theodore Roosevelt's Presidency, *The Promise of American Life* was strangely filled with a sense of crisis. From Croly's suggestion near the beginning that concentrated wealth might end America's historic promise to his warning near the end that democracy itself might disappear in a maelstrom of class warfare, the book echoed with grim forebodings. These were no mere literary device. Repeatedly Croly insisted that the United States in 1909 faced a national crisis as extreme as that before the Civil War.

Croly's fear reflected in part the common anxiety of a middle class that in the early 1900's felt itself threatened by radicals and reactionaries on either side. But, for Croly, the threat of a class struggle was merely one symptom of the general disintegration of modern society he had described in the *Architectural Record*. America's "social problem," said Croly, went far deeper than the corruption and poverty the muckrakers exposed. "In its deepest aspect," he wrote, "the social problem is the problem of preventing such divisions from dissolving ... society—of keeping such a highly differentiated society fundamentally whole and sound."

Seeking, therefore, to find for the United States some semblance of the communal unity that had made past cultures great, Croly charged that most reformers were working in a contrary direction. Such men were well on the way to being unwitting reactionaries, while their programs were merely "a species of higher conservatism." They had a naïve belief that reform meant the return of "the American political and economic system to its pristine purity and vigor."

When progressives launched massive assaults against the boss and his machine or the tycoon and his trust, they were attacking the very organizations that kept modern society from flying apart. Concentration of political and economic power was necessary and inevitable in a maturing capitalistic economy. Bosses and tycoons were actually unrestrained exponents of new social forces in themselves desirable. Their excesses, which so concerned the muckrakers, arose less from personal iniquity than from a struggle to survive in a society dominated by laws and ideas inherited from an agrarian past. Progressives who insisted on the enforcement of such laws were as stupidly archaic as the feudal nobles of the Old Régime before the French Revolution.

Croly did not, as many recent analysts of progressivism have done, question the sincerity of the progressives' desire for real reform. Instead he thought them misguided. They were in all sincerity trying to reform twentieth-century evils by means of ideas they had inherited from late eighteenth-century Jeffersonian reformers. The progressives, for instance, had invariably assumed the Jeffersonian "principle of 'equal rights for all and special privileges for none' as the absolutely sufficient rule of an American democratic political system." Yet, oddly enough, the same individualistic slogans came from the mouths of the robber barons and their political henchmen. Political machines waxed fat amid the multitudinous rights of popular democracy, while labor unions found themselves locked in an ironic battle with "employers . . . [who were] extremely enthusiastic over the individual liberty of the workingman." Americans who half a century later still see the right of workers to organize challenged by specious "right-to-work" campaigns may appreciate what Croly was getting at.

Croly's attack on the Jeffersonians, in fact, was savage, thorough, and for the most part sound. He took strong exception to the Jeffersonians' indiscriminate fervor for both liberty and equality. Jeffersonian progressives, he argued, had seldom sensed that the two principles might actually conflict. The enjoyment of liberty might lead to inequality, while, conversely, the preservation of equality might entail a sacrifice of liberty. Croly believed that wherever the Jeffersonians had made any choice between the principles, they had sacrificed liberty to a monotonous egalitarianism, suppressing "fruitful social and economic inequalities . . . in favor of intellectual and moral conformity."

Point after point, for page after page, Croly ticked off his objections to the Jeffersonian tradition. He had no patience with the pacifism that had been part of the tradition ever since Jefferson's abortive experiment with the embargo. Even less did he approve of the isolationism with which latter-day Jeffersonians had sought security for America in an increasingly dangerous world. He believed that the Jeffersonians' dedication to such things as strict construction of the constitution and states' rights had so hamstrung the government that little could be done to thwart the tyranny of allied business and political interests. Equally disastrous was the longevity that

Jefferson's prestige as a democratic hero had given his notions of economic laissez faire. Even in the highly integrated American economy of the twentieth century, Jeffersonian reformers expected that the mere abolition of special privilege for business would bring about an automatic distribution of "the good things of life . . . among all the people."

Jeffersonianism, however, had not been the only strand in the American political heritage. With seventy-three pages of detailed historical analysis Croly showed how Jeffersonianism in American history had consistently been opposed by a nationalistic tradition derived from Alexander Hamilton. "I shall not disguise the fact," he wrote, "that on the whole my own preferences are on the side of Hamilton rather than of Jefferson." Under modern conditions, Croly argued, the Hamiltonian reliance on a strong national government was necessary for attaining ends admittedly Jeffersonian, ends "essentially equalitarian and socialistic."

The pursuit of Jeffersonian ends by Hamiltonian means, therefore, became Croly's prescription for a new liberalism. He was aware of the risks of preaching such a nationalistic philosophy to his own generation. Having thoroughly schooled himself in history after college, he knew well that in both the United States and Europe nationalism had become increasingly the tool of the conservatives. Yet Croly insisted that nationalism was "far from being merely a conservative principle." The spirit of nationalism was a great power in the modern world. Croly wanted American progressives to exploit it for their own ends before reactionaries exploited it for theirs.

Croly believed—in fact he staked his entire career upon it—that nationalism could be made to work in tandem with democracy. Here, he thought, was where the Hamiltonians had erred. For if the Jeffersonians had been indiscriminate in their enthusiasm for democracy, the Hamiltonions had been almost indecent in their neglect of it. Hamilton had based his national program upon the very forces that progressives had to fight, upon "that concentration of wealth, and of the power exercised by wealth" that threatened American democracy. Croly had the wit to see, even before Fascism made nationalism a withering scourge, that nationalism without democracy was essentially destructive.

In elaborating upon his theory of democratic nationalism, Croly focused on those aspects of American life that had changed most in the twentieth century—the nation's new world position, its business consolidations, and its growing labor movement.

The new century, Croly thought, had much changed the role of the United States in world politics. While the surrounding oceans still gave the country "military security," its new and far-flung empire, its foreign policies, its trade, and its interest in world democracy, all confirmed "the merely comparative nature of . . . [America's] isolation."

Croly was a strong believer in power politics in the international realm, so much so that he has sometimes been misunderstood. He has been pictured as an amoral genie of *Realpolitik*, as wanting "a persistent and unappeasable expansionist program" for the United States. Such criticism, however, confuses his means with his ends. It ignores his own criticism of any foreign policy that failed "to foresee that . . . the United States must by every practical means encourage the spread [in world affairs] of democratic methods and ideas."

No lust for expansion or national glory underlay Croly's belief in power politics. He was moved instead by a rational conviction that shifts in the pattern of power among nations were the determinant force in world politics. He called for a foreign policy that would advance "a positive concept of the national interest," one, in other words, that would help make the world safe for democracy. Like Woodrow Wilson later, Croly thought peace and democracy inseparable, since "a decent guarantee of international peace . . . [was] precisely the political condition which would . . . release the springs of democracy."

Croly's thinking on foreign policy was considerably in advance of its time. Together with Captain A. T. Mahan and Theodore Roosevelt, he anticipated such recent critics of American foreign relations as George F. Kennan and Hans J. Morgenthau. Either of these modern critics could have written the many passages where Croly decried "the American habit ... [of] proclaim[ing] doctrines and policies, without considering either the implications, the machinery necessary to carry them out, or the weight of the resulting responsibilities." Croly believed that world peace could be won only by the intelligent and circumspect exercise of American power.

Croly's concern for peace and distaste for expansion came out most strongly in his analysis of the Monroe Doctrine. Strangely enough for a nationalist, even a democratic nationalist, he attacked the Doctrine for giving a "dangerously militant tendency to the foreign policy of the United States." He considered it not inconceivable that the Doctrine might at some point involve the United States "in a war against a substantially united Europe." He rejected, too, Roosevelt's famous Corollary to the Monroe Doctrine, which had committed the United States to a unilateral policing of the western hemisphere to block foreign interventions. Instead the publicist looked ahead to a co-operative organization of the Latin American countries and their North American neighbors that was prophetic of both the ideas of Woodrow Wilson and the "Good Neighbor" policy of Franklin Roosevelt.

Toward the American imperialism that had arisen with the Spanish-American War, Croly in *The Promise of American Life* took a more equivocal attitude. He partly ducked the issue by refusing "to raise the question as to the legitimacy in principle of a colonial policy on the part of a democratic nation." Where, however, a people had clearly shown themselves "incapable of efficient national organization," he argued (echoing Theodore Roosevelt), then foreign dominion might be justified. Cuba and Puerto Rico he saw as cases in point. He might have added such countries as Spain and Tsarist Russia for good measure.

About the addition of the Philippines to the American empire, however, Croly was nowhere near so sure. Critical of the bloodshed by which the islands had been conquered, he saw their chief value in awakening Americans to the possible cost of their "Open Door" policy in the Far East. "During the life of the coming generation," wrote Croly with a foresight that spanned three decades, "there will be brought home clearly to the American people how much it will cost to assert its own essential interests in China."

With respect to European politics, the complexities of which he would face as editor of the *New Republic*, Croly's words were equally prophetic. He predicted that the United States might sometime face "the obligation of interfering . . . in what may at first appear to be a purely European complication . . . [as a] result of the general obligation of a democratic nation to make its foreign policy serve the cause of international peace." Specifically, Croly saw either Germany or Russia as powers that might resort to aggression, since they had the most "to gain by war." If in the past the United States had remained isolated because of a desire for peace, the same desire might someday "demand intervention." Croly's foresight gives him some claim to Delphic augury.

Such was the meaning of Democratic nationalism for American foreign policy. Just as at home Croly sought ends essentially Jeffersonian through Hamiltonian means, so abroad he would strive for the ends of world democracy and peace by means of an exercise of national power. "If [a nation] . . . wants peace," wrote Croly, "it must be spiritually and physically prepared to fight for it."

Croly's sense of being adrift in a world of mounting complexity and danger was part of that mood of crisis with which he argued for his nationalized democracy. Here again he was a true disciple of Hamilton, who had justified his highly centralized political and economic system partly on the grounds of foreign dangers. A weak nation "under modern conditions," Croly argued, "does not gradually decline . . . it usually goes down with a crash."

Strength for the United States, Croly believed, required a radical change in the government's policies toward business and labor. Jeffersonian reformers had to abandon their illusion that a governmental policy of "equal rights for all" discriminated against nobody. Such a policy, Croly argued, merely left the great mass of the people at the mercy of strong political and economic interests. In its place he favored a program of "constructive discrimination" that would frankly favor the weak against the strong in the interests of "national efficiency."

"Constructive discrimination" toward business meant first of all a major redistribution of the economic functions of the national, state, and local governments. Since the states were largely artificial political units with no real relation to industry, Croly suggested that they be deprived of virtually all control over economic matters. To the towns and cities would be given the control or ownership of local utilities, while the rest of the economy would be regulated by a much strengthened government in Washington. Here, too, if one considers the massiveness of the federal government today compared to the states, Croly's prescription seems at the very least prophetic.

Having sliced with one blow the Gordian Knot of the Constitution's commerce clause, Croly was equally forthright about federal economic responsibilities. He wanted the federal government to cease its feckless war on large corporations. He called for the repeal of the Sherman Anti-Trust Act and the encouragement of huge corporations for the benefits they would bring. Progressives were advised, too, to get rid of the sentimental affection for small business that four years later became, at least in theory, the focus of Wilson's New Freedom. "Whenever the small competitor of the large corporation is unable to keep his head above water," said Croly stoutly, "he should be allowed to drown." Time has certainly justified Croly's skepticism about the Sherman Act, but both the plight and the bathos of the small businessman very much remain.

Croly's plan for industrial consolidation smacked somewhat of the ruthlessness of John D. Rockefeller's efforts for Standard Oil, yet the publicist did not propose that the resultant business giants go uncontrolled. Instead, the very lives of such companies would be placed in the hands of the government by a national incorporation act. Along with federal incorporation would come federal regulation.

"Regulation" for Croly meant that corporations should either be placed under "official supervision" of the kind bank examiners held over banks or be completely expropriated with government ownership and management. Neither alternative would cause that confusion of public and private authority that had so bedeviled past efforts to regulate business by means of commissions. Expropriation with compensation would come when a corporation grew so large as to be a "natural monopoly." Only the railroads, Croly believed, were in 1909 "approximating to such a condition," but with increased consolidation other industries would inevitably be nationalized. Croly's prescription for nationalization has not been realized. But certainly his prediction that corporations would both grow huge and be at least nominally regulated by the federal government has been justified.

Croly recognized that the problem of the large oligopolies and monopolies arose not only from their irresponsible industrial power, but also from the massed power of their wealth in society generally. Characteristically he saw the problem in terms of social fragmentation. Unearned wealth and extreme poverty, he declared, "breed class envy on one side and class contempt on the other; and the community is divided irremediably." The encouragement of large corporations required, therefore, severe limits on their monopolistic earnings, a limit best set by a very high graduated tax on company incomes.

In order to curb the power private wealth enjoyed in society Croly thought that federal inheritance rates up to 20 per cent would be the best solution. Huge inherited fortunes while common in "aristocratic countries" were "hostile both to the individual and public interest of a democratic community." Croly had, however, no liking for the individual income tax then being put forth by other reformers. He thought that such a tax would redistribute the nation's wealth "both less efficiently and less equitably" than the inheritance tax and would conflict with the more desirable levy on corporations. In the last of these arguments Croly anticipated the way conservatives since have used the "double taxation" argument in their efforts to relieve the "tax burdens" of the wealthy.

Taxation to redistribute the national wealth would go far toward stopping social disintegration. But there was a greater threat to "national unity." The United States faced a labor problem that required "immediate and direct action." In the case of labor unions, "constructive discrimination" meant "substantial discrimination in their favor." Croly considered the unions "the most effective machinery . . . for the economic and social amelioration of the laboring class." Here, too, as in the case of business, the acceptance of consolidated bigness was the theme. The non-union worker received no more sympathy than the small businessman. He was a "species of industrial derelict" whom Croly would suppress "as emphatically, if not as ruthlessly, as the gardener rejects the weeds in his garden for the benefit of the fruit- and flower-bearing plants."

At the same time that Washington placed business under federal incorporation it was to give the labor unions "legal recognition." Croly wanted, however, less a curb on unions than a program of legalization and government support much like that of the Wagner Act almost three decades later. Labor was to have the specific right to negotiate contracts that required the employment of "only union men," though the employer would still be ensured "as much labor as the growth of his business required." In effect, though he did not use the terms, Croly favored not the "closed shop" but the "union shop" now standard for American industry.

Even so, Croly did not propose to give the workers free rein. The government would have "to discriminate between 'good' and 'bad' unions" by setting definite (though not very arduous) standards for union action. Where unions violated such standards, they would be deprived of recognition and their members kept from employment. In fact, Croly went even further, skirting as close as anywhere to Fascism, when he suggested that in the case of particularly recalcitrant unions the government might organize "counter-unions" whose members "alone . . . [would] have any chance of obtaining work." Though the creation of rival unions by government has only taken place indirectly, certainly the Taft-Hartley Act initiated the trend toward restraint of the unions by the government that Croly advocated.

Croly's discussion of possible restraints on unions together with government encouragement was still another sign of the way his basic cultural concern kept him non-partisan. He knew that most union leaders were doughty Jeffersonians who feared the government. They would be inclined to compare governmental "recognition," said Croly, to the "recognition which the bear accords to the man whom he hugs to death." But neither was Croly's labor policy likely to attract management, since it anticipated by a quarter-century tactics of the New Deal hardly popular with business. Most employers of 1909 preferred to go on fighting the unions, chanting all the while their Jeffersonian litany to the freedom of the workingman. His policy, Croly argued, was not intended "to further the selfish interest of either the employer or the union, but rather the interest of the nation as a whole."

In this sense Croly's "national reconstructive policy" remained faithful to the end to that vision of a nationalized America that had stirred him almost a decade earlier. He was moved not by the plight of the impoverished, nor of the beleaguered unionists, nor even by the evil of the bosses and tycoons that bestrode the land. His values were not political, or economic, or merely sentimental; they remained primarily cultural. National cohesion, the creation of a setting where creative art and life might flourish, was his essential goal.

The creation of a strong, centralized government, the promotion of labor unions, the restraint and eventual nationalization of big business—such was the three-pronged program of "reconstructive legislation" that Croly advocated for progressives. "An organic unity," he wrote, "binds the three aspects of the system together." Business consolidation would require "the completer unionizing of labor." Similarly, consolidation would require increased government control "to appropriate the fruits of . . . monopoly for public purposes." The powerful government needed to discipline the corporations could aid the unions. And, finally, the increased strength of both capital and labor "would demand a vigorous and responsible . . . [government] to maintain a proper balance." "The majority of good Americans," Croly admitted in a key passage of his book, "will consider that the reconstructive policy . . . is flagrantly socialistic. . . . It should be characterized [however], not so much as socialistic as unscrupulously and loyally nationalistic." Most of the creative and prophetic ideas of Croly's book had been borrowed from socialism, but it was as a nationalist that he preferred to seek the fulfillment of America's promise.

Croly's dream of revitalizing American democracy by nationalizing it had definite dangers—particularly for the dreamer. From the time of Socrates on, men who would improve democracy have been vulnerable to charges of subverting it. Not surprisingly, Croly and his work have been pilloried many times over for having "totalitarian implications" or at least a "taint of Fascism."

The publicist left himself most open to such charges in the parts of *The Promise of American Life* where he outlined the tactics reformers would have to use to bring the United States around to his program of democratic nationalism. Here again Croly anticipated many future critics when he charged Jeffersonian progressives with seeing reform as merely an "uplift movement," as a kind of "politico-moral revivalism." Croly, like his hero Theodore Roosevelt, had little respect for the muckrakers. Though he accepted the grim picture they had painted of American society, he doubted that the moral outrage their exposés provoked would bring any meaningful or lasting reforms. Effective democratic action required something more than an aroused and virtuous electorate. The whole idea of democratic nationalism had implicit within it a new set of tactics for progressivism. Reformers of the future would have to rest their hopes upon three tactical elements—a democratic elite, strong executive leadership, and the Republican party.

Croly's concept of a democratic elite took him farthest from commonly accepted notions of democracy. Not surprisingly, it was Croly's cultural nationalism that set him off here, as in so many other places, from other progressives. What he wanted was a multiplication of the Wilbur Littletons throughout the land, an increase in the number of dedicated men of talent who might lead the United States toward "regeneration."

Haunted by the ghost of the unfortunate Littleton, Croly, like so many novelists and cultural critics since, made the architect the prototype of his new elite breed. If the architect would stick to his ideals while at the same time promoting and profiting from the flowering of nationalism, then he would find himself serving "the nation in the very act of contributing to his individual fulfillment." "The case of the statesman, the man of letters, the philanthropist, or the reformer," said Croly, "does not differ essentially from that of the architect."

Croly called the work of his elite "constructive individualism." He thought such leadership to be an answer to the "devil-take-the-hindmost" individualism of the Jeffersonians, whose narrow and selfish view of the individual had caused men not only to be "victimized . . . by unlimited economic competition," but, worse, had robbed even the winners in the struggle of "any value in their work . . . [except] its results in cash." Only some impulse beyond self-interest, argued Croly, could bring the best from a man.

In fact, he carried the selflessness of his elite to an extraordinary extreme. Good middle-class progressive though he was, he so detested the profit motive that he wanted for an "ultimate end" something close to the Communist ideal of "from each according to his ability, to each according to his need." "The only way in which work can be made entirely disinterested," Croly wrote, "is to adjust its compensation to the needs of a normal and wholesome life." In this respect he seemed to verge on the utopianism of that American nationalist of a decade or so before, Edward Bellamy.

Croly's tactical faith in an elite might seem suspect enough to any believer in democracy, yet actually it contained none of the "totalitarian implications" of either Communism or Fascism. As for the former, Croly conceded immediately that the ending of the profit motive was "far beyond the reach of contemporary collective effort." His speculations on the profit motive, in fact, boiled down to the pious, but hardly radical, hope that nationalism might provide a substitute for the cash values that dominated American life.

Croly's leaders were also very different from the elitist corps of Fascist ideology. The patriotic disinterestedness of his elite required no total subordination to the nation. Accepting as he did pragmatism's pluralism of means and ends Croly had no love for a monolithic, all-absorbing state of the Hegelian variety. While rejecting the extreme individualism of the Jeffersonians, Croly kept the focus of his own theory on the individual. "A democracy," he wrote, "like every political and social group, is composed of individuals, and must be organized for the benefit of its constituent members."

Croly, furthermore, sincerely believed that his leading group could remain democratic. The influence of the elite would rest upon talent and effective leadership, not upon inherited position or some "rigidly limited electoral system." His elite was to have only delegated powers, which could only be "used, under extreme penalties, for the benefit of the people as a whole." Yet while Croly's intentions may have been above reproach, he ignored the fact that the idealistic Wilbur Littletons of the land are seldom leaders and that actual leaders are seldom idealists. The gifts of artists and philosophers are not the same as those of the masters of coal and iron and men.

Oddly enough, when Croly finished describing his elite, it

resembled nothing so much as that "natural aristocracy among men" that Thomas Jefferson once called "the most precious gift of nature, for the instruction, the trusts, and government of society." If Croly knew Jefferson's mind on the matter, he missed a chance to quote the sage of Monticello against latter-day equalitarian Jeffersonians.

Croly's second tactical recommendation to progressives— the need for strong executive leadership in reform—also opens his political theory to serious question by believers in democracy. At times in his book Croly called for leadership in enthusiastic, semi-religious terms that are suspect in a later age weary of "fuehrers," "duces," and other willful men of power. He called again and again for some "national reformer . . . in the guise of Saint Michael" or "some democratic Saint Francis . . . some imitator of Christ" to lead America toward "national regeneration."

Yet, for all his rhetoric, Croly wanted for his executives not Nietzschean demi-gods of will and power, but instead humble, dedicated truly superior men of whom the "uncommon common man," Abraham Lincoln, became the prototype. Croly was asking for no mere man of action, no "man on horseback" to quash threats to middle-class tranquility. When he called for a leader, "something of a saint and something of a hero," the emphasis invariably fell on "saint" and not on "hero."

Even Croly's deep and abiding admiration of Theodore Roosevelt was clouded by a certain horror of the former Rough Rider's lusty militancy. He failed to find in Roosevelt that desirable balance between the will and the intelligence that had been "so finely exemplified in Abraham Lincoln." Croly never quite lost the suspicion that Roosevelt much preferred the role of hero to that of saint.

Roosevelt's performance as President, together with that of such earlier men as Jackson and Lincoln, was enough to make Croly feel that at the national level strong executive leadership was possible without major constitutional changes. At the state level, however, Croly called for so thoroughgoing a reform of the existing machinery that it constitutes one of his more important contributions to progressive thought. Boiled down, what Croly proposed was that the state governors become "official bosses," who would replace the machine bosses then in control of most of the state capitals.

Croly's governors were to be given extraordinary powers, including the sole initiative in proposing legislation and great power over subordinates. Such powers would make it possible for the governor to ram through and administer a program despite the opposition of special interests, while leaving to the people the clear-cut choice of supporting or rejecting the man and his program. Applying his principles of nationalism and democracy, Croly once again blasted the indiscriminate enthusiasm of Jeffersonian progressives for pure democracy. He attacked the initiative and the direct primary as merely multiplying the trivial choices that confronted the voters, while at the same time he approved the referendum and recall as providing efficient checks on his governors' great powers.

In sum, Croly wanted a government that was capable of meeting the people's needs while at the same time remaining responsive to their will. His suspicion that such devices as the direct primary and initiative would merely open new avenues for manipulation by the old-line bosses has been largely justified. Since he wrote in 1909, he may be forgiven the perversion of his dream of strong state executives by such a man as Huey Long.

At the national level, however, Croly's search for the great leader became a neurotic obsession that often badly distorted his political perspective. Again and again Croly measured politicians against the half-saint, half-hero image of Lincoln, and more often than not he found them wanting. When his work brought him close to men of power like Roosevelt or Wilson, he seemed to try to transcend his own oddly impassive intellectuality in a passionate plea for the President to lead, to provide inspiration and guidance for the legions of reform. Much of the drama and not a little of the tragedy of Croly's career arose from the inevitable failure of such leaders to fulfill his ideal vision.

Croly's third tactical specific, that progressives place their hopes for reform in the Republican party, seems rather odd after nearly a half-century of Republican conservatism. Even in 1909, the party had enjoyed only a brief holiday from the reactionary sway of Conkling, Blaine, Hanna, and McKinley, while the still unbroken leadership of Senator Aldrich and Speaker Cannon kept pungently alive the memory of a Nean-derthal past. Not even the pyrotechnics of Theodore Roose-velt's presidency seem enough to justify either the strength of Croly's Republicanism or his marked reluctance to abandon it in later years.

Yet such partisanship had come naturally to Croly, as to many other intellectuals of the day. He had reached political consciousness as a reformer in 1890, when Tammany Hall once more ruled New York with much of the corrupt aplomb of the Tweed ring of two decades before. Croly's concern for clean government, his lack of sympathy with the "raw and un-approachable foreigners" that swarmed the Democratic halls, precluded much enthusiasm for the party that had been one with the Sons of Saint Tammany from the time of Jefferson on. Nor was Croly likely to be stirred by the mid-'nineties success of the western agrarians in overthrowing the staid "hard-money" faction that had ruled the Democrats under Seymour, Tilden, and Cleveland. The farmer's plight was remote to the city-minded young Croly. He had little liking for what he called the "financial heresies" of William Jen-nings Bryan's 1896 campaign.

By 1909, Republicanism had become one of Croly's strong-est prejudices. He believed that the party of Lincoln had been from the beginning "the first genuinely national party." During the Civil War it had asserted the supremacy of the nation over sectional and class interests, and, despite its late-nineteenth-century factionalism, had never lost its original nationalistic impetus. The Jeffersonian Democrats, on the other hand, could hardly "become the party of national responsibility without being faithless to . . . [their individualistic] creed."

The Promise of American Life called on the Republicans once again to fulfill their "historic mission," to assert the pre-eminence of the nation over those modern forces of business and labor that threatened, like the slaveholders and abolitionists before the Civil War, to tear the country asunder. Nor were Croly's hopes for the Republicans entirely unreasonable. A party that numbered Theodore Roosevelt, Charles Evans Hughes, George Norris, and Robert M. La Follette among its members might well become an effective instrument for reform.

Even so, the publicist's nationalistic vision was not unsullied by prejudice. When, for example, Croly criticized the Democratic party for alternating opportunistically between liberalism and Bourbonism, for "trying to find room within its hospitable folds for both Alton B. Parker and William Jennings Bryan," he might as easily have sought out the mote in the Republican eye. Only recently the Republicans had hugged both Roosevelt and Mark Hanna to their companionable bosoms, and, in 1909, their progressive-conservative split was if anything wider than that of the Democrats.

Such were the tactics Croly wanted for progressivism. Taken all together they appear to contain a contradiction. Croly was asking that a relatively small group of men—his elite, his strong executives, the liberal wing of the Republican party—convert an enormous country to nationalism. Like his hero Alexander Hamilton, however, Croly had an abiding faith in the powerful few. If only a minority of influential men could be made to see the promise of the new liberalism, Croly had little doubt that in time other Americans would follow.

Croly's confidence in such tactics derived in part from his pragmatism. He was advocating an instrumental approach to politics that anticipated much that John Dewey later had to say about general education. "The national school," wrote Croly, "is the national life." "The nation, like the individual, must go to school . . . [and] its schooling consists chiefly in ex-perimental collective action aimed at the realization of a collective purpose." Americans, in short, were to be converted to nationalism not by words but by deeds. The United States was to learn by doing.

If the country was to be educated to nationalism primarily by deeds, then a relatively small group of men might carry on the process of education. Once such a group had gained control of one of the major parties and of the government, then they could start a course of frank experimentation in politics that would test and presumably vindicate the philosophy of democratic nationalism. Croly was calling for that crusade for the "New Nationalism" that Theodore Roosevelt waged after 1910. The strengths and weaknesses, successes and failures, of the Bull Moose movement would provide the test of the new liberalism's tactics.

8. Nationalism and Democracy

Such then was the book that transformed Croly from architectural critic to political philosopher. Such were the outlines of the new liberalism that became the focus of his later work with Walter Weyl and Walter Lippmann. Such, too, was the work that Theodore Roosevelt praised strongly both in private letters and in print and promised to use as a basis for speeches. Such, finally, was the book that became the unofficial bible of those who would cheer Roosevelt and the "New Nationalism" in 1912.

The Promise of American Life, however, has a deeper import than its transitory prominence during the Bull Moose campaign. In it Croly managed to engage the central political problem of a war-ridden twentieth century—the question of the relation between democracy and nationalism. Fascism has since resolved the matter by exalting nationalism to the extinction of all real democracy, while Communism, despite its pretense to class internationalism, has swallowed democracy through totalitarian state systems strongly nationalistic in flavor. Even within relatively free states, democracy has faced the challenge of a militarist, conformist nationalism of a kind that Croly in 1909 could hardly have foreseen.

The whole point of *The Promise of American Life*, however, lay in Croly's realization of the great power of nationalism. With remarkable insight he saw how difficult it would be to make democracy and nationalism work together. Yet he believed the United States in 1909 to be a nation that could only be saved by mobilizing the sentiment of nationalism behind a social democratic program. By grappling so formidably with a problem few men then even recognized, Croly well earned a top rank among American political thinkers.

In his realistic measure of the forces then molding America's future Croly stands high as prophet. Yet he betrayed at times the tendency toward mystical excess also characteristic of prophets. An attack he made on the secret ballot, for instance, suggests a certain isolation from the saloons and smoke-stained rooms where the real work of the democracy he loved was carried on. And his disdain for the profit motive, however admirable, reflected the intellectual's remoteness from the mundane forces that move most men, even the intellectuals.

These criticisms, however, might have come from Croly himself. The stern realism that made him believe in the creative potential of corporations, unions, political machines, and battleships was no mere realism of acquiescence. Croly did long for a better world. He dreamed of an America where men might vote in the open, where they might value their work and their service to others more than mere personal gain. As a nationalist he thought patriotic sentiment might help inspire Americans toward such ends. As a pragmatist he saw "experimental collective action" as the best tactic to follow. As a realist he would work with the materials at hand rather than pursue the impossible ideals of a vanished agrarian past. Yet the realistic, pragmatic nationalist was at odds with the latent mystic. Croly still had within him that impulse toward a "religion of humanity" his father had fostered in him. The closing section of *The Promise of American Life* admitted that the final triumphs of reform would have to wait "until the conviction and feeling of human brotherhood enter[ed] into possession of the human spirit." It was the aura of his father's Positivism that explained Croly's occasional visions of a society unblemished by greed, ruled by political choices made publicly and proudly, and led by "some democratic evangelist— some imitator of Jesus." In 1909, however, the pragmatic nationalist was dominant over the mystical humanist.

Croly's "religion of humanity" like his cultural emphasis tempered the force of his nationalism. Nothing is more remarkable about *The Promise of American Life* than the things that are not there. Though Croly was not yet *au courant* with modern ideas about the equality of the races, his book betrayed none of the racism that has usually been part of twentieth-century nationalism. Croly never fell afoul of such Aryan notions as those expressed by the "grass roots" democrat, William Allen White, who in *The Old Order Changeth* of 1910 ascribed American superiority to the greater purity of its racial strains over those of the "mongrel" populations of South America. Neither did Croly's nationalism involve any overweening worship of the state. His view of the state was instrumental, and he held its worth to lie in its service to individual citizens. The imperialism that was part of Croly's nationalism, futhermore, was (as far as such is possible) reasoned and moderate. He wanted to secure American interests in the Western Hemisphere through co-operative internationalism rather than through conquest. Finally, while Croly's love of country was strong, his pride of country was restrained. At times Croly's criticisms in *The Promise of American Life* foreshadowed that echo his title would find in the 'thirties when Archibald MacLeish wrote the poem, "America Was Promises."

Out of such criticisms Croly evolved an economic policy that meant a kind of middle-class or state socialism. Though he denied that he wanted any mere "compromise . . . between individualism and socialism," he certainly had no sympathy for proletarian socialism. Certain passages directly engaged the claims of the Marxists. The appeal of "the most popular form of socialism" for an "international organization of a single class," he wrote, "is headed absolutely in the wrong direction." Nationalism, not class interest, was the force that would unite men for real reform. His largely cultural desire for a cohesive society made him abhor the Marxist acceptance of "revolutionary violence." While he believed that "revolutions . . . [might] at times be necessary and on the whole helpful," violence itself was too socially disruptive to be anything but the last resort of any political movement.

Yet, if Croly attacked socialism for promoting a "class interest" rather than the "national interest," how well did he meet his own disinterested standard? How much did *The Promise of American Life* merely reflect the interests of Croly's own middle class? Certainly Croly's desire for stronger unions reflected in part the ordinary middle-class fear of the violence that follows from repression. His reforms of both government and business, furthermore, would lead to the replacement of the reigning tycoons and bosses by respectable middle-class managers and politicians. The seeming squeeze of the middle class by the very wealthy was to be relieved by the gradual expropriation of huge fortunes and the taxation of unearned corporate wealth, while the absence of an income tax would leave the vigorous middle-class businessman with few limits to his lifetime horizons. Finally, middle-class intellectuals like himself would gain enormously in status, for the social critic, said Croly, would "in a sense become the standard bearer of the whole movement."

All such gains for his class and type, however, were as consistent with Croly's nationalistic vision as with middle-class bias. Had he condemned labor unions as disruptive of national unity, Croly's objectivity might have been questioned. Ob-

viously, however, he intended labor to make real gains relative
to the higher economic groups. Nor is there any reason to
doubt the sincerity of his repeated demand for a thoroughgoing redistribution of the nation's wealth. Croly's aims transcended the limits of class, and his later career would become a
further proof of his sincerity.

Immune to any pronounced class bias, Croly, nevertheless,
suffered from a New York parochialism of view that had been
evident in his earlier *Architectural Record* essays. In one of
these he had shown himself to be an early prophet of that cult
of "metropolitanism" that enthralled so many intellectuals of
the time. Croly saw the rapid growth of his own native New
York as a sign that it was becoming a new focal point for a
nationalized culture. He dreamed that New York might become what Paris was to France, what Berlin was to Germany,
a metropolis that "might not only reflect large national tendencies, but . . . sum them up and transform them." All of
which would have been fair enough had Croly's residence in
the metropolis given him a truly national outlook. Instead it
seems to have focused his own attention largely on problems
of interest to the city dweller. Croly's concern with political
corruption, his faith in a new managerial elite, his consciousness of a labor problem, all reflected a city environment. Rising
prices and the plight of the consumer alone among urban-
reform problems failed to attract his attention.

Most incriminating in this respect, perhaps, was Croly's almost total neglect of critical problems that bedeviled the
country outside the Northeast. The tariff issue, already in 1909
being resoundingly agitated in Congress by western insurgents, received only passing mention. Conservation, of vital
interest to even such easterners as Theodore Roosevelt and
Gifford Pinchot, was entirely ignored in *The Promise of American Life*. Nor did the publicist have anything to say about
currency and banking, a question much agitated in the East
since the panic of 1907 but of even more interest to agrarian
sections of the nation. Even agriculture, still the means of

livelihood for a majority of Americans, was mentioned but once. In short, Croly's book failed to resolve a contradiction that had long existed between his New York-centered "metropolitanism" and his nationalism.

The actual nature of Croly's democratic nationalism, however, cannot be explained in terms of class or sectional interests. The values Croly strove to realize were not primarily those of locale or caste, but, instead, they were ethical and esthetic. While it often seemed obscured and partly compromised, Croly never forgot his initial vision of a vital culture where art and life might flourish. Viewed in any other light Croly's ideas often seem contradictory; only the recognition of his cultural emphasis gives his program the unity it had in his own mind.

Croly's thought suffered, in fact, not from contradictions but from polarities, polarities that could never be entirely resolved. The schism in his thinking went back at least to his break with his father during early manhood. It had been accentuated by the intensity of his response to the plight of Wilbur Littleton. Croly remained the aspiring mystic in his inner heart, however much he turned the face of the stern realist to the world. The softness inside tempted him to exaggerate the outer hardness. When discussing world peace, for instance, Croly could accept with remarkable equanimity the prospect that "the road to any permanent international settlement . . . [would] be piled mountain high with dead bodies." Yet here again Croly was merely accepting the reality that peace was something for which a nation might have to fight. The notion of waging war for peace involved, of course, difficulties both logical and practical, but the dilemma into which Croly plunged so confidently was hardly his alone. All America and most of the world has shared it for much of the twentieth century. Croly, who defined the problem sooner than most, was also to suffer its heartbreaks more poignantly than most during the first of America's "wars to end war."

For the time being, however, *The Promise of American Life* stood as the culmination of eight years of rigorous thought, during which Croly had formulated the new theory of liberalism from which the rest of his career would grow. All the polarities of his thought had been bound together as best he knew how. American imperialism had been transformed into a policy of international co-operation. The incompatibility of liberty and equality he had found in the old Jeffersonian liberalism had been resolved by a willingness to sacrifice some freedom for an approximate equality. His desire for strong reform leadership had been tempered by a prayer that the leaders themselves might display the moral restraint of Abraham Lincoln. His instrumentalism had been set off from mere opportunism by the hypothetical goal of a nationalized democracy. The cultural aspects of his nationalism had been joined with the political in the "constructive individualism" of the Wilbur Littletons who would lead America toward "national regeneration." And, finally, nationalism had been combined with democracy through the central claim that Hamiltonian means might serve for the attainment of essentially Jeffersonian ends.

Twentieth-century political theory has followed two broad paths in resolving such contradictions or polarities between political principles. On the one hand, many men have tried to resolve the contradictions through various dialectical processes derived from Hegel. Other men, however, have followed the line of the pragmatists. They have shifted from principle to practice and tried to take the measure of truth in experience. Croly's own combination of nationalism and democracy in *The Promise of American Life* had taken the latter course, for the pragmatism of his Harvard years stayed with him. Nationalism and democracy were not merged dialectically into a new and absolute ideology; instead, they were left as separate but interacting aspects of an experimental theory.

Wilbur Littleton was to find expiation not in some absolutistic, nationalistic faith, but instead through the patient, experimental contrivance of dedicated intellectuals. "I cannot expect to hold my ground unless I obtain support," wrote

Croly a few weeks after his book was published. "The idea when it came to me seemed to have some power. . . . I have always hoped that it would win some converts, because then I should feel encouraged to seek other applications and fortify the position already assumed." Converts there would be, and collaborators, too, for *The Promise of American Life* had established the basic ideas of a new liberalism. The philosophy in the years ahead would guide both Croly and the men like Walter Weyl and Walter Lippmann who gathered around him. These years were to be the test of his pragmatic faith; they would test too whether democratic nationalism was the best path from the crossroads that confronted liberalism.

TWO

Walter Weyl: Democratic Liberal

1900-1912

1. A MAGAZINE AND A MAVERICK

"I . . . received yesterday a letter from Croly," wrote Walter Weyl in his diary late in September 1913. "A new paper. Wants me to go on it if it comes out. . . . I am in entire accord." Weyl was a natural choice for the *New Republic*. He had become one of those "converts" to the new liberalism that Croly had wished for when he finished *The Promise of American Life*. Though too independent and original in his own thinking to be merely a follower, Weyl by 1912 had found himself in general accord with the "New Nationalism" of Croly and Roosevelt and the Progressive party. He, too, along with Croly, had pledged his support to what he called Roosevelt's "struggle for national reorganization and regeneration." His *The New Democracy*, published in February of the campaign year, had ranked second only to Croly's book as a manual for the Bull Moose movement.

Weyl, like so many progressives, had developed a marked respect for Herbert Croly. Croly's work had been the scale by which Weyl had measured his own accomplishment in the anxious months after *The New Democracy* appeared. Noting that, while *The Promise of American Life* had sold relatively few copies, Croly was known everywhere, Weyl confided to his diary: "I am pretty sure that this book of mine will reach a far wider public and will have a deeper influence." Later Weyl took pride in the fact that Roosevelt in a speech had called the "Promise of Amer. Life & New Democ. . . . the true books of the [Progressive] movement."

Though the two men had not known each other long before 1913, Croly realized the special contribution Weyl might make to the *New Republic*. Weyl had written for years with notable success for most of the muckraking and progressive journals. *The New Democracy* had proven his capacity both as writer and thinker. Furthermore, he possessed capacities and interests lacking in Croly and the third member of the intellectual triumvirate, Walter Lippmann. A well-trained economist, he was a convenient foil for the other two men, who had approached politics through philosophy and the arts. His loquacious irreverence, his insistence that generalizations be given a firm ground in facts, helped counteract the sober abstractions of Croly and the brilliant fancies of Lippmann. Weyl, the product of a lower-middle-class Jewish family, who had studied at Pennsylvania's Wharton School of Commerce and Finance, relieved somewhat the *New Republic*'s aura of Harvard gentility.

Weyl's most marked intellectual trait was his passion for statistics. He constantly embarked upon new "projects," more often than not several simultaneously, and he faced each with the statistician's love for accumulating data. A plan for a play in 1911, for instance, brought the diary resolve: "I shall immediately open up cards for this. . . divided into theme, incidents, characters, general . . . & [later] make a new classification." The several novels he attempted during his life were similarly approached. The journal he kept from day to day was filled with mathematical calculations, from estimates of the number of hours he took to write a magazine article to averages of the time consumed in driving to the railroad station. He invariably buttressed the conclusions of his political writing with neatly handled statistics.

Yet, strong as was the statistical habit in Weyl, he was anything but a drab and humorless compiler of facts. His rather extrovert personality contrasted markedly with the gnome-like imperturbability of Croly or the omniscient blandness of Lippmann. Weyl was a handsome man, slender and of average height, with strong, aquiline features that were set off by a neat moustache and a dark goatee. He had a warm, outgoing manner, and a knack for making people feel that he was interested in them and their problems. His friends remembered him for "his quick laugh, his nervous chuckle," for his habit of starting conversations with a "suave, tentative, 'well, dear friend.' "

Weyl's friendly yet imposing exterior, his predominant intellectuality, concealed a character that remained throughout his life oddly youthful and guileless. Almost every day was New Year's day for Walter Weyl. His diary was larded with resolutions and good intentions. Hardly a month went by that he did not announce to himself and the world his firm intention to give up smoking. Friends knew well his habit of "boasting that he had been two days and a quarter [or some longer period] without a cigarette." Various projects for personal improvement were a constant absorption. At one time he embarked enthusiastically upon elocution lessons; at another he took up the study of Latin; still other days he spent gardening, or improving his automobile driving. Typical was a passage in his diary when toward the end of his life he brooded about psychoanalysis: "I have a strong desire to be psycked," he wrote. "I am sure that I have all sorts of inhibitions that if corrected, would make me more effective." Weyl's restless urge for improvement was part of a tendency that friends noted to "underrate himself seriously."

Relations between Weyl and the two other political editors of the *New Republic* were for the most part cordial. He had a deep respect for Croly and often turned to him for advice on matters both personal and professional. At times, however, Croly's unvarying impassivity wore upon Weyl's own rather volatile spirits. He complained that Croly tended to be "excessively cautious," or fulminated on the danger of the *New Republic's* becoming "a middle-aged journal."

Towards Lippmann, Weyl's attitude was more complex. Outwardly the two men were fast friends, and Lippmann showed his warm feelings in a memorial essay after Weyl's death. Weyl had much admiration for Lippmann, an admiration that may have been mixed with a certain envy. "Walter Lippmann," he wrote at one point, "is my ideal of a man who writes easily, because he is big and strong and full. He gives the sense of merely giving his overflow.... He does not hammer it out; it comes (or seems to come) out automatically by mere gravity." Yet beneath the admiration there lurked a definite distrust. "Walter has the faculty for taking what he can without giving any credit whatsoever," Weyl noted in one of the very few censorious passages of his journals. "I have not the slightest desire to be exploited at his pleasure."

Weyl's occasional impatience with Croly and his latent distrust of Lippmann were probably matched by their restive feeling toward him. Croly, who always considered the *New Republic* "supreme in importance," probably resented the frequent interruptions in Weyl's work for the magazine. Lippmann, too, had the impression "that fully half the time ... [Weyl] was away [from the paper]. He was not a good member of the team and he knew it, because the work of the team interested him only in spurts."

Lippmann, however, recognized Weyl sympathetically for what he was, "an incorrigible free-lance." What resentment there was among the three intellectuals rarely came to the surface. Other men on the *New Republic* thought of Weyl with affection and respect. Robert Morss Lovett, fairly close to the *New Republic* men during the war years and a member of the board later, believed Weyl's "intellectual authority and powerful political articles [had] contributed to the unity of the board." Alvin Johnson, an editor after 1915, remembered Weyl as a man "who looked like a saint and fundamentally was one."

Genial, even saint-like, Weyl even so became the maverick of the three intellectuals. Though all three placed a high value on their independence, it was Weyl who more often than the others demanded that the *New Republic* take a fighting stand. He assumed for himself a role as the magazine's "conscience," especially during the years of the war and afterwards. He remained, in spite of his natural friendliness, always a little apart from the other two men and the magazine. An incorrigible independent, he prodded and goaded Croly and Lippmann when their closeness to men of power seemed to threaten their will to criticize. He was the one who insisted that a bold policy for the *New Republic* would be not its ruin but its salvation. "It is better to die fighting," said Weyl of the magazine at one point, "than to die of inanition and sterility."

2. A German-American Francophile

When in the days before his work with Croly and Lippmann Walter Weyl wrote articles on immigration for *Harper's Magazine* and the *Outlook*, he was telling the story of his own family. His father, Nathan Weyl, son of a farmer of "moderate circumstances" in the German Palatinate, had emigrated to America in 1851 at the age of sixteen. In the United States, Nathan Weyl, like so many of the immigrants his son would later write about, was looked after by a fellow-countryman, Julius Stern, a Philadelphia merchant. In time Nathan Weyl married his patron's daughter and set up housekeeping on a street nearby. There, on March 11, 1873, Walter Edward Weyl was born.

Weyl's father, known for his "idealistic" temperament and his poor luck in business, died when young Walter was seven. Weyl's mother then took Walter and his five brothers and sisters to live with Grandmother Stern in a large house near the heart of Philadelphia. Old Julius Stern had died, but the rising publishing business of his son Edward helped provide enough to support the seven Weyls, the grandmother, and three uncles in relative comfort. The Stern house, large enough to hold its eleven inhabitants, lay in what had once been a "preferred residential district," and "was considered distinctly desirable."

Some of Walter Weyl's later irrepressible gregariousness may have resulted from his youth in so large a family. Though never strictly Orthodox, the Sterns and the Weyls developed much of their family cultural life around their Jewish faith. There were Friday evening chamber-music sessions in which the musicians of the family were joined by friends and neighbors. Uncle Simon Stern, who for many years was editor of the *Penn Monthly*, was the "dominating influence of the family" and was said to have had "great effect in the shaping of Walter's career."

In later years when Walter Weyl was jotting down impressions for an abortive autobiographical novel, he remembered his childhood as a happy one. "He went to the Mercantile and Apprentices' Library as I did," wrote Weyl of his intended hero. "[He] loved cherry pie, played Indians in the park . . . read Scott & Cooper, lived much alone . . . liked history, philosophy, but above all mathematics." Weyl remembered himself as having "wept over Mill's Logic," and thought his fictional character should show "a certain tendency to tears stirred by merely intellectual proceedings."

Unlike Herbert Croly, Weyl never was subjected to strong religious influences. He recalled that as a boy he had "believed in God, but did not picture him forth; said his prayers mechanically; [and] was not taught religion." In later life Weyl was to declare himself an "agnostic" and meet the humorous jibes of a Christian wife who chided him for being "a heathen." Religion neither obtruded upon nor perceptibly influenced Weyl's political writing the way it did Croly's, yet Weyl was not entirely without religious sentiments. Through much of his life, for instance, he worked sporadically at an allegorical novel about a modern Christ, who would bring to the world a renewed sense of redemption. Weyl had a habit, too, which his wife and friends knew, of keeping a Bible in the pocket of his car to be read at idle moments.

Though only conventionally religious, the Sterns and the Weyls had a large measure of that respect for learning that Weyl himself would later find typical of Jewish immigrants. Weyl was the precocious member of his family, the only one of his brothers and sisters to go beyond high school. His elders recognized his brilliance early and did everything possible to advance his education. A room, once the children's playroom on the second floor of the Stern house, was set aside as his study, and Weyl was later to remember working "up in the 'Verandah'. . . under that gas light." He came to be "looked upon . . . as a dreamer" by the rest of the family.

Weyl entered Philadelphia Central High School at the age of thirteen and rewarded his family's confidence in him by winning a scholarship for the Wharton School of the University of Pennsylvania after four years. Entering the Wharton School of Commerce and Finance as a junior in 1890, Weyl was graduated with a Ph.B. two years later, having, despite his youth, received "distinction" in two thirds of his subjects.

Unlike Croly and Lippmann, who centered their studies at Harvard on philosophy and aesthetics, Weyl developed an early interest in history, politics, and economics. Seven of his courses at the Wharton School were in economics, seven were in history; only one of them covered philosophy. His remarkable precociousness was demonstrated when as a senior aged nineteen he won first prize in a national essay contest on tax problems. The average age of the other prize winners was thirty-seven.

Weyl, like Croly, had looked forward to "an academic career" after college, but the ambition was temporarily frustrated when his family dragooned him into studying law in the office of Mayer Sulzberger, a prominent Philadelphia attorney. He found, however, "no joy in the study of law"; in fact, he "conceived a most vigorous distaste for it." After several months his elders relented and sent him off to the University of Halle in Germany for graduate work to "end in a professorship."

Weyl was saved from the toils of the law largely through the influence of his former economics professor, Simon Nelson Patten. Patten, who had himself been forced by family to study law on two unhappy occasions, had an understandable sympathy for Weyl's plight. He promised Weyl a fellowship if he would agree to take "his doctorate at home." But the Halle experience was to come first for the young German-American. Patten had returned with a Ph.D. from Halle seventeen years before, inspired "to help in the transformation of American civilization from an English to a German basis." In effect, young Walter Weyl was placed in the center of that conflict between German and Anglo-French cultures that would reach its tragic climax during World War I.

Weyl's immersion in the traditions of Germany was heavy. Financed by family to the extent of "nine dollars a week . . . with a few exceptional extra amounts," he studied for more than three years at the universities of Halle and Berlin, with side trips for research in London and Paris. Though Weyl "knew practically no German" at first, so thorough was his indoctrination that by the time of his return to America in 1896 his "English had become decidedly German in character."

Yet, significantly for his future development, Weyl's contact with actual German scholarship was relatively light. Since he was not working formally for a Ph.D. abroad, he made his stay in Europe more a poor man's "grand tour" than a serious academic exercise. Weyl saw more of the people and the countryside than of professors and universities, though he also managed to do research on European railway traffic for his dissertation. In later years he liked to tell stories of scrapes with restaurant proprietors over luncheon checks or of the adventure of a passage from Germany to England on the open deck of a North Sea steamer.

Weyl did acquire at Halle and Berlin a fascination with German life and problems that stayed with him the rest of his life. He acquired a definite sympathy for German culture. In marked contrast to Herbert Croly, who saw democracy nullified in Germany both by the militarism of its leaders and the socialism of its workers, Weyl in *The New Democracy* believed "the German masses ... a more capable democratic group than ... the English, because the Germans, though perhaps poorer, and with fewer political rights ... [were] better educated."

The conflict within Weyl between his German background and education and the Anglo-Saxon heritage of his own nation came forth most poignantly in a diary entry during World War I. Commenting that "certain newspapers always ... [referred] to the Germans as Huns," Weyl wondered how "the most studious of all nations, ... the strongest believer in progress, the blindest advocate of ... modern civilization ... [could be called] the defender of Barbarism." "We ourselves called her civilized," wrote Weyl. "We read her books and sat at the feet of her teachers." His earlier faith in Germany, he concluded, could not have been wrong; instead the "war cries ... [were] all false, all ... false because of their very purpose."

For all his sympathy for Germany, however, Weyl did not come back to the United States in 1896 the prophet of German *Kultur* his mentor Patten had hoped for. Instead, oddly enough, France was the country Weyl came most to admire, the country that had the most profound impact on his political thought. He considered the French the people with the most advanced and appealing civilization. With his passion for statistics and population problems, he was impressed by the fact that France seemed to have most rationally of all adjusted its population to available resources. "France aspires to be comfortable and civilized," he wrote in 1912. "She has the choice of being populous or democratic, and she is choosing the latter.... France, growing wealthier daily and dispersing its wealth over larger and larger millions, represents a financial democracy."

"That way," concluded the German-American economist, "lies civilization."

3. THE DISMAL SCIENCE UNFOLDS A PROMISE

Weyl was twenty-three when he returned by steerage from Europe in 1896 to complete his Ph.D. His work for the doctorate plunged him deeply into economics, a science that by its parade of inevitabilities is perhaps the most innately conservative of all. Simon Patten provided the promised fellowship, and Weyl went to work on railroad economics under Emory Johnson, a friend of the early Halle days who had become a professor at the Wharton School. Within a year Weyl finished a dissertation later published as *The Passenger Traffic of Railways*.

In the dissertation Weyl ran up against the chronic tragedy of the scholar—the conflict of fact with theory. He had hoped initially to prove that the reduction of passenger rates would have the same stimulating social effects that the lowering of postal rates had had a generation or so earlier. But the elaborate statistics that Weyl gathered on the railroads of eleven nations were stubborn. He was forced to concede that lower rates were not the only, or even the most important, way to encourage railroad travel.

Even the dissertation, however, held signs of the later publicist. Weyl had already developed an easily flowing style and a knack for decisive phrasing. He had the journalist's talent for dealing with multiple variables gracefully. The reformer was evident in his charge that the rates of American railroads were unjustifiably high. Yet Weyl's chastening contact with the realm of conflicting facts would often inhibit in him later the formulations of the grand generalizations so necessary to the publicist. As a result, for such is the irony of the intellectual's work, he often seemed less perceptive and creative than the philosophically trained Croly.

A solid grounding in economic theory, study in Europe, the scholar's chastening necessity to reconcile theory with reality— all these helped make Weyl what Walter Lippmann later called him, "by far the best trained economist of the progressive movement." Study in the "dismal science," however, seems to have quenched for a time Weyl's characteristic buoyancy and optimism. A friend at the University of Pennsylvania, Martin Schutze, remembered Weyl as being the pessimistic realist among the other young instructors and graduate students. He liked to squelch high-flown harangues against the McKinley Republicans with the flat statement, "But that is the way it is done." What reformist bent the young economist had, Schutze believed, came through the very strong influence of Professor Patten.

The philosophy of *The New Democracy* reflected a multitude of influences—Weyl's omnivorous reading, ideas from friends, experiences with immigrants and workers, the notions of other reformers. Yet the central core of the book was derived from the teaching of Simon Nelson Patten at Pennsylvania. When Weyl introduced *The New Democracy*'s central thesis "of progress through prosperity" he paused to make "the fullest possible acknowledgment of his deep indebtedness to that great teacher," citing Patten's *The Theory of Social Forces* of 1896 as the "original statement" of the concept. In a letter to Patten a month after *The New Democracy* was published, Weyl credited him with being the source of "the very best of my poor stock of political and social philosophy."

Patten had helped free Weyl from the pessimism of the classical economists, particularly the grim prophecies of David Ricardo. Ricardo, writing in early nineteenth-century England, had predicted the gradual contraction of capitalism through inherent contradictions between industrialization and agricultural production. The close relation of wages to food costs, argued Ricardo, bound the manufacturer as well as the farmer to an iron law of diminishing returns. Patten, however, held the law of diminishing returns to be untrue for modern capitalistic economies. Even on the farms, he contended, improved methods and shifts in mass-consumption habits could increase production enormously by allowing a greater variety of crops. Completely reversing Ricardo's prediction of contraction, Patten showed that lowered food prices from increased farm production would expand the market for industrial products and thus allow manufacturers as well as farmers to expand their production and profits.

From Patten's basic attack on Ricardo certain corollaries followed that were reflected in Weyl. Anticipating to a certain degree the Keynesian revolution in economics of America's New Deal, Patten stressed consumption over production as the source of progress. The emphasis was later reflected in Weyl's faith that the new consciousness of "consumers" would be the main hope of progressive reform. Furthermore, like Weyl later, Patten thought the encouragement of consumption would so stimulate the economy generally that the existing miseries of the poor could be ended without any direct redistribution of wealth. "Where wealth is growing at a rapid rate," said Weyl in *The New Democracy*, "the multitude may be fed without breaking into the rich man's granary." Both Patten and Weyl, furthermore, went beyond their rejection of the pessimism of Ricardo to quarrel as well with the optimism of Adam Smith. They denied that progress could come through a free competitive economy. Instead, co-operative action by the people and direct economic intervention by government were essential for continued prosperity. Weyl, in fact, went somewhat further than Patten in rejecting laissez faire. He argued in *The New Democracy* that "the industrial goal of the democracy . . . [was] the socialization of industry."

Weyl's belief in the need for stronger economic intervention by government may have stemmed in part from another disagreement with his professor. Patten had little patience for the bugaboo of overpopulation and resultant poverty predicted by Ricardo and, more particularly, by Ricardo's friend and rival,

Thomas Malthus. Patten held that greater wealth would come from the growth of populations, whereas for Ricardo greater numbers had meant only a rise in landlords' rents at the expense of society, while for Malthus it meant only misery and death for the masses. Fascinated by the statistical analysis of population figures, Weyl for a long time remained convinced by the Malthusian strictures against over-population. Only after many years of research and analysis did he come to accept Pattern's more optimistic conclusions about the effects of greater populations. Even in *The New Democracy* Weyl was still enough of a Malthusian to select France as the best model of a democracy largely because that country had prudently restricted its birth rate.

Even so, the ultimate result of Weyl's years at Pennsylvania was a new freedom from the "iron laws" of classical economics, plus an enduring urge to search in the facts of economic life for the ways of progress. Largely through Patten's influence, the "dismal science" had shown that the promise of American life lay in the great and growing wealth of the United States.

4. A Scholar Adrift

For five years after he earned his Ph.D. in 1897, Weyl was an aimless wanderer. He abandoned his resolve to be a professor. Despite two years at the University on a senior fellowship and teaching a successful course at the Law School, Weyl decided in 1899 to put academic life once and for all behind him. Years later he was glad that he had so decided. "I am not obliged to consult anybody as to what I say," he reflected in his diary. "I am not obliged to consider the effect of my words upon the revenues or prestige of the University. . . . One stands better alone."

"Drift-wood" was Weyl's own word for himself in the immediate years after he left Pennsylvania. "That is one of the elements," said Weyl's sketch for his autobiography. "—Sheer *drift*. Rudderless. Two poles of Self-interest & Social spirit. Lying between. Passive. Mere pleasure in impact." He ranged over much of the world—to France, to Puerto Rico, to Mexico —making statistical surveys for the United States Bureau of Labor. Carroll D. Wright, head of the Bureau and an important pioneer statistician, made Weyl a protégé and encouraged the researches.

Weyl's reports on his surveys suggest some of the things that were stirring in his mind during his years of wandering. Very probably his intimate contact with the poverty and misery of places like Puerto Rico and Mexico fixed in his mind the contrast with America's enormous prosperity that motivated so much of his later thinking. More specifically, an article on "Labor Conditions in France," written after a trip to Europe in 1898, revealed the intellectual underpinnings of his life-long resistance to Marxian Socialism. Weyl concluded from a long statistical breakdown of a six-volume French report on wages, hours, and employment opportunities that the real wages, the actual standard of living of French labor, had risen considerably in the latter half of the nineteenth century. This conclusion became the first link in the long chain of evidence he would marshal in *The New Democracy* to prove that, contrary to the Marxist prediction, "no progressive impoverishment of the working clasess, no 'increasing misery, oppression, servitude, degradation and exploitation'. . . [had, in fact,] taken place."

Such tentative conclusions, however, did little to establish Weyl in a definite line of work. His family found it increasingly difficult to understand how a man in his late twenties could still be without a settled occupation. A standing offer from his brothers to join the family publishing firm in Philadelphia went unheeded. When an uncle staked Weyl to a search for mineral deposits in Mexico, the venture was profitless. Equally stillborn was a plan of Weyl's to capitalize on his knowledge of railroading by doing a study for Stuyvesant Fish, the highly successful president of the Illinois Central.

The turn of the century found the young economist working in Washington for the Bureau of Statistics, but within a year he decided that the life of a low-paid bureaucrat hardly resolved his inner conflict between "Self-interest & Social spirit." He wandered on then to New York, where like so many intellectuals of the day he worked at the University Settlement, meeting there and becoming fast friends with the young socialists Ernest Poole and William English Walling. In 1902 Weyl was just on the point of accepting another assignment from Carroll D. Wright, when he suddenly found himself, as he said later in his diary, "caught in a vortex that carried him into real life."

On May 15, 1902, John Mitchell of the United Mine Workers called the anthracite coal miners of America out on strike. By the following evening Weyl had reported to the coal fields and offered his services to the union leader. Many others came to the aid of the miners—John Graham Brooks, Henry Demarest Lloyd, Louis D. Brandeis, John R. Commons, Clarence Darrow—men who had already done much to create the vortex that now whirled Weyl into life. There was, in fact, a stirring among the intellectuals in 1902 that presaged much to come. Many felt like Weyl that this strike was different, that the public, as well as the workers and owners, would be involved. The Coal Strike of 1902 had a great deal to do with starting the era of the muckrakers.

The strike itself was something of a miracle. When John Mitchell had first come to the anthracite fields two years before, there had been little hope. The miners had suffered a demoralizing defeat in 1892; in 1900 they had seen the best-organized workers in the country, the steel workers, beaten down by the steel trust. Differences of nationality and religion, the chronic sores of the American labor movement, divided the miners badly and seemed to make effective unionization impossible. John Mitchell, however, had come to Pennsylvania armed with the prestige of earlier victories in Illinois. His skillful leadership had soon given the miners a new union and new hope.

The union had to be strong, for Mitchell's opposition this time was far more vigorous than it had been in Illinois. The anthracite companies were united under the control of seven coal-carrying railroads, which were themselves combined under the Morgan and Vanderbilt interests. The owners were determined not to yield, for to do so would encourage the organization of workers throughout the great new corporate empires.

The strike was a turning point in Weyl's life. Drift and uncertainty gave way to the challenge of a cause. He was welcomed by John Mitchell, who "had no scorn for intellectuals." Weyl's wanderings in Europe, his work in the University Settlement, his talent for languages now came into their own. He could speak many of the tongues of the foreign-born miners, while Mitchell knew only English. Living with and talking for John Mitchell, Weyl found himself useful at last.

Weyl's statistical bent was also helpful, for cold figures could measure some of the misery of starvation wages and inhumanly long hours. The use of statistics by reformers was of course nothing new, but Weyl brought to the business the professional's touch. The number of company-owned houses could be counted, or the number of company-owned stores, or the deductions made from pay checks for medical services seldom received. The number of children in the mines could be totaled; the death and accident toll of their fathers measured. Such were the statistics Weyl helped organize and present before President Roosevelt's Board of Arbitration in 1903.

The Coal Strike of 1902 probably did more to fix Weyl's attitudes toward labor than all his earlier academic work. Behind such attitudes there lay the strong affection and respect he developed for John Mitchell. "I have roomed with him for several weeks at a time," wrote Weyl of Mitchell several years later, "and have seen him at work from early in the morning until deep into the night, when he was suffering pain that would have sent an ordinary man to bed." Weyl admired Mitchell's driving energy, his compelling honesty, but most of all he was impressed by Mitchell's single-minded devotion to the union and its miners.

Weyl considered it a virtue that the union leader refused to use his power in the interests of general social reform. He lauded Mitchell's "willingness to limit his efforts to the immediately obtainable"; he approved Mitchell's lack of rancor against the coal-company bosses. "His philosophy," said Weyl, "is like that of the trained prize fighter who feels no hatred against his antagonist, even though he is attempting to disable him temporarily." Living and working with Mitchell, Weyl favored such tactics, not from conservative bias or fear of labor, but because the tactics seemed to work. Since Mitchell's methods seemed ultimately the most effective, Weyl liked and trusted John Mitchell in 1902, just as he would at first dislike and mistrust the revolutionary Bill Haywood in the Lawrence strike of 1912.

Beyond fixing the general ideas about labor that he would express in *The New Democracy*, the anthracite strike also gave Weyl a start as a publicist. In July 1902 he argued effectively in the *Outlook* for recognition of the miners' union by the coal companies. *Charities* for September carried Weyl's description of the union's strike-relief program, where he stressed the fact that non-union miners were given equal benefits with the rest.

Though the country late in 1902 was just on the brink of the muckraking movement, Weyl wrote of the coal strike not as a muckraker but as an avowed partisan of the labor cause. His difference from the ordinary muckraker is dramatized by the contrast of his writing on the strike with an article on the miners' union by Ray Stannard Baker. Baker's piece was one of the three exposé articles in the January 1903 *McClure's* that started muckraking as a recognizable movement.

Baker also had visited the coal fields in 1902, as an observer, not a partisan, and he came away with a very different picture from Walter Weyl's. While conceding "all the glaring injustices of the coal fields—low wages, company houses, company stores, poor schools, wretched living conditions," *McClure's* muckraker was more concerned with the "17,000 . . . men in the anthracite fields . . . [who] doggedly refuse[d] to support the strike." Thus Baker's "The Right to Work" became an attack on alleged union intimidation and racketeering, rather than, like Weyl's articles, a defense of unionization. The contrast is a measure of how unusual it was for a middle-class intellectual of the day to support even Mitchell's "conservative unionism."

Labor problems became the center of Weyl's life and thinking. Ernest Poole, later a brother-in-law, tells of Weyl's "talking . . . to English Walling and myself on a night train to Boston when all three of us ought to have been in our berths." "We were headed that night for the A.F. of L. Convention in Boston," Poole explained; "and Walter, fresh from his big job for the coal miners, told us of the strike, and a lot about John Mitchell, Wilson, Darrow, and the rest." So strong was Weyl's enthusiasm that the talk went on most of the night and continued unabated in Boston all the next day.

Weyl spent most of 1903 ghostwriting for John Mitchell the union leader's *Organized Labor: Its Problems, Purposes, and Ideals,* a monumental compendium that covered the entire history of trade unionism both in Great Britain and the United States, while dwelling on the aims and methods of labor organizations in exhaustive detail. The book, in arguing strongly for Mitchell's conservative unionism, rejected political action for labor and looked forward to an era "of industrial peace."

In June 1904, Weyl and Mitchell went off together on a jaunt to Europe, a trip that brought complaints from the UMW that "Mitchell stayed abroad two months, writing, with the assistance of Dr. Weyl, articles which he sold for two hundred dollars each, while he was receiving a salary from the mine workers for the protection of their interests." Weyl, in fact, remained Mitchell's friend through the rest of the union leader's life, though as the years advanced he became skeptical of Mitchell's close association with the very conservative Civic Federation.

Weyl's doubts about Mitchell's brand of single-minded, non-political unionism were slow to rise, but they did begin stirring even before he began *The New Democracy.* His long monographs for the Bureau of Labor maintained the same general position, but an article in the *Review of Reviews* on Samuel Gompers suggests that by 1905 certain reservations were forming in Weyl's mind. He lauded Gompers's career as head of the A.F.L.; he praised the union leader for his sturdy refusal of all "political and business honors"; he argued that the steady growth of the A.F.L. seemed a vindication of Gompers's methods. Yet, at the end of the piece, a cautionary, almost critical note appeared, when Weyl suggested that, in order to survive, the A.F.L. would have to organize unskilled workers as well as the skilled.

5. A Scholar Becomes Publicist

In 1907, at the age of thirty-four, Walter Weyl entered into a marriage not without consequences for his future career. Weyl took as his wife Bertha Poole, the daughter of a wealthy former member of the Chicago Board of Trade. Weyl had met young " B. P.," as she had been known at Jane Addams' Hull House, though her brother Ernest, Weyl's friend and fellow worker at the New York University Settlement. During the courtship there were difficulties with some of the members of Bertha's family, who objected to the marriage on religious grounds. From the prospective bride's father, Abram Poole, there even came rumbling threats of disinheritance. Yet in the end the Pooles relented sufficiently to allow their daughter to be married in an elaborate ceremony at Forest Hills, Illinois, in September 1907.

Marriage meant a change for Walter Weyl. Habits of life that had alternated between isolated scholarship and the gregarious male world of YMCA gymnasiums, political conventions, union halls, and settlement houses gave way in part to domesticity. The freedom and pleasure Weyl had found in his proven ability "to live on seven dollars a week" was replaced by the necessity of supporting a wife and eventually a child as well. Personal adjustments had to be made. Weyl later planned as a major theme of his autobiographical novel "the problem of W & B, coming from two absolutely distinct social territories, with different heredities, different points of view."

Many factors, however, made for the remarkably close and happy life the Weyls found together. Bertha Poole had also done settlement house work and written for magazines on labor problems. She was even on one occasion a behind-the-scenes leader of a strike in the New York garment trades. Sharing so many of her husband's interests, Bertha Weyl was able to give his work a direction and momentum it would otherwise hardly have had. "The ordinary ambitions were not strong enough in Walter Weyl," Lippmann writes, "to carry him over that dead center where the original ambition is frayed and all the words are dust and ashes." Gently, firmly, Bertha Weyl supplied both the ambition and the discipline Weyl so conspicuously lacked. In 1912, for instance, when Weyl had taken up self-expressive singing he noted in his diary: "Bertha is more and more opposed to this stunt of mine. . . . She thinks it is a fad, which makes me unsolicitous about my work." In time Weyl came to depend on his wife to an unusual degree.

Marriage had a galvanic effect upon Weyl's literary output. The disapproval of the staunch Presbyterian Pooles meant that little money came from Chicago in the early years of the marriage. Settling in the artists' colony of Woodstock, New York, where they had gone for their honeymoon, the Weyls managed to live comfortably as free-lance writers. For Walter Weyl, the long monographs in the *Bureau of Labor Bulletin* or the *Annals of the American Academy* were quickly replaced by more popular and profitable articles in the *Outlook*, the *Saturday Evening Post*, or the *Survey*. The scholar had become publicist, and the publicist was not above the occasional production of potboilers.

Weyl soon made a success of popular magazine writing. By 1911 he was earning an average of $250 an article from such journals as the *Outlook*, the *Post*, or *Harper's*. "I am in a position of complete independence financially and otherwise," said Weyl at the end of that year. By 1913, rates such as $450 from *Harper's* and $500 from the *Post* convinced Weyl that among magazine writers he had "advanced to the first rank."

In the period before he joined Croly and Lippmann to define further a new liberal philosophy, Weyl's conscience was occasionally troubled by the writing of such popular pieces as "The Corner Grocery" or "The Up-to-Date Druggist." He justified the work in a variety of ways. Frequent estimates were made of the number of days it took him to make enough money to leave the rest of his time for serious work. He subscribed to a newspaper-clipping service and noted happily that one of his articles had been "the basis of 6 or 8 editorials" or that another had been "reproduced all over the country, 5 or 6 papers so far." By 1912 Weyl had decided that "even a mere magazine writer . . . [could] be a man of enormous influence in the community."

Weyl needed the income from his writing, if only to give him an independence he much desired. After 1911, however, he was rarely under real pressure to produce and publish. By then Bertha Weyl's family had become reconciled to her marriage and had set up a trust fund that relieved Weyl of much of the responsibility of supporting his wife and newborn son. In 1911 the Weyls bought a farm on the side of Ohayo Mountain near Woodstock for $3,000 and the next year began building a large house that Weyl anticipated would cost $10,000. When finished, the house was unusually handsome and impressive. Set on a knoll at the end of a long sweeping drive, it commanded on clear days a view of the Hudson far away through the Catskills. Thus comfortably endowed, Weyl was able in 1913 to turn down a salary of $7,500 a year from the New York garment workers' Protocol. "It is . . . a satisfaction to me to know that I could make $10,000 a year if I wanted it," wrote Weyl, when he had offered to serve without pay. "As a matter of fact I already have enough & do not want money."

Economic security and a happy marriage modified but did not entirely change Weyl's earlier ways of living. The press of outside events provided many excuses to get away from Woodstock and the palpable misery of serious writing. There were still strikes that had to be seen, immigration stories that had to be watched and analyzed. Ernest Poole later remembered one trip with Weyl to the Socialist party convention of 1912, where "for days and nights . . . [they] barely slept." "In the hall and in the lobbies outside, and up in the galleries packed with a wild 'Wobbly' crew cheering on their leaders below, and later in the hotel rooms—I remember Walter getting both sides, Walter smoking himself to death, Walter tense, his muscles taut—listening, questioning, listening—antagonizing no one, gradually breaking through reserves, suspicions, restraints—friendly, so plainly and honestly fair—but boring, boring, boring in—critical—untangling—in a tense but patient search for all the facts and all the human values."

Weyl became increasingly fascinated by the problems of immigration. Like so many of the other young intellectuals of the time he wandered through the danker streets of New York and brought back stories for the American middle-class world. Most of the stories Weyl wrote were merely case studies, with little attempt at analysis or effort to point a moral. Frequently the articles seemed to reflect their intended market. Writing his first study for the social-work magazine *Charities*, for instance, Weyl described the life of Simon Ginsburg, a Jewish broom peddler, in tones of unrelieved despair. For the more popular *Outlook*, however, Weyl struck a consistent note of optimism. The Italian immigrant rose from being exploited by corrupt labor bosses to become a prosperous but honest *padrone* himself; the Greek acquired a successful cigar business; the Jew a restaurant chain. Whatever the story, the theme, at least for the *Outlook*, was one of brutal struggle relieved in the end by success and gradual assimilation.

Weyl not surprisingly was far more penetrating in his treatment of immigration problems in magazines like the *Review of Reviews* and the *Atlantic Monthly*. During a trip to Europe with his wife late in 1908, he studied and wrote about the effects of emigration upon European countries. Once more, however, he was most fascinated by France, in a way that had prophetic significance for *The New Democracy*. From France there had been almost no emigration, yet its population had declined. Weyl ranged over all the problems related to such a decline. He denied the common claim that France's reduced population would leave it at the mercy of Germany, arguing instead that the relative power of the two nations depended on resources rather than numbers of people. He believed that France's voluntary reduction of its birth rate, rather than inviting degeneration or military destruction, had ushered in "a new era for mankind."

In the imperial age of Kaiser Wilhelm and Theodore Roosevelt, Walter Weyl was concluding that the strength and wealth of nations depended on something other than fecundity and ferocity. "The development of the race is away from bloody international conflicts"; said Weyl, "away from poverty, ignorance, disease, and crime; away from excessive families and excessive populations, to which these human miseries have always been linked." France's salvation lay not in matching Germany in the breeding of cannon fodder, but rather in the creation of a "new democracy" that could strive for international peace. "The new democracy demands for the man freedom from providing for excessive families"; wrote Weyl, "for the woman freedom from the burden of bearing many children; for the child, the care and the attention that limit inevitably the number of his brethren.... The new democracy does not want an array of unemployed men; of useless and unusable men and women to fill the gutters, to swell the ranks of the criminals, and to promote the decay of the social body." In such a fashion did Weyl first sound the questioning yet hopeful note of *The New Democracy*.

6. THE PUBLICIST AND PROGRESSIVISM

Sometime before 1911 Weyl, like Croly before him, began writing a book on American democracy. His speculations on the "new democracy" of France suggest that as early as 1909 he was turning over in his mind those broad questions of population, resources, and civilization that he tried to resolve in his book. Patten's *The New Basis of Civilization* of 1907 was probably the original inspiration for what became *The New Democracy*, for Weyl confessed at one point that he had started out merely to give a "statistical foundation" to Patten's first chapter on natural resources. Certainly, too, Bertha Weyl must have helped bring from Weyl's wonderfully discursive mind a clear statement of his political philosophy. Ernest Poole expressed more than brotherly pride when he doubted whether "if Bertha had not taken him in hand . . . [Weyl] would have written 'The New Democracy.' "

As important as anything in motivating Weyl, however, was the progressive movement that had grown up all around him. Like Croly before him, and Lippmann after, Weyl had a strong sense of the incoherence of the movement, of its lack of positive direction and form, of its need for a new liberal philosophy. He saw "a new spirit . . at work in America," which was "still inchoate . . . [speaking] with many voices." When, late in August 1911, the book had been accepted by Macmillan and needed only a month's revision, Weyl wrote of *The New Democracy*: "It will be an argument for an American point of view in dealing with American conditions. It will be an argument for the Progressive Movement."

Weyl was himself, of course, very much part of the movement he now tried to analyze and define. In his early years after college he had suffered the congenital alienation that explains so much of the intellectual's protest. He planned to stress in the hero of his autobiographical novel the "academic attitude ... the self-centered quality ... the non-emotional quality. Then ... all the powerful forces that bring him into direct contact with gripping problems." Weyl's closeness to John Mitchell had helped. The University Settlement may have brought to Weyl some of the emotions Ernest Poole expressed when Poole spoke of the settlement's "genial crowd." "They took me in," said Poole, "and made me feel I was not alone in tackling this baffling life." Magazine writing had filled Weyl with a sense of independence and accomplishment, but in those magazines where he had been able to reach the largest audience, he had been able to say least about problems that concerned him. *The New Democracy* consummated Weyl's marriage with the progressive movement. "I am quite astounded at the change in my reputation and standing during the last year," wrote Weyl seven months after his book had appeared. "*The New Democracy* is everywhere meeting with enormous recognition. ... My prices have doubled in the magazine world. My position in the Prog. Party is very secure —one of the 50 leaders."

Much that Weyl said in *The New Democracy* was built on the work of other progressives. He knew the historical heresies of J. Allen Smith's *The Spirit of American Government*, and, like Croly, Weyl saw the Constitution as undemocratic and economically motivated before Charles Beard made the view a progressive commonplace. Frederick Jackson Turner's frontier thesis had had a deep, though fortunately negative, influence on Weyl's thinking. The muckraker Lincoln Steffens had revealed to him the anatomy of American political corruption; Upton Sinclair's researches into American industrial brutality added extra dimensions to Weyl's own impressions from the coal fields of Pennsylvania and the slums of New York. The conservation doctrines of Gifford Pinchot and the theories of "conspicuous waste" of Thorstein Veblen also found a place in *The New Democracy*.

Weyl made his book, however, far more than merely a vivid summation of the progressive agitation of the foregoing years. His intimate knowledge of socialism, both native and foreign, let him argue for multi-class democratic reform far more cogently than, say, Croly, who had made only infrequent and rather vague references to "international socialist theories." Weyl raised and refuted directly the doctrines of American socialists like William J. Ghent and John Spargo, men who were his personal friends in spite of political differences. *The New Democracy* referred frequently and specifically to the ideas of Karl Marx, Friedrich Engels, or Eduard Bernstein and demonstrated with calculated glee how even the revolutionary socialists of Europe were adopting programs of democratic reform.

Weyl, like many progressives, was a pragmatist. Ernest Poole remembered a time in Chicago when Weyl, the Illinois progressive Raymond Robins, and others "were talking of William James and his Pragmatism . . . and Walter was defending that." When Robins had reached a "thundering climax about the Cosmic Verities," Weyl had jibed " 'Yes . . . but what have the Cosmic Verities ever done for me?' " During the final revision of *The New Democracy* Weyl promised in his diary to "glance over Dewey's Ethics," and his interest in the pragmatist philosopher continued in later years. *The New Democracy* contained even more of the pragmatist's pluralism of means and ends than Croly's *The Promise of American Life*, but pragmatism did not mean for Weyl, any more than it did for Croly, the mere expediency and drift of America's later New Deal era. "The democracy, though compromising in action," wrote Weyl, "must be uncompromising in principle. . . . What the democracy needs is a consistent and constructive policy, changed from time to time as new exigencies or new interpretations of the social facts require, but carried out unflinchingly, and realized as opportunities permit."

Weyl was a typical progressive in rejecting the fixed dialectics of Marxism and in accepting the relativism of pragmatism, but he departed from the usual progressive ideology in one significant respect. He was not a Jeffersonian. Though Weyl has often been placed in the Jeffersonian camp, very little of his political theory invites such an interpretation. *The New Democracy* revealed none of that admiration for Jefferson that might be expected of a loyal disciple of the sage of Monticello. Furthermore, just as Croly had done before him, Weyl attacked American individualism in a specific rejection of the Jeffersonian creed. "The inner soul of our democracy," he wrote, "is not . . . unalienable rights, negatively and individualistically interpreted, but these same rights . . . extended and given a social interpretation. . . . This social interpretation . . . makes . . . [the new democracy] different in kind from the so-called individualistic democracy of Jefferson and Jackson." At another point, to give a further example, Weyl held the American "emphasis upon the natural, unalienable, uncontrollable right of property" to be the primary source of American social and political evils, and Thomas Jefferson was pilloried as "a leading exponent of this political anarchism." For Weyl, too, the old Jeffersonian liberalism had to give way to a new liberalism.

7. "THE NEW DEMOCRACY"

Weyl's *The New Democracy*, like Croly's *The Promise of American Life*, was an effort to fashion a new philosophy of middle-class liberalism. Weyl's main concern, however, was to advance a new idea of the necessary dynamics of progressivism. He made little effort to center reform on a single idea, as Croly had done with nationalism. Nor did he have much of Croly's strong sense of crisis. "Like other evolutions," said Weyl of his program (adding his own emphasis), "it is simply a quicker turn of the wheel *in the direction in which the wheel is already turning.*"

Like Croly, like most progressives, what Weyl sought was a middle road between Manchester liberalism and Marxian socialism. "The old *laissez-faire* liberal philosophy is done for," he wrote, "and the old absolute socialism is dying in the embrace of its dead adversary." Weyl's attack on the shibboleths of individualism was if anything stronger than Croly's had been. American individualism had been the source and justification of the "monopolist" and "railroad wrecker," of the inhumanities of the sweat shop and the chicanery of graft and rebates. It deluded Americans into seeing equality and democracy where exploitation and oppression actually ruled. As Croly had done, Weyl saw all the efforts of reformers as blocked "by ancient political ideals which still cumber . . . modern brains, by political heirlooms of revered—but dead—ancestors."

For all his congenital optimism, Weyl joined Croly in finding the United States a land of unfulfilled promise. "Europe does not learn at our feet [any more] the facile lessons of democracy," said Weyl, "but in some respects has become our teacher." "Why have the promises of the rash young democracy . . . remained unfulfilled?" he asked. "Why has the tortoise Europe outdistanced the hare?"

German-trained, as much the product of the nineteenth century as Croly, Weyl inevitably sought the answer to his question in history. America in its beginnings, he found, had hardly been the democratic commonwealth modern Americans romantically looked back upon. Twentieth-century Americans saw the Constitution as a sacred democratic compact; yet, said Weyl, "the Constitution . . . was in intention, and is, in essence, undemocratic." And though the Jeffersonian and Jacksonian periods had marked some progress toward democracy, Weyl found that "only slowly . . . [was America] freeing . . . [its] larger, newer democracy from the trammels placed upon it by the raw, crude democracy of that day."

"All of this has a somewhat familiar sound," said one reviewer about *The New Democracy*'s historical chapters. "The somewhat trite topics have already been thrashed out in a hundred periodicals and newspaper articles." Certainly the muckrakers had made generally familiar the picture of a "plutocratic reorganization," with which Weyl ended his historical analysis. Only in his view of the frontier did Weyl depart from the stereotypes familiar to progressives. He agreed with the historian, Frederick Jackson Turner, on the vital significance of the frontier in American history, but, speaking from New York rather than the Middle West, Weyl believed the influence of the frontier to have been largely bad. American democracy had not been born on the frontier, as Turner and his disciples had suggested; rather it was there that American democracy had been betrayed. "The westward march of the frontier," Weyl wrote in one of his more brilliant insights, "gave the Americans a psychological twist which was to hinder the development of a socialized democracy."

Weyl's analysis of the frontier experience brought him to the heart of his political theory. Unlike most progressives, Weyl found the end of the frontier a cause for hope rather than despair. The frontier, in spite of its harmful effects on the American character, had left America with a great material legacy that promised much for the future. This legacy Weyl called the "social surplus," and the "social surplus" became the basis of his version of the new liberalism.

By the social surplus Weyl meant the increment of wealth the United States had produced over basic human needs. The surplus was social because it was the product of all society and not of particular individuals. Being surplus, futhermore, it could easily be directed toward social ends. Such unprecedented wealth meant that America, and to a lesser extent other industrialized nations, had broken the grim circle of overpopulation and resultant poverty Malthus had decreed to be the world's fate. Striking once again the theme of his earlier essays on France, Weyl declared that the social surplus had released America from what he called "the fateful force of human fecundity."

Here, thought Weyl in 1912, was the answer to Karl Marx. The pattern of American capitalism had not been one of decay, but of continuing material and social progress. Marx had taught that progress would come through poverty. Weyl now answered with the doctrine of "progress through prosperity." Marx's crucial error, an error that Weyl believed Marx himself had ultimately recognized, was his faith in an impoverished proletariat as the source of social revolution. The truth was that Marx's proletariat would have lost all capacity for revolt in the depths of its own misery. "A man or a class crushed to earth—," said Weyl succinctly, "is crushed to earth."

Though Weyl borrowed his notion of the social surplus largely from Simon Patten, he came closest to making an original contribution to progressive thought in his concept of the "levels of democratic striving." Marx had failed to realize until too late that his brutalized proletariat would be below such levels. A class, to be effective either for revolt or reform, had to be economically above the poverty line, intellectually above the literacy line, and politically above the suffrage line. In America, almost alone, had the great mass of the people been lifted by the social surplus above these levels. Calculating roughly, Weyl thought perhaps twenty of America's ninety millions were either too rich or too poor to concern themselves with democratic reform. Seventy millions, however, remained for the purposes of the "new Democracy."

Weyl, nevertheless, trod the brambled paths of economic determinism cautiously. The social surplus represented the *opportunity* for progress, not the actuality. Much of the nation's surplus wealth had already been pre-empted by a ruthless class of plutocrats, who had monopolized America's resources and perverted her democracy. Meanwhile less affluent Americans took comfort from such individualistic slogans as "from shirt sleeves to shirt sleeves in three generations." America had almost lost its chance for a new democracy.

Yet Weyl in 1912 found the situation anything but hopeless. The very malignancy of the plutocracy had bred a reaction that was the progressive movement. Furthermore, the social surplus itself had given rise to a new social consciousness. Men could now rationally believe in the idea of a "full life for all the members of society." Out of the chance for a full life, Weyl declared, had been born the desire, out of the desire the "moral idea," and out of the idea had come the "impetus for action." "For," said Weyl, making his compromise between economic determinism and freedom of the human will, "it is ideas born of conditions that rule the world."

Both the impulse and the opportunity for a new democracy existed. Only one difficulty remained. How could seventy million Americans, who were neither too rich nor too poor to desire reform, be united in an effective movement? The impulse for reform could not come from an idea alone; it must also arise from circumstance. What motivating circumstance did the seventy million Americans share? The answer, for Weyl, followed immediately upon the question. They were all consumers. Why had Americans protested against the tariff, the trusts, the rape of the nation's resources by the few? The progressive movement, said Weyl, with apparent plausibility, represented the protest of the consumer against the prices of monopoly. "A new insistence," Weyl wrote, "is laid on the rights of the consumer, and political unity is based upon him. . . . Men who voted as producers are now voting as consumers."

Weyl was not politically obtuse. He conceded that man's common lot as a consumer might be a tenuous political bond. He recognized the discouraging tendency of Americans in the past to think of themselves mainly as producers and to place their productive interests first. But his recognition of the difficulty did not make him abandon his theory. Instead he argued that the tenuousness of the bond among consumers would force on reformers a gradualist program. The great diversity of the democratic group would, more often than not, make flanking movements, rather than frontal assaults, the desirable "tactics of democracy."

To revolutionary socialist critics who would reject such "gradualism," who would deny that the bourgeoisie could be deprived of property and power without violence, Weyl again found an answer in the social surplus. The very vastness of America's social surplus would allow the nation's industry and resources to be brought under public control without forcible dispossession of the wealthy.

"What I had to say," said Weyl of *The New Democracy* a week after it had been published, "I put in the last three chapters." There Weyl presented his program for America. The program, however, despite Weyl's confidence in it, remained peculiarly vague and diffuse. In essence Weyl demanded an enormous expansion of the welfare state, plus a gradual program for the socialization of industry. Yet, perhaps because he had lived much closer to many of the problems than had Croly, Weyl was less able to formulate sweeping and didactic prescriptions for their cure.

Weyl's labor policy, for example, lacked the reassuring simplicity of Croly's idea of federal recognition and encouragement of trade unions. Weyl apparently was satisfied that the unions could make their own way without government aid, though even here he at no point stated his position clearly. In place of Croly's program for frank government discrimination in favor of unions, Weyl advocated laws against woman and child labor and for maximum hours and minimum wages, laws chiefly beneficial to those outside the range of union activity.

Toward political reform, too, Weyl's attitude was remarkably indecisive. He valued "efficiency" and "responsibility" as much as did Croly and other progressives, but he could distil from such words no certain clues for distinguishing between one reform and another. Without definite principle, therefore, but with varying degrees of enthusiasm, Weyl favored the direct primary, the initiative, referendum, and recall, the direct election of senators, easier amendment of the Constitution, and a more precise division of powers between state and federal governments.

When he took up the problem of the "trusts," Weyl spoke with greater certainty and conviction. Here he definitely shared the views of Croly and supported Roosevelt's New Nationalism. He derided attempts to smash the plutocracy "by merely 'smashing' the trusts." In place of "trust busting," Weyl wanted a long-term policy of nationalization of major industries, with the degree of government ownership or control to depend on the circumstances of each business. For the railroads and coal mines (significantly those industries he knew best) Weyl suggested direct government ownership "in the very near future"; other less monopolistic businesses might continue under government regulation for an indefinite period. In rounding out his economic program, Weyl argued that increased conservation measures and much heavier taxation would help curb the power of the propertied few over American democracy.

Taken all together, Weyl's program meant very gradual progress toward democratic socialism. Its spirit remained pragmatic throughout. Reforms were to be judged not so much by their logical consistency as by their results. Changes were to be pressed only so hard as the diversity of the democratic mass would permit. The program, in effect, was the opposite of the doctrinaire.

Sharing the pragmatism of progressivism, Weyl, furthermore, put more emphasis upon democracy than was usual for many progressives of the time. The "expert," the "strong administrator," the other quasi-authoritarian heroes of progressivism were absent from Weyl's pages. He advanced no theory of a democratic yet dominant elite of the kind Croly commended in *The Promise of American Life*.

The strong emphasis upon democracy probably explains why Weyl has so often been typed a Jeffersonian. Certainly he was not an avowed Hamiltonian like Croly, but then Croly himself was a Hamiltonian only in so far as Hamiltonianism seemed the most practical path toward Jeffersonian ends. Weyl's belief that the great mass of the people could be the impulse behind reform seemed to breathe the "spirit" of Jeffersonianism, yet it would be hard to find a democratic group more dissimilar from Jefferson's small, property-owning farmers than Weyl's embattled consumers.

Weyl's faith in the consumer, moreover, fortified his pronounced lack of sympathy for small businessmen, who would become the ideological targets of Woodrow Wilson's Jeffersonian New Freedom. Weyl thought the protests of such petty entrepreneurs hollow; he denied that trusts and monopolies were the source of their troubles. Taking the case of the tobacconist, Weyl showed that, even if the United Cigar Store chain were dissolved, its "place would immediately be taken by thousands of small competitors, and the average cigar store dealer would be but little better off." More sophisticated than many analysts of his time, Weyl argued that the small businessman's problems in a corporate economy were more psychological than economic. And wherever economics did rule, competition, not the corporations, was the source of the *malaise*.

Weyl suffered from much the same eastern, urban myopia that had characterized Croly's *The Promise of American Life*. Like Croly's, Weyl's prescriptions were supposed to apply to the country as a whole. Yet farming was mentioned in his book only where agricultural statistics could help refute the bleak prophecies of Malthus and Ricardo or the Marxian prediction of the "proletarianization" of the farmers. For Weyl, as for Croly, the problems of major concern were those of the city.

Just as Croly's "metropolitanism" contradicted his nationalism, so Weyl's emphasis upon urban problems conflicted with his theory of mass consumer protest. Weyl nowhere tried to reconcile his hopes for seventy million consumer reformers with the fact that the still large and disproportionately powerful farm population of the United States had obviously different interests. High prices for hogs and corn would hardly delight those who dined in the shadow of an elevated line.

Weyl's questionable faith in consumer protest, however, merely demonstrated the most salient quality of his philosophy —its pervasive materialism. "In the final analysis, however it may be clothed in legal rights and political immunities," he wrote, "democracy means material goods and the moral goods based thereon." The Francophilia that came so oddly from Weyl's German-American background, for instance, meant a fondness for France's "civilization" not its "culture." Weyl valued not so much the art, the literature, or the philosophy of France as the over-all prosperity and enlightenment of its people. The genius of French life lay in the capacity of the French to adjust their numbers to available material goods.

In the last chapter of his book Weyl raised the same questions for the United States that as early as 1909 he had asked for France. Could the United States by limiting immigration and restricting its birth rate become a sane and civilized democracy like France? Could America's vast resources be turned to nurturing not more people but better people? Would the nation turn away from expansionist imperialism abroad to cultivate contentedly its gardens at home? On the answer to such queries, said Weyl, marking the crisis of his own times, hung the fate of the "new democracy."

Weyl's concern for such material and social ends contrasted vividly with the cultural values that moved Croly's thinking. Where Croly attacked a materialistic America for stifling talent and originality in art and thought, Weyl cherished America's bountifulness for its promise of happiness for all. Croly saw economic progress chiefly as a means to a higher culture; Weyl preferred to postpone cultural questions "until the material problems which beset mankind ... [were] solved." Weyl's materialism reflected the statistician's habit of measuring things by quantity rather than quality; it came naturally to one trained in economics rather than philosophy and the arts. His intimacy with strike and sweatshop, tenement and miner's hovel had constantly impressed on him how little the latest novel or play could mean to a man in fear for his daily bread. Weyl, too, had little of that strong religious impulse that occasionally carried Herbert Croly beyond the practical to the sublime.

Concerned, thus, with the more prosaic needs of man, Weyl's political philosophy had less sweep and grandeur (and therefore, unfortunately, less potential impact) than that of the man whose cause he would join in 1913. He was no less brilliant than Croly; he had, perhaps, a firmer grip on reality. Not personal intellectual incapacity, but rather the enormous variety of the wants he tried to satisfy, explained the general imprecision of Weyl's program for reform. Dedicated by his materialism to provide for the masses, Weyl also could rest his reform upon mass support. His philosophy had no need for inspired leadership to guide and cajole the people to some higher destiny; *The New Democracy*'s homely aims were readily negotiable democratic coin. Weyl's difference from Croly, therefore, was not that of a Jeffersonian from a Hamiltonian; instead, the difference arose from the forces the two men would rally for reform. Whether one or the other or neither was right hung upon the future.

THREE

Walter Lippmann: Voluntarist Liberal

1909-1913

1. THE TRIUMVIRATE'S PRODIGY

Walter Lippmann was the bright young man of the intellectual trio. Though his twenty-fifth birthday came but six weeks before the *New Republic*'s first issue, Lippmann was already a man of experience and accomplishment. His academic work at Harvard had been distinguished. He had already published two much-praised analyses of current politics, *A Preface to Politics* in 1913 and *Drift and Mastery* a year later. Four months as secretary to a Socialist mayor of Schenectady, New York, had given him some insight into practical politics. After a period of apprenticeship under Lincoln Steffens, he had joined the staff of *Everybody's Magazine* at the age of twenty-two. To his work with Croly and Weyl, Lippmann brought a quick and erudite mind and a facile pen.

In spite of youth and relative inexperience, Walter Lippmann made a major contribution to the new theory of liberalism upon which the three men were working. Together with Weyl, Lippmann helped counteract for the *New Republic* the effects of the tortured abstractness of Croly's writing. Lippmann's talent for broad generalizations, his fondness for paradox, his dexterity with the pithy quotation were the essence of weekly journalism. Called by Theodore Roosevelt in 1915 "on the whole the most brilliant young man of his age in the United

States," Lippmann added more than a little luster to Croly's band of intellectuals.

Insofar as the triumvirate's influence was a compound of the reputation of its members, Lippmann's adherence was not all advantage, however. While most intellectuals of the time respected Lippmann's mental keenness, he was generally neither liked nor trusted. Though Lippmann had been a confirmed Socialist at Harvard and for several years afterwards, the Socialist William J. Ghent in 1915 dismissed him with a brief: "Lippmann I have never had any use for and judged him capable of anything." John Reed, Lippmann's friend during a short Bohemian period after Harvard, jibed in verse at the young publicist's bland omniscience:

> . . . Lippmann,—calm, inscrutable,
> Thinking and writing clearly, soundly, well;
> All snarls of falseness swiftly piercing through,
> His keen mind leaps lightning to the True;
> * * *
> Our all unchallenged Chief! But . . . one
> Who builds a world, and leaves out all the fun,—
> Who dreams a pageant, gorgeous, infinite,
> And then leaves all the color out of it,—
> Who wants to make the human race and me,
> March to a geometric Q. E. D.

Mabel Dodge, whose Manhattan salon Lippmann helped organize, ticked off her young confidant with the remark: "Walter is never, never going to lose an eye in a fight. He might lose his glow, but he will never lose an eye."

The reactions of the other two members of the trio to Lippmann were mixed. Weyl's chronic distrust has already been noted. Croly's responses over the years varied. When he first asked Lippmann to join the *New Republic*, the older publicist was both skeptical and enthusiastic. He agreed with his friend Learned Hand that Lippmann was an interesting combination "of maturity and innocence." "The Preface to

Politics is an astonishing book for a fellow three years out of college to write," said Croly, "but no matter how he turns out as a political philosopher, he certainly has great possibilities as a political journalist. ... He has enough real feeling, conviction, and knowledge to give a certain assurance, almost a certain dignity to his impertinence, and, of course, the ability to get away with impertinence is almost the best quality a political journalist can have."

As he worked with Lippmann on the *New Republic*, however, Croly's confidence much increased. Philip Littell, probably the closest of any of the other editors to Croly, thought that Lippmann, among Croly's "intimate friends ... in those early days [was the] only one to whom ... [Croly] would have attributed any turn for sustained thought." Yet much as Croly came to respect Lippmann as a journalist, he never apparently lost his doubts about the younger man as a political philosopher. Croly's reading of Lippmann's *A Preface to Morals* in 1930, for instance, provoked the comment: "Walter's journalistic habit of mind does not fit him to deal with ... [the subject] in a satisfactory manner. ... Unless he stops journalism soon he will only continue to write introductions and prefaces as long as he lives."

The mild irritation Lippmann roused in Walter Weyl was matched in the attitude of other *New Republic* men. When Harold Stearns worked for the magazine in 1916, he found Lippmann "a little ... stuffy and bowed down with the cares of the world." Robert Morss Lovett, an editor after the First World War, believed that between Lippmann and Francis Hackett, the *New Republic*'s early literary editor, "there was inveterate opposition." Such reactions, however, were perhaps the inevitable lot of an intellectual as precociously brilliant as Lippmann. Even the talented Alvin Johnson believed, when he joined the staff late in 1915, that he "could never compete with Walter Lippmann, then unfolding his wide wings." Harold Laski, who worked on the magazine during the war and knew most of the editors intimately, concluded in 1920 that "of all the *New Republic* bunch .... [Lippmann's] mind is the wisest and most profound."

Lippmann's own feelings toward his work with Croly and Weyl can only be surmised. Evidently he never quite shared Croly's absolute dedication to the *New Republic*. Like Weyl, he took time off from the magazine to write a book on the war; in 1917 he left for a variety of jobs with the War Department, Colonel House, the army, and the Peace Commission. Though even Weyl during the war's hysteria came to think the *New Republic*'s possible influence of supreme consequence, Lippmann stayed away until 1919, when he returned to help blast Woodrow Wilson's dying peace efforts. Where Croly was the consecrated philosopher of the intellectual trio, and Weyl its conscience, Lippmann tended to be the ambitious doer. Whether pressing a labor program on Roosevelt, advising Wilson on war aims, maneuvering with House on peace terms, or sapping German morale on the Western Front, Lippmann instinctively gravitated to the centers of action and power. Personable, vigorous, remarkably intelligent, the young publicist was never entirely content to be a mere dreamer of dreams among the "movers and shakers."

2. CONSERVATIVE GENESIS

Lippmann, like Weyl, came from a German-Jewish background, but significantly he was of the third rather than the second generation. Born in New York City on September 23, 1889, Lippmann belonged to the wealthy middle class. His grandfather Louis Lippmann, a native of Berlin, had emigrated to America after the German revolutions of 1848. Walter Lippmann's father was "an able and successful businessman, a manufacturer," while the mother has been described as "a woman of unusual intelligence, witty, cultivated, interested in the arts." An only child, the young Lippmann was surrounded by every comfort and advantage. He attended a small private school in New York and spent many of his vacations traveling with his parents in Europe.

In later years Lippmann tended to glory a little in his success at having risen above a conservative middle-class background. In 1914 he recalled that he had been "a child of four during the panic of '93," when Cleveland had been "a sinister figure . . . [whose] name was muttered with monstrous dread in the household." Bryan, too, had been "an ogre from the west," and Lippmann remembered "waiting for the election returns of 1896 with a beating heart." "To this day," wrote Lippmann in *Drift and Mastery*, "I find myself with a subtle prejudice against the Democrats that goes deeper than what we call political conviction."

His early religious training was another evil Lippmann later used his pen to exorcise. He wrote feelingly of a family servant who used the fear of God to punish boyhood iniquities. He remembered how the maid would begin "to talk in a solemn voice." "I would have preferred a thousand beatings to that voice," Lippmann recounted some twenty years afterwards. "And for years God was the terror of the twilight."

Yet religion, at least for the first half of Lippmann's life, was never so important as it was for Croly. Lippmann rarely mentioned religion in his first two books, and then only to assert the inability of Christianity to combat modern materialism or to condemn the Catholic church as "hostile to democracy and to every force that tended to make people self-sufficient." Lippmann's early approach to religion was wholly pragmatic. Strongly echoing William James, he declared the truth or falsity of religious beliefs to be unimportant. The real question about religion was "the effect it had on men." Where has it helped them, where hindered?" Lippmann asked in *A Preface to Politics*. "What needs did it answer?"

Much of Lippmann's early radicalism seems to have been a reflex from his conservative upbringing. Remarkably bitter passages in his first books, for instance, condemn secrecy in sex education. Such secrecy, Lippmann charged, built up "the sense of sin and furtiveness of sex" and made the body an "object of sneaking curiosity, of a tingling embarrassing interest." Or elsewhere Lippmann poured contempt upon the ordinary middle-class citizen who worried as to "who . . . [were] 'the best people' and who . . . 'the impossible,'" and taunted the lowly bourgeois for his sleepless nights over whether or not he would "be invited to be seen with Mrs. So-and-so." Liberality about sex and disdain for snobs were very much part of Lippmann's age; what was unusual was the violent derision he expended on such human commonplaces.

Young Walter Lippmann did brilliantly in his early studies at Dr. Julius Sachs' School for Boys in New York. He wrote for and edited the school paper, was a leading debater, and won several academic prizes before his graduation in 1906. Though trained and confirmed at the reformed Jewish Temple Emanu-El during his youth, Lippmann abandoned the faith soon afterwards. As in the case of Weyl, neither the Jewish religion nor the problems of the Jews played much part in Lippmann's intellectual life. In 1922 he contributed to a symposium of leading American Jews on anti-Semitism by asserting that leaders of the Jewish people seemed "supersensitive to trivial prejudice in non-Jews, and extraordinarily insensitive to the faults of the Jews." In the 1930's he suggested colonization in Africa as a partial solution of the problem of Jews under persecution by Hitler. Strong passions raged beneath Lippmann's cool exterior, but they were rarely those of sentiment.

Between his mother and father the young Lippmann faced the tug of rival ambitions. Devoted to art, his mother bent his interests in that direction. His businessman father, however, looked forward to a career in law for his brilliant son. That the struggle never became irreconcilable is suggested by the fact that Lippmann continued to live with his parents on New York's East Eightieth Street just off Park Avenue until his marriage in 1917.

3. MIDDLE-CLASS INTELLECTUAL AT HARVARD

In any case the maternal influence prevailed, for Lippmann, like Croly and Weyl, started off in life with the goal of an academic career. He entered Harvard in 1906 with the firm intention of becoming "an art critic or professor." Eleven of twenty-three courses Lippmann took at Harvard reflect his early fascination with art. Eight other courses in philosophy and five in economics, government, and history, however, suggest that political subjects rapidly became of equal interest.

Lippmann found Harvard just as intellectually insurrectionary as had Croly two decades before. He recalled later the confusion stirred in him by his first course in the history of philosophy. When another student complained that he had agreed with each of the philosophers in turn and yet knew that they couldn't "all be right," Lippmann confessed that he also "was too much puzzled with the same difficulty to help him." Only later did Lippmann realize that he had vainly been searching for "the philosopher's stone . . . [for] an absolutely true philosophy of politics."

Lippmann's class of 1910 at Harvard was distinguished. It included John Reed, radical, war correspondent, author of *Ten Days That Shook the World*; the poets Alan Seeger and T. S. Eliot; the stage-designer Robert Edmond Jones; and the humanitarian journalist Heywood Broun. H. V. Kaltenborn, a contemporary of Lippmann's at Harvard, remembered him as "an earnest, hard-working intellectual who was known in Cambridge respectfully as one of Harvard's bright young boys." Conrad Aiken, a classmate, later dubbed Lippmann "the darling of English 12."

Lippmann took full advantage of Harvard's opportunities. Under President Eliot's elective system the ambitious could finish the undergraduate requirements in three years. Lippmann did so with ease, taking more courses than needed for a degree and earning a Phi Beta Kappa key in the process. He became an editor of the *Harvard Monthly* and while taking an extra year of graduate work in 1910 assisted George Santayana in a course in the history of philosophy.

Harvard was in turmoil during Lippmann's years there, a turmoil that caught in microcosm the progressive forces at work everywhere. Lippmann's class was the last to study under Eliot's relaxed régime, and even John Reed thought later that individualism had been carried almost to the point of anarchy. The undergraduates, he said, "could live pretty much as they pleased, and do as they pleased—so long as they attended lectures." Yet, while the undergraduate body was, in Reed's phrase, made up of "all sorts of strange characters, of every race and mind," the "aristocrats," the rich and "well-born," held the positions of honor and power in the university. Walter Lippmann, a Jew, could not be one of these.

The ferment at Harvard, however, was more than the struggle between "clubmen" and "hoi polloi" that a few years before at Princeton had helped start Woodrow Wilson toward the Presidency. Spreading beyond the quiet streets of Cambridge, the movement took on social and political overtones. While at college young Lippmann worked in Boston's Hale House and Civic Service House and, like Weyl in New York shortly before, learned something of the squalor that lay just beneath America's blatant prosperity. Relief work after a great fire that swept one of Boston's slums apparently turned his interests during college definitely toward politics and social reform. At Harvard many of his fellow students rose in general revolt. They "criticized the faculty for not educating them, attacked the sacred institutions of intercollegiate athletics, sneered at undergraduate clubs so holy no one dared mention their names." At the forefront of the agitation Walter Lippmann soon found a place.

Socialist doctrines became a symptom of the unrest. The British Fabians H. G. Wells and Graham Wallas, visited the Harvard campus and, as Englishmen, made economic heresy respectable. Lippmann was later convinced that even William James had been "converted" to socialism by the dynamic

Wells. Inspired by such examples, the more thoughtful students turned away from mere "Oscar Wildean dilettantism" to a world of squalid but interesting fact. "Some men," wrote John Reed, "notably Walter Lippmann, had been reading and thinking and talking about politics and economics, not as dry theoretical studies, but as living forces acting on the world, on the University even." In 1909, Lippmann, Alan Seeger, Edward Eyre Hunt, and others banded together to form the Harvard Socialist Club, with Walter Lippmann its president.

The club tried to be more than just a college forum for theoretical debate. Reflecting their Fabian antecedents, the leaders delved immediately into active politics. They drew up a Socialist platform for the city elections. They had social legislation introduced into the Massachusetts legislature. They challenged undergraduate ideals in the college papers and "muckraked" the university for not paying its servants living wages. As the club grew in numbers and gained some influence in campus affairs, only the "clubmen and athletes," according to John Reed, escaped its stimulus.

Lippmann himself wrote much for the college magazines. He championed "Socialism at Harvard," attacked the commercialism of college athletics, defended Fabian socialism over Marxism, and advocated women's suffrage. In his last year he became the center of a factional struggle with traditional campus leaders over the election of class officers. Though the results of the battle were inconclusive, the fight probably gave Lippmann some training in politics. Harold Stearns, watching the struggle as a freshman, found it a better "introduction to class and personal politics . . . than even an apprenticeship in a local Tammany organization in New York City would have given."

Among the intellectual influences that played on Lippmann at Harvard, William James, George Santayana, and Graham Wallas were the most important. Like Croly before him, Lippmann emerged from Harvard a pragmatist, but his pragmatism derived much more directly from James than had Croly's. Though Lippmann had no courses with the philosopher, it appears from one account that James himself sought out the brilliant young student. An attack by Lippmann in one of the college papers on a book justifying capitalism so stirred James's enthusiasm that he stalked into Lippmann's room and announced, "I'm William James. I liked that review." Lippmann joined those students who made frequent pilgrimages to James's house the last two years of the retired professor's life.

Lippmann demonstrated both his closeness and indebtedness to James when in 1910 he was asked to write his first article for *Everybody's* on a subject "well within his personal knowledge." Writing on James, Lippmann celebrated the philosopher's "open-mindedness," his willingness to give "all men and all creeds, any idea, any theory, any superstition, a respectful hearing." With an enthusiasm that became the touchstone of his own early career, Lippmann welcomed most of all James's call to action in "The Will To Believe." James had shown the impossibility of waiting until all the evidence was in, of evading action in academic detachment. "Our daily life is full of choices we cannot dodge," said Lippmann. "Who shall refuse us the right to believe what seems most adapted to our needs?" Out of the whirling experience of pragmatism, the dreamer of dreams would become doer.

Lippmann's first two books on politics cited James so frequently, and referred so often to Santayana, Wallas, and others, that little space was left for ideas Lippmann could call his own. Both books were essentially attempts to apply the pragmatic method to politics, with James's theories elaborated in terms of the insights of Graham Wallas and Sigmund Freud. "No creed possesses any final sanction," declared the young Lippmann in *A Preface to Politics.* "It is more penetrating, in my opinion, to ask any creed whether it served than whether it was 'true.' " In *Drift and Mastery,* written as he was joining Croly and Weyl to organize the *New Republic,* Lippmann was equally sure that "the only rule to follow . . . [was] that of

James: 'Use concepts when they help, and drop them when they hinder understanding.' "

Though associated as assistant and professor during Lippmann's final year, Lippmann and Santayana never became really intimate, perhaps because a certain coldness in both precluded close communion. Lippmann himself has since said, according to an interviewer, that, while Santayana's influence on him "was profound," it "would have been just as great . . . if he had never known him."

The marked similarity of professor and student, nevertheless, invited influence. Both were devoted to art and poetry, Santayana as a poet himself, while Lippmann's first book was an edition of the works of a minor French poet. Like Lippmann, Santayana lived apart from the main stream of Harvard life. Catholic by tradition, half-alien by birth, wholly alien in spirit, the philosopher was never at home in genteel, Protestant Cambridge. Furthermore, the thoughts of both men in 1910 were tending in similar directions—Santayana toward the brief political phase of his career that later found expression in the *New Republic*, Lippmann from the artistic to the political in philosophy and in action.

Lippmann's work with Santayana answered the riddle of the sophomore course in "The History of Philosophy." The key, Lippmann said in *A Preface to Politics*, lay in Santayana's treatment of Platonism as nothing more than "a very refined and beautiful expression of our natural instincts." "In some such way as this," wrote Lippmann, "the sophomoric riddle is answered. No thinker can lay down a course of action for all mankind—programs if they are useful at all are useful for some historic period." The same idea was the culminating note of Lippmann's introduction to the book where he adjured his readers "never to forget that all philosophies are the language of particular men."

Naturalism, in the sense that all theories are created by living men and respond to specific human desires, became a cornerstone of Lippmann's thinking. Derived perhaps from

Santayana, it was fortified by the similar insights of James, Wallas, and Henri Bergson. Much of the argument of *A Preface to Politics* can be reduced to the single point that politics must satisfy basic human wants, not abstract political rights and concepts. Lippmann never carried naturalism as far as Santayana, whose epiphenomenalism denied that ideals could control action, but the philosopher's skepticism was always on the borders of Lippmann's thought. How far could reason guide political action? This question obsessed Lippmann more than any other during the years he worked with Croly and Weyl. Lippmann's resolution of the problem in *Public Opinion* in 1922 retained the flavor if not the substance of his Harvard master's doubts.

Santayana's ideas, however, had less immediate impact on Lippmann than did the pragmatism of William James. At best Lippmann merely recognized that Santayana was a mine of quotable remarks. In *Drift and Mastery*, for instance, he used a long passage from Santayana to support his own conviction that rational science was the crowning achievement of the age. In *A Preface to Politics* a year earlier, however, when Lippmann took a less happy view of science, he had used Santayana with equal facility to prove that "reason itself is an irrational impulse."

The cool detachment of Santayana's "socialistic aristocracy," which so stirred the impassive Croly, had less immediate appeal for the vibrant, ambitious Lippmann. In 1910, the ultimate meeting of minds between master and student was foreshadowed by little except surface similarities of style and manner. Lippmann had the same air of authoritative objectivity, the subtle vein of irony that gave Santayana's writing its distinctive cast. Lippmann, sharing Santayana's distaste for the merely technical, wrote of politics as Santayana wrote of philosophy in the ordinary vocabulary of life and letters. Even Lippmann with all his facility, however, could no more imitate the particular cadences of Santayana's writing than he could apply the philosopher's concept of "essence" to the problem of ballot-box stuffing.

Lippmann's closest and most influential friendship at Harvard developed with the English Socialist, Graham Wallas. When Wallas came to Harvard in the spring of 1910 to give a course on the relation of psychology and politics, Lippmann became his protégé. Lippmann's precociousness was such that the worlds of age and experience between the two men seemed not to matter. When Lippmann went to Europe in the summer of 1914, he visited Wallas in his suburban London home. The same year Lippmann prefaced *Drift and Mastery* with a quotation from the Englishman's *The Great Society* and acknowledged "the privilege of reading Mr. Wallas's book in manuscript while . . . revising this one." Wallas in turn dedicated *The Great Society* to Lippmann and began the book with an admonitory letter to his young disciple.

Two years before his lectures at Harvard in 1910, Wallas had published *Human Nature in Politics*, a book Lippmann subsequently hailed as "marking a turning point in the history of politics." The book had grown from the twenty years Wallas spent as a leader of the Fabians, a group of English intellectuals who stood for a gradual, non-revolutionary brand of socialism. Wallas, however, had been discouraged by the inconclusive results of Fabian attempts to apply theory to practical politics. He decided that reform to succeed needed a more realistic basis in human nature. His main purpose in *Human Nature in Politics* became to show "the danger . . . of the 'intellectualist' assumption 'that every human action is the result of an intellectual process, by which a man first thinks of some end which he desires, and then calculates the means by which that end can be attained.' " Wallas tried to demonstrate instead that men's political actions were more often than not the result of irrational impulses. Recognition of this fact required a thoroughgoing revision of political theory.

"Mr. Wallas has called a halt," said Lippmann in *A Preface to Politics*. "I think we may say that his is the distinction of having turned the study of politics back to the humane tradition of Plato and Machiavelli—of having made man the center of political investigation." Wallas's book and his teaching at Harvard had opened for Lippmann the Pandora's box of twentieth-century irrationalism. The English Fabian had prepared the young publicist's mind for all the more voluntaristic notions of Georges Sorel, Henri Bergson, and Sigmund Freud that would bedeck the pages of *A Preface to Politics.* So ardent became Lippmann's discipleship, in fact, that Wallas himself a few years later found cause to warn him against "certain forms of twentieth-century anti-intellectualism."

Wallas's ideas, plus the pragmatism of James and the urbane skepticism of Santayana, were the things that most filled Lippmann's mind as his last year at Harvard came to an end. He left Harvard in 1910 much taken with all that was new in modern thought. There was no match in Lippmann's experience for Croly's early commitment to the rationalism of Comte or Weyl's to the classical economics of Ricardo and Malthus. Lippmann did not have the same hard struggles with nineteenth-century survivals as did Croly and Weyl. Such struggles gave the liberalism of Croly and Weyl a muscularity Lippmann's sophomoric triumphs could hardly claim. A socialist from the start, without conservative beginnings except those of family and status, heavily imbued with the relativism of James and Wallas, Lippmann would later prove more susceptible to conservative strains of thought than either of his colleagues.

4. MUCKRAKING AND SOCIALISM

Even before his Harvard commencement Lippmann, like Croly and Weyl before him, had abandoned his early plan to be a professor. Eschewing what Santayana called Harvard's "normal school for future professors," Lippmann decided to train himself for journalism. While his friend John Reed took a cattle boat for Europe, in the first of a series of adventures, and another friend, Alan Seeger, who had been class poet, romantically wandered off to France and ultimate death in the French army, Lippmann, neither anarchist nor poet, remained in Cambridge as a reporter for the Boston *Common*.

The decision to work for the new reformist newspaper had been made on the advice of another of Lippmann's collection of notables, the muckraker Lincoln Steffens. With an old newspaperman's sentimental dedication to the discipline of the "cub reporter," Steffens had advised his young protégé not to miss the chance "to see the various departments of a paper [all] at once." But as Lippmann worked part-time on the paper during his last months at Harvard, he soon became bored with sitting "all day in the office, reading newspaper clippings, and trying to restate the facts as colorlessly as possible." With something close to desperation he wrote Steffens of how he had "dreamed" of working under him. "Money," he said, "does not happen to be an important consideration for me at the present time. Opportunity to work and to learn is the thing I am looking for."

Soon Steffens decided to take on Lippmann as his secretary. As usual the muckraker was bent on proving a point. He had bet the editor of *Everybody's*, which he served as associate editor, that he could create within six months an accomplished magazine writer from some intelligent college graduate. He wanted magazines to train their men just as newspapers did their "cubs." In the "keen, quiet, industrious" Lippmann, who "understood the meaning of all he learned," Steffens felt he had a sure thing.

Steffens at the time was investigating the "Money Power" on Wall Street, and Lippmann became his "leg-man." As Lippmann later explained, he and Steffens were attempting something "different from ordinary 'muckraking' "; they were trying to elicit not "the evils of Big Business, but . . . its anatomy." Steffens wanted to prove that the "invisible government" he had found operating in America's states and cities was duplicated in the control of large business. "We found," wrote Lippmann in *A Preface to Politics*, "that the anatomy of Big Business was strikingly like that of Tammany Hall; the same pyramiding of influence, the same tendency of power to center on individuals who did not necessarily sit in the official seats, the same effort of human organization to grow independently of legal arrangements." The work gave Lippmann one more proof of Graham Wallas's thesis that official institutions ignored the facts of human nature.

Lippmann enjoyed assisting a man who, as he said, "had seen as much of actual politics as Mr. Steffens." They lived and worked closely together, and the fledgling journalist dotted his later writings with the fruits of Steffens's keen political eye. When Lippmann came to thank Steffens at the end of the year as his secretary, he acknowledged that Steffens had helped humanize more than his view of politics. "Whenever I understand a man and like him, instead of hating him or ignoring him," wrote Lippmann, "it'll be your work. You've got in my blood, I think, and there'll be a little less bile in the world as a result."

Never one to hide his light under a bushel, Steffens soon moved to win his bet with the editors of *Everybody's*. He sent an article of Lippmann's on William James through the editorial mill without a name, waiting until the final proof to add the correct one. When the article appeared in the magazine as "by Walter Lippmann," the editors were forced to concede that Steffens had won his wager. His triumph became complete when during the summer of 1911 Lippmann was hired as an editor.

The era of the muckrakers was already on the wane, but *Everybody's* was still basking in the glow of Tom Lawson's famous Wall Street series, "Frenzied Finance." The investigations Lippmann carried out in the financial district for Steffens were intended to carry Lawson's process further, to go beyond mere exposure to analysis and understanding. The work was probably the beginning of Lippmann's long search

for "constructive" solutions. In *Drift and Mastery* he dismissed
all the data of the muckrakers with the quip "that if anyone
really desired that kind of proof, a few German scholars, young
and in perfect health, should be imported to furnish it." While
Steffens was not yet sure, as he would be later, that the "reformation of politics and business by propaganda and political
action was impossible," he was probably close enough to the
conclusion to add to Lippmann's already healthy skepticism.

Lippmann, rapidly disenchanted with muckraking, found
his position on *Everybody's* less than happy for other reasons
as well. The promotion from Steffens's assistant to editor
turned out to be a comedown. Lippmann soon became bored
with being the "first reader of manuscripts and the sorter-out
of jokes for a funny column." Furthermore, *Everybody's* had
already begun to succumb to those subtle restraints that within a year or so largely ended the muckraking movement. The
year before Lippmann joined it, the magazine was sold to new
owners, and in 1911 its muckraking editor, John O'Hara
Cosgrave, resigned in protest against "a pressure to which he
was totally unaccustomed." Lippmann also suffered from the
change. "I have seen the inside workings of business pressure,"
he wrote later of *Everybody's*. "Articles of my own have been
suppressed after they were in type."

Most of his articles that did appear in *Everybody's* were
rather routine pieces on the evils of arson and pension frauds
or the virtues of scientific management. Beyond the initial
essay on William James, only one of them showed much about
the bent of Lippmann's mind at the time, an article on Henri
Bergson entitled "The Most Dangerous Man in the World."
Lippmann thought the French philosopher the prophet of the
real revolution of the day, a revolution going on in the minds
and hearts of men. "Bergson," he wrote, "is . . . a herald in
whom the unrest of modern times has found a voice." Bergson
had shown that ceaseless change was "the very principle of
life." "It is the conservatives who violate the spirit of life when

they want institutions to stay frozen tight," said Lippmann, "not the radicals who want them fluid."

While a few of Lippmann's *Everybody's* articles expressed the philosophical heresies he had come across, more than philosophical heresy filled Lippmann's mind in 1911. His leadership of the Harvard Socialist Club had led him after college to membership in the Socialist party in New York State and a position as secretary to the party's "cabinet." In January 1912 the New York Socialist Morris Hillquit urged George R. Lunn, recently elected Socialist mayor of Schenectady, to hire Lippmann as his assistant. Bored by his work on *Everybody's,* Lippmann accepted the new post with alacrity.

Men like Hillquit were excited by the prospects of the new Schenectady administration. Except for Milwaukee, Schenectady was the largest city in the United States where Socialists had an opportunity to put their theories in practice. But as he worked closely with Mayor Lunn, Lippmann began to see some of the handicaps of practical politics. "I have lived with politicians," he wrote in *A Preface to Politics,* "—socialist politicians whose good will was abundant and intentions constructive." The "petty vexations" and "distracting details" of politics so engrossed the Schenectady reformers, however, that "the mere problem of exercising power ... [crowded] out speculation about what to do with it." Lippmann reached the same conclusion at Schenectady that Herbert Croly had drawn earlier: practical politicians had to have someone do their thinking for them.

Still much the radical, Lippmann soon decided that the actions of the Schenectady Socialists were actually betraying socialism. Mayor Lunn and his lieutenants had concentrated on "immediate demands" in order to attract non-Socialist votes, but once in power their reliance upon non-Socialist voters tended, as Lippmann complained in the *Masses,* "to impregnate the movement with half-baked people who ... [didn't] understand Socialism." The whole Schenectady campaign, he wrote in 1913 to a Socialist friend, had turned "on keeping the progressives in line." Mayor Lunn had been forced to placate property owners and reduce taxes, when the real "business of a Socialist administration . . . [had been] to cut into the returns on property, [to] take as much of them as possible to be spent for social purposes." When the progressives won out on a critical issue, Lippmann decided that Schenectady was no place for a sincere Socialist.

Thus, oddly enough, Lippmann first broke with the Socialists in 1912 because he believed them not radical enough. The Schenectady Socialists, he argued in *A Preface to Politics*, had sought "obvious success"; they had won political office through voters not thoroughly indoctrinated with Socialism. The Lunn reforms had "had to pass the judgment of men who did not see life as the officials did." "To me," wrote Lippmann, "it always seemed that we were like Peer Gynt struggling against the formless Boyg—invisible yet everywhere—we were struggling with the unwatered hinterland of the citizens of Schenectady."

Socialists, in effect, were to hew to principle and accept defeat until the time became ripe for victory. Lippmann's Schenectady experience convinced him that his Fabian friends, Graham Wallas and H. G. Wells, had been right in their disillusionment with Fabian tactics. "I understood then, I think," Lippmann wrote, "what Wells meant when he said that he wanted 'no longer to "fix up," as people say, human affairs, but to devote his forces to the development of that needed intellectual life without which all his shallow attempts at fixing up were futile.' " After four months as Mayor Lunn's secretary, Lippmann quit the job and set out to promote the revolution in men's minds that he believed had to come before any revolution in their politics.

5. SOCIALISM AND PROGRESSIVISM

The Lippmann of 1912 was in real danger of being a revolutionist without a cause. His own political beliefs were much in flux. Though his protests at Schenectady made him seem more radical than the Socialist Mayor Lunn, actually he was quarreling more about tactics than principles. And, strangely enough, at the same time Lippmann was advising the Schenectady Socialists to take political defeat rather than compromise their Socialism, he himself was drifting away from their cause. Even at Harvard, Lippmann had never been a Marxist; by the time *A Preface to Politics* was finished, in October 1912, he had jettisoned most of the tenets of even his Fabian creed.

One after another in his book Lippmann ticked off his objections to various socialist shibboleths. He rejected what he called the socialist "myth . . . that initiative springs anonymously out of the mass of the people," a delusion he thought led socialists to ignore the need for inspired leadership in politics. He was convinced that the usual socialist vision of "the misery of the country as a deliberate and fiendish plot" much exaggerated "the will, the intelligence and the singleness of purpose in the ruling classes." Neither could he accept the usual socialist argument that just as the French Revolution had been the rising of the bourgeoisie against the nobility so inevitably a day would come for the proletariat to rise against an oppressive middle class. "Just because the capacity for aggression in the middle class ran away with things, and failed to fuse into any decent social ideal," he wrote, "is not ground for trying as earnestly as possible to repeat the mistake."

By the closing months of 1912, therefore, Lippmann seemed to be approaching the ordinary progressive hope for some political theory that would benefit all classes, not just the working masses. What fragments of his earlier socialist enthusiasm survived seemed to attach themselves to the guild socialism of England's G. D. H. Cole. Guild socialism, said Lippmann, called "for co-management of industry by the state and by the labor union." It avoided the "socialist danger" of "exploitation by a bureaucracy in the interests of the consumer" and at the same time "the syndicalist danger" of "oppressive monopolies by industrial unions." Since it gave consumers as well as others some say in industry, guild socialism was "an example of statesmanlike dealing with a new social force."

Yet even in the case of guild socialism Lippmann refused "to argue . . . either for or against the scheme." His tactic in *A Preface to Politics* was to capitalize brilliantly on his own uncertainty by decrying all programs and theories until some basic thinking had been done about the facts of human nature. The Progressive campaign of 1912 that so excited Croly and Weyl failed to provoke any public enthusiasm from the young political thinker. He was still enough the Harvard radical, of course, to find Taft beneath consideration. For Wilson, he had some respect. But as a presidential candidate Wilson had "slackened into commonplace reiteration" while running on "a futile and intellectually commonplace platform." Roosevelt, whom Lippmann most admired, also had betrayed his better self and failed to live up to the radical program of the Bull Moose Chicago convention. So, beyond a possible practical awareness of the advantages of keeping his book nonpartisan, Lippmann probably was still too close to his Socialist past for an open progressive avowal.

Lippmann's criticisms of socialism, however, made it clear enough that if he was moving anywhere it was toward the right. Essentially Lippmann had reached the same conclusions about America that Croly and Weyl as progressives had reached. He had become sure that socialism was as hopeless as Croly and Weyl believed liberalism to be, unless American ways of thinking changed. For Lippmann, as for Croly and Weyl, the trouble did not arise as much from the corrupting influence of the special interests as from the miasma of outmoded belief and stultifying tradition in the American mind. What Lippmann sought in his first book, therefore, was not a practical political program, but "a preliminary sketch for a theory of politics, a preface to thinking." The onetime Socialist was well on the way to being a prophet of the new liberalism.

6. "A Preface to Politics"

Disenchanted with the Socialists, still uninspired by the Progressives, basically unsure of his own theories, Walter Lippmann forsook the clangor of politics and retired to the Maine woods to write a book during the summer of 1912. The problem he addressed was the one Graham Wallas had raised at Harvard. How, Lippmann asked himself, could politics be made a living, breathing reality and not merely "a personal drama without meaning or a vague abstraction without substance?" He considered the widespread apathy of the people, not the depredations of the special interests, to be the real cancer of American politics.

Rather fortuitously, a solution to the young writer's problem accompanied him to his backwoods retreat. Along with Lippmann went a friend, Alfred Kuttner, who was working on an English translation of Sigmund Freud's recently published *An Interpretation of Dreams.* "I read the translation as ... [Kuttner] worked on it," Lippmann has since related, "and discussed it with him and began to see how much Freud had to contribute to the psychology which I had learned at college." Freud seemed to provide the new psychology for politics Wallas had demanded four years before in *Human Nature in Politics.* By October, Lincoln Steffens reported that Lippmann was back in New York with a completed book. "He dined with me last night," wrote Steffens to a friend, "and he is in a bully state of mind."

Lippmann had cause to feel "bully," for *A Preface to Politics,* in spite of serious limitations, was a remarkable work for a man barely twenty-three. The book brought an admiring letter from Theodore Roosevelt the next year. Sigmund Freud himself referred to it in his magazine *Imago* as the first practical attempt to apply Freudian psychology to politics. The *Forum* serialized three chapters of the book early in 1913. When it was reprinted a year later, the *North American Review* belatedly cited it as "The Book of the Month."

Though a few reviewers made fun of the pretentiousness of Lippmann's manner, comments generally were very favorable. The staid Boston *Transcript* declared *A Preface to Politics* to be "in many respects . . . the ablest brief book of its kind published during the past ten years." Bliss Carman in the New York *Times* found it "a refreshing book, first, because of its temper, secondly, because of its soundness."

In writing *A Preface to Politics* in less than six months, Lippmann had accomplished a *tour de force.* Within the book's covers he had brought together much of the most advanced thinking of William James, George Santayana, H. G. Wells, Graham Wallas, G. K. Chesterton, Friedrich Nietzsche, Henri Bergson, Georges Sorel, and Sigmund Freud. He had pieced out the insights of the other men with his own rather limited experience at Harvard, on *Everybody's,* and with the Schenectady Socialists. The uncritical conjunction in a single book of the ideas of men so remarkably different was perhaps a mark of Lippmann's youth; it may also have been the sign of a mind more facile than profound.

Only one review was critical. The *Nation* alone wondered what the end would be of a " 'modern philosophy' which . . . placed the will in its new found 'freedom' on the throne of the universe, wholly autonomous, wholly creative, wholly loosened from the trammels of the past which concerns it not, and wholly lord of the future which lies at its feet." The *Nation* pardoned Lippmann's "rather juvenile and cocksure pronouncements" only on the ground that he would "probably outgrow most of them." Lippmann himself may have agreed, for some twenty years later he humorously jibed at his first book as "covering pretty nearly all human problems."

If, with the *Nation* as an exception, the general critical acclaim accorded *A Preface to Politics* were an index of the sentiments moving intellectuals at the time, rather serious questions could be raised about the progressive movement. Few of Lippmann's reviewers probed deep enough, however, to realize that beneath the haze of authoritative references and broad generalizations there lurked a political theory with disturbing implications.

What reviewers noticed most was Lippmann's use of Freud. Lippmann's Freudianism meant a call for a "new freedom" far more profound than that sought by Wilson on the stump in 1912. Freud's theories, Lippmann believed, explained the apathy toward politics of the great mass of the people. Politicians throughout history had attempted to govern by the "taboo." They had made laws for what people ought not to do, thus inviting a first-class neurosis. Prohibitory legislation stirred all the social evil Freud had found in the "repression" of individual psychology. The real hope of politics was evident in Freud's theory of "sublimation"—the direction of society's evil impulses toward desirable ends.

Critics hailed without hazard Lippmann's use of Freudian "repression" and "sublimation" in politics, for there was little new in the thought except its penumbra of semi-scientific jargon. Lippmann himself conceded that Freud had merely further documented the ideas implicit in James's psychology and Wallas's *Human Nature in Politics*. Two decades before, furthermore, the sociologist Lester Ward had attacked legislation for being "negative rather than 'attractive,' " for being "more concerned with preventing crime than with releasing the energies of men for constructive work." Another sociologist, Edward A. Ross, had made the same idea the main theme of his *Sin and Society* in 1907. Lippmann was striking a theme that Croly and Weyl had already made familiar when he suggested that a government that turned "away from the sterile tyranny of the taboo" would be a "government totally different from the ideal of Jefferson." For Lippmann as for Croly and Weyl the example of government "repression" most frequently cited was the Sherman Anti-Trust Act.

While Lippmann's Freudianism only added a new dimension to the protest of many progressives against individualistic theories of government, it suffered from limitations less evident in the theories of Croly and Weyl. Lippmann assumed too easily a parallel between social forces and the individual instincts of the Freudian analysis. He equated the suffrage movement, industrial consolidation, and labor unrest with irrational impulses Freud had discovered in the human psyche. In advising that such social forces be "sublimated," Lippmann ignored vital differences between individual and social phenomena. The suffrage, trust, and labor movements, for instance, were too recent to count as aboriginal social instincts. Certainly the demand by women for equal rights was hardly a force that had been simmering repressed through all the centuries. The feminist movement could more sensibly be explained as a response to the new economic status of middle-class women in the twentieth century. Lippmann was undoubtedly right in stressing the danger of ignoring such new forces, but his use of Freud was mere "window-dressing."

Lippmann's application of Freud to politics, moreover, carried the young publicist into some rather dark and troubled waters. In addition to the Viennese psychologist, James, Wallas, Santayana, Nietzsche, Bergson, and others had all helped convince Lippmann that man's irrational impulses were stronger than reason. The task of statesmanship became to search out the "dynamic currents" in society and to "shape and direct and guide them." One such current that Lippmann stressed was the new character of modern businessmen. He was convinced that the leadership of industry had passed to "the hands of men interested in production as a creative art instead of as brute exploitation." "That subtle fact," said Lippmann, "—the change of business motives, the demonstration that business can be conducted as medicine is,—may civilize the whole class conflict." Suggested in *A Preface to Politics* as only one of many "civilizing forces," Lippmann's faith in "far-sighted businessmen" became a major theme of *Drift and Mastery* a year later. As such it indicated how utopian Lippmann's bravely critical world of irrational relativism might become.

Even more striking was the statesman that Lippmann believed his theory of politics required. What was needed, Lippmann said, was a politician equipped in every way by education and instinct to understand and direct the real "motor currents of social life." Most important of all, Lippmann's statesman would become a man of "creative will and insight," a man not hampered by a mere fetish for logical consistency, but willfully creative enough to relate his program to "human passions" and give it reality in a world of "human desires."

"Creative will and insight" most distinguished Lippmann's statesman from the ordinary politician. Taking very much to heart Bergson's notion of the superiority of intuition over reason, Lippmann believed that an aesthetic insight into the "stream of life" would give the statesman a sense of "the springs from which conduct flows." The will of the statesman would dominate his intelligence. He would inaugurate a program, not because reason had shown it right, but because his intuition of society's "dynamic purpose" revealed it as necessary. Often the statesman's program could not be presented to the people in honest and rational terms, but only through some "myth" that would capture their enthusiasm. The statesman's knowledge of human nature would reveal the appropriate myth and his ultimate aims would justify its use.

Though Freud's ideas on dreams and fantasies bolstered the argument, Lippmann's notion of the creative function of the "myth" was derived largely from the French syndicalist Georges Sorel. In his *Réflexions sur la violence* Sorel had confounded his critics by admitting that the syndicalist call for a General Strike was a conscious myth. He had conceded "without a blush" that the General Strike might "never take place, that it . . . [was] not a true picture of the goal of the socialist movement, . . . [but instead was] simply a 'myth.' " "Revolutionary myths . . ." Sorel had explained, "enable us to understand the activity, the feelings, and the ideas of a populace . . . *they are not descriptions of things but expressions of will.*" Having added his own italics, Lippmann went on to assure his readers that for a real grasp of the use of myths it would be "necessary to read M. Sorel with great sympathy."

Since Lippmann's statesmen would rule even through calculated deceit if necessary, the young writer's idea of leadership went considerably beyond ordinary liberal notions. Even Herbert Croly had stressed the extreme importance of keeping the leader's will "the handmaid of his intelligence" and not vice versa. Croly's call for leadership had boiled down to a pious wish for another Lincoln to lead the nation further toward nationalism. Lippmann's desire tended more toward the virile, voluntaristic superman of Friedrich Nietzsche. "I have put it negatively, as a counsel of prudence," Lippmann explained at one point in his attack on the repression of human instincts. "But he who has the courage of existence will put it triumphantly, crying 'yea' as Nietzsche did, and recognizing that all the passions of men are the motive power of a fine life." In 1912, at least, the young Walter Lippmann had the courage of existence in full measure.

Lippmann freed his statesman even more from ordinary democratic restraints by insisting that the ultimate ends of government were beyond definition. Here again he contrasted markedly with Croly, who impressed on progressives the need for defining the ends of reform, however tentatively, so that the people could judge them. Lippmann, on the other hand, insisted that politics was "not concerned with prescribing the ultimate qualities of life." He denied that government could be based on ideals, even ideals so hazy as "life, liberty, and the pursuit of happiness." "Every abstraction," said Lippmann, "every rule of conduct, every constitution, every law and social arrangement, is an instrument that has no value in itself. . . . Each man in his inward life is a last judgment on all values. . . . The goal of action is in its final analysis aesthetic and not moral—a quality of feeling instead of conformity to rule."

Lippmann entered into the free and whirling world of Nietzsche, Bergson, and Sorel with an ardor only the invariable blandness of his manner concealed. He had passed far beyond his master William James, who insisted always on the practical efficacy of "old truths" and the vital need for a rational ordering of experience. Lippmann was undoubtedly right that the ends of government must of necessity be vague, and that "life, liberty, and the pursuit of happiness" mean many things to many men. What he ignored was that even vaguely defined principles imply an *agreement* among men upon ends, and within the limits of such agreement the statesman is restrained. Subtle as the difference may be in practice, such a ruler is different from one who obeys only the decrees of his own intuition.

Perhaps Lippmann should be held no more responsible for the dangers inherent in his ideas than Croly, for Lippmann also was writing before Fascists had carried the ideas of Sorel, Bergson, and Nietzsche to their ultimate extremes. The measure of responsibility, however, lies in the difference of the two men. Croly saw the perils of the ideas he used. He conceded that the leadership he proposed "was by its very nature liable to become perverse and distracting." He insisted on definite personal qualities in the leader and definite democratic restraints upon his power. He believed, finally, that "in a country whose traditions and ideals ... [were] democratic such leadership ... [could] scarcely go astray." In the wondrous cosmos of Lippmann, ideals and traditions were dismissed, at best with youthful jocularity, at worst with a sneer.

Lippmann, however, did not seriously desire a leader totally without restraint. Yet the restraints were entirely personal, the product of the statesman's education and of his intuitive insight into the needs of society. Lippmann in a sense merely magnified that common middle-class progressive desire for a leader to save the class from its own stupidity. In the back of Lippmann's mind, as in the minds of many progressives, there lingered a fear that otherwise some sterner, less tractable master, some demagogic man of the people, might usurp the defaulted power.

For all his recent socialism, Lippmann's susceptibility to ordinary middle-class fears of class warfare was shown by his praise of Theodore Roosevelt. Roosevelt, said Lippmann, had never spoken "more wisely or as a better friend of civilization" than when early in 1912 he condemned the folly of France "in splitting into the two camps of unreasonable conservatism and unreasonable radicalism." Thus the impulse behind Lippmann's philosophy of endless change was not only to promote reform but also to prevent that "hard-shell resistance to change which . . . [would bring] it explosively." The impulse seemed quite different from the one that had led him to quit the meliorist Schenectady Socialists only a few months before.

Roosevelt, in fact, was the American leader closest to Lippmann's ideal. "You can readily see from my book," wrote Lippmann to the Colonel in 1913, "that it owes a great deal to you, and for that very reason I was very eager to have your opinion of it." Roosevelt's genius had lain in his marked sensitivity "to the original forces of public opinion." His success, Lippmann argued, "had to be judged by the size of his task, by the fierceness of his opposition, and by the intellectual qualities of the nation he represented." Roosevelt had been "the working model for a possible American statesman at the beginning of the Twentieth Century."

Though, like Croly, Lippmann found a certain crudeness in Roosevelt's thinking, he tended to admire the very militancy in Roosevelt that Croly feared. Whereas Lippmann praised "Woodrow Wilson's . . . elegant and refined intellect" and Wilson's liking for "a world of gentlemen," he feared at the same time that Wilson lacked the vital insight into "the inward mutterings of the age" that was Roosevelt's chief distinction. Such insight made Roosevelt "a man of will in whom millions of people . . . felt the embodiment of their own will, . . . a man of destiny in the truest sense."

Beyond the already familiar idea that reform should turn from "destructive" measures like the Sherman Act to more "constructive" ones, beyond the emphasis on leadership and the use of the myth, Lippmann's *A Preface to Politics* offered little in the way of a constructive program. He obviously believed in a definite centralization and expansion of government of the kind Croly and Weyl had called for. He wanted government to go beyond merely political and economic issues and handle "social and moral questions." "They are what politics must deal with essentially," he wrote, "now that it has found a way."

Like Croly and Weyl, Lippmann much wanted to find a substitute for socialism. "A new philosophical basis is becoming increasingly necessary to socialism," said Lippmann, "—one that may not be 'truer' than the old materialism but that shall be simply more useful." As a creed the new philosophy would develop in men "no less energy . . . than that of the war of class against class." It would capitalize upon the kind of zeal men felt "in the building of the Panama Canal." It would allow men's "domineering impulses" to "find satisfaction in conquering things, in subjecting brute forces to human purposes." "This sense of mastery in a winning battle against the conditions of our life is," concluded Lippmann, "the social myth that will inspire our reconstruction."

All of which was well and good. Lippmann undoubtedly captured something of the spirit of the new day he celebrated so enthusiastically. Yet, in what sense was Lippmann's exhortation to Americans to put their creative, domineering impulses foremost a myth? Where in such an ideal was all the faith and illusion that made up the "Christian myth," the "democratic myth," or the "socialist myth?" Removed from the context of Lippmann's hortatory prose, his "myth" contrasts pallidly with any of these.

Compared with the mature and seasoned works of Croly and Weyl, Lippmann's *A Preface to Politics* inevitably suffers. Writing with more facility than either of the other two men, Lippmann triumphed more by his manner than by his meaning. Beneath the surface sheen of quip, quote, and paradox lay a mass of rather puerile and often dangerous ideas. Though,

like Croly and Weyl, Lippmann sought essentially a new
formulation of middle-class democracy, he ended with ideas
both destructive of middle-class values and of democracy itself.
Lippmann in 1912 was a synthesizer of the ideas of other men.
Far less than Croly or even than Weyl was he an originator of
his own. The sign of Lippmann's youthful fatuity lay in the
rapidity with which he fulfilled the *Nation*'s prediction that
he would soon "outgrow" his ideas. Only a year later in
Drift and Mastery Lippmann abandoned the anti-scientific
Bergsonian world of drift and fantasy for the more prosaic
scientific experimentalism of John Dewey. In doing so he
came closer to the new liberalism of Croly and Weyl.

BOOK II

THE NEW LIBERALISM IN PRACTICE

FOUR

Bull Moose Nationalism

1909-1912

1. "You Certainly Hit the Game"

"Your response to the book overwhelmed me," wrote Herbert Croly to Learned Hand in December 1909, when his friend had finished reading *The Promise of American Life* and praised it volubly. "Is it really," he continued, "as good as that? . . . Naturally I hope that it is really good not merely because I have my own share of vanity, but because it needs to win friends." Though three editions of Croly's book brought total sales to "only about 7,500 copies," it did win friends, friends influential enough to make the book a significant part of the progressive movement.

For all the ponderousness of its style and organization, *The Promise of American Life* was widely and favorably reviewed. The New York *Times* spoke for all the reviewers when it found the book "worth studying seriously, . . . a sincere and forcible argument based upon fresh and honest thought." Even more impressive was the amount of serious analysis the book brought from reviewers. From the first, however, the reactions suggested how much Croly's message would be changed through absorption by the progressive movement. American reviewers without exception took up the political and economic aspects of Croly's nationalism; they were blind to the cultural emphasis that gave Croly's theory coherence, that distinguished his nationalism from oppressive and militant varieties.

It took an Englishman to catch the real drift of Croly's arguments—specifically, a reviewer for the irascibly anti-American London *Saturday Review*. The *Review*, while conceding that attacks on irresponsible millionaires and corrupt politicians were nothing new from an American, lauded Croly's "chief reason for disliking the millionaires." "It is perfectly true," the English journal declared, "that if the one object aimed at by every male in the nation is the making of money, individuality disappears . . . [that] if the national civilization produces only one type, the money-maker, it is a failure." The reviewer thought "literally true" Croly's conclusion "that in no country in the world has the opinion of the educated man less weight in real affairs than in the United States." Significant for Croly's future was the fact that only in England was he completely understood. The cultural emphasis of his nationalism had real meaning only to a country whose stultifying aristocratic tradition he himself had roundly attacked.

There were men in America, however, who caught the substance of Croly's elitist appeal. They did not boggle at the last sentence of *The Promise of American Life*, with its call to "exceptional fellow-countrymen" for "acceptable examples of heroism and saintliness." For the most part they were men close to Theodore Roosevelt. Henry L. Stimson, who ran in 1910 with Roosevelt's support for governor of New York, was one of them. Felix Frankfurter, Stimson's "brain trust and factotum" during the New York campaign, was similarly stirred. Somehow, too, Croly's book fell into the hands of the young diplomat and financier Willard Straight, a Roosevelt protégé, who was at that time the representative of American banking groups in China and who would later finance the *New Republic*. Judge Learned Hand reflected the impact of the book on the whole group of young, upper-middle-class, eastern progressives when he confessed to Croly: "I find that in my talk and in my thought about political matters, since I have read it, I am constantly borrowing whole cloth what you say."

Such support was heartening, but Croly had even more

heroic hopes for his book's influence. In a section of *The Promise of American Life* entitled "The Reformation of Theodore Roosevelt," the publicist had called on the politician to carry his presidential "Square Deal" further toward thoroughgoing nationalism. Like many Americans, Croly did not think that Roosevelt's political career was over. The Colonel was to be the instrument for teaching the lessons of nationalism to the people.

The problem was to get *The Promise of American Life* into Roosevelt's hands. In early 1910 the ex-President was still off on safari in Africa. Learned Hand volunteered to be, as Croly later gratefully acknowledged, "the instrument that forged the bond." As the closest of friends, visiting each other back and forth in New York and Cornish during the winter and spring of 1910, the Judge and the publicist hatched a minor conspiracy. When late in March the American press blazed accounts of Roosevelt's emergence from the jungle and the beginnings of a European tour, they decided to act. Judge Hand mailed Croly's book to Roosevelt and sent at the same time a letter that recalled "an acquaintance, long since past," in order to urge the book's virtues on the ex-President. Croly, he wrote, dealt with a "set of political ideas which can fairly be described as neo-Hamiltonian, and whose promise is due more to you, as I believe, than to anyone else."

Within three weeks Hand had received two letters from Roosevelt from the Netherlands and France thanking the Judge first for his letter and then for the book. Croly and Hand were hopeful. Though Roosevelt's replies were merely the conventional few lines of a man who received many letters and many books, they believed their tactics had worked. "I have great confidence," Croly wrote, "in the fact that he has got to supply copy for the *Outlook* and the book would be one of those subjects prized by every editorial writer which are up-to-date without being contentious." "You certainly hit the game," Croly told Hand after Roosevelt's second letter had arrived. "Now let's see whether he drops."

Yet, oddly enough, it was probably not the gentle conspiracy of publicist and jurist that actually brought *The Promise of American Life* to Roosevelt's attention. Eleven days after Hand had written Roosevelt and mailed the book, the eminently conservative Henry Cabot Lodge also wrote Roosevelt. "I have just finished a book called 'The Promise of American Life' by Herbert Croly, of whom I have never heard before," wrote Roosevelt's intimate friend and close political adviser. Praising the book as containing "an amount of hard and careful thinking about things past, present, and to come ... rarely met with in any study of American democracy," Lodge continued: "There are plenty of things in the book with which you will disagree as I do but you will not say of any of them that the writer has not thought hard about it. . . . You can get it in London . . . and read it on the voyage. It will repay you I am sure."

Lodge's words were probably decisive, for when Roosevelt replied eight days later, he had either forgotten or was unaware that Hand had promised to send him the book. "I have at once ordered Herbert Croly's 'The Promise of American Life' from the Macmillans of London," wrote the Colonel, thus ensuring himself of two copies, since Hand's gift reached him in Paris within a day or so. In his second letter of thanks to Hand, Roosevelt assured him that he looked "forward with real pleasure to reading it."

Read the book Roosevelt did, though probably not so soon as Lodge, Hand, and Croly hoped he might. Visits with most of the crowned heads of Europe, a review of the German army with the Kaiser, lectures, speeches, the funeral of Edward VII, and finally a triumphal and tempestuous return home in mid-June, all were enough to challenge even Roosevelt's prodigious energy. Not until the end of a relatively quiet July spent at Oyster Bay did the Colonel write Croly about *The Promise of American Life*.

"I do not know when," declared Roosevelt, "I have read a book which I felt profited me as much as your book on American life." Though there were points on which he could not "entirely agree," such disagreements were "on minor matters, indeed chiefly on questions of emphasis." "All I wish," he continued, "is that I were better able to get my advice to my fellow countrymen in practical shape according to the principles you set forth." "I shall use your ideas freely in speeches I intend to make," said the Colonel, adding that he hoped Croly might visit him, for he wanted "very much to have a chance to talk."

The "game" seemed very definitely, as Croly said, to have been hit, but the telling shot paradoxically had come from the rather reactionary Henry Cabot Lodge. What was the common strand in *The Promise of American Life* that could attract so strongly both the deeply conservative Lodge and the increasingly progressive Roosevelt? Why had both Lodge and Roosevelt, who equally abhorred socialism, praised a book Croly himself had called "socialistic"? In all probability, neither could detect much of socialism in a book that mirrored so well Roosevelt's own thoughts and convictions. Furthermore, the impulse behind Croly's "socialistic" theories was at one with the basic motives of the two eastern politicians. Croly's version of Santayana's "socialistic aristocracy" was concerned, after all, more with preserving and advancing what the publicist considered the finer elements of society than with elevating the masses. Lodge and Roosevelt, at least privately, could only agree.

Both politicians shared all of Croly's disdain for the "new rich," his faith in the middle class, and his latent fear of the masses. Considering themselves members of the upper class, they resented the new power of industrialists in America and appealed to the great middle group for resistance. In Vienna that spring, Roosevelt had been amused to find "what in America was regarded as a democratic movement against the powerful and arrogant aristocracy of wealth was among ... [the Viennese nobility] looked upon as a movement fundamentally in the interests of the right kind of aristocracy." Lodge on occasion wrote feelingly of the "lawlessness," the "disregard for the rights of others" of those he called condescendingly "the modern, *very* modern plutocrats."

Moreover, though Croly's nationalism differed considerably from the militant, imperialistic variety of Lodge and Roosevelt, it had enough "blood and iron" to be acceptable to the two jingo politicians. Both men had helped foment the Spanish-American War, and neither of them would have taken Croly's internationalized imperialism seriously enough to be bothered by it. Though Roosevelt accepted joyously what Croly faced with resignation, there was similarity between Roosevelt's remark in 1901 that he was "not in the least sensitive about killing any number of men if there . . . [were] adequate reason" and Croly's realistic though cold-blooded feeling that the road to international peace would be "piled mountain-high with dead bodies." The publicist's desire for a strenuous foreign policy to help promote national efficiency had something of the flavor of Roosevelt's sentiment that "an occasional war . . . [was] a good thing for the moral fibre of a nation." As Roosevelt had said, any differences were those of "emphasis."

Certainly, too, Roosevelt had found much in the book to stroke his vanity. The Colonel had been made the hero of the Hamiltonian revival Croly desired. Even Croly's program for the trusts, thought by so many since to have influenced Roosevelt, was described in *The Promise of American Life* as merely an extension of the "Roosevelt-Taft policy of recognition tempered by regulation." Croly granted the Colonel the ultimate accolade when he declared Roosevelt's "devotion to the democratic and national ideas . . . [to be] more thoroughgoing and absolute . . . [than that of] any other American political leader, except Lincoln."

Thus, Roosevelt's note praising Croly's book and promising to use its ideas in speeches brought to a climax a long courtship by the diffident political philosopher. Croly's reaction to Roosevelt's praise showed just how prayerfully he had awaited such a culmination. "Whatever gratification I may feel as an author in receiving such a letter," he wrote Hand, "is entirely swallowed by my sentiment of personal loyalty to the man in his position who could lend me so firm & cordial a hand." Croly's demand for leadership and his faith in a democratic elite seemed about to be realized in the rally of Roosevelt and his followers to the banner of democratic nationalism.

2. A Question of Influence

Roosevelt did come out with a dramatic political program he called the New Nationalism within a month of his letter of praise to Croly. Most historians have assumed since, what Croly may then have believed, that he and his book were the inspiration for Roosevelt's seeming new departure. Again and again Croly has been hailed as the man who inspired Roosevelt's New Nationalism, the man who led Roosevelt down the paths of radicalism to Armageddon in 1912.

The judgments of influence have had small warrant, however, for even Roosevelt's letter promising to use Croly's "ideas freely in speeches" has heretofore been unknown to scholars. That there was a profound similarity between the ideas of *The Promise of American Life* and Roosevelt's New Nationalism is true, that Roosevelt proclaimed his policy after the publication of Croly's book is also true, but similarity and sequence alone cannot be the measure of influence. To be significant *similarity* has to be set off from mere coincidence of reasoning, from ideas that arise simultaneously from similar sources, or from patterns of influence that are interacting rather than direct. For *sequence* to count, a definite change has to be shown in the supposedly derivative thought. Such a change has to be linked above all other causes to the impact of the ideas held to be influential. None of these tests is adequately met in the case of Croly, Roosevelt, and the New Nationalism. The unraveling of the evidence, furthermore, suggests much about the nature of the relationship between intellectuals and politicians.

When in August 1910 Roosevelt proclaimed his New Nationalism at Osawatomie, Kansas, he had in fact long been turning over in his mind the very ideas Croly had brought forth the previous November. Over and over again in his private correspondence, Roosevelt had rung the changes on Hamilton and Jefferson that *The Promise of American Life* composed into a progressive philosophy. Through all his mature life Roosevelt had held Croly's conviction that Jeffersonianism was the cardinal vice of American politics. "I think the worship of Jefferson a discredit to my country; and I have small use for the ordinary Jeffersonian," wrote Roosevelt in 1906 to the English author of a book on Alexander Hamilton. Moreover, while Roosevelt admired Hamilton's national policies and faith in strong government, he again anticipated Croly by confessing a lack of "sympathy with Hamilton's distrust of democracy."

For Roosevelt as for Croly, furthermore, the epitome of all political virtue was Abraham Lincoln. "Lincoln . . . unconsciously carried out the Hamilton tradition," Roosevelt declared three years before Croly's book appeared. "[He] . . . was superior to Hamilton . . . because he was a politician and was a genuine democrat and therefore suited to lead a genuine democracy." Roosevelt in fact summarized his political faith in a manner almost identical to Croly's eight months before *The Promise of American Life* was published. "I think you have struck it exactly right as regards Jeffersonianism and Hamiltonianism," Roosevelt wrote to his friend William Allen White. "I have no use for the Hamiltonian who is an aristocrat, or for the Jeffersonian who is a demagog. Let us trust the people as Jefferson did, but not flatter them; and let us try to make our administration as effective as Hamilton taught us to have it. Lincoln . . . struck the right average."

Quite obviously when Roosevelt later spoke of his effort "to get a proper mixture of the principles of Hamilton and Jefferson into the political movement of the present day," he reflected not Croly's ideas but his own. Even the ghost of Wilbur Littleton, so crucial to Croly's philosophy, had cast its spell on Roosevelt, for the Colonel held *Unleavened Bread* among his favorite novels, terming it the "strongest study of American life that has been written for many years." Croly himself recognized the great empathy of his thought with Roosevelt's. "He is the original and supreme Hamiltonian revivalist," wrote Croly to Learned Hand in 1910. "I have just been reading his life of Gouverneur Morris, written about 1887, and have been amused to find how closely I merely followed after many of his judgments of the Federalist epoch."

Among those who have ignored such pre-existing similarities, many have been most misled by Croly's coinage of the phrase "New Nationalism." "Colonel Roosevelt ... gives credit for this phrase to Mr. Croly," declared the *American Magazine* in 1912, and the claim has often been echoed since. Yet, though Croly did use the words "new nationalism" when discussing Roosevelt in *The Promise of American Life,* nowhere in speeches, writings, or letters did the politician credit the publicist with originating the phrase. In fact, since Croly used the particular construction but once in a four-hundred-and-fifty-four-page book (and then as an afterthought), the publicist had something less than an absolute claim.

The single usage came where Croly argued that Roosevelt's nationalism was more democratic than Hamilton's. "The new Federalism or rather new Nationalism is not in any way inimical to democracy," said Croly. "On the contrary ... the whole tendency of ... [Roosevelt's] program is to give a democratic meaning and purpose to the Hamiltonian tradition and method." While the phrase occurred at a place likely to catch Roosevelt's eye, Croly was probably more prophet than phrase-maker when he used it to describe Roosevelt's career.

In sum, the marked similarity of the New Nationalism and *The Promise of American Life* arose largely from a coincidence of reasoning, from a parallel response of publicist and politician to currents of nationalism then stirring in the United States. When the measure of Croly's influence on Roosevelt is taken, moreover, the profound impact of Roosevelt's own career on the philosopher has to be counted. The relation of the two men was one of interaction, with Roosevelt's impress much the stronger. Croly was quite consciously trying to formulate and carry further tendencies that had been manifest in Roosevelt's Presidency. He managed to catch and make articulate ideas that Roosevelt and men like him had long held. But philosophers more often define the spirit of an age or movement than make it. Croly, in this respect, deserves full honors among the breed.

3. THE NEW NATIONALISM

Very probably Croly's trenchant argument for a new liberalism did help clarify Roosevelt's thinking as the ex-President pondered the political situation during the summer of 1910. Yet to argue that *The Promise of America Life* inspired the New Nationalism not only exaggerates Croly's originality but also distorts Roosevelt's motivations. Theodore Roosevelt was not a man in the grip of some new and powerful political persuasion, but rather a working politician bent on saving his party. The New Nationalism that emerged from his speaking tour through the West that summer was more than anything a politician's attempt to meet a practical political situation. Croly's book and Roosevelt's new program did follow in sequence, but the book was at best a minor pin prick among a multitude of massive pressures.

Upon his return to the United States in June Roosevelt found himself in a position of "inconceivable difficulty." President Taft, his hand-picked successor, had badly split the Republican party by signing and defending the Payne-Aldrich tariff. In the agrarian West, Republicans were in open revolt. Taft's dismissal of or failure to reappoint men close to Roosevelt, plus other more personal factors, made renewed intimacy between the fighting Colonel and his political heir difficult. Yet Roosevelt knew that a break with Taft would make the split in the Republican party irrevocable. Worse, as Roosevelt saw clearly, such a break would make Democratic victory in 1912 almost certain.

Convinced like Croly that a Democratic victory would be a national calamity, Roosevelt resolved to bring the warring factions of his party back together. Importuned by both administration and insurgents for his open support, Roosevelt found he could satisfy neither side and still maintain a united party front. As he explained over and over again to political intimates, an unqualified endorsement of Taft would deprive him of all control over those insurgents still willing to follow the Roosevelt lead. Loss of such control would in turn end his power to help the beleaguered President. On the other hand, the endorsement of the insurgent position would further divide the party and probably evoke such extremes of radicalism from the insurgents that they would lose much public support. "I am . . . convinced," wrote Roosevelt to a friend just before the congressional elections of 1910, "that we shall get beaten if we cannot find a common ground upon which Insurgents and Regulars can stand."

Beyond the needs of the party Roosevelt had to consider his own relationship to the American people. Though probably without immediate political ambitions in 1910, Roosevelt still could not easily forswear the habit and joy of leadership. Taft had failed as a leader of the progressives at the very time America was becoming more and more progressive. Roosevelt sensed the change in American opinion soon after his return from Europe. "The revolt is not merely among political leaders," he wrote Nicholas Longworth in July, "but among the masses of the people. I am not prepared to say that the masses of the people are Insurgents, [but] a very large portion of them are." Facing a disunited party and an aroused public, Roosevelt assured Longworth that "the safest thing . . .

[seemed] to be to [dwell] as far as possible on the future." Out of the decision to stress future over present came the New Nationalism.

While the elaboration of a program for the future evaded the immediate embarrassment of supporting either Taft or the insurgents, it offered no real solution for Roosevelt's problems. Unwilling to abandon Taft, Roosevelt on his tour of the West could placate the insurgents only by becoming more radical. "The progressives . . . felt they had a right to expect me, un-equivocally, to declare for the principles for which they stood," Roosevelt explained. "Not to have done so would have given them the feeling I had betrayed them." Thus the New Nation-alism was largely Roosevelt's testament of good faith to the insurgents, not an expression of new and irrepressible con-victions.

With the need for party unity uppermost in his mind, Roose-velt apparently had some idea that the new program he developed during the summer would unite discordant factions in the national interest. Some such notion was implicit in his frequent private use of the theme, perhaps derived from Croly, that the Republican party in 1910 faced a crisis as severe as that of the Whigs before the Civil War. With a sense of sym-bolic fitness, Roosevelt chose to launch the New Nationalism in a speech during the dedication of John Brown's battlefield at Osawatomie, Kansas. "At the moment," wrote Roosevelt of the speech a few weeks before he delivered it, "I am endeavor-ing to prevent the John Browns among the insurgents getting themselves in a position from which the Abraham Lincolns cannot extricate them." Yet, however much Roosevelt saw himself at Osawatomie in the moderate guise of Lincoln, his oration became what one historian has called "probably . . . the most radical speech ever given by an ex-president."

Roosevelt began his address with a remarkably radical quo-tation from the first Republican President. "Labor is prior to, and independent of capital," quoted the Colonel. "Labor is the superior of capital and deserves much the higher consider-

ation." Though he immediately went on to the rest of the
Lincoln passage that stressed property as "the fruit of labor
... desirable ... a positive good," the first part had set his
theme. Roosevelt was still for "righteousness and justice"; he
temporized and moralized as of old—but this time with a difference. "The American people are right," he declared, "in
demanding that New Nationalism, without which we cannot
hope to deal with new problems."

Most of the nostrums of the New Nationalism as outlined at
Osawatomie were already familiar to progressives everywhere.
Roosevelt himself later insisted to Lodge that he had proposed
there nothing but measures already advanced in his presidential messages. His support of the direct primary, however, was
relatively new, for he had only come out for it that summer.
He stood now, too, for a definite revision of the tariff, something that as President he had never pressed. Roosevelt at
Osawatomie backed the income tax, though like Croly he
preferred a graduated inheritance tax as "far more easily col-
lected and far more effective." A thoroughgoing conservation
policy, a strong army and navy, prohibitions against political
contributions by corporations, workmen's compensation acts,
measures to restrict woman and child labor—all these Roosevelt had championed before.

On the already much-agitated question of the trusts, Roosevelt's position had become somewhat stronger. He repudiated
his own earlier fame as a trust buster by admitting that "the
effort at prohibiting all combination ... [had] substantially
failed." "The way out," he declared at Osawatomie, "lies, not
in attempting to prevent such combinations, but in completely
controlling them in the interests of the public welfare." While
this was essentially the program Roosevelt had advocated before Congress in 1908, he now seemed to favor total abandonment of the Sherman Act, whereas earlier he had protested only
its use against "good" combinations. The "effective and thorough-going supervision" of trusts recommended two years be-

fore had become "complete control." The means for such control, however, were left scrupulously vague.

For the moment, the New Nationalism meant at best a shift of emphasis in reform, a drawing together of things Roosevelt had long supported under the single banner of nationalism. He put a stronger stress, perhaps, on national discipline, though discipline had always appealed to Roosevelt's militant soul. "I ask," the Colonel declared, "that civil life be carried on in the spirit in which the [Civil War] army was carried on." The New Nationalism would not only make corporations stand for inspection, but it would "regulate the terms and conditions of labor . . . directly in the interests of the common good." Leadership, a guiding elite, even tycoons were justified in the image of "great generals who gained . . . promotion by leading the army to victory." The federal government was made what it had always tended to be for Roosevelt, the main focus of reform. "The betterment we seek," Roosevelt declared, "must be accomplished, I believe, primarily through the national government."

Probably few of the good Jeffersonian insurgents of the West who cheered Roosevelt so lustily in 1910 actually felt the strong nationalistic impetus behind their hero's thinking. What most roused them was Roosevelt's greater economic radicalism. "I believe in shaping the ends of government to protect property as well as human welfare," he declared, paraphrasing Lincoln once more, "but whenever the alternative must be faced, I am for men not property." The needs of human welfare, in fact, brought Roosevelt at Osawatomie remarkably close to the socialism he had always attacked. "Every man," he said, "holds his property subject to the general right of the community to regulate its use to whatever degree the public welfare may require it."

These were unusual words indeed from Roosevelt. They set the insurgents cheering, while conservatives everywhere mourned. Though Roosevelt assured Lodge that "the tour of the West . . . [had] been a very material help toward securing a fairly united support for the Republicans," he must have known better. While the Osawatomie speech satisfied many insurgents, it merely sharpened the contrast between Roosevelt and Taft. In truth, Roosevelt could not placate the strong progressives without both injuring and alienating the President. The Colonel was straddling not a fence but a chasm, and as the breach widened he was forced to choose a side.

Probably Roosevelt himself did not foresee either the wild enthusiasm or the fierce condemnation his New Nationalism would provoke. Clinging to the hope that comon ground might still be found, he temporized on the Osawatomie speech to his conservative friend Lodge, saying that he had not made his "point clear" and had allowed "good men to go wrong from misunderstanding." Yet a month later he told his more progressive friend Benjamin Wheeler: "I stand for every word of that speech. I am sure that in the end the people will endorse the policies there enunciated." Roosevelt had proclaimed the New Nationalism to heal a rift in the Republican ranks. He did not yet realize that at Osawatomie he had started on a road from which there was no turning back.

4. A MEASURE OF INFLUENCE

While Croly had neither inspired the New Nationalism nor determined its essential outlines, Roosevelt undoubtedly learned something from his reading of *The Promise of American Life*. Quite possibly the strength of Croly's reasoning gave Roosevelt further confidence to make fully known convictions about nationalism he had long held privately. Possibly, too, the recommendation of Croly's book by both the liberal Learned Hand and the conservative Henry Cabot Lodge suggested to him how widely his own and Croly's notions of democratic nationalism might appeal.

The prevalence of such ideas was evident in Croly's own use of the "new Federalism" as well as the "New Nationalism" as a name for his policy. The New Federalism was the program of the *Outlook*, the very religious and moderately reformist magazine Roosevelt had joined as contributing editor in March 1909. The *Outlook*'s New Federalism called for a policy of trust regulation similar to Croly's and Roosevelt's. But Croly's total program of social reform went much further than anything dreamed of by the *Outlook* editors. Roosevelt at Osawatomie spoke more in the spirit of Croly's prophetic radicalism than of the *Outlook*'s meliorism when he called for regulation of property "to whatever degree the public welfare may require it."

Roosevelt himself, however, had another rather revealing explanation for his increased radicalism. "As you know," he wrote an English friend a few weeks before Osawatomie, "I am a genuine radical. I believe in what you would call an 'imperialist democracy.' " And elsewhere Roosevelt indicated that England's "Democratic Imperialism" was the same as the "Democratic Nationalism" he wanted for America.

Roosevelt's description of himself as both a "radical" and an "imperialist" suggests the dangers of democratic nationalism as a political doctrine. Even Croly admitted that nationalism could be either very radical or very conservative, the outcome depending on who gained control of the great state machine. Croly believed in democratic reform as strongly as he did in nationalism. Roosevelt believed in himself. He saw nationalism as a slogan capable of drawing both conservatives and liberals to his support. His close connection with tycoons like George Perkins and Frank Munsey in 1912 made many men, including Croly, wonder just how democratic or radical the New Nationalism would be.

To attract the reformers, however, Roosevelt at Osawatomie had to revamp his political philosophy in a definitely democratic direction. In doing so he used words so close to Croly's that the publicist may have contributed at least a guide line or two for Roosevelt's revamped liberalism. In the section of *The Promise of American Life* called "The Reformation of

Theodore Roosevelt" Croly had argued that in its ultimate meanings Roosevelt's "Square Deal" had implied "a conception of democracy and its purposes very different from the Jeffersonian doctrine of equal rights." Whether he knew it or not, Roosevelt actually had been calling not for a Square Deal but for a "revision of the rules of the game." The Colonel may have been merely paraphrasing Croly when at Osawatomie he redefined the Square Deal to mean not only "fair play under the present rules of the game, but ... having those rules changed so as to work for more substantial equality of opportunity and reward."

In other important respects, however, the politician proved himself remarkably immune to the advice of the publicist. The New Nationalism of the innately conservative Roosevelt never contained anything even approaching Croly's key scheme for direct government aid to unionization. Moreover, though Roosevelt shared Croly's desire for leadership and a strong and efficient government, he refused to discriminate between such measures as the initiative, referendum, recall, and direct primary. By 1912 Roosevelt had given his blessing to all of these in a fashion Croly thought irresponsible.

Since much of the difference between the New Nationalism and Wilson's New Freedom revolved around the trust issue, Roosevelt's divergence from Croly on that issue is of major significance. The one important change Croly might have wrought in Roosevelt's thinking about the trusts would have been to convince him of the evils of regulation by commission. Yet Roosevelt's letters fail to show that he ever seriously considered the Croly doctrine. Instead, the politician came out for the very extreme of detailed regulation Croly had condemned. By 1912 the Bull Moose candidate wanted a regulatory commission able to set both maximum prices and the wages and hours of labor.

Ironically Roosevelt came closest to a public avowal of influence by Croly on the very issue of the trusts where he most rejected Croly's ideas. The policy of pervasive regulation

Roosevelt championed in 1912 reflected a multitude of influences. The Morgan partner, George Perkins, a heavy financial backer of the Progressive party, made clear as early as 1911 his desire for repeal of the Sherman Act and regulation of corporations by commission, a commission, as he said "composed largely of businessmen." Early the same year Roosevelt hailed a speech by William Dudley Foulke as "the first really practical way out of this matter of monopolies" and included many of Foulke's suggestions in an *Outlook* article. At the Progressive party convention of 1912 Roosevelt documented his own stand on the trusts with three long paragraphs from Charles R. Van Hise's *Concentration and Control*, which had been published the same year. But in 1913 Roosevelt divided the honors between Croly and Van Hise when he defended the origins of his trust policy. Stung by a Wilson attack that accused him of getting his ideas on the trusts "from the gentlemen who . . . [ran] the United States Steel Corporation," Roosevelt retorted: "Does Mr. Wilson pretend that Mr. Van Hise and Mr. Croly got their ideas from the Steel Corporation?"

Roosevelt's mention of Croly and Van Hise, however, was less an ascription of influence than a recognition that both had given intellectual respectability to a policy of controlling rather than breaking the trusts. Roosevelt himself gave the best statement of the origins of his trust policy in the same article. "Why the ideas that I have championed as to controlling and regulating . . . [the trusts]," he wrote, "have been in the air of this country for a quarter of a century. I was merely the first prominent candidate for President who took them up." What the Colonel said for his trust policy could have been said for his New Nationalism as well. The coincidence of his views with Croly's, however, became the making of the reputation of the political philosopher.

5. AN INFLUENTIAL PUBLICIST

Probably only Roosevelt himself and a few of his closest friends knew how little Croly had actually had to do with originating the New Nationalism. Among progressives generally, the publicist became known as the intellectual genie behind the politician. The first meeting between Croly and Roosevelt in October 1910 was duly noted by the press, and fairly frequently thereafter Croly's name appeared among Roosevelt's advisers. In the January 1911 *Outlook* Roosevelt gave substance to the impression of influence by proclaiming *The Promise of American Life* "the most powerful and illuminating study of our national conditions which has appeared for many years." Learned Hand thought Roosevelt's praise a "splendid send-off" and humorously warned his friend that the enthusiasm of the "local insurgents" for Croly's ideas was such that they were "in some danger of canonizing [him]." The publicist's fame reached a climax in 1912 when the serial of Roosevelt's *Autobiography* in the *Outlook* singled Croly out along with Weyl for special praise and when the *American Magazine* published a full-page picture of him as the philosopher behind Roosevelt's New Nationalism.

Croly's reputation probably grew in part by a circular process not uncommon to the history of ideas. The coincidence of Croly's thoughts with Roosevelt's, plus the obvious merits of *The Promise of American Life*, first attracted attention to the obscure architectural critic. Then Roosevelt himself, admiring the book and finding Croly becoming a personage among the faithful, praised Croly and thus fortified the initial appearance of influence. As the rumor of influence grew, so too did the publicist's reputation, and the circle became complete as Roosevelt found it ever more politic to have the influential publicist among his supporters.

The Promise of American Life did bring to Croly a considerable expansion of activity. The book had stressed the central role a social critic might play as the "standard bearer" for the whole progressive movement. Croly was not one to take his responsibilities lightly. He knew how little most politicians could risk the "candid and constructive thinking" he thought to be the country's chief need. "The task of plain speaking," wrote Croly, "must . . . devolve largely upon men who have from the political point of view little to gain or lose by their apparent heresies." Croly's notions about the independent role of the intellectual were sound, but both he and his later *New Republic* colleagues would have trouble sticking to them.

Even before Roosevelt's return from Europe there had been the *Outlook* editorial that had called for a "great debate" between Croly and Woodrow Wilson on their "two principles of National action." In May 1910 Croly did his best to further the debate with an article in Walter Hines Page's *World's Work* and another in the *North American Review*. In the last of these, under the title "Democratic Factions and Insurgent Republicans," Croly once again measured various reform groups against the standard of nationalism.

The publicist still had little respect for the Democrats. Bryan's recantation on the nationalization of the railroads, the party's devotion to the spoils system, and its continued love of Jeffersonian laissez faire, all proved the Democrats "incapable of formulating a national policy." The Republicans, however, were little better, for the split Croly had predicted had come sooner than expected. Taft was hopeless, Croly believed, but his insurgent opponents were little better. The insurgents had made a "bug-bear of monopolies"; they often represented purely local interests; they tried to array the agrarian West against the industrial East. Worst of all, they suffered from a common progressive penchant for fuzzy thinking. In short, the insurgents had "the earmarks of agitators rather than statesmen." "Not one of them can be named," declared the publicist, "(unless Theodore Roosevelt is still to be classified an Insurgent) who is capable of inspiring general confidence and becoming a leader."

Croly early in 1910, however, was still the philosopher not

far removed from his study. Roosevelt's return in June and the proclamation of the New Nationalism two months later quickly widened Croly's horizons. A request from the Hanna family to do a biography of Mark Hanna brought him into increasingly intimate contact with Roosevelt and other political leaders. The Cleveland *Leader* asked him to write a political series; the American Political Science Association invited him to deliver a paper on state political reform; the ever-loyal Learned Hand arranged a dinner for Croly to be attended by political notables in New York. When early in 1911 the publicist went on a jaunt to California with his wife, he plunged naturally into lengthy conferences with William Kent and Francis J. Henney, two of the state's outstanding progressive leaders.

Closer contact with politics changed many of the recent architectural critic's preconceptions. The meetings with Roosevelt brought the politician into more realistic perspective. By October 1910 the Colonel had become thoroughly embroiled in the Republican factional struggle. Croly, much discouraged, admitted that "the result would not have been essentially different if Roosevelt had never returned from Africa." He was no longer so sure, as he admitted in a letter to Hand, that Roosevelt "had the quality which I always credited him with possessing, of being able to unite right-minded and disinterested people on a program of national reform."

A few weeks later things seemed even worse. Having consulted in Cleveland with "all sorts and conditions of people . . . —moderate reformers, fanatics, Bourbons, and some very fair-minded stand-patters," Croly decided that Roosevelt's "peculiar influence was really trembling in the balance." "He has got to go about things differently," Croly told Hand, "and if I get a chance I shall tell him so." By early 1911 the publicist's ideas had suffered so much among the politicians that he wanted nothing more than to "rescue . . . the New Nationalism from the disfigurement that infant had received at the hands of T.R. and his critics." Planning a pamphlet to be called "The

Old Nationalism and the New," Croly was ready to take "another whack both at the stand-patters and the insurgents." A marked scarcity of Wilbur Littletons was besetting Croly's crusade for a new liberalism.

Croly's stand against both conservatives and insurgents was, of course, a characteristic posture. It meant, however, no mere longing for some happy mean between the two groups. Instead Croly, as a consistent if prejudiced nationalist, stood somewhat to the left of both factions. The western insurgents, he thought, had shown their real nature when they rejected Taft's reciprocity agreement with Canada. By refusing a reciprocal lowering of agricultural duties the westerners had revealed "what kind of tariff reformers they . . . were when the interests of their own locality . . . [were] affected." To Croly the insurgents were as narrow a special-interest group as the stand-patters they battled; neither faction had any real vision of the "national interest." The Progressive Republican League, with which the insurgents hoped to rally their forces for La Follette, was for the publicist "simply a new ebullition of the old Jeffersonian spirit." From his eastern viewpoint, Croly could not see La Follette for what he was, the most sincere and effective reformer on the national scene.

Oddly enough, however, the prophet of the New Nationalism in the days before Armageddon was more concerned with past politics than present. Most of Croly's time between 1910 and 1912 was spent doing the research and writing of a family-sponsored biography of Mark Hanna. Hanna's son Dan, a newspaper publisher and moderately progressive friend of Roosevelt, was responsible for choosing Croly. The choice, considering the publicist's somewhat "socialist" views and his unconcealed distate for the "new plutocracy," might seem peculiar. Dan Hanna, however, was sophisticated enough to perceive Croly's essential fairness as well as to realize the value to Mark Hanna's memory of fair treatment from a reputed radical. He placed Hanna's papers at Croly's disposal, plus interviews gathered by another man from Hanna's friends, and gave the publicist a regular salary while he was doing the work. Croly supplemented the accumulated materials with further interviews, particularly with Roosevelt, who had him spend several nights at Sagamore Hill during their consultations. Thus aided and abetted, the publicist finished the book with dispatch. "I am particularly pleased that you like Croly's manuscript of your father's life," wrote Roosevelt to Dan Hanna early in 1912. "I look forward to the appearance of the book."

The younger Hanna had cause to be pleased, for Croly's book was in many ways an apologia. Croly gave most of the sordid details of Mark Hanna's career—the corrupt franchises, the brutal business tactics, the political chicanery—but he defended Hanna by placing him in his own time. He denied that Hanna was merely "the sinister, corrupt type of money-man in politics." He argued instead that Hanna had been a simple, relatively honest patriot—considerate, normally unselfish, kind to his employees, not unusually venal, an "industrial pioneer." Hanna, insisted Croly, was a man who had lived beyond his own time to suffer from the morality of a new day he did not understand. Yet Croly, like many historians who have treated Hanna similarly since, may have been overdoing the admitted relativity of morals.

When the biography was published the *Nation* remarked that its "singular interest . . . [lay] less in the subject than in the author," an observation that had much truth. For Hanna, as Croly made clear, represented everything the publicist disliked. No taint of intellectual snobbery, however, marred Croly's picture of Hanna as a gregarious, sincere, unexceptional man of homely tastes and habits. Mark Hanna was the opposite of the Wilbur Littletons of the land, yet by setting the politician in context Croly was able not only to justify him but also to suggest the need for new types for a new age. The sociable yet independent Hanna, Croly argued, had been the expression in an early industrial age of an old frontier breed. Hanna had held sincerely to the pioneer faith "that in doing well for himself he was also doing well for society." "Business was in his eyes not simply money-making," said Croly, "but the most necessary type of social labor." Thus, through something of a *tour de force*, the publicist was able to treat Hanna with plausible sympathy while at the same time supporting the refurbished values of the progressive era.

Yet for all its dialectical dexterity, Croly's *Marcus Alonzo Hanna* was not a notable success. The American mood of 1912 was hardly receptive, perhaps, to a rehabilitation of the much-maligned "Dollar Mark." "It seems to me that Croly's book on Hanna has fallen rather flat," noted Walter Weyl in his diary not long after the book appeared. Scattered reviews, while for the most part favorable, were not enthusiastic. The reviewers in general remained skeptical of the resurrected Hanna. "Croly's . . . capital biography," wrote Thomas Beer some years later, "was exposed on the lacteal quagmire of American criticism and sank therein through a scum of tepid reviews."

6. Ideas, Intellectuals, and a Movement

A sympathetic biography of a recent Republican Old Guard leader, then, became Croly's main contribution to the campaign of 1912. His capacity to treat Hanna so favorably brings home the dangers of nationalism as a creed. Nationalism, taken in the abstract, could justify almost anything. Thus Mark Hanna, abstracted into the national life as a pioneer, was somehow no longer the corrupt manipulater of men and money, but instead a benign, misplaced frontier democrat. The very ambiguity of nationalism, however, may have given it a certain strength. As the faith of Croly and Roosevelt in 1912, it could accommodate as well the diverse enthusiasms of Walter Lippmann and Walter Weyl.

Croly, Weyl, and Lippmann knew little of each other before 1912, when the furor of the campaign helped bring them together. Working independently, however, they had created a definite school of political thought quite at variance with majority progressive sentiment. Responding to similar conditions, absorbed by the same problems, influenced by like intellectual currents, they had arrived at remarkably parallel conclusions.

All three were avowedly pragmatists, relativists in morals, and anti-Jeffersonian in their liberal persuasion. As eastern, urban intellectuals, they saw the middle class as the focus and fulcrum of reform. Even the quasi-socialist Lippmann had decided by the summer of 1912 that no leverage from labor was needed for social change. All three believed that national problems could be solved by a strong national government under popular (thus middle-class) control.

Yet there were also definite differences in the thinking of the three men, which only the dangerous ambiguity of nationalism could conceal. Certainly the cultural and aesthetic values that moved Croly and Lippmann had little in common with the unabashed materialism of Walter Weyl. Both the onetime students of philosophy at Harvard tended to be more theoretical than the graduate of the Wharton School of Commerce and Finance. More removed from immediate reality, their thought contained a certain ruthlessness alien to the gentle spirit of Walter Weyl.

On the other hand, Weyl shared with Croly certain significant differences from Lippmann. Both older men were rationalists, that is, they viewed politics as primarily a matter of rational calculation by individuals of demonstrable ends. Their pragmatism had not led them to accept the irrationalism of such Lippmann heroes as Nietzsche, Bergson, Wallas, and Freud. Consequently, Croly and Weyl were more democratic in their thinking than Lippmann. Weyl with his great middle-class mass of consumers and Croly with his Wilbur Littletons were far removed from Lippmann with his "creative myth" and his intuitive, virtually omnipotent statesman.

Such differences among the three might have made collaboration impossible. As pragmatists, however, they shared an in-bred tolerance for conflicting opinions. As prophets of a new liberalism they were less prone to rabid doctrinal disputes than thinkers further to left or right. On immediate practical measures, moreover, they were in virtual agreement. A power-ful national government, a stronger labor movement, encour-agement of corporate consolidation, a lower tariff, higher tax-es, increased social welfare, more federal intervention in the economy—on all the major tenets of the new liberalism the three publicists agreed.

Nor, to say the least, were the three intellectuals immune to the blandishments of a dynamic political leader. Roosevelt's leadership of the Bull Moose crusade of 1912 more than any-thing else welded Croly, Weyl, and Lippmann into a united junto. By the summer of 1911 Croly had recovered somewhat from the discouragement of the year before. Though too hard at work on the Hanna biography to attend a meeting with Roosevelt and other progressive leaders, Croly asked Learned Hand to "keep a good account of it for me."

The end of 1911 found Croly virtually hovering on Roose-velt's doorstep. He wrote to his friend Hand that he was "wait-ing for a possible summons from that gentleman to pay him straightway another visit." January 1912 brought news from Dan Hanna "positively that TR had consented & that he was working . . . for the nomination." Croly was skeptical about the politician's chances. He feared that Roosevelt might "as usual be deceiving himself." "That he will run [however]," the pub-licist wrote Hand, "appears inevitable to me—unless some very stout resistance develops. I don't like it, but if he does run, a good strong argument can be made on his behalf."

When Roosevelt's candidacy became official the next month, Croly waited only a day to pledge his support. "I am glad it has become an open fight," he wrote Roosevelt on February 28, "and I am glad of the opportunity of wearing a Roosevelt button." The publicist's enthusiasm, however, was not un-qualified. He had been disturbed by Roosevelt's recent advocacy of the recall of judicial decisions. He assured the Colonel that he agreed "absolutely with the purpose" of the recall, but he had "doubts about . . . submitting constitutional decisions . . . to popular vote." He had been "delighted, "therefore, that a more recent speech had revealed in Roosevelt "an obvious willingness to shift . . . [his] ground."

Croly's objection to the recall of judicial decisions was not exceptional. Roosevelt's stand probably more than anything else deprived his candidacy of the strong conservative support he had always enjoyed. But Croly, of course, did not even consider joining Lodge, Root, and other conservatives who broke with Roosevelt on the judicial issue. Even when Roosevelt the next day answered Croly's letter by substantially maintaining his position, the publicist was unshaken in his loyalty. Agreeing with Roosevelt on the need to restrain the courts, Croly objected that the Colonel's means might diminish national power. The demurral, however, suggests how much Croly's nationalism kept him separate from those Roosevelt later called the Progressive party's "lunatic fringe." The publicist was more "radical" than the politician, but his radicalism was very different from that of such Jeffersonian liberals as Amos Pinchot.

Walter Weyl, too, eventually clambered aboard the Bull Moose band wagon, but, like so many progressives, only after first working in the cause of Wisconsin's La Follette. On the recommendation of the labor historian John R. Commons, the Senator had asked Weyl in September 1911 for help in analyzing the Aldrich currency plan, which La Follette expected conservative Republicans to present to the next session of Congress. Though still writing *The New Democracy*, Weyl plunged into the task with his usual enthusiasm. He began spending six or seven hours a day in reading on currency and banking, hired a secretary to organize his notes, consulted bankers in New York, and traveled to Washington several times for conferences with La Follette and Commons. Within two months Weyl evolved an alternative banking scheme and forwarded it to La Follette with a lengthy memorandum.

Weyl admired La Follette and enjoyed the sense of importance and usefulness the work with the Senator gave him, yet his relation to the Wisconsin insurgent was never a very happy one. In part, Weyl, like Croly, tended to be skeptical of the partisan spirit of the insurgents. "He does not say that he wants an analysis," Weyl protested at one point when La Follette asked for a report, "but he does say that he wants me to riddle it. To riddle it would presuppose a merely antagonistic attitude." What split Weyl from La Follette, however, was the Senator's failure to answer letters and to credit Weyl with the large amount of work he had done. Though he realized that La Follette was "probably fearfully worried about his presidential chances," Weyl became increasingly annoyed by such slights. When in February 1912 La Follette's supposed breakdown before a publisher's meeting in Philadelphia seemingly ended his chances for the Republican nomination, Weyl wrote in his diary: "I am awfully sorry for poor Senator La Follette. I am afraid he realizes it is pretty well over. He has no chance for 1912 & in 1916 he will be sixty."

To turn as did so many other progressives from La Follette to Roosevelt, however, was not easy for Weyl. Roosevelt's militarism must have offended the pacifism that pervaded so much of Weyl's writing. Roosevelt's theories on "race suicide," his belief in the need for a large and virile population, also contrasted markedly with Weyl's admiration of the stable population of France and its prosperous and pacific civilization. On many issues that were prominent in 1912, however, particularly on the trust problem, Weyl and Roosevelt saw eye to eye. And, doubtless, an attentive and charming politician like the Colonel was more alluring than the dedicated but brusque La Follette. By the middle of the summer Weyl had made a pilgrimage to Oyster Bay, but, perhaps because he sensed the important differences between himself and Roosevelt, he withheld complete support until after the Progressive party convention. "I have been waiting only the outcome of the Convention," he wrote to Roosevelt in August, "to be entirely assured the third party movement was a real struggle for national reorganization and regeneration. I am now thoroughly convinced." Weyl had carefully made the Progressive party rather than its leader the object of his loyalty. He did not yet realize how completely Roosevelt (plus the shrewd financial support of Perkins and Munsey) *was* the party. Certainly, like many other progressives, he would have been truer to his own principles had he stuck to La Follette.

Walter Lippmann, off in the Maine woods writing *A Preface to Politics*, evidently made no definite commitment to any candidate. Croly, on the other hand, was willing to follow Roosevelt even into the limbo of the Bull Moose crusade. Roosevelt's bolt from the Republicans and the organization of the Progressive party in July stirred the publicist to enthusiasm. Yet he strove valiantly to maintain the detachment that he rightly knew to be essential for the intellectual in politics. The new party was the thing, he argued, not its unpredictable and pugnacious leader. He even confessed to Hand what was for him the highly heretical judgment, that had "Roosevelt . . . been the regular Republican nominee, there would have been much justification in voting for Wilson."

All the same, Croly thought that the new third party "even under the existing somewhat dubious conditions" contained "more promise . . . than any recent movement in American politics." The party, he assured Hand, would be "driven by the logic of its own work and situation towards nationalism." A friend had reported that "at one of the Chicago conferences the idea of calling it the 'National' party without any Progressive . . . [had been] strongly supported." Croly's dreams in *The Promise of American Life* seemed to be coming true. He was more than ever convinced that the issue of nationalism had "much more reality underneath the surface of American politics than most people suspected." He did not yet realize how much that "reality" was merely the attractiveness and expediency of the nationalist theme to Roosevelt.

Though Walter Weyl's initial skepticism about the Bull Moose crusade had been much greater than Croly's, characteristically, once he had made up his mind, he plunged into the movement with all his energy. For two and a half months he labored in the Progressive party headquarters in New York, organizing an "educational" campaign among the foreign-born. He became a member of the party's national committee; he traveled with Roosevelt on a campaign tour; at one point he was suggested as the Progressive candidate for secretary of state of New York. When the canvass was over, Weyl estimated that his volunteer services represented "a contribution of $2000 to the cause," since he "could have made that much by writing magazine articles."

Much less equipped for practical politics than Weyl, Croly spent most of the campaign months at his summer retreat in New Hampshire. He was at work on several articles, as well as the Godkin Lectures, which Harvard had asked him to deliver in the fall. The publicist found Cornish "hot and dull" and complained that he had hardly "a single person to play tennis and golf with." He saw little of Roosevelt. In July he reported humorously to Hand that the presidential candidate had asked him to lunch "and announced the important fact" of their meeting, but the invitation had been phoned to Croly's club in New York on the day of the "festivities," the proposed guest being, as Croly said, "in Cornish."

Later the same month when the two men did get together, a misunderstanding arose that must have wrenched the ever-sensitive Croly's heart. Croly left the interview with the impression that he had been asked to become Roosevelt's official biographer. He wrote the Colonel that he had been "preoccupied ever since" with the idea and "touched . . . very deeply." But Roosevelt's reply a few days later dashed the enthusiastic biographer's hopes. The Colonel admitted to being "both pleased and surprised" by Croly's suggestion but had not supposed Croly "would pay any attention to . . . [a] half-jesting remark." Softening the blow, he assured Croly if ever a biography were written there could be no one better for the work. "I think you understand," said Roosevelt, "as no other literary man does, the kind of thing I am striving for in politics."

Just before the voting Croly published an article on the campaign in the *American Magazine*. Though privately he had doubts about the new third party, which seemed to be trying to do "too many things" under "any name . . . & any method," publicly he put the Progressive organization at the center of the struggle. He reasserted his conviction that even Wilson's leadership could not keep the individualistic, boss-ridden Democratic party from splitting asunder. The Progressives then would inherit progressive Democrats as well as Republicans, and the United States at last would have a permanent "party devoted exclusively to the work of constructive liberation." The Progressive party and its platform, said Croly, called "more loudly for allegiance than . . . any single leader." "The cause itself," he declared, ". . . was old when Mr. Roosevelt was born, and it will be going when he is dead."

Yet for all their statements to the contrary, it was the personality of Roosevelt the leader that led Croly and Weyl to stand with the Progressives at Armageddon in 1912. For Weyl the stand meant the sacrifice of many cherished principles; for Croly it meant watching ideas he shared with Roosevelt being much perverted by the pull and sway of practical politics. If his memory much later is to be trusted, even the pseudo-socialist Walter Lippmann fell under Roosevelt's spell before the campaign ended. Roosevelt, removed temporarily from the campaign by a fanatic's bullet, returned just before the balloting for one last large rally in New York. Lippmann afterwards recalled "that great night in Madison Square Garden when . . . Roosevelt spoke after he had been shot in Milwaukee." "I was his unqualified hero worshipper," confessed the publicist. He could have spoken for Croly and Weyl as well.

The publicists' qualifications on their admiration at the time were at best sops to their proper roles as independent and critical intellectuals. None of them was capable of a really unprejudiced consideration of the alternatives that La Follette or perhaps even Wilson offered to Roosevelt. The moths swooped and swerved in all directions, but in the end they were drawn unerringly to the bright promise of Roosevelt's power. Croly and Weyl felt sure in 1912 that their new liberalism had taken a strong hold on the minds of Roosevelt's followers. Lippmann soon enough agreed. It would take them a long time to realize that it was Roosevelt's blinding charm that captured the minds of most Progressives, including their own.

With Roosevelt behind it the new liberalism had taken on an impressive (if illusory) momentum. A decade earlier the philosophy had been little more than a series of contradictions in the minds of two men. Croly had been bedeviled by the plight of America's Wilbur Littletons, Roosevelt by the many restraints on his own dreams of national glory. By 1910 Croly's book and Roosevelt's speeches made the New Nationalism the subject of wide discussion. Two years later Lippmann and Weyl joined the chorus together with tens of thousands of loyal Bull Moose followers. So rapid had been the rise of their ideas and themselves to prominence that the three intellectuals would not easily abandon their delusions of ever-growing influence.

Whatever the results of the Bull Moose campaign, Croly, Weyl, and Lippmann were certain that the new liberalism would have an early triumph. Even before the election results were in, Croly began searching for some means by which its themes could be given wider currency. The search would lead to the founding of the *New Republic*. "We started," wrote Lippmann of the magazine's founding, "as loyal, though we hoped critical, members of the Progressive movement. We thought the movement was established. We thought that Roosevelt would continue to lead it."

FIVE

Toward a New Republic

1912-1914

1. A LOYAL BULL MOOSE TRIO

Soon after the election of 1912 a friend visited Theodore Roosevelt at Sagamore Hill and talked of Progressive victory in 1916. Roosevelt, however, demurred. "The fight is over," he assured his friend. "We are beaten. There is only one thing to do and that is to go back to the Republican party." Roosevelt easily understood the hopelessness of the Progressive cause. Though, because of Roosevelt's popularity, the Progressive party had polled more votes than Taft in the Presidential election, it had no strong, permanent organization to help it in the future. Roosevelt knew better than most men that favors, patronage, and interested contributions were the bone and sinew of political parties, that ideals for the most part were the froth of politics. He could afford to confide his feelings to few of his loyal Bull Moose followers, however, unless he was willing to return to the Republican fold alone.

Croly, Weyl, and Lippmann, as they came together to found the *New Republic*, were among the most loyal. "Now that the first skirmish is over and the long campaign begun, I feel that the moment has arrived to consider the question of organizing the party on a permanent, democratic, and self-supporting basis," wrote Weyl to Roosevelt the day the returns came in. Within a week he had been invited to Oyster Bay for lunch and, as he noted in his diary, talked with the Colonel on "the

Perkins matter . . . [and] other things . . . largely confidential."
A fortnight later he submitted a paragraph on party finances
for the politician's speech at the Progressive post-campaign
conference in Chicago

Croly, always more comfortable as philosopher than partisan, turned away from the campaign with something like
relief. "I am getting to work again," he wrote Hand several
weeks after the election, "& I don't propose to be interrupted
until Christmas—unless the country really needs me—which
it won't." Yet Croly continued working for the Bull Moose
cause. In December 1912, Weyl numbered him among thirty-
five Progressive leaders at a "high brow" party dinner. The
following month found Croly making elaborate plans to attend
another party function with Hand, George Rublee, and other
Progressive partisans.

Croly retained his pre-election feeling about the need for
the new third party. An encounter with Henry L. Stimson
made Croly snort disdainfully that Stimson had "illusions
about re-organizing the Republican party." Nor did he find
much to praise in the new Democratic Administration. Wilson's
choice of William Jennings Bryan for Secretary of State seemed
a "grave mistake." Some of Wilson's pre-inaugural statements
made Croly wonder whether Wilson might not try "to out-
Teddy T.R." but the inaugural address itself he dismissed as
"fascinating rather than convincing." Soon his mood was one
of deep depression. "I have a hunch," he wrote Learned Hand,
"that 1913 is to be a year of riot & bloodshed." Revolution in
Mexico, unrest in China, unpredictable chances for violence
in Europe seemed to promise that "the Almighty . . . [was]
going to have a little laugh on W.J.B." "The only consolation
is," he concluded, " (and it is a damned poor one) it will make
us nationalists more necessary."

Such forebodings made Croly focus his hopes all the more
strongly on nationalism and the Progressive party. His next
book, *Progressive Democracy*, published in October 1914,
argued that the ultimate triumph of the new third party was

very probable. The election of 1912 had shown the overwhelming strength of general progressive sentiment. His predictions about a nationalist wing of the reform movement seemed to have come true. No matter what accomplishments Wilson and the New Freedom might make, the Democrats would founder on the contradictions of their own philosophy. Wilson had no intention "to substitute for an automatic competitive regime one in which conscious social purpose ... [would] play a decisive part." Wilson's failure to swing to nationalism, Croly maintained, gave Progressives their continuing opportunity.

Walter Lippmann, his socialist phase now definitely over, also developed an increasing confidence in Roosevelt and the Progressive party. Writing to Roosevelt in May, 1913, just before the Bull Moose leader left for a trip to the Amazon, Lippmann expressed his hope when the Colonel returned "to have an opportunity of talking over some things." By 1914, along with Croly, Weyl, and others, Lippmann was loyally at work on a "labor policy" for Roosevelt and the Progressives.

2. CROLY AND DEMOCRACY

All three of the Bull Moose intellectuals undertook after 1912 revisions of their versions of the new liberalism. Heartened by the growth of the progressive movement, influenced by thinkers like John Dewey, stirred by new forces on the labor front, Croly changed perhaps the most. The sum total of the changes made for a philosophy considerably more optimistic than that of *The Promise of American Life*.

The Croly of *Progressive Democracy* was still a democratic nationalist, but now democracy was stressed far more than nationalism. Though in 1914 he still spoke of the "national ideal" and of the need for America to be "nationalized," more regularly he called for a "progressive democratic faith" or a "social democratic ideal." The shift of phrase was a significant mark of the revision of his thinking.

In part Croly's changed emphasis reflected a further post-ponement of the cultural aims that had originally inspired his nationalism. He stressed now that western nations (and by implication his own book) were necessarily "excessively pre-occupied with the economic mechanism . . . [because of] its wretched maladjustment to human needs." Yet he still looked forward to the new day that might come when such basic needs would be met. In the last paragraph of *Progressive Democracy* he returned to his old dream of an America where art might flourish as it had "in classic Greece . . . [or] in Venice of the renaissance."

The religious overtones of Croly's thought were also much less pronounced. No more was heard of the "democratic St. Francis" who might lead America toward "regeneration," while religion itself was dismissed as a form of "moral co-ercion" used by the dominant privileged classes. Croly still, however, put his father's "religion of humanity" at the heart of democracy. "The progressive democratic faith . . ." he wrote, "finds its consummation in a love . . . which is at bottom a spiritual expression of the mystical unity of human nature."

Croly's delayed succor for the Wilbur Littletons and his de-emphasis of religious values were part of a general abandon-ment of the elitist notions of *The Promise of American Life*. He still believed in strong executive leadership and perhaps even more in the use of "experts" in government, but gone now were such ideas as the "imitation" by the masses of "democratic saints and heroes" or the "ideal participation" of the common citizen in the country's greatness. Influenced ap-parently by John Dewey and the sociologist Albion Small, Croly stressed the need for "active participation" by ordinary men in all aspects of social and political life. In *Progressive Democracy* the "national school . . . [was] the national life" as before, but by 1914 Croly's national school had many more active pupils. "Democracy is not government by peculiarly qualified people or by a peculiarly qualified part of the people," he wrote, eliminating with one stroke of his pen the once brave elite of *The Promise of American Life*.

Croly's new accent on participation much modified his ideas on government. He now approved of the direct primary on the ground that it tended to prevent unofficial rule by political machines. He condemned the initiative and referendum not as before for their inefficiency but rather for promoting minority rule, since only minorities had the interest and unity to use them. His state governors would be as before the representatives of majority opinion, responsible for presenting a program to the lawmakers in a form the people could understand. But Croly now advocated a much less qualified recall as keeping "administration closely in touch with public opinion without any necessary sacrifice of efficiency."

The national government in *Progressive Democracy* remained the strong, centralized organ of many functions Croly had wanted in 1909. Yet through the federal halls as well fresh winds of democracy were blowing. Citing the researches of J. Allen Smith and Charles Beard, Croly came out for a definite limbering of the amendment clause of the Constitution. He also reversed himself on earlier strictures against commission control of industry. No longer attacking regulatory commissions for dividing power and responsibility in industry, Croly now pictured them as supplanting "rigid regulations on factory operations . . . [with] the possibility of flexible and articulate human adjustments." Here again Croly was adopting one of Roosevelt's ideas, rather than the reverse.

Nowhere was Croly's added emphasis on democratic participation more obvious than in his labor policy. While he wanted stronger unions and the complete unionization of labor as in *The Promise of American Life*, Croly in 1914 went much further. Striking a note that became major in the joint philosophy he worked out on the *New Republic* with Weyl and Lippmann, Croly called for thoroughgoing "industrial democracy." Influenced perhaps by Bill Haywood of the I.W.W., whose leadership of the Lawrence and Paterson strikes of 1912 and 1913 impressed so many intellectuals, Croly predicted a "deplorable result . . . [if] the American democracy fail[ed] to recognize the peculiar promise and nobleness of the syndicalist ideal." Though he rejected the violent tactics of syndicalists like Haywood, Croly thought that militant unions, a co-operative government, and enlightened employers could gradually attain the syndicalist goal of giving labor a powerful voice in management. The scheme was no mere plan for labor-management "co-operation" at the expense of labor's power, for Croly wanted unions to maintain their "independence and . . . whenever necessary . . . be strong enough to declare war." If employees could join employers in the running of business toward a common goal of higher productivity, then workers might escape from the monotony of modern industrial life to a new sense of "the dignity and serviceability of their calling." The problems of America's Wilbur Littletons had spread even to the assembly line.

Another mark of Croly's changed thinking that became central to the philosophy he would share with Weyl and Lippmann was his attack on the two-party system. Though in the past the two-party system had been a main bulwark of democracy, in the present he thought the system operated automatically "in the interest of the existing property owners." Croly proposed that state legislatures be apportioned not geographically but in terms of the interests of "associations of business men, or farmers, and of wage-earners,—of civic societies, voters' leagues, ballot associations, women's suffrage unions, single-tax clubs, and the like."

At the national level, Croly analyzed the future of the two-party system shrewdly, yet inconclusively. He believed the danger of gains by the Progressive party had been a strong force behind the reforms accomplished by Wilson. But Wilson's very successes had weakened the Bull Moose legions and left Wilson at the mercy of conservatives within his own party. Whatever the upshot, reformers would have to realize that some other form of national organization than the two-party system was necessary if progressivism was to become permanent. For the moment, however, Croly remained vague about the way such a change would come about.

In *Progressive Democracy* Croly still clung to his pragmatism. But by 1914 he was even more aware of the possible incoherence of pragmatic reform. Having pictured a government freed from legalistic Jeffersonian restraints and intimately responsive to the popular will, Croly went on to suggest that such a government "might escape one danger only to be involved in another." "Its career might degenerate into a succession of meaningless and unprofitable experiments, which would not get enough continuity either to accomplish stable results or to teach significant lessons." Croly was not only calling for the experimental nationalism of the New Deal of the 'thirties but he was cautioning against the feckless opportunism that would lessen the New Deal's meaning.

Perhaps the most remarkable thing about *Progressive Democracy* was its optimism, an optimism that contrasted with Croly's depression of the year before when only "riot & bloodshed & sudden death" seemed to lie ahead. In 1914 Croly was much less the stern master of *The Promise of American Life* who had preached hard truths to fellow reformers. Instead Croly's notions of an interest-centered government and nonviolent syndicalism put him in the optimistic vanguard of reform, a position only his ideas on labor organization and trust nationalization had suggested before.

Croly was so optimistic largely because of his great hopes for the future of progressivism. In spite of Roosevelt's defeat, Croly thought the election of 1912 had proven most Americans to be radically progressive. Reform no longer seemed "doctrinaire"; reformers no longer staked "the welfare of the country on a rigid political and economic creed." Even Woodrow Wilson's Jeffersonian New Freedom, said Croly, "has approximated in certain respects to the New Nationalism." Everywhere the old liberalism seemed to be giving way to the new.

During the fateful summer months of 1914, as he read the

final proofs of *Progressive Democracy* and worked with Weyl, Lippmann, and others on organizing the *New Republic*, Croly was relatively lighthearted. Even the bloodshed and death that followed Sarajevo failed to shake his confidence. The European war, he wrote Learned Hand, "will tend to dislocate conventional ways of looking at things, and to stimulate public opinion to think about the greater international problems which are now pressing for solution." Yet as the horror of the guns spread throughout the world after 1914, even to the shores of the land of promise, the prophet of democratic nationalism was to find his new liberalism much tested. *Progressive Democracy* was the new testament of the faith; in the pages of the *New Republic* Croly, along with Weyl and Lippmann, would pit his new hopes for democracy against the problems of nationalism rampant.

3. WEYL AND CLASS WAR

Weyl, too, attempted to revise his version of the new liberalism during and after the Bull Moose campaign. *The New Democracy* was hardly in page proofs late in 1911 when Weyl began a new book to be called "The Class War." Though he wrote two other books on the World War, though he started several books on feminism, the Far East, and other subjects, this was the book Weyl turned to again and again until his death eight years later, and thought his most important. It was also the book he could never finish. Weyl's diary comments on the various drafts of "The Class War" provide a clinical account of the fate of his liberal philosophy in the years after 1912.

At first Weyl wanted his book to be a counterattack against the challenge of socialism to middle-class liberalism. By January 1912 he had resolved to make it "a pretty big book" and hoped to have it finished by the following October. Almost immediately, however, events obtruded to upset such plans. A violent strike led by the syndicalists Haywood and Ettor of the I.W.W. had broken out in Lawrence, Massachusetts. As the first test of the radical union in the East, the strike aroused much interest. Within two weeks of its start Weyl was off to Lawrence as a reporter for the *Outlook*.

Weyl returned from the strike much impressed, but he was still unshaken in his long-held faith in conservative unionism. "It was one of the most fruitful experiences of my life," he wrote in his diary. "It was my first experience with the I.W.W. & with Revolutionary Syndicalism. It excited my enthusiasm, but I am sure there is nothing to it. The Lawrence strike would be won by a man like [John] Mitchell but will be lost by Haywood and Ettor."

When Weyl revisited the strike three months later, however, he could not so readily discount what he saw. The strike had lasted longer than expected; there had been violence, misery, and suppression; yet the workers had not deserted the I.W.W.'s red banner. "My experiences in Lawrence shook me up mightily," Weyl confessed in his diary. "I feel that it compels me to test all my theories." What, he asked, was "labor—especially unskilled labor—to do? To what extent should it accept the banner of the class war and to what extent not?"

Weyl went about the revamping of his theories energetically. Through the early months of 1912 he read the writings, both foreign and American, of as many socialists as he could find. He resolved "for the sake of . . . [the] book on the Class War . . . [to] go to one strike after another . . . to one manifestation after another of the class struggle." In March an article he had written for the *Survey* on the strike brought an invitation to testify before a House Committee in Washington. He turned it down, however, as distracting him from his book. He went to socialist meetings in New York, but more often than not came away disgusted. "The evening left me with a sense of utter contempt for the methods of this little group," he wrote after one such meeting. "They are Parlor Socialists—& that is all there is to it." In May he traveled to the Socialist party convention in Indianapolis and watched the parliamentarian Berger faction drive out the Haywood syndicalists.

Weyl's studies and speculations bore little fruit. March 1912 found him still merely blocking out the early chapters and deciding that just as in his first book he had personalized American history "in the figure of the Pioneer so . . . [he] would figure him this time as the Proletarian." Another month brought little further progress. "Bertha is pushing me to make a draft," wrote Weyl after a conference with his wife, "and perhaps she is right." But first he resolved to read several more books on socialism and labor, among them William English Walling's *Socialism as It Is*. Two weeks later he was still "working steadily through Walling's book and getting lots of good through . . . opposition to it." His own book, however, just would not jell, and by August he was caught up in the great Bull Moose crusade.

After the Progressive campaign Weyl again became "deeply engrossed" in "The Class War." Late in November he found its central problem "a simple one in a certain sense." The whole issue resolved itself into the single question: "Are we to have peace or war in our industrial life?" For the moment Weyl's solution was the same as in *The New Democracy*—the social surplus, the idea of progress through prosperity. "Prosperity means peace," he noted: "poverty means war."

A week later he believed that the real aim of his book was to awaken the middle class, "to appeal to other people than the workingman to face the problems." "We shall have a class war unless we prevent it," said Weyl. "It is up to us." He decided like Croly that what was needed was "industrial democracy." He wanted a system where worker and employer could stand "shoulder to shoulder," where the workman would become "an equal citizen . . . [in spite of] a worse environment." "I really believe I have it now," said Weyl of his idea on industrial democracy. "It is a thing on which I must work immediately."

Off and on for much of 1913, until in September he began

intensive work with Croly, Weyl continued to struggle with "The Class War." Yet, while he was sure that the American middle class could work together with labor to thwart revolutionary unionism, he was never quite able to spell out the theory. He filled his diary with speculation; he accumulated piles of notes and half-completed manuscript. At one point he decided that a fundamental revolution in the wage system was necessary. Seeking a "reformation & improvement . . . of the very nature of paid labor," Weyl like Croly found the ideas of John Dewey suggestive. "Education became pleasant," wrote the publicist in his diary; "why not labor?"

Croly's call for Weyl to join the *New Republic* late in 1913 found the economist with "The Class War" still unfinished. Distractions during the summer had been numerous. Work with Louis Brandeis for the garment workers' protocol, six days spent revising the labor chapter of Roosevelt's autobiography, conferences with the Progressive party's Legislative Service, the writing of magazine articles—all conspired to prevent definite progress. By the end of July Weyl thought "28 days of actual work" might bring a first draft, but such days were not forthcoming. The final drift of his conclusions, at least for 1913, is evident in the shift of title from "The Class War" to "The Social Concert." Weyl had turned from merely attacking the socialists to working out a positive theory of his own. The book "will stand or fall on its *Constructive Labor* Program," said Weyl in August in what was for the moment his last mention of the project. Had the book been finished in 1913, it would probably have much resembled Croly's *Progressive Democracy*. The agitations of the I.W.W. during the Lawrence strike had moved Weyl beyond the conservative unionism of John Mitchell, but they had little damaged his basic faith in middle-class reform.

4. LIPPMANN AND MASTERY

Walter Lippmann also found strong grounds for optimism in the months after the campaign of 1912. Like Croly he at times veered toward the utopian. His *Drift and Mastery*, published in the early fall of 1914, showed none of those nagging doubts about middle-class reform that had plagued Weyl. Instead Lippmann saw cause on every hand for impassioned re-affirmation.

While Croly in *Progressive Democracy* had stressed how very much progressivism still had to do, Lippmann in *Drift and Mastery* believed the battle to have been largely won. The need for further agitation had passed; the consolidation of gains should begin. "The battle for us," Lippmann proclaimed, "does not lie against crusted prejudice, but against the chaos of a new freedom."

Looking about him in 1914 Lippmann saw many things that made continued agitation meaningless. There was, for instance, a "widespread rebellion against the profit motive." Business was increasingly "being administered by men who . . . [were] not profiteers." "The motive of profit is not their motive," said the young publicist of the managers of "gigantic enterprises." "That is an astounding change." Astounding indeed, but Lippmann saw still more. The new industrial system was also "organizing private property out of existence," thus making all the wrangling about "property rights" virtually senseless. Lippmann saw "no essential difference between holding the securities of the Steel Trust and those of the United States Government." "The government bonds are if anything," he added, "a more certain investment."

Drift and Mastery's first chapter brushed aside all the revelations of the muckrakers as irrelevant to the needs of "mastery." Lippmann's own conclusions, however, suggest that the task of exposure had barely begun. Weyl's friend Louis Brandeis, for instance, had shown before the Stanley Committee only a year earlier that 65 per cent of the workers for United States Steel earned "less than the minimum cost of living." At the same time the corporation over a ten-year period had paid $220,000,000 in dividends on 200,000 shares of heavily watered stock and had averaged a profit of 40 per cent on every pound of steel made. Lippmann may have been right in recognizing the increased professionalism of corporation management, but he dismissed too easily the importance of the profit motive in American industry.

Oddly enough, part of Lippmann's greater optimism came from his new association with Weyl. In *Drift and Mastery* Lippmann approved of the way Weyl had attacked Marxism through the notion of "levels of democratic striving." At the very time Weyl was wondering whether he had been right in *The New Democracy* to discount the proletarian so thoroughly, Lippmann was quoting the Weyl dictum that "a class crushed to earth—is crushed to earth." Lippmann also was much taken with Weyl's ideas about the consumer. "We are finding, I think," Lippmann wrote, "that the real power emerging today in democratic life is just the mass of the people who are crying out against the high cost of living." Lippmann thought the force of consumer protest was "far from being an impotent one"; in fact, it was "destined to be stronger than the interests of either labor or capital."

Lippmann, like Croly, therefore, moved farther toward democracy in 1914. His shift, however, occurring in less than a year and starting from a position much less democratic than Croly's, was considerably more dramatic. Gone now was the inspired, willful leader who would translate the "dull mutterings of the multitude" into a dynamic program. Instead Lippmann asserted that mastery was to be attained "not by some wise and superior being but by the American people themselves." Now as in Croly's *Progressive Democracy* cooperation and participation became the theme.

Like Croly and Weyl, Lippmann also now embraced the idea of "industrial democracy." For Lippmann as for the others the stimulus was Bill Haywood, the I.W.W., and the Lawrence and Paterson strikes. Lippmann was part of the group—John Reed, Robert Edmond Jones, Edward Hunt, and others—that in 1913 put on a Madison Square pageant to dramatize the plight of the Paterson silk workers. Mabel

Dodge remembered how Lippmann brought Bill Haywood to her salon one evening the same year and "tried to draw him out." Haywood, however, could talk to the genteel intellectuals only "as though he were wading blindfolded in sand." Mabel Dodge recalled that Lippmann, "remarkably certain in his judgments . . . and very definite in his speech, . . . gave Big Bill several leads." The colloquy between bantam intellectual and strike leader, however, turned out to be "useless," with Haywood helplessly inarticulate.

In *Drift and Mastery* the tactics of Haywood and the I.W.W. were dismissed with scant ceremony. The radical union, Lippmann argued, was nowhere near so effective as "conservative unions" like the railroad brotherhoods. The revolutionary I.W.W. was "quite ready to destroy a union for the sake of militancy." Haywood's violence was less a threat than the sign of labor's general desperation. It could be cured only by giving workers "power in the life of the nation."

Power for labor meant for Lippmann, too, a system of "industrial democracy." Such a system might in time mean that employees would "demand the right to choose their own foremen, perhaps to elect some of the directors, and to take not only wages, but a percentage of the profits." Lippmann was unclear as to whether he would support such demands, but he immediately added that labor's "assumption of power . . . [could not] go to indefinite limits." "The consumers will have a control," wrote the young publicist," and the state too will have a say about the control of industry."

Lippmann's new call for democratic participation, his faith in consumer protest, his espousal of industrial democracy brought him more in line with the thinking of Croly and Weyl. Yet *Drift and Mastery* revealed an even more significant change. Though less than a year separated the two books, the young publicist had by 1914 abandoned most of the anti-intellectualism of *A Preface to Politics*. No longer did he emphasize the "irrationality of reason" or the "creativity of instinct." His former irrationalist idol Henri Bergson was mentioned but once and then apologetically. Completely absent was the master myth-maker Georges Sorel, while even Sigmund Freud, upon whom Lippmann's first book had been centered, was mentioned but thrice. So fell the heroes whose influence had most set off Lippmann from the older publicists.

Lippmann's English mentor Graham Wallas was largely responsible for the change. The Fabian intellectual used a letter to Lippmann as a preface to *The Great Society*, published in June 1914. In the letter Wallas credited the inspiration for his new book to a "discussion course" Lippmann had joined during the Englishman's "stay at Harvard in the spring of 1910." Wallas had had second thoughts about the psychological emphasis of *Human Nature in Politics*. "The earlier book . . .," Wallas wrote, "turned into an argument against nineteeth-century intellectualism; . . . this book . . . has turned, at times, into an argument against certain forms of twentieth-century anti-intellectualism" Wallas hoped Lippmann might undergo a similar change. "I send . . . [my book] to you," he wrote, bringing his preface to a close, "in the hope that it may be of some help to you when you write that sequel to your *Preface to Politics* for which all your friends are looking."

Even Wallas must have been surprised by the alacrity with which his young disciple took the suggestion. In *Drift and Mastery* Lippmann was still a pragmatist, but much less aggressively so. He noted now the objections of those who claimed one could not "judge rules or beliefs by their results, because many an idea of the greatest value may be at first disagreeable." Less cocksure, Lippmann could only reaffirm his faith on the rather lame note that pragmatism was the most possible belief among a welter of impossibilities. If anyone can evolve a more absolute answer, Lippmann declared, "well, then, surely, no pragmatist will object."

Even more astonishing was the way *Drift and Mastery* celebrated objective science over the aesthetic intuition that had been the dominant note of *A Preface to Politics*. No longer did Lippmann find society's salvation in the "creative myth,"

but instead in "science"—a science, as he said, that could
"distinguish fact from fantasy." The earlier book had sneered
at "the efficacy of 'scientific' demonstration and logical proof"
in politics. In 1914, however, Lippmann found "the scientific
spirit ... [to be] the discipline of democracy.... This is what
mastery means."

Science became the matrix of all Lippmann's new enthusiasms. Science implied a "common discipline"; it meant co-
operation; it was men's only assurance "that from the same set
of facts ... [they would] come approximately to the same set
of conclusions." As such, science was democracy's necessary
faith. Science in fact could arouse the "same loyalty and courage to which religions of old could point as their finest flower."

Lippmann's reversal of field in so short a time showed an
admirable disdain for the consistency Emerson called "the
hobgoblin of little minds." Undoubtedly the Bergsonian
doctrine he had abandoned was the direct antithesis of the
science he now espoused. It was equally certain that a politics
based on "myth" was markedly different from one that relied
upon scientific proof. Lippmann's myth, however, had never
been very mythical, nor was his science now entirely scientific.
Obscuring the violence of his own transformation, Lippmann
stressed the subjective aspects of scientific inquiry. "Before the
scientific spirit can reach full bloom," he wrote, "it will have
to acquire an honest sense of the role that fantasy plays in all
its work." Human desires still ruled Lippmann's world, with
science simultaneously their servant and master. "If thinking
didn't serve desire," Lippmann concluded, "it would be the
most useless occupation in the world."

Thus Lippmann in effect had merely shifted from the
"creative instincts" of the artist to those of the scientist. Reason
still had its impulse in desire and instinct, but science had now
become its discipline. Lippmann was as concerned as ever in
Drift and Mastery with "the blind mutterings and brute forces
that move beneath the surface of events." Science and the
people, however, rather than myth and master, were to keep

such forces "welded and disciplined to the other interests of civilization."

Lippmann was as optimistic as Croly about the great upsurge of progressivism in the campaign of 1912. Though he had stronger reservations than Croly about Woodrow Wilson, he was equally confident of the ultimate triumph of the new liberalism. In *Drift and Mastery* he broke completely from the socialism he had championed only two years before, arguing, as had Weyl in 1898, that none of the socialist predictions had come true. "The middle class has not disappeared," wrote Lippmann. "[Instead] it is the dominant power expressing itself through the Progressives and through the Wilson administration." The middle class had "put the 'Money Power' on the defensive," while business was "losing its control of the government." There had been no tendency toward that "great line-up of two hostile classes" Karl Marx had so confidently predicted but, on the contrary, "an unexpected burst of sheerly democratic impulse which . . . [had blurred] class lines." Lippmann, like Croly and Weyl, turned to the work of organizing the *New Republic*, convinced that middle-class liberalism held the key to America's future.

5. A MEETING OF MINDS AND MONEY

The thinking of Croly, Weyl, and Lippmann had moved toward a common center in the two years between the Bull Moose campaign and the beginning of their collaboration on the *New Republic*. Croly largely abandoned his notions of a guiding elite, while his nationalism merged with less militant strains of "social democracy." Lippmann forgot the voluntaristic leader of *A Preface to Politics* and, like Croly, came out for a broadly based reform movement of which co-operation and participation were the themes. He modified the aggressive irrationalism of his earlier work and compromised between pragmatism and absolutism in a manner substantially similar to Croly's. Both Lippmann and Croly after 1912, in fact, moved closer to that idea of a rational and beneficent democratic society that Weyl had sketched in *The New Democracy*.

Yet it was Croly's democratic nationalism, the New Nationalism of 1912, that became the heart of the creed the three men worked out in the *New Republic*. The magazine itself, furthermore, was born of an impulse stirred by Croly's earlier and more virile thinking in *The Promise of American Life*. The publicist's weaving together of an internationalized imperialism with democratic nationalism appealed strongly to young, idealistic Willard Straight, who in 1910 was exercising his idealism for an American banking group in China. Straight was struck by Croly's argument that a strong national policy in foreign affairs required a similar policy at home. When he returned to the United States in 1912, Straight looked up the writer and, as Croly records, "asked . . . [for] a report . . . on the kind of social education which would be most fruitful in a democracy."

Though Straight was only thirty-two in 1912, there was little presumption in his request for a "report" from the prominent political philosopher. He spoke, first of all, for wealth, since the year before he had married Dorothy Whitney, daughter of the Wall Street capitalist, William C. Whitney, who had him-self benefited from an alliance with Standard Oil millions. Straight himself, furthermore, was not without importance. Orphaned at ten, he had largely worked his way through Cornell, and though he had left college without money or powerful connections had soon become a favored protégé of both Theodore Roosevelt and the railroad magnate, Edward H. Harriman. By a remarkable combination of ability, charm, and good luck, Straight, before he was thirty, had been successively American Consul General in Manchuria, acting chief of the State Department's Division of Far Eastern Affairs, and the main representative in China for such notably demanding institutions as Kuhn, Loeb and Company, and the J. P. Morgan firm.

Willard Straight, in fact, was a Wilbur Littleton. He met remarkably well Croly's specifications for those men whose "constructive individualism" might save America. His rather obscure beginnings accorded with Croly's notion that the democratic elite be "ceaselessly replaced." His intense patriotism was, as Croly had asked, "instead of being something apart from his work, absolutely identified therewith." The young banker-diplomat sincerely believed that the hegemony he sought for American interests in China would be of a different quality than that of other countries, that it would do "tremendous work in furthering the Chinese Renaissance." Straight's talent for leadership, his daring, his humane yet hard-headed flair for empire building eminently qualified him for the company of Croly's "saints and heroes."

Straight probably found an appealing moral for his own work in the nationalism of *The Promise of American Life*. The irresponsibility and sentimentality of the Jeffersonian tradition seemed to cripple American efforts even in China. In the Far East, Straight combatted a laissez-faire Open Door policy he thought analogous in folly to the trust-busting enthusiasms Croly deplored at home. Free competition among nations in Manchuria, Straight believed, merely meant that the strongest would win. The Open Door, without the support of American power and money, would ultimately ensure the conquest of China by Russia and Japan.

Wealthy, public spirited after the fashion of his class and kind, Straight undoubtedly saw in Croly an avenue by which to impress his own imperialistic convictions on the American public. His return to the United States in 1912 marked the apparent triumph of what Croly later in a biography of Straight called "the outstanding project of his life," a consortium of bankers of the United States, Great Britain, France, Germany, Russia, and Japan for the joint exploitation of China. By 1913, however, the great scheme had gone sour. Fearing losses, the "American Group" of bankers wanted to quit, while the incoming Wilson administration seemed certain to repudiate the Taft-Knox policy of "dollar diplomacy." "Bankers, as you know," wrote Straight in February 1913 to a friend, "are at this time under a cloud in this country."

Straight, in fact, expected nothing better from the Democratic party in foreign policy than Croly, Weyl, and Lippmann expected at home. Soon enough Wilson did repudiate the Consortium with a ringing condemnation of "dollar diplomacy," an act Croly a decade later still thought to have been the death of the banker-diplomat's pet project. Straight, however, must have known better, for his own banking associates in February 1913 had put off their withdrawal from the Consortium only to avoid embarrassment of the Taft administration, while a year later he himself conceded that "any administration, if confronted at the very outset by a question such as . . . [the Consortium] propounded, would doubtless have given the same reply." Even so, the Wilsonian attitude seemed to him symptomatic of a general malaise infecting the country. As Croly put it, Straight became interested in plans for the *New Republic* in 1913 largely because the young banker found "the results he wished to see achieved . . . more and more impeded or barred by the indifference or hostility of public opinion."

As an arch-exponent of American imperialism and in 1913 an employee of J. P. Morgan and Company, Straight might seem a strange figure to have made possible Croly, Weyl, and Lippmann's elaboration of a new liberalism in a "magazine of opinion." Like most progressives, however, Straight saw no necessary contradiction between imperialism abroad and progressivism at home. Nor was it unusual at the time for the rich to support seemingly radical causes. The Morgan partner George W. Perkins, after all, had been a major supporter and manager of Roosevelt's Bull Moose campaign, while Straight's brother-in-law, Harry Payne Whitney, had in 1912 begun to subsidize the avowedly socialist *Metropolitan*. Furthermore, Straight himself quickly adjusted his own beliefs to the progressive movement he found all around him upon his return from China. Prodded by his idealistic wife, Dorothy, increasingly in contact with Croly in planning for the *New Republic*, Straight by 1914 had adopted the ideas and even the phraseology of the intellectuals he would soon be supporting. "The country needs more than anything else," he wrote Roosevelt, "Construction—Nationalism—Americanism, hopeful, effective, and above all things sane. The old vocabulary about monopolies, the wicked interests, and corrupt big business, is pretty well out of date. . . . We need and must have something new—constructive and helpful, not mean and envious, and withering."

In their first talks together Croly and Straight played with the idea of a daily newspaper, one of large circulation, which through its news and the weight of its editorials might help save the country from the Jeffersonian cant of Wilson's New Freedom. In the end, however, they decided a weekly magazine might more practically serve their end of converting America to Croly's nationalistic vision.

The immediate stimulus for the latter plan came from their distaste for the work of Norman Hapgood, who in 1913 was trying to revitalize *Harper's Weekly* into an organ for the Wilson progressives. Hapgood had resigned from *Collier's* the year before when financial pressures and decreased public interest began to curb that journal's muckraking career. Turning to *Harper's* he gave the old magazine a "striking new format" and a liberal policy that led many to "expect great things from . . . [his] bold editorial initiative." Croly and Straight, however, could hardly be impressed by the efforts of so strong a partisan of Woodrow Wilson and the New Freedom. An attack by Hapgood on a prominent conservative in 1913, for instance, struck Croly as "a dirty and malign bit of writing . . . [that] sounded to . . . [his] ears like the barking of a yellow dog." During one of his visits with the Straights at their Long Island estate, Croly gave "a weighty and convincing statement of what Harper's weekly should be but wasn't." "Why don't you get out a weekly yourself, Herbert?" Dorothy Straight asked the publicist, and before the conversation was over financial backing had been promised and rough plans for the magazine made.

The problem the Straights and Croly wanted to tackle with the *New Republic* was in many respects real. At least it was so for those who thought continuing progressivism and the expression of "independent" opinion vital. Most of the muckraking magazines either had disappeared by 1913 or were about to do so, while others, like *Pearson's* or the *Metropolitan*, had turned to more radical agrarian or socialist interests. The *American Magazine*, which had become the co-operative refuge of many muckrakers, had only about a year left of independent existence. The *Masses* had been founded as a new and rather exciting socialist periodical, but it had little appeal for the old middle-class audience of the muckrakers. The *Outlook* had attained a certain glory after 1909 when Theodore Roosevelt joined it, but it was more a "family magazine" than a serious political organ. The *Nation*, patterned on English liberal weeklies, offered the *New Republic* its closest domestic model, but it was largely literary and no longer the voice of upper-middle-class protest it had been under Godkin.

Many of the men who joined Croly in founding the *New Republic* had suffered personally from the economic restraints and waning public interest that ended the muckraking movement. Lippmann, as already noted, had seen on *Everybody's* "the inside workings of business pressure," though typically he had found mass resistance to new ideas more depressing than the machinations of the bankers. Weyl had had that struggle with his conscience over his profitable pieces for the *Saturday Evening Post* that had led him finally to abandon merely popular writing. Robert Hallowell, who became the *New Republic's* business manager and art editor, was a refugee from the collapsing *American Magazine*. Francis Hackett, the first literary editor, had in 1911 taken over the editorship of the muckraking *Human Life* in what proved a futile effort to save it. While none of these men regretted the demise of "unconstructive" muckraking any more than Croly, their experiences made them receptive to any organ that provided for the free expression of opinions.

In their general plans for the *New Republic* Croly and Straight hoped to evade the existing restraints on independent journalism. They forswore any mass appeal of the kind that had thwarted Weyl and Lippmann on the large-circulation magazines. Instead they aimed for the teachers, professors, civil servants, social workers, enlightened politicians and businessmen—the Wilbur Littletons in all fields upon whom Croly had always counted. They hoped that the *New Republic*, inexpensive in format and liberally subsidized, would be immune to those pressures that had had much to do with ending the muckraking movement. In April 1914 Croly told the New York *Times* that "sufficient funds to guarantee four years of publication had been obtained."

There were some among those who joined Croly in founding the *New Republic*, however, who were not so sure that subsidy by a banker would end the problem of banker control. Francis Hackett, as he reported several years later, had from long experience "strong feelings about the intellectual dishonesty of most American journalism. In the main," he continued, "Walter Weyl shared those feelings." Another of the original staff, Philip Littell, was also skeptical. He could not see how a man of Straight's "energy and will and decision of character" could avoid insisting on expressing his own views on the proposed magazine. Croly himself was sufficiently concerned by the problem to decide to limit official editorial meetings strictly to staff in order to "prevent W.D.S. from inviting men like Ogden Mills & Lloyd Griscom." Croly could remember what had happened in Bull Moose councils when George Perkins and Frank Munsey had their powerful say.

The other founders, however, were not to be satisfied either with Croly's maneuvers or with tacit understandings. Several of them threatened to "withdraw from the start" unless the whole relationship to Straight "was made man-to-man and democratic." Late in 1913 a meeting was held with Straight in New York during which the issue was thrashed out to the satisfaction of all. An explicit agreement was reached that both Straight and his wife together would have but one vote in editorial conferences. They were to be consulted on all important matters of policy or management, but they were not to have a veto over the other editors.

The agreement, while as satisfactory as possible under the circumstances, rested ultimately only on the good faith of the Straights. "They could always," admitted Croly, "withdraw their financial support, if they ceased to approve the policy of the paper." Without a subsidy the *New Republic*, self-supporting for only one brief period in 1920, would almost inevitably have collapsed. The fact is, however, that in spite of strong disagreements over policy during World War I, the Straights never did withdraw their support. Firm in their devotion to Croly, in basic accord with Croly's new liberalism, while Croly lived both Straights denied themselves a measure of the power of wealth in a way that did them credit. Croly managed to be relatively lighthearted about the whole arrangement. "The . . . vision I have of the New Republic . . .," he wrote Learned Hand, "will, I fear, set angel Dorothy back some hundreds of thousands of dollars . . . but she will get a little education for her money and so will I and so, I hope, will you and others."

Croly, Weyl, and Lippmann made their compromise with the realities of life, therefore, on terms that left them an unusual degree of intellectual freedom. Yet the possibility remains that the subsidy behind their philosophizing became a governor on their radicalism. William J. Ghent, the California socialist, claimed, for instance, that the policy of the " 'polluted and polluting' . . . [*New Republic* was] determined by the terms of the subsidy from Willard Straight." In a sense, Ghent's instinct was true, for Straight, an ardent nationalist, a slightly skeptical progressive, a second-echelon functionary of the Morgan empire, consistently held views to the right of the intellectuals he supported. Even his altruism and his devotion to Croly might not have survived, say, a sudden conversion of the editors to Marxian socialism. The measure of the restraint the Straight money may have imposed on the minds of the trio, however, was never taken. In the period of the war and after the outer limits of the philosophy of the three were set, if by anything, by a common dedication to middle-class liberalism.

SIX

Nationalism and the New Freedom

1914-1916

1. IDEAS AND MEN

"We'll throw a few firecrackers under the skirts of the old women on the bench & in other high places," wrote Croly early in 1914 of his plans for the *New Republic*. The jest caught the spirit with which he, Weyl, and Lippmann started their new venture. The firecrackers of reform, not the bombs of revolution, were to be their weapons.

Croly knew what he wanted such critical firecrackers to do for American life. Oddly enough for a founder of a "magazine of opinion," he had little hope that mere words could sway mass opinion. Americans, he had argued in *The Promise of American Life*, were to learn by doing, or, more accurately, by having done for them. The critical intellectual would serve best by being a force behind the reforms of an elite.

Though by 1914 Croly wanted mass participation in reform, his purpose in the *New Republic* harked back to his earlier elitist instrumentalism. The *New Republic* would be directed toward the Wilbur Littletons, toward those "exceptional fellow-countrymen" Croly had addressed in *The Promise of American Life*.

"We shall be radical without being socialistic," wrote Croly in June 1914 of his intended magazine, "and our general tendency will be pragmatic rather than doctrinaire." Lippmann, writing a friend at about the same time, seemed to contradict the leading editor when he declared the magazine would be "in direction socialistic." The difference, however, became inconsequential when he immediately added, but "not so either in allegiance or in method or phrase." Both men, whether they described their ideas as "radical" or "socialistic," meant to work pragmatically toward what Croly described as "a more thoughtful and radical form of progressivism." By immersing themselves pragmatically in the stream of events, Croly, Weyl, and Lippmann hoped they might distil from the experience itself further sanctions for their new liberalism.

By 1914 the three publicists had carried their theories about as far as their pragmatism, their nationalism, and their middle-class liberalism would allow. Though they tried, Croly and Weyl were never again able to publish revisions of their political philosophies. When Lippmann revised his more than two decades later, he spoke in different accents to a different generation. For the moment the test of the new liberalism rested in the hands of the practitioners. Unequipped themselves for leading roles in the world of action, the best the *New Republic* men could hope for was a chance for continuing consultation. The readers of their books had been numbered in the thousands; in their magazine the editors hoped to reach tens of thousands. The "dreamers of dreams, . . . world losers and world forsakers" were still to be "movers and shakers."

Even intellectuals do not live by ideas alone. The new venture had for each of the publicists certain practical advantages. For the dedicated Croly, oddly enough, the immediate advantage was money. The generosity of the Straights saved him from acute financial embarrassment. Though a man of property and anything but poor, by 1913 Croly was living more comfortably than he could afford. A delayed legacy, slow payment of his fee for the Godkin lectures, and the failure to find a buyer for one of the houses he owned in New York reduced him to such a state that early in the year he was posted for debt at the Harvard Club. Only a $2000 loan from Judge Learned Hand saved him from even greater difficulties. "Probably I would never have the courage," Croly confessed to Hand, "to hitch myself to a desk in New York again if my money matters were in better shape. It is a solace to know that I shall actually be earning during the next few years our expenses."

To Walter Weyl the *New Republic* salary made little difference. In 1913 he and his wife were just moving into their large new house at Woodstock. His wife's income was sufficient to afford a car and a chauffeur. The quickness with which Weyl accepted Croly's invitation to be an editor sprang from frustrations other than financial. He had not been able to complete a draft of his book "The Class War"; personal frictions and union factionalism marred his service on the garment workers' arbitration board; and he still resented the coldness of magazine editors toward his more "dignified" pieces. Croly's personality alone was enough to guarantee that the *New Republic* would be serious and dignified.

Walter Lippmann in 1913 was equally well off. Not only did he still live with his wealthy parents in New York's East Eighties, but his remarkable precociousness was paying off. *A Preface to Politics* was about to be reissued by a more prominent publisher. *Drift and Mastery* was nearly done. Magazine editors greeted his lucid prose most cordially. Among the younger intellectuals he was winning a formidable reputation. Well might Croly have thought Lippmann a "gift from Heaven" for the launching of the *New Republic*. For the young writer, in turn, the editorship meant prestige and a chance for greater influence. To rank equally on a magazine with Croly and Weyl was quite a coup for a young man of twenty-five. "He is certainly in fine fettle these days," a friend reported a week after the magazine began publication. "Whether it is the book or a regular job or the responsibility of finishing up the incomplete work of the Creator, I don't know. But I have never seen him happier or nicer."

With the choice of Weyl and Lippmann as editors late in 1913, Croly's stellar rockets were at hand. Croly realized, however, that the 25,000 words planned each week for the *New Republic* would require more writers. His literary editor, Francis Hackett, could help. A well-educated Irishman who had come to America thirteen years before, Hackett had settled in Chicago, where he edited for the *Evening Post* one of the most distinguished literary supplements of the day. The strongest political voice on the board beyond the dominant trio, he too had cheered Roosevelt and the New Nationalism in 1912.

Less important than Hackett in policy making, though theoretically equal members of the original board of six, were Philip Littell and Charlotte Rudyard. Littell, a Harvard contemporary of Croly's who had become a close friend in Cornish, made his largest contribution through a weekly column called "Books and Things." His deep loyalty to Croly also often made him a peacemaker during heated editorial discussions. Charlotte Rudyard, a Vassar graduate who had been associate editor of *Harper's Weekly*, became, in Lippmann's words, "a kind of assistant managing editor." Her influence on policy was slight.

In addition to his six "regular Republicans," Croly soon found others to help. Robert Hallowell, a Harvard classmate of Lippmann's and later a member of the same Greenwich Village group, was signed on as business manager and unofficial art editor. Croly also wanted Learned Hand to join the staff. "I would be particularly happy," he wrote, "in case you discarded the dignity of being a judge and threw your fortunes in with the Republic." Hand did attend staff meetings and make contributions, but basically he preferred the hard realities of the bench to the airy firmament of a journal of opinion.

Hand brought Croly into touch with Felix Frankfurter. While never officially on the staff, Frankfurter became an important member of the early *New Republic* group. When Croly met him early in 1913, he thought him "one of the most completely alive men . . . [he had] ever met." Frankfurter, about to leave a lame-duck post with the outgoing Taft administration for a law professorship at Harvard, helped much with the planning of the *New Republic*. He also worked behind the scenes with the others on policy statements for Roosevelt, and ultimately contributed both signed and unsigned articles to the magazine. His importance to the venture was shown when the *New Republic*'s first statement of ownership listed him with Croly and Straight as a trustee for the other editors' stockholdings.

Finally, there were a few men, either younger or less well established than the others, who by joining the magazine actually helped make their reputations. The fledgling economist George Soule came to the staff a month after publication began. Two years later he was made an assistant editor. Alvin Johnson, then teaching economics at Cornell, agreed during the summer of 1914 to serve as a regular contributor. In September of the next year he became the first addition to the original board. Croly's and Hand's close friend George Rublee helped with initial planning and later became an important connection for the magazine with the Wilson Administration. Lippmann's Harvard friend, Lee Simonson, was signed up for "a definite amount of writing" on art. Randolph Bourne, but two years out of college in 1914 and not yet the figure among the younger intellectuals he would become during the war, was pushed strongly by Ellery Sedgwick of the *Atlantic* and Charles A. Beard for a place on the staff. Bourne had to be satisfied, however, with a vaguely defined salaried contributorship.

If ideas like men can be known by their friends, then the general tone and bent of *New Republic* policy was already evident. By birth, marriage, or attainment all of the men Croly had gathered belonged to America's upper-middle class, that narrow stratum of society where men have ample means and often ample talent, but not the peculiar power of long-held wealth. All of the native-born among them except Alvin Johnson were graduates of "Ivy League" colleges, institutions often as efficient in perpetuating the privilege of class as in education. They could move easily in the genteel air of the Harvard or

Players Clubs, where many of the magazine's early conferences were held, while only Weyl and Hackett among them could feel really at ease at a Socialist party convention or a union strike meeting.

Beyond such similarity of status, the *New Republic* men were also mostly products of the eastern seaboard, particularly of the metropolis New York. Only Johnson, with his Nebraska background, served to temper the markedly eastern cast of the group's views. The nationalistic *New Republic* helped fulfill Croly's long-held vision of New York as America's nationalizing metropolitan hub.

As upper-middle-class easterners, the *New Republic* editors worked within a controlling world view. They shared an image of the social and economic levels above and below them that often made them more sensitive to the misery of the masses than the masses were themselves. Beneath this sensitivity there also lay an undercurrent of mistrust and fear. Toward the upper stratum, too, the *New Republic* men were characteristically ambivalent. Observing the American capitalistic system, yet knowing and often admiring the men who ran it, the magazine's writers usually charged the evils of the system to "capitalism" and not to the "capitalists." Only gradually, for instance, were Croly and Lippmann to abandon their notion of the new "responsible" or "disinterested" businessmen who would promote "industrial democracy."

Insulated by both status and conviction from working-class movements, separated geographically from the agrarian radicalism of the West, Croly's group could be expected to stay within the confines of liberalism. They were all, of course, progressives. Most of them had supported Roosevelt and the New Nationalism in 1912 and to that extent shared the demands for regulated trusts and a strong welfare state that Roosevelt had popularized. Croly had rallied around him men much in his own image.

2. Plans and Politics

The physical plans that were worked out for the *New Republic* early in 1914 nicely reflected the genteel tastes of Croly and his new associates. The Straights further alleviated their leading editor's pressing financial predicament by buying for the magazine's offices a property on West 21st Street Croly had been trying to sell. A substantial, four-story, yellow-brick house set across a quiet street from the General Theological Seminary, the building was refitted to resemble a gentleman's club as much as an editorial plant. A kitchen run by a French couple provided elegant lunches for the editors and their guests. Croly wanted his guiding elite to be "social" as well as intellectual.

Full-scale conferences of "all future 'Republicans' " were held in January and April to hammer out editorial procedure. Perhaps as a result of the stand against Straight domination, certainly as a reflection of Croly's own retiring disposition, the magazine was organized to give free expression to the opinions of a group. There was to be no editor-in-chief, though in practice Croly soon became as much. All important policies were to be discussed in weekly editorial meetings where each editor would have an equal vote. "After the discussion," as Croly explained, "a special writer . . . [would] be assigned to the topic." All contributions and leaders were to be read by the entire staff, and nothing was to be published except "by practically unanimous consent." In organizing their magazine the three publicists veered close to that anarchism in liberalism their own writings deplored.

Finding a name for their publication gave the editors trouble. Had it not been pre-empted, Croly of course would have chosen the *Nation*, but as second best tried the *Republic*, only to find that also in use. When the final name was settled upon, it was done, as Lippman admitted later, despite a "positive dislike for the suggestion of utopianism."

By mid-April plans were firm enough to begin advertising.

Under the head "New Weekly a Radical" a New York *Times* reporter quoted the leading editor on intended policy. "The magazine," Croly declared, "is to represent progressive principles, but it is to be independent of any party, or individual in politics." It was to be "strongly in favor of woman suffrage . . . [and] radically progressive."

The *Times*'s rendering of "radically progressive" as "radical" in its headline probably gave the *New Republic*'s initial announcement more punch than Croly intended. As he explained to Hand of a similar statement later, it did "not seem . . . wise . . . to go into too much detail." "If, for instance," he wrote, "I should say that we intended to preach self-government in industry, the nationalization of the railroads, a minimum wage, and all the other specific economic and social reforms which will constitute our program, I think we would run the danger of making both illusory friends and unnecessary enemies" For the moment the *New Republic* men intended to be the most cautious of Fabians. The actual radicalism of a new liberalism that would give unions a say in management and socialize the railroads was to be broken gently to the magazine's middle-class readers.

The general confusion of the progressive movement of the time seemed to justify such caution. The year 1914 marked another slack point in the progressive tide, a lull in momentum that might mean either retreat or new surges in unforeseen directions. The Wilson Democrats had done far better than Croly and his friends had expected. Yet by the spring of 1914, with the difficult waters of tariff, banking, and anti-trust legislation successfully navigated, the Administration's future course was uncertain. Theodore Roosevelt's Bull Moose crew lay in even more dubious straits, with its most faithful members unsure whether the bulk of their fellows would return to the Republicans, defect to the Democrats, or pull loyally forward to a victory in 1916. A serious lag in economic activity that seemed to presage a major depression was also having its usual inhibiting effects on middle-class reformers. Publication was best held off until the fall Congressional elections had given some clue as to the prevailing currents. "If we did go into the campaign," Willard Straight explained, "we would have to take sides, which, of course, means making enemies and it seems to us wise that we should take up this controversy, summarize its results and be ready for the fight in '1916.' "

The fight in '16, of course, was to be for Roosevelt. However much the editors publicly disavowed support of "any party . . . or individual in politics," they remained supporters of the Colonel and his Progressive party. Their prospective publication of a magazine if anything strengthened their ties with the Bull Moose leader.

In spite of President Wilson's many accomplishments, Croly still favored the heroic Colonel over the saintly ex-professor. Wilson, the publicist wrote early in 1914, was a "moral pedant and pedagog" whose words made "T. R.'s platitudes seem really human." When Roosevelt returned in May from an exploring expedition in Brazil, the entire *New Republic* group hastened to rally around him. Within a few days of the Colonel's return Walter Lippmann joined him at a breakfast meeting at the Harvard Club and then moved on with Felix Frankfurter for a further conference at Roosevelt's *Outlook* office. Willard Straight also gave an enthusiastic welcome. "It seems to me," he wrote a week after Roosevelt had landed, "that the country is weary of uplift, weary of the high moral tone upon which, we are led to believe, affairs are at present being conducted. . . . You can sound the note and eunciate the broad policy that is required and I believe the people would respond." Walter Weyl, too, immediately got in touch with the Colonel, and when at the end of the month Roosevelt sailed on a short trip to Spain, the economist sent a farewell note wishing him "a safe, sane but not conservative return."

Doing everything in their power to make Roosevelt both active and progressive in politics, Croly, Weyl, and Lippmann worked hard with him during the summer of 1914 on a labor policy for the Progressives, a policy that, as Weyl said, would "be really big and statesmanlike." Its keynote, of course, was "industrial democracy." As Lippmann outlined the policy in June, it would demand better conditions for labor in order to keep the United States from facing "in the future a class structure imperiled by insurrection.... "Industrial democracy," the young publicist wrote Roosevelt, meant acceptance of the labor union "with all its crudities" as the most promising instrument for worker "representation in the management of business."

Early in July, Lippmann sent Roosevelt a "somewhat more detailed draft" of the labor program. Approved by Weyl and Frankfurter, it had been submitted first to "three manufacturers," two of whom had "agreed with it in its essentials." In August, Croly, Weyl, and Frankfurter traveled to Oyster Bay for lunch to talk over the general labor situation with the Colonel. The day after the meeting Weyl wrote that he and the others were still seeking "a dynamic labor policy for the Progressive Party" and looking forward "to the real fight in 1916."

The relationship between the politician and the intellectuals, however, had its tensions. In 1914 Roosevelt was as uncertain about the political future as the *New Republic* men. Only his loyalty to his friends and his own need for a following led him to keep the waning Bull Moose dream alive. In the face of such uncertainty the hovering about of the *New Republic* group may have seemed as much nagging pressure as welcome support.

Inevitably, too, the practical politician preferred moderation, the nice balancing of one side against another. When, for instance, Weyl wanted to remove "a few qualifying words and phrases" from one of Roosevelt's statements on labor, the politician was annoyed. "Now, my dear fellow," he wrote back. "You were a little surprised and rather a little shocked, when I told you how the bulk of the labor men sides with the McNamaras, and had previously sided with Moyer, Haywood, and Pettibone." He continued with a lengthy homily on the taste for violence among workers and the consequent need, irrespective of political expediency, to denounce "the murders and outrages of the strikers."

3. THE FIRST FIRECRACKERS

When the first issue of the *New Republic* appeared on November 7, 1914, the noise of Croly's reform firecrackers was almost drowned out by the ominous boom of guns in Europe. But the *New Republic* men, like Wilson in the White House and most reformers in general, were resolved for the moment not to be distracted by the European war. The stalemate in the fighting by November, moreover, helped the editors keep the focus on the national scene.

Croly's article on the war, therefore, came only second among the editorial articles and placed its emphasis on the consequences at home of the fighting in Europe. The war, wrote Croly, had served to reveal the tragic weakness of the American "national organization." The government under the Democrats had floundered helplessly in the face of the war's economic disruption. A grim winter loomed ahead with no provision made for the many men thrown out of work. Most Americans had reacted foolishly to the coming of the war, facing it not in a mood of "national responsibility," but instead with incoherent plans for "national self-assertion."

For the most part, however, the European crisis obtruded little upon the *New Republic*'s general air of assurance. Except for a brief introductory appeal to "all those who feel the challenge of our time," the first issue plunged into the swim of events without fanfare. Even the four major leaders that outlined *New Republic* policy contained no suggestion of new beginnings. The following signed articles went without introduction, while the reviews at the end covered a random selection of books such as any established magazine might note. A casual newsstand reader who brushed over the very brief opening statement might easily have imagined he was reading a well-established journal.

Among random notes and articles on such matters as the unemployed, the dearth of accurate news from Mexico, and a national conference of the Woman Suffrage Association, the editors sketched out in broad and cautiously imprecise strokes their general policy. For those who knew the men and their books there were few surprises. Though they did not flaunt the fact before their largely Jeffersonian audience, they were, of course, nationalistic prophets of a transformed liberalism.

The editors turned first, as they had planned, to the meaning for progressivism of the recent Congressional elections. They found a decided run of the tide against reform, a rejection of progressive candidates almost everywhere, plus a disconcerting near-collapse of Roosevelt's Progressive party. In explaining the reversals, the editors hinted at but did not define that belief in the decline of the two-party system and the rise of nonpartisanship that Croly had expressed in *Progressive Democracy*. To lay the groundwork for their later barrage on the subject, the editors charged Woodrow Wilson with most of the responsibility for the progressive setback. Much damage had been done by the President's "scrupulous loyalty to his own party." The result had been, declared the editors, "the recrudescence of merely partisan Republicanism."

Having, with magnificent aplomb, blamed Wilson for the unregenerate character of many Republicans, the editors went on to blast the New Freedom. Conceding that the Democrats had made "a surprisingly good record," the *New Republic* still quarreled with Wilson's "delusion" that his program "contained a complete and final solution for the problems of American democracy." The New Freedom had even severer tests before it, the editors predicted, and, in order to survive, the Democrats would have to abandon "many of their traditional shibboleths and . . . [seek] an access of inward light and grace." The discerning could easily hear the muffled drums of the New Nationalism rumbling in the background.

The magazine's new version of liberalism came forth even more strongly in an unsigned editorial called "The Tolerated

Unions." Following the pattern of their books, the editors defended labor not so much against its overt reactionary enemies as against those reformers who saw the worker's salvation in employer benevolence and welfare capitalism. With welfare capitalism and scientific management on one side and the unions on the other, America faced the task of choosing the best instrument for social progress. After an incisive analysis of common misconceptions of union tactics and attitudes, the *New Republic* concluded that whatever their faults the unions remained the best path to "industrial democracy."

The *New Republic*'s friendly attitude toward unions neatly met the test labor policy sets for all middle-class liberals, particularly those of nationalist persuasion. The editors' nationalism could just as logically have required, in place of "industrial democracy," an attack on unions as inefficient and disruptive of national unity. Croly, Weyl, and Lippmann, however, revealed themselves as *democratic* nationalists—nationalists, that is, who would accept even the inefficiency and confusion of union-management warfare if democracy were thereby strengthened. Their position on labor was considerably more favorable than that of the Wilson Administration in its first two years in office. The policy, in fact, both anticipated and went beyond that of the New Deal two decades later.

Croly's first fireworks display was impressive. The issue by its very temper, solemn here, humorous there, yet dignified throughout, seemed destined to attract serious attention. Even so, the success of the new venture hardly seemed certain. An advertising campaign before publication had attracted only 875 subscribers, and during the first weeks circulation was a matter of vital concern. Freda Kirchwey recalls going to a Harvard-Yale football game with Walter Lippmann soon after the first issue appeared. The excitement of the game itself, she later wrote, "was overshadowed by the major sport of the afternoon—a rapid canvass of the newsstands of New Haven to discover how many carried the newborn NR."

Strangely enough, the staid and stately journal won quite a following among New York's younger intellectuals. Randolph Bourne, who a year before had thought Norman Hapgood's New-Freedom-oriented *Harper's Weekly* "curiously infantile and sentimental," greeted the *New Republic* as "just . . . the opportunity . . . [he had] wanted to get . . . [himself] expressed," and only hoped "to be big enough for the opportunity." Amy Lowell, in 1914 a leading fomenter of the Imagist movement in poetry, was so enthusiastic that she tried unsuccessfully to become the magazine's poetry editor. Young Edmund Wilson became from the first "a regular reader," and to Van Wyck Brooks the magazine, "as one first heard of it, seemed already the symbol of a great coming epoch." Mabel Dodge's friend, Robert Rogers, probably expressed the feelings of most of the younger generation when he wrote his mentor: "I think the *New Republic* people are to be congratulated on their first number. There is certainly nothing like it in America."

A much less happy view of the *New Republic*, on the other hand, was taken by Lippmann's Harvard classmate and friend, John Reed. Lippmann's editorship, Reed felt, meant desertion of the socialism they had championed together since college. He wrote his friend chiding him for leaguing himself with the "capitalist" Straights, to which Lippmann wrote back cuttingly that "when Reed had burned himself out in the radical cause, he [himself] would still be active and useful in his own way." For a time the friendship of the two came to an end, a circumstance Reed gleefully ceremonialized by framing Lippmann's reply for the wall of his Washington Square room.

Reed, however, was in a minority, for Croly, Weyl, and Lippmann soon found an audience. "The New Republic is getting to be a best seller," wrote a friend of Randolph Bourne's two weeks after publication began. "It will be getting smug and complacent soon!" By 1915 the magazine's circulation had climbed to 15,000 and increased fairly steadily thereafter to a 1920 peak of 43,000. For the three publicists the thought of being read week after week even by so few was enough. Croly particularly must have had a sense of communing with those Wilbur Littletons in all walks of life to whom he had appealed so passionately in 1909.

4. THE LIGHT THAT FAILED

Though the *New Republic* did attract a good portion of the intellectual elite on whom the editors centered their hopes, within a month it lost one supporter who meant almost as much to Croly, Weyl, and Lippmann as all the rest. Roosevelt's heroic figure had quickly come to dominate their magazine's pages. The Bull Moose leader's example was evoked, for instance, in an attack on Wilson's policy of neutrality. Roosevelt knew, said the editors, "that treaties will never acquire sanctity until nations are ready to seal them with their blood." America under Roosevelt's leadership would have protested the violation of Belgium's neutrality and thus "given ruthlessness . . . the severest jolt it ever imagined."

Roosevelt, of course, was delighted, not, perhaps, so much for the praise of himself as for the condemnation of Wilson, for whom the Colonel was developing a vehement hatred. Within a week of the first issue the three editors were invited for dinner and the night at Oyster Bay, where undoubtedly their efforts were lauded as "Bully!" A joint review in the *Outlook* of Croly's *Progressive Democracy* and Lippmann's *Drift and Mastery* put the two books in a class with the greatest. They were so good it was impossible "to review them"; Roosevelt could only summarize and "call attention to their excellence."

Yet even in the throes of such approval, Roosevelt had one reservation about the two publicists that foreboded trouble. Conceding the impossibility "even for reformers of lofty vision and sane judgment to treat of everything," Roosevelt complained that Croly and Lippmann had not sufficiently em-

phasized "the need for prosperity in the nation." Exhibiting
the chronic neurosis of a reformer in a capitalist society, he
warned his readers that "reformers whose reforms interfere[d]
with the general prosperity . . . [would] accomplish little."
Unions particularly, with the United States in an industrial depression, should concern themselves "with a return to good
times, and not with any plans for securing social and economic
justice."

Roosevelt had always been capable of taking a swipe at the
unions, even during his most progressive phase after 1910. But
now his blow at the very vitals of the editors' "industrial democracy" showed the strong conflicts that underlay the surface
intimacy. The Colonel's friendliness, in fact, lasted only a few
more weeks, when it too was devoured, along with much else
that was fine in him, by his consuming enmity for Wilson.

The break came over a New York *Times* article that Roosevelt published early in December, which, in attacking Wilson's
and Bryan's policy in Mexico, practically, as Lippmann later
suggested, charged "them with personal responsibility for the
rape of nuns in Mexico." The *New Republic* claimed that
Roosevelt was too sophisticated not to know the dangers of
drawing "the Catholic Church into a political controversy."
In short, Roosevelt had struck "blindy and unfairly."

Roosevelt's reaction to the magazine's censure was "savage."
Meeting Francis Hackett soon afterwards, he accused the
editors of "personal disloyalty." Croly answered by denying
that the editors had any obligation to dance blindly in at-
tendance on Roosevelt. "In writing and publishing that critical
paragraph," he wrote to the Colonel, "we all of us considered it
merely the same kind of criticism which candid friends contin-
ually pass upon one another, and we had no idea that any
question of loyalty or disloyalty could be raised by it. . . . The
New Republic has never pretended to be a party organ, and
its whole future success in life depends upon the impression
which it makes upon its readers of being able to think disinter-
estedly and independently." Croly admitted that there were

times "when the fruits of such independent thinking . . . should not be expressed," but concluded by denying "that any such reasons had any force at the . . . time." Croly was saying, in effect, that a leader out of power had no right to expect the intellectuals' unquestioning allegiance.

Explanations, however—particularly explanations that emphasized the magazine's independence—were not enough. The brief flight of the *New Republic* intellectuals in the bright light of Roosevelt's power was over. In the months that followed, the editors continued to praise Roosevelt over Wilson, but the ex-President was no longer interested. His attitude at first was merely cool; in time it became rabidly hostile.

Though the personal relationship was at an end, Roosevelt had played too vital a part in the lives of Croly, Weyl, and Lippmann to be forgotten. Many years would pass before the dramatic fire of Roosevelt's personality faded entirely from the editors' eyes. His image long remained to bias their attitude toward Woodrow Wilson. Walter Lippmann admitted as much two decades later. "He became for me," said Lippmann, "the image of the great leader and the prototype of Presidents. . . . In any complete confession I think I should have to say that I have been less than just to his successors because they were not like him."

5. LIBERALISM AND LEADERSHIP

The question of leadership has been a major dilemma for twentieth-century liberals. Those of Jeffersonian persuasion have generally, despite the example of Jackson, resisted the idea of a strong executive. Roosevelt's presidency led quite a few progressives besides Croly to accept the need for a strong guiding hand. The old liberalism, however, with its roots in resistance to monarchy, with its individualistic, equalitarian bias, could not easily adjust to the vibrant figure of the modern politician-statesman. In the 'thirties liberals would once again divide among themselves over the forceful sway of another Roosevelt.

The quarrel with the Bull Moose leader, plus Wilson's unexpected strength, made the question of leadership particularly acute for the *New Republic* men in 1915. Though they still dreamt that Roosevelt might return to active politics and need their support, the editors had to decide whether leadership of the Roosevelt or the Wilson variety was best for liberalism.

Even while working with Roosevelt, the editors had not entirely neglected the question. With an insight to match the hindsight of later historians, the editors had neatly dissected both leaders' strengths and weaknesses just before their fight with Roosevelt. Wilson's genius, they wrote, lay in his capacity to work with Congress, in contrast to Roosevelt whose very ability at marshaling public support often alienated the legislators. Wilson, on the other hand, often seemed to be controlled by Congress. He badly compromised his reforms to win legislative consent, while, unlike Roosevelt, suffering from "a remoter relation . . . [with] popular opinion." What the editors wanted, of course, was a leader who could bend both Congress and the public to his will, who with Roosevelt's vigor and Wilson's skill could rally both people and politicians behind reform. Neither of the older editors would live to see that second Roosevelt of the New Deal era who came perhaps closest to their ideal, while a later, much more conservative Lippmann would remain singularly unimpressed.

The inability of the editors to be satisfied with either man gave a judicious, and for their magazine undoubtedly healthy, ambivalence to their comments on Roosevelt and Wilson. Roosevelt, during the early part of 1915, got mingled doses of praise and blame. Wilson was treated similarly, but in time the negative side became discernibly heavy. The editors admitted the President's legislative successes, they conceded the fineness of his intellect, but could never find him quite adequate to the Roosevelt image. Bringing all the advantages of their own new liberalism forward, they condemned Wilson as a "dangerous and unsound thinker." They scourged him for breaking his campaign pledges to the Negro and for the alleged failure of his policy of "watchful waiting" in Mexico. Even Wilson's fight with the Senate over appointments was eventually dismissed as merely a battle "against the specific effects of a bad system . . . not on behalf of a better system."

Not surprisingly the editors found Wilson most inadequate where he most contrasted with Roosevelt—in his personality. In words that re-evoked Lippmann's vision of leadership in *A Preface to Politics*, they accused Wilson of lacking the "quality of reacting vividly to a thousand varying stimuli, of showing an unflagging interest in the surroundings, the sense of boundless energy—. . . endowments which democracies ask of their leaders." Placed in the metaphor of Croly's comments on Roosevelt in *The Promise of American Life*, Wilson for the *New Republic* men was too much the saint and too little the hero.

The editors' emphasis upon a strong executive leadership was one of their more realistic contributions to a transformed liberalism. In a nation where anti-liberal forces have increasingly exploited a decentralized and complex constitutional system, vigorously progressive governors and presidents can help (if they will) to arouse the public and force legislative action. But the *New Republic*'s realism in this respect was diminished by the editors' illusion that leaders could lead other than through such available instruments as the committee chairmen and blocs in the legislature and bosses and machines in the states and cities. The *New Republic* had yet to learn the lessons in political accommodation evident from the later liberal careers of Al Smith and Franklin Roosevelt.

Croly, Weyl, and Lippmann, however, were men of the progressive era; they had developed their ideas in an aura of optimistic moralism hardly known to Americans since. Having risen themselves with the progressive tide, they had seen by 1912 so seemingly thorough a conversion of America to liberalism that even the coming of the war and the decline of progressivism in 1914 could not break their confidence. As late as 1915 they still dreamed that bosses, machines, legislative cabals, and all the other excrescences of a working democracy belonged to a vanquished past, and that liberal leaders at the head of a cleansed body politic held the promise of the future.

So strong was their optimism, in fact, that even political parties—and not just their corruptions—were held to be unnecessary. Building from the attacks on the party system in *Progressive Democracy* and *Drift and Mastery*, the editors were able to face without undue dismay the collapse of their own Progressive party. An unsigned editorial in the second issue, marked with the labored cadences of Croly's prose, became the official obituary. The party during the 1914 Congressional campaigns had failed to offer "a sufficiently attractive and compelling alternative" to traditional party loyalties, and "the failure . . . [was] likely to be decisive and irreparable." By August 1915 the *New Republic* doubted that the Progressives could nominate a candidate for 1916 and cited the party's "gradual and inexorable disintegration" as a sign of the "hopelessness of all third-party movements."

The editors would have been more candid had they spoken of the "hopelessness of all party movements whatsoever." Underlying their easy acceptance of the Bull Moose demise was a conviction that the major parties also deserved extinction. With a tendency, common to most liberals, to be stronger on diagnosis than prognosis, the *New Republic* men easily showed that the party system was outmoded for the twentieth century. Roosevelt, Taft, and Wilson, as official heads of state, had all been forced to fight their own parties to obtain reforms desired by a large majority. Some way had to be found to circumvent the admitted strength of the old parties. "Executive leadership, expert administrative independence, and direct legislation" were the means suggested in the *New Republic*'s second number.

Historically such an attack on the party system had much validity. Certainly Roosevelt, Taft, and Wilson had expended much of their energy fighting parties theoretically pledged to their support, and for most Presidents since the struggle has continued. Significantly, however, Croly, Weyl, and Lippmann had great difficulty developing viable nonpartisan alternatives. Readers who missed the early editorial on parties must often have been confused by the magazine's political criticisms, for rarely again were either the rejection of the party system or the possible alternatives made articulate. When, for instance, the editors praised Wilson for his strong executive leadership and at the same time condemned his "partisan tactics," the absence of a clear restatement of the magazine's nonpartisan enthusiasms invited confusion. Equally ambiguous was the magazine's habit of attacking Congress as hopelessly inefficient while at the same time upholding the Senatorial filibuster as a desirable protection for minority opinion. The apparent contradictions of such positions were diminished only by the editors' conviction (and hope) that the major parties were dying.

Croly, Weyl, and Lippmann wanted "great national organizations of teachers, social workers, business and professional men, farmers and trade-unionists" to replace legislatures and political parties as "the really representative members of . . . [the] political body." In effect, the combination of leadership with nonpartisan reform meant a melding of the political theories of the three men. The strong leaders featured by Croly and Lippmann were now placed at the head of Weyl's great band of reformist consumers. Men of good will from all walks of life were to move without partisan strife toward a progressive millenium. Nothing, perhaps, so much revealed the utopian bent of writers who were in so many other respects stern realists. Nor did anything more clearly demonstrate the all-important faith of Croly, Weyl, and Lippmann in the continuing promise of middle-class liberalism.

6. A National Renaissance

More than the triumphs of the reforming hosts, however, lay behind the *New Republic*'s abiding optimism. In the years just before the magazine began, America had been enjoying a cultural revival, a flowering in literature and the arts often hailed since as the "little renaissance." Definitely encouraging to Croly and Lippmann, who had turned to politics from the bleakness of American architecture and art, the general cultural awakening probably moved even the somewhat philistine Weyl.

Signs of the rebirth were everywhere in the years before America entered World War I. Art reached a kind of apogee in the great New York Armory Show of 1913; poetry rang forth in the fresh meters of Robert Frost, Carl Sandburg, Vachel Lindsay, Edgar Lee Masters, Amy Lowell, and Ezra Pound; the drama seemed born anew in the work of Eugene O'Neill and the Provincetown Players; while the "modern dance" took on a sudden excitement with the eruption of Isadora Duncan upon the land. Promising novelists like Sinclair Lewis, Sherwood Anderson, Ernest Poole, and Willa Cather were publishing their first books. And in all the arts new critics seemed bent on hastening the renaissance—men like Hiram K. Moderwell and Paul Rosenfeld in music, Francis Hackett, Van Wyck Brooks, H. L. Mencken, and Floyd Dell in literature, and Lee Simonson and Leo Stein in art.

The cultural revival, like most such movements, was markedly self-conscious, with a consciousness that had strong overtones of nationalism. Edna St. Vincent Millay, for instance, sensed the general awakening when in 1912 she entitled her first long poem *Renascence*. Randolph Bourne's first book, *Youth and Life*, the next year caught the nationalistic theme with a protest against the "cultural humility" of America toward Europe, while John Macy, Lippmann's successor as secretary to the Socialist mayor of Schenectady, struck the same note in *The Spirit of American Literature*. Even the expatriate poet Ezra Pound in 1913 wrote *Patria Mia* to announce an "American Risorgimento," and two years later Van Wyck Brooks brilliantly summed up all the artistic and patriotic hopes of the new generation in *America's Coming-of-Age*.

Well might the *New Republic* nationalists have been optimistic, for they seemed to be riding the crest of that combined political and cultural revival Croly had called for in *The Promise of American Life*. The Wilbur Littletons of 1915, moreover, were hardly the isolated, thwarted martyrs of the dark turn of the century. Instead there were the united, enthusiastic prophets of a national renaissance. They followed now the pattern of Croly's "constructive individualism" to work fervently in both politics and the arts. Lee Simonson or John Macy could write of art one day and of socialism the next, just as Weyl's brother-in-law Ernest Poole dealt naturally with the awakening of a young socialist in his first novel *The Harbor*. Whether submitting articles to the poet Max Eastman who edited the *Masses*, catechizing the I.W.W. leaders at Mabel Dodge's salon, or organizing a Madison Square Garden pageant for Paterson strikers, the younger intellectuals seemed to feel everywhere a new harmony between art and the nation's life.

Croly caught the mood exactly when he told Randolph Bourne in September 1914, that he wanted the *New Republic* to have "a certain amount of conscious patriotism" in its criticism of the arts. The battle cry of the movement was sounded in the third issue with an editorial called "Our Literary Poverty" that demanded an end to America's "cultural vassalage" to England. For the last hopeful years before America's entry into the war, the *New Republic* became a major rallying ground for the young cultural nationalists.

Though the *New Republic* men had refused Amy Lowell an editorship, they willingly published her poetry and her broadsides for the "imagist" movement. By publishing Robert Frost's "Death of a Hired Man" in 1915, they suddenly made him a literary "sensation." Lincoln McVeagh and Conrad Aiken, who were to be prominent in the 'twenties, were given space to praise the poetry of Edwin Arlington Robinson or to define the "Limits of Imagism." As the magazine's literary editor, Francis Hackett put an official stamp of approval on all that was new in poetry when he expressed delight at the way

Carl Sandburg had found the fog in Chicago coming in "on little cat feet."

Painting, too, met a bright new day in the pages that followed the political articles of Croly, Weyl, and Lippmann. Though Lee Simonson saved his socialist writing for the *Masses*, his pieces in the *New Republic* bravely defended "cubism," "impressionism," "futurism," and most of the other schools of modern art. Editorial notes and leaders gave the blessing of the whole board to the growing acceptance of modern painting or, in the nationalistic vein, contrasted the state support of artists in France with their neglect in America. The new music also had its defenders, from H. K. Moderwell's appreciations of the dissonances of Schoenberg to Paul Rosenfeld's reiterated pleas for the "moderns" over the "romanticists." In the dramatic arts the old similarly lost out to the new, with attacks on the established and popular impresario David Belasco set against warm praise for Robert Edmond Jones's designs in an experimental Shakespeare production or for David Wark Griffith's original work in the movies.

Characteristically for America, where the novel has led the parade of the arts, the themes of the young cultural nationalists came through most clearly in their literary criticism. Strong in most of them was a tendency to depreciate past American writers. Just as Croly in *The Promise of American Life* had tempered his patriotism with a rather reserved view of the American past, so now his younger followers stressed the inadequacies of Irving, Cooper, Hawthorne, Twain, Wharton, and James. Only in Walt Whitman did budding critics like Van Wyck Brooks find a literary match for Croly's hero Lincoln who had resolved nationalism and democracy into an American philosophy. John Dos Passos, fresh from Harvard in 1916, blasted forth upon the theme with a *New Republic* piece called "Against American Literature," wherein he pled for America to meet the challenge of Whitman's "Democratic Vistas," rather than merely mimicking the art of other people in a materialistic welter of steel, and oil, and pork.

Brooks and Dos Passos well expressed the mood of the new generation of critics, but the *New Republic*'s back pages also had room for a dissenting voice, that of the philosopher George Santayana. Santayana had taught many of the magazine's writers at Harvard—Brooks, Simonson, Aiken, Stearns, and Mason, as well as Croly and Lippmann—but he hardly shared their patriotic enthusiasms. "Nationalism," he wrote in 1913, "has become of late an omnivorous, all pervading passion. . . . Of this distinction our contemporaries tend to make an idol, perhaps because it is the only distinction they have left." Santayana did not share the *New Republic*'s vision of America as a land of promise, even of unfulfilled promise. Its "moral and intellectual atmosphere everywhere . . . seemed to be uniform: earnest, meagre, vague, scattered and hopeful," said the Spanish-American philosopher in 1912; and, having little hope for the country, he left it.

Croly, Weyl, and Lippmann evidently made Santayana an expedient exception to their rule against printing anything at odds with general policy. The philosopher defined culture, for example, as something belonging to the individual, not the nation, as something a cosmopolitan, cultivated man could hardly find within a cramping national tradition. Even more at odds with the *New Republic*'s cultural nationalism was the philosopher's notion that culture so defined was the peculiar product of modern freedom, of the liberated mind fostered by the old laissez-faire liberalism. With a pointed reference to Germany's "dragooned" nationalistic *Kultur*, Santayana suggested that just as "the days of [the old] liberalism . . .[were] numbered, so too might be those of the promising liberal culture for Western man."

The *New Republic*, however, could afford in Santayana's case a compromise with principle, for the philosopher's urbane arguments hardly stimulated controversy, while his prestige compensated for the embarrassment. As their own advocate, moreover, the editors had Randolph Bourne, a brilliant young hunchback armed with ideas often as cogent as Santayana's, plus a prose style of greater force if less elegance. At twenty-eight he was already emerging as "the spokesman of the younger generation." "Our 'intellectuals' will have to sharpen up their knowledge and stiffen their fibre a good deal," declared Bourne after a trip to Europe, "before they can take the commanding place of leadership . . . they fill in France."

Spurred by such a mission, Bourne believed that the old liberalism was a creed outworn—stultifiying, constricting, long emptied of that power of liberation Santayana claimed for it. An ardent believer in the instrumentalism of John Dewey, a promoter of Dewey's "progressive education" as a new force for liberation, Bourne was well equipped to weave together in the *New Republic* all the social and aesthetic strains of younger America's new sense of destiny.

The mental vigor that brought Bourne so quickly to the fore among the younger New York intellectuals was evident in his *New Republic* pieces. With the ruthless clarity of a superior mind, he took up without fear the grim question of how cultural nationalists were to face a world seemingly gone mad with nationalism. Early in 1915, he contrasted the attitudes of genteel Americans with those of Europeans, who rightly, as he said, saw the struggle "in terms of national culture rather than morality." "Now this," Bourne declared, "is exactly as it should be." "The war from this point of view," said the young writer in words that would have a bitter irony two years later, "may be a vast liberating movement, clearing the way for . . . [a] more conscious, intenser world." What was needed for Europe, and what the war might bring, was for "political nationality . . . [to] be made to coincide with cultural unity." Cultural nationalism, he wrote as the guns boomed away in Europe, remained "the brightest promise of a twentieth-century Western civilization."

Thus in 1915 spoke the youngest and most brilliant of the recruits to Croly's band of romantic nationalists. Though the times and the terms of discourse had somewhat altered, the burden of Bourne's thought was strikingly similar to Croly's of six years before. There was the same central cultural impulse as in *The Promise of American Life*, the same dream of a "constructive individualism," the same call for experimental collective action toward social ends, the same urge to bring nationalism and democracy together for a new cultural millennium. If young Bourne spoke for his generation in 1915, he spoke in an accent long familiar to Croly.

There were, of course, exceptions to the general pattern of hopeful chauvinism. Ezra Pound, despite the contrary note of his *Patria Mia* in 1913, had left the country in 1908 for what was eventually permanent expatriation. Lippmann's Harvard classmate T. S. Eliot was studying at Oxford in 1915. Though still largely unknown, despite "The Lovesong of J. Alfred Prufrock," Eliot was already moving toward that identification with England that would make him for his generation the symbol Henry James had been for Croly's. Closer to the *New Republic* group was Alan Seeger, another Harvard contemporary of Lippmann's who had been poet for the class. He, too, found little that was hopeful in pre-war America. With a "white, mask-like face and stony eyes" he wandered for a time with Lippmann, Reed, Hallowell, and the rest through their Washington Square Bohemia, but he shared few of their dreams. With Pound and Eliot he helped mark the trail to Europe that Hallowell, Simonson, Stearns, Hackett, and many others would follow in the 'twenties. Settling in France in 1912, he came to love Paris and French culture so much that he joined the French army when war broke out. He expressed something of his love for France in an article in the *New Republic* in 1915; he confirmed the love by his death at the front not long afterwards.

Seeger, however, was out of tune with his generation; he was disillusioned before disillusionment became endemic. His expatriation had more of the flavor of Santayana's or of Henry James's; it was motivated more by a love of an ancient culture than by disdain of a new one. Seeger's young American compatriots knew as much of foreign cultures as he; they had all read widely at college; Bourne, Stearns, Simonson, Aiken, and Brooks had all made extended "grand tours" once college was over. They, too, admired the cultures of France, of Italy, sometimes of Germany or England. For the moment, however, they shared the dream Croly had had so many years before them, the dream of a politically unified, aesthetically and intellectually awakened America. Wilbur Littleton now had new champions.

7. PROGRESSIVES AND THE NEW LIBERALISM

However much the cultural renaissance fortified the editors' optimism, culture itself was no longer their main concern. For Croly as for the others, winning converts to the new liberalism was the pressing interest. They had called their magazine, after all, the *New Republic*, not something like the *Seven Arts*, the name given still another journal founded in 1916 by Bourne, Brooks, Simonson, and others of the cultural nationalists. Reform, the creation of a new republic, had once for Croly been merely a means to an ultimate cultural end. Now, however, the *New Republic* pragmatists were more and more absorbed by their means, while aesthetic goals tended less and less to control their thought. They saw their real challenges in the war abroad and in Wilson's rival brand of liberalism at home.

If nationalism was to be the ground on which the *New Republic* attacked Wilson's New Freedom, the magazine itself would have to be not only nationalistic but national. Such in fact was the editors' plan, and they suffered from the illusion that they had fulfilled it. In the otherwise friendly editorial with which they greeted the *Seven Arts*, for example, the *New Republic* men chided the new paper for "the preponderance [on it] of a group of eastern writers whose quality . . . [was] keen, but outlook not national." Also, Alvin Johnson later claimed the *New Republic* in its early days had served as a kind of "committee of correspondence" for "leading liberals and progressives . . . in every part of the country."

If, as the editorial on the *Seven Arts* implied, residence else-where than in the East for its writers was the measure of being "national," then the *New Republic* might well have sought out the beam in its own eye. Of the original editors and close sup-porters, only Hackett and Johnson had lived for any extended period in other parts of the country, and both of them had returned to the East several years before. Contributors were equally heavily concentrated in the eastern centers, partic-ularly New York.

Even less was the magazine successful in providing a national focus for all the regional centers of progressivism. During the first planning conferences, Charles J. McCarthy, the intel-lectual spokesman of Wisconsin progressivism, had suggested a system of regional offices and editors to make "the *New Republic* a national instead of a Washington-New York week-ly." But Croly and the others did little to implement the idea. In fact, neither in its relation to leading progressives nor in its coverage of progressive news did the *New Republic* become the "committee of correspondence" McCarthy wanted and Johnson later described. Such prominent progressive thinkers beyond the eastern seaboard as Raymond Robins, William Allen White, Charles McCarthy, and William Kent had little or no connection with the *New Republic* group in its early years. Regular reports on reform movements throughout the country might have given the magazine a more convincing national flavor, but the politics of the city and state of New York alone received adequate coverage.

Undoubtedly such marked parochialism handicapped a journal that hoped to convert a nation to a new liberalism, especially when the rival Jeffersonian creed daily gained prestige from Wilson's successes. Possibly the costs of a system of regional reporting and co-operation restrained the editors, but probably as important was their own eastern provinciality. But in any case, as long as they clung to their nationalism, they could not have expected much help from outside the north-east. With the bulk of progressives in West and South still wed to the laissez-faire individualism of the old liberalism, the available recruits for a nationalistic crusade against the New Freedom were not plentiful.

Not only were there geographical limits to the *New Republic*'s appeal, but also ideological—even within the East. There, where Croly, Weyl, and Lippmann had most of their friends and found the most support, definable groups among the reformers had little voice in the *New Republic*. Such groups significantly were largely represented by people close to Weyl, not to Croly and Lippmann, the more nationalistic prophets of the new liberalism. From the diffident Croly's circle came Philip Littell, Alvin Johnson, George Rublee, Learned Hand, Felix Frankfurter, and Amy Lowell either as editors or writers for the magazine. Walter Lippmann, too, though never so well liked as either of his colleagues, attracted eminent and stalwart helpers. George Stantayana's contributions were probably to his credit, while close friends like Robert Hallowell, Charles Merz, and Harold Stearns helped out with both contributions and editorial work. Other men close to Lippmann, such as Graham Wallas, Edward Hunt, Lee Simonson, and Alfred Kuttner, wrote for the magazine, and by 1915 even John Reed was sufficiently reconciled to make a contribution.

Walter Weyl, gregarious and widely beloved, probably had more friends among reformers than either Croly or Lippmann. Few of them, however, were willing to help the *New Republic*. Two of his closest friends, Robert Bruère and William Hard, eventually joined the magazine's staff, and several of his Woodstock neighbors and acquaintances—James Shotwell, Gertrude Atherton, and Howard Brubaker—made occasional contributions. For the most part, however, the men and women Weyl had known best either kept away from the magazine or complained about its policies in its correspondence columns.

Louis Brandeis, for instance, whom Weyl had come to know through the garment workers' protocol, would have nothing to do with the *New Republic* during its early days, when the lines between the New Nationalism and the Wilson-Brandeis New

Freedom were still fairly clearly drawn. Even the Bull Moose leader Amos Pinchot, with whom Weyl had worked closely during the Roosevelt campaign, sent a letter for publication early in 1915 that attacked the magazine for not being sufficiently radical. Nor did Weyl's socialist friends follow those of Lippmann, like Lee Simonson and John Macy, in becoming contributors. His brother-in-law, Ernest Poole, made but one contribution; his other socialist crony of settlement house days, William English Walling, made none; while the socialist intellectual, William J. Ghent, could only express surprise at "the venality of Walter Weyl."

The issues of neutrality also brought dissent from some of Weyl's oldest friends. His main sponsor at the University of Pennsylvania, Simon Patten, sent several letters irascibly attacking the magazine's foreign policy, while his closest student friend there, Martin Schutze, charged the *New Republic* with pro-Allied sympathies. William English Walling, on the other hand, berated the magazine for being pro-German, while Crystal Eastman, another good friend of Weyl's at the University Settlement, roundly denounced the editors' support of military preparedness. Whatever the issue, foreign or domestic, Weyl's companions of the exploratory years that had led to *The New Democracy* seemed likely to be at odds with *New Republic* policy.

The resistance to the *New Republic* of most socialists, settlement workers, pacifists, Germanophiles, and Jeffersonian liberals was significant, for it indicated how narrow was the base for the editors' fireworks barrage against the New Freedom. Yet within the limits of its largely eastern, Bull Moose orientation, the magazine attracted to its columns some of the outstanding thinkers of the day. Charles A. Beard, who had helped Croly and the others organize their magazine, started as a regular contributor in the second issue with an article that attacked in a nationalist vein the Jeffersonian antecedents of Wilson's New Freedom. When in 1915 the editors wanted a restatement of their magazine's purposes, they could turn to another contributor, James Harvey Robinson, who rivaled Beard in prominence within the new school of history. John Dewey, the unchallenged leader among pragmatic philosophers, made the *New Republic* the major outlet for his social and political writings, while Lippmann, Hackett, and Bourne in various articles showed the *New Republic*'s dedication both to the philosopher's educational theories and his scientific instrumentalism.

So large an outpouring from academics often threatened to give the *New Republic* a rather professional, even professorial, tone. Yet the more sprightly writing of Lippmann, Weyl, Johnson, and Bourne, the thoughtful eloquence of Hand and Frankfurter, the essays of established novelists like Robert Herrick and Theodore Dreiser, along with the efforts of Brooks, Simonson, Stearns, Lowell, Frost, and other young poets and critics, leavened the whole into an attractive and impressive sampling of American thought. Whatever the limits of the new liberalism's appeal to progressives of the West or South or to certain others of the reformers, it was not without formidable spokesmen.

8. LIBERALISM AND NATIONALISM

"That part of the *N.R.* that shapes our destinies I generally skip," wrote Justice Holmes to a friend in 1917. Olympian detachment was a favorite pose with Holmes. Yet he had admitted the year before: "God knows I have as deep a respect as anybody for the ability of Croly and Lippmann." The editors themselves were often equally Olympian, but they were rarely detached. To them the editorial notes and leaders at the front of their magazine were of supreme importance. There they could blast the pernicious dogmas of Wilson's New Freedom, there they could develop the beguiling alternatives of their own new liberalism, and there, too, they had the most hope of winning a real sway over the minds of men of power. Even if a Holmes refused to listen, a Roosevelt, a Wilson, or some other practical and powerful man just might. More gyrating moths than gadflies, the *New Republic* men always veered toward the brighter centers of power.

Yet mixed with the ambitions that kept the editors laboring week after week were certain strains of doubt. Their middle-class liberal faith had already undergone a series of shocks that threatened all their optimism. Roosevelt's defeat in 1912, while not unexpected, had been one blow; the rude intrusion of the I.W.W. upon the eastern labor movement at Lawrence and Paterson had been another. The collapse of the Progressive party in 1914, followed so soon by Roosevelt's defection, had left the editors much in limbo. But worst of all had been the dawning fear, first stirred by the Congressional elections of 1914, that the entire progressive movement was waning.

By the early part of 1915, the editors found only more cause for gloom. "The tide of reaction which began last spring seems still to be rising," they declared. The 1913-14 recession was over, however, and could no longer explain the bleak climate of opinion. The editors thought the trouble might have arisen in part from the effect of progressive measures upon consumers. Reform had turned out to be "expensive"; tariff reduction had tended to "injure business"; while trust-busting had "if any-thing . . . increased the cost of living." But the real cause of the progressive malaise, declared the *New Republic*, was Wilson and his New Freedom. The voters' pique reflected an effort to dissuade the President from his "plausible but uncandid at-tempt to convert progressivism into a Jeffersonian Demo-cratic revival." Americans were not feeling less liberal; they were just feeling less Jeffersonian in their liberalism, or so the editors manfully argued.

The editors, nevertheless, faced a hard task in making their case. Even before they began to publish, Wilson had amassed a legislative record that included a lowered tariff, an income tax, a new Federal Trade Commission, a revision of the anti-trust laws, and a major reform of the banking system. But Croly, Weyl, and Lippmann felt that they could spurn even so salutary a record if it failed to meet the dictates of their new liberalism.

The *New Republic* dismissed the Democrats' new anti-trust Clayton Act as likely to do "more harm than good," as merely a piece of well-written but "destructive legislation." The editors also noted with mounting glee during 1915 and 1916 Wilson's marked tendency to abandon his earlier trust-busting enthusiasms. Even better for setting off their liberalism from the President's was their early stand for government ownership of the railroads, a program they soon expanded to include operation "by an organization of railroad employes."

The editors also used the government-ownership issue to contrast their own pragmatic flexibility with what they saw as the New Freedom's doctrinaire devotion to principle. Wilson's Postmaster General, for example, had proposed the nationalization of the telephone and telegraph industries. But the editors rejected the idea on the pragmatic grounds that the growing telephone business might better be left to "private initiative," while, conversely, the government would be "ill-advised to invest in an industry with so dubious a future [as the telegraph]." Applied thus pragmatically, the demand for the ultimate expropriation of monopolistic industries remained much a part of their new liberalism. But the gesture of the Wilson Administration in the same direction raised the danger that the *New Republic* dissents might seem more cranky than consequential.

To meet more immediate problems raised by business, the editors continued to demand pervasive government economic intervention. Both delighted and amused by Wilson's move in the same direction through the Federal Trade Commission, the editors insisted that their new liberalism required far more. They demanded on various occasions powerful commissions for aiding immigrants, making the tariff more flexible, controlling waterpower sites, regulating overseas banking, and supervising general government operations. Again, however, they refused to make government control an absolute.

They were very cautious, for example, about government interference in labor relations. Though they had no objection to a commission's regulating the *causes* of labor unrest, they resisted any toying with the results. Fearing that federal interference in strikes would weaken rather than strengthen labor, they wanted compulsory arbitration restricted to the railroads and to industries using woman and child labor.

A strong aggressive labor movement independent of government continued to be the focus of the *New Republic* "industrial democracy." "The idea is," wrote the editors, "that the management of modern industry is a problem of government. ... We do not expect to jump straight from the present [industrial] absolutism into a cooperative democracy ... but we must at least start on the road to democracy before we can command the loyalty of the people." In the theme of "loyalty" the magazine's nationalism and its democracy were joined.

The *New Republic*'s "industrial democracy" was a strange blend of progressive euphoria and I.W.W.-inspired syndicalism. Of the two elements, however, liberal optimism remained for the moment dominant. The editors continued to stress the stern discipline of their expert, authoritative administration, but even more strongly they demanded moves toward a popular, nonpartisan democracy. They campaigned enthusiastically for such reforms as woman suffrage, liberalization of the Constitution's amendment clause, limitations on judicial review, and various devices for direct government and the free expression of minority opinion.

The editors' strong emphasis upon direct democracy, however, made them seem at times more fecklessly Jeffersonian than the Wilson Democrats. For all their pro-labor feelings, Croly, Weyl, and Lippmann still did not see labor as a separate, or even less a dominant, political force. Out on the hustings the unions were to be only one of many nonpartisan, progressive groups, made up of teachers, social workers, farmers, and businessmen, as well as workers, that in time would rule the nation. As Wilson caucused and conferred in the anterooms of Congress, the *New Republic* men rested their hopes on the massed pressure of middle-class progressivism.

In some respects, however, the *New Republic* men were better able to set off their liberalism from Wilson's. During their first month of publication, the President provided a welcome opening when he publicly proclaimed the program of the New Freedom to be substantially complete. The President's statement reflected in part his own laissez-faire convictions, but also the usual fatal need of liberals in power to preserve or restore prosperity by conciliating businessmen. The *New Republic* men suffered from neither restraint. They at once used Wilson's statement as a springboard for setting new goals for liberalism. These goals, which transcended their own day, caught the spirit of a reform movement that would come into being two decades later.

Even more prophetic was the new liberalism's sensitivity to the ups and downs of the economic cycle. Croly, Weyl, and Lippmann saw the inherent instability of unregulated capitalism more clearly than did most liberals of their day or even of the depression 'thirties. The mere threat of a downturn in late 1914 led them to call for a whole spate of recovery measures. They demanded federal labor exchanges, federal unemployment compensation, and a national minimum wage both to provide relief for workers and as "cushions" for the economy. Even after Allied war orders brought the booming prosperity of 1916, the *New Republic* continued to call for a stand-by program of federal public works. Such later New Dealers as Felix Frankfurter, Raymond Moley, and Donald Richberg, who supported and wrote for the magazine in its early years, may have owed as much to Croly, Weyl, and Lippmann as to the later much celebrated John Maynard Keynes.

The editors also foreshadowed somewhat the "technocrat" movement of the 'thirties. Prophets of Dewey's dream of applying science to everyday life, they plumped for scientific training in education, scientific administration in government, and scientific management in industry. In October 1915 they anticipated to a degree the later C.C.C. by proposing that the tramp be taken from the road and retrained by "a corps of expert scientific managers" until he could be "restored to society with his full complement of . . . industrial habits." The editors were certain that "not even the most dogmatic exponent of laissez-faire" would object to such a harnessing of scientific management "for public use."

Though a taint of authoritarian inhumanity marked such plans for the possibly quite happy American hobo, any real streak of authoritarianism in the new liberalism was belied by its strong concern for civil liberties. Croly, Weyl, and Lippmann, in fact, were considerably more strenuous in their defense of individual rights than the prophet of the New Freedom in the White House. In this respect as well, their new liberalism was more prophetic of the future than characteristic of the progressive movement.

The notorious Leo Frank lynching in 1915, for instance, brought a scathing series of *New Republic* editorials, while the editors the same year strongly and repeatedly protested the University of Pennsylvania's dismissal of the economist Scott Nearing. Denials of free speech to I.W.W. leaders, unfair trials of union officials, and violations of aliens' rights were also frequently and roundly condemned. Cases of discrimination against the Negro also stirred the editors in a way not yet common for liberals, and they had no patience at all with the sociologist E. A. Ross's racist views toward southern European immigrants.

So strong a defense of individual liberty might seem odd coming from critics of the equal-rights philosophy, but here, too, the editors were essentially consistent. They based their fight for civil liberties not upon an absolute concept of natural right but rather upon a pragmatic calculation of the practical effects of suppression. Pragmatism, nationalism, and democracy all worked together in their argument that the denial of freedom to anyone would "sunder the national bond." So defined, their new liberalism held both promise and problems for future liberals. The promise lay in their realization that freedom was something for which men should organize and fight. It rested too on their realization that absolute concepts of rights were more useful to reactionaries than radicals. A real problem remained, however, in their emphasis on nationalism, in their failure to see how easily appeals to the "national interest" might swallow up all liberty.

Yet, even as the *New Republic* men argued for their new liberalism from week to week, events at home and abroad began to sap its foundations. In America, the most serious threat came from the continued popular retreat from progressivism. By October 1915 even the normally optimistic Weyl was wondering whether a "negligent and sometimes distracted electorate . . . [could] run the country at all." In November Lippmann struck a theme that would dominate the rest of his career by explaining progressive troubles in terms of a "division in what we call our democracy between the insiders and the outsiders." The well-informed "insiders" actually ran the country, he declared, while the "outsiders" merely "listen[ed] to the largest hope and follow[ed] the most magnetic personality." Quite clearly Lippmann was moving toward the elitist notions that had once enthralled Croly.

Almost as distressing to the editors was the reactionary cast of mind they detected in certain of the "insiders," particularly the nation's businessmen. Reporting now week by week on actual business practice, they could no longer find those "new businessmen" Lippmann's and Croly's books had praised. Instead they made fun of George W. Perkins, Roosevelt's friend and supporter, attacked the paternalism of Judge Elbert H. Gary of United States Steel, exposed as a sham John D. Rockefeller, Jr.'s pose as an enlightened businessman, and condemned for "social irresponsibility" even Willard Straight's employer, J. P. Morgan. In moving from their studies to the *New Republic* offices, at least two of the editors had had a chastening brush with reality.

Abandoned by Roosevelt, disliking Wilson and his New

Freedom, much less sanguine about middle-class progressives or enlightened capitalists, the *New Republic* men were much adrift. A shift to the left might have given them new momentum. They were themselves convinced, however, that the left was moving steadily right. Writing on "Socialist Degeneration" in an early issue, they found the Socialist party no longer "a revolutionary party, or even a party of wage-earners," but instead a "vague, ungeneralized, democratic organization." With calculated derision, they showed how American Socialist strength had shifted from the industrial areas of orthodox Marxist theory to "brand-new, corn-growing, hog-raising Oklahoma."

With their own pragmatism making a virtue of apparent inconsistency, the editors could perforce reject all the better defined systems to right or left. They could argue that the Socialists' devotion to dialectical materialism would prevent "constructive action" just as completely as did the Democrats' dedication to Jeffersonian individualism. Denying any dogmatism in their own nationalism and still seeing it as the best hope for progress, the *New Republic* liberals condemned all other persuasions as "caught in the embrace of outmoded traditions." They declared it to be a "matter for comparative indifference" which group of reformers among the many would become "the democratic socialized party for which . . . [they were] looking."

In effect, the *New Republic* men were confessing the domestic bankruptcy of their new liberalism. While their nationalism seemed to suggest promising goals beyond the accomplishments of the New Freedom, most such ideas had been borrowed from socialist thinkers. With the collapse of the Bull Moose movement and the eclipse of Roosevelt, nationalism no longer promised anything as a stimulus behind reform. It was much more likely, as it had already done with Roosevelt, to distract men from reform to diplomatic and military concerns. In September 1915, for instance, the *New Republic* men were themselves willing to speculate that the very conservative Elihu Root might "in certain respects [be] better qualified to act as President in the . . . emergency than . . . Mr. Wilson." "The immediate present problems," they declared, "concern foreign affairs, military preparedness and administrative reorganization." On such matters they found Root's record "exceptionally good."

Yet none of the three leading editors had become so conservative as their qualified endorsement of Root might imply. Instead, as the imbroglio with Germany deepened, their pragmatic flexibility allowed them to subordinate their social desires to their nationalism, to a quest for a militantly conceived and executed foreign policy. By mid-1916 they were willing to concede the futility of their earlier dream of a nonpartisan progressive democracy. The national nominating conventions during the summer seemed to prove the durability of the two-party system. Since at best the party system was merely a device to allow "the dominant middle class to perpetuate its domination," the editors found "the immediate outlook for radicals with convictions . . . not . . . very encouraging." "The next step in American party development," said the *New Republic,* "is likely to be the formation of independent labor and agrarian partisan organizations who will agitate on behalf of a perfectly definite class program and try to control enough votes to hold the balance between the national parties."

For the moment, however, the prophets of the new liberalism left undeveloped this fresh and promising resolution of old tactical problems of liberalism. The vital question as to whether pressure for reform should come from bottom, middle, or top was begged during the crises of war and peace. It was not raised again until, in the disillusionment that followed the war, the three editors groped toward different and divergent solutions. Meanwhile, with only pragmatism's confident lack of confidence to sustain them, they gave up the grander home dreams of their new liberalism to search for the party and leader best for meeting the looming challenge of war.

BOOK III

THE DECLINE OF THE NEW LIBERALISM

SEVEN

Nationalism and Internationalism

1914-1917

1. NATIONALISTS AND A WAR

The *New Republic* men were quite right in their insistence that firm principles were needed to keep pragmatism from being mere opportunism. The experimental program of reform that they wanted was very different from the later haphazard experimentalism of the New Deal. But their own admission by 1916 that nationalism had failed as a stimulus for reform left the domestic applications of the principle much in doubt. A desire for national unity (as well as middle-class prejudice) kept them from following up their own prediction that farm and labor groups would provide the leverage for reform in the future. To have done so would have made them democratic socialists rather than democratic nationalists. Instead, the editors followed the bent of their own nationalism toward diplomatic and military adventures. Though frustrated as reformers, they could still hope that nationalism might prove a viable guiding principle for foreign affairs. Nationalism might still be the source and focus of the power-oriented internationalism that Croly had suggested in *The Promise of American Life*.

To be a nationalist amidst the carnage that followed Serajevo, however, was no longer so easy as it had been in the innocent days that gave birth to the new liberalism. Croly's philosophy of democratic nationalism had first fed on the virile deeds that brought the hero of San Juan Hill to the Presidency. It owed much to the man who had used the office to expand and consolidate an empire, to flaunt American power with a great White Fleet, and to work pugnaciously for peace both in Europe and Asia. But the bloody explosion of nationalistic hatreds in Europe made nationalism, whether new or old, somehow not the same. "Even nationalism we saw in innocent terms," confessed the editors in 1915, "unsaturated by the menace of today."

Whatever confessions of innocence the *New Republic* men might make as a group, Croly had some claim to absolution. In *The Promise of American Life* he had seen the dangers of nationalism. A chapter entitled "Militarism and Nationality," for example, had described as "the chief threat to European peace" the mixed nationalities of Austria-Hungary and the temptations such would offer to "the national ambitions of Russia and Germany." Stern realism rather than naïveté governed Croly's belief that "the ultimate object of a peaceable and stable European international system . . . [could] not in all probability be reached without many additional wars."

Croly, however, had refused to see nationalism as the rival of internationalism. Instead he had anticipated the later preachments of men like George Kennan and Hans Morgenthau in his belief that only strong, responsible, nationalized states could create a peaceful international system. Such nations through a politics of power should realistically pursue their "national interest," argued Croly. Nationalism and internationalism were joined in his claim that the major national interest of countries like the United States, Great Britain, and France was international peace. Even in 1909, therefore, Croly had foreseen the possibility that the United States might one day face danger from the collapse of the balance of power in Europe. "Under such circumstances," the doughty publicist had declared, "a policy of neutrality would be a policy of irresponsibility and unwisdom."

For Croly, therefore, the war of August 1914 was not the

sudden plunge it seemed to so many. The time of "riot and bloodshed" he had feared a year before had come. Yet the oddly imperturbable Croly immediately saw a creative side to the bloodshed in Europe. "My own interest in it," he wrote Learned Hand in mid-August, "is becoming more and more a matter of seeking its probable results in making over the European international system." As for its effect on liberalism and his magazine, Croly thought the war might prove "in the end an actual help to the 'New Republic' " "It will create . . .," he wrote, "a state of mind in which a political and social agitation will find its words more influential and more effective in modifying public opinion."

Walter Weyl, much more volatile and openhearted than Croly, met the European war with far less detachment. He felt the actual human agony of the war so intensely that "for weeks, after the outbreak of hostilities, he slept little." Yet, with an ambivalence essential to sanity, Weyl, too, could face war issues with something like Croly's spirit of pragmatic realism. "He could," said Lippmann, "play chess with the war as brilliantly as the rest of them."

In this, Weyl was hardly a match for Croly. Though as early as 1909 he had feared the enmity of France and Germany in Europe, he developed in *The New Democracy* no real theory of world politics. While he ended his book on the question whether the democratic nations with their low birth rates could resist the more "frugal, prolific, and undemocratic" ones, he saw no need to answer. "For the time being," said Weyl two years before the war, "the danger is too shadowy and hypothetical to justify any slackening of our progress toward a socialized democracy. We need not put on our armor for battles which our children must fight."

Walter Lippmann was even less prepared for the war than Weyl. "I came out of college," he admitted many years later, "thinking . . . that war was an affair that 'militarists' talked about and not something serious minded progressive democrats paid any attention to." Lippmann's first two books well illustrate his innocent unconcern. *A Preface to Politics* had only two brief and inconclusive mentions of foreign affairs. *Drift and Mastery* had but three, the last of which revealed Lippmann's own view of the relationship between nationalism and internationalism. "Internationalism," he wrote, "is still a very distant dream, and while men are less provincial, it is doubtful whether the national idea is any weaker." Like Croly, Lippmann saw nationalism as beneficent both at home and abroad. With an optimism to match Weyl's, Lippmann found "ground for supposing that love of country . . . [was] coming to mean love of country and not hatred of other countries."

Unaware of the strength of the accumulated national hatreds of Europe, the young publicist left early in July 1914 for a two and a half months' tour of England and the Continent. When the war came four weeks later, Lippmann admitted that "it all seemed like a terrific plunge, let loose by a few men who consulted nobody." He was in London on the eve of Britain's declaration of war, dining and talking with reform leaders at the National Liberal Club. His traveling companion, Harold Stearns, wandered the same night through the streets of the capital, where he found great crowds of ordinary people "tipsy, . . . singing cheap little catchpenny songs . . . almost hysterically gay." When, later, Lippmann reported that the mood of the reformers at the club had been not nationalistic but "sad and depressed," Stearns could only wonder, "Why didn't he look out the window?"

Another friend also saw the war as a challenge to Lippmann's usual bland omniscience. "Walter, with his ideas of bad education [as the cause of all evil]," wrote Robert Rogers to Mabel Dodge in November 1914, "was beginning to shake me in my very firm belief in *original sin*—this war has restored it triumphantly." The war had shown Rogers that all the hopes and fears and hatreds of men "blend together . . . into one thing we call patriotism . . . which finds expression in joyous fighting." "How," he asked, "is Walter going to quench this fundamental and illogical passion of us all?" The question faced not only Lippmann but all the *New Republic* nationalists.

2. NATIONALISM AND NEUTRALITY

As the editor who had thought most about world problems, Croly dominated the *New Republic*'s views on foreign policy as much as domestic. His editorial of the first issue, "The End of American Isolation," set forth the major themes. Croly still held his old belief that American isolation was over. The impact of the war on America's economy and its effect on American opinion had, he thought, put the point beyond dispute. Furthermore, as he had predicted to Hand the year before, war had made "nationalists more necessary." An "unregenerate" America had failed on every hand to meet a crisis its own weakness had partly invited.

Croly's real bent, however, only became clear when he turned from the problems of war to those of peace-making. Both during the war and after he wanted American power to be used to get a peace favorable to the American "national interest." Any treaty at the end of the war that "made militarism even more ominously threatening," would force the United States to seek "a better substitute." For Croly as well as the others the end of American isolation meant strong American intervention in world politics.

The key assumption, of course, was the claimed end for American isolation. Here once again Croly set off the new liberalism from the old, from the strain of liberal thought that went back at least as far as Jefferson's gunboats and embargo. Jeffersonian liberals, however, were not as ready as Croly to forego a prudent isolation. They might agree with him on the damage done to America by the war. But they could not follow him in seeking to remedy the domestic malaise by curing all the ills of the world.

In truth the isolationists had a strong argument against the first World War. One of the most prominent of Croly's group of writers in the pre-war period, Charles A. Beard, would later contend that they had had the best argument. Though as internationalist as Croly in 1914, the historian came to feel that he had been wrong once the war was over. By the 1930's isolation was for Beard not what Croly had called it, a "myth," but instead the main hope for the country.

Beard's points in *The Open Door at Home* reveal how little necessary connection there was between the *New Republic*'s nationalism and its internationalism. Actually the magazine's demands for a strong government, a regulated economy, and a benign welfare state were exactly what Beard meant by an "open door" at home. Beard challenged directly the dreams of men like Willard Straight who wanted to extend the blessings of American trade and democracy to China and the rest of the world. The historian argued instead that American trade should be much reduced to avoid the bloodshed that usually went with it. Americans, he believed, had quite enough to do in curing the ailments of their own economy and their own democracy.

Clearly, too, the *New Republic*'s nationalism was well adapted to the strenuous national policy required by Beard's "open door at home." The strong government wanted by the editors could easily have kept America out of war. Probably a ban on American travel on Allied ships would have been enough, but a firm denial of loans to the Allies or even an arms embargo would have been well within the *New Republic* credo of vigorous government. The depression that might have followed upon the latter actions would have presented few problems to men who even during the slight recession of 1914 had advocated deficit financing, labor exchanges, unemployment compensation, and federal public works.

Whatever its logical consistency, isolation was unthinkable to the founders of the *New Republic*. The sources of their new liberalism in the imperialism of Theodore Roosevelt, the dependence of their magazine upon the bounty of the Anglo-

phile interventionist Willard Straight, and their own intimacy
with the largely pro-Allied educated classes of the Northeast—
all made for militant internationalism rather than isolation.

Theoretical considerations, furthermore, were of vital
moment to publicists so bent on a revision of liberal theory.
Croly, Weyl, and Lippmann had no use for the pacifism of the
Jeffersonian tradition. Leaders like Jefferson who thought war
could be prevented by refusing to fight stood for "passivism,"
not "pacifism," declared the *New Republic*. They repeated "in
the larger region of international politics the error which
advocates of *laissez-faire* . . . [had made] in domestic policies,"
an error that "in both cases . . . [invited] the triumph of the
predatory power or interest."

The *New Republic*'s cultural nationalism also, rather oddly,
set it against isolation. True, the magazine wanted a distinctively American art, an end to America's cultural dependence
on Europe. But the hoped for renaissance was not to be
parochial. Croly believed the wellsprings of culture lay not in
isolation but in the kind of competition that had existed between the city-states of ancient Greece or Renaissance Italy.
Randolph Bourne caught the same theme for the *New
Republic* when he hailed the conflict of cultures evident in the
European war as "the brightest promise of a twentieth-century
Western Civilization."

Even the editors' "metropolitanism" militated against
isolationism. Seeing the great port city of New York as a focus
and inspiration for a new national culture, they could hardly
welcome the idle wharves and financial stagnation real withdrawal from Europe would entail. Similarly, the belief in
democracy that always restrained the editors' desire for strong
national action would have made even them hesitate to accept
the regimentation necessary for a thoroughgoing Beardian
isolation. A war, a boom, and a bust, after all, lay behind the
conviction of the thoroughly democratic Beard that only an
enforced disentanglement from foreign trade and problems
could save American democracy.

For the *New Republic* men in 1914, however, the booms and busts, recurrent crises and wars of future decades were but a flicker on the horizon. The only real hint of impending storms came from an unexpected reaction to Croly's first editorial on isolation. Though Croly had been carefully neutral in his expressions, his article had at least one reader who had no doubts about the essential meaning, who thought the exercise of American power in the world could only favor the British. Soon after the first issue appeared, a "distinguished English publisher" visited the magazine's offices and suggested that if the editors "would promise to produce an article a week in the same vein as Croly's he would be prepared to buy fifty thousand copies a week for the duration of the war."

So crude a bribe offer could only insult intellectuals who so much valued their independence. Yet it may also have brought home to them the delicacy of their role as journalists in a neutral nation. They at once made clear that the end of isolation did not mean the end of neutrality. They argued, in fact, that if Americans were to seek ways to make the war lead to permanent peace an attitude of realistic neutrality was vital. Neither the Allies nor the Central Powers, declared the *New Republic*, could "claim exclusively to represent the interests of a better international order."

During the first months of publication the editors urged that the war be discussed "not in relation to its 'moral' causes, but in relation to its realistic results." Trying to be consistent nationalists, they exhorted their readers to analyze the war "as Americans, instead of as pro-Germans or pro-Allies." Americans had to weigh impartially the consequences for their own country and for the world of either an Allied or German victory. In sum, the *New Republic* assumed the duty of being "something more than a credulous follower of one of the belligerents."

However proper such a position might be for ardent nationalists, it ill accorded with the editors' private sentiments. Practically everything in the pasts of Croly, Weyl, and Lippmann made them sympathize instinctively with the British and French. Croly had spent several years of his youth in Paris, and his later travels took him there or to England again and again. Weaned on Comte, he retained throughout his life an "addiction to French philosophy" and once confessed to a friend that he considered his "culture [to be] mainly French." "In the years 1914-17," Lippmann later wrote of him, "there was never any question in his mind, I think, that under certain circumstances, such as the threat of a German victory, it would be necessary for America to enter the war."

Walter Weyl, German in background and partly so in education, surrounded by friends of pacifist or Germanic persuasion, might have counteracted the Croly bias. He did, in fact, manage to be fairer to Germany than most of the other editors. Yet basically his sympathies were with the Allies. The example of a pacific, prosperous, democratic France, after all, had first roused in him the dream of a "new democracy." Throughout the war he remained opposed to German "militarism" and "hoped for her defeat."

If Walter Lippmann's ideas on world politics were still a bit ill-defined, his prejudices were not. Though he was like Weyl of German descent, an extra generation, family wealth, and a Harvard education had rid the heritage of any poignancy. Significantly, Lippmann's intellectual heroes were mostly English and French; only Freud and Nietzsche among Germanic thinkers had had any appeal. Soon after the war, while passions were still warm, Lippmann boasted of his lack of neutrality. "If there were not bound volumes . . . to prove it . . ." he wrote, "I should be afraid to say that the 'New Republic' was never neutral in thought."

Luckily for the editors, Willard Straight more than shared their sentiments. Had he not, the violent emotions roused by the war might have strongly tempted him to end the magazine. Straight, however, was four-square for the Allies, so much so that Croly later believed the young banker "might have enlisted in the British army . . . had [he] not been married." As one of the negotiators that made the Morgan firm the American purchasing agent for the Allies, Straight strongly believed that common interests bound the United States irrevocably to Great Britain.

None of the other men close to the magazine quite matched Straight in commercial and emotional involvement, but they did little to lessen the *New Republic*'s pro-Allied bias. Felix Frankfurter, Learned Hand, and Alvin Johnson all strongly favored the Allies, and even the Anglophobe Irishman Francis Hackett confessed to detesting "the Germans most of all." Only Harold Stearns and Randolph Bourne among the *New Republic* regulars were really neutral in thought and unalterably opposed to involvement. American "war with Germany," wrote Bourne in August 1915, "seems to me the last calamity to which this teetering world of ours could come."

What little influence the two salaried contributors might have had, however, was more than counterbalanced by two Englishmen much closer to the magazine's inner councils. Norman Angell, famous as a "pacifist" before the war through his book *The Great Illusion,* arrived in America in the spring of 1915 bent on changing the neutral policies of the United States. A loyal Englishman, actually more anti-imperialist than pacifist, Angell in the fall of 1915 was invited to take part in editorial discussions, and "for about a year" became "virtually a member of the staff." The other Englishman, Harold Laski, started as a book reviewer, but when in 1916 Frankfurter got him an instructorship at Harvard, he began regularly spending vacations in the *New Republic* offices. Thereafter hardly an issue appeared without an article or review from the Englishman's pen. Eventually Laski was asked to write leaders and join policy discussions, until he too, like Angell, became "almost a member of the staff."

Angell and Laski contributed only part of the magazine's general Anglophile cast. As the *New Republic* merged its nationalism with internationalism, it managed to be no more representative of world opinion than of national. During the months before publication began, the liberal English journalist, S. K. Ratcliffe, was made London correspondent, while such other English writers as Alfred Zimmern, Rebecca West, and Graham Wallas were asked for regular contributions. Most of the magazine's military news came from two British reporters, Gerald Morgan and H. N. Brailsford, while such famous Britons as James Bryce, George Bernard Shaw, H. G. Wells, John A. Hobson, and Hugh Walpole were much in evidence during the period of neutrality. More than one quarter of the *New Republic*'s non-staff contributions during the first year came from Great Britain.

Yet there were Englishmen and Englishmen (as well as Irishmen), even in the midst of Great Britain's struggle against Germany. Significantly, almost all the British contributors— Brailsford, Zimmern, Ratcliffe, Wells, Wallas, Shaw, and Hobson—came from the English left. Though in general loyal sons of Great Britain, they were often skeptical of their country's aims and methods. Shaw, for instance, actively opposed the war and was praised by the *New Republic* for his courage. Ratcliffe and Brailsford opposed conscription and bluntly accused British conservatives of prolonging the war for private ends. Though the heavy concentration of British writers on the *New Republic* made real neutrality unlikely, the attitudes of such writers made the magazine something less than a "credulous follower" of the Allies.

Considering how violently partisan most of the American press became even at the start of the war, the *New Republic* did not do too badly—at least for the first half year or so when neutrality was still its aim. The editors' uncertainty about the war and their pragmatic distaste for absolute judgments helped them to seem at least as neutral as, say, the Wilson Administration. They refused to accuse Germany of starting the war. Toward atrocity tales from Belgium, so important in the battle of opinion, Croly, Weyl, and Lippmann kept a commendable skepticism.

On the more vital but less emotional issues of neutral com-

merce and the blockades the *New Republic* men also seemed
relatively balanced, at least if measured against most of the
Eastern press or many high figures in the Wilson Administration. The *New Republic* attacked proposals for an American arms embargo, for instance, not as being damaging to
the Allies but rather as being unfair and unneutral. Croly,
Weyl, and Lippmann even managed to be critical of the
British blockade, but they agreed with the private desires of
such Anglophiles in the Administration as Robert Lansing and
Walter Hines Page, who wanted to water down protests against
Great Britain's actions in a deluge of legalisms. Even so, the
normal American sentiments of the time were such that a
Literary Digest survey credited the *New Republic* with having
made "the strongest denunciation of Great Britain."

The magazine responded quite placidly in February 1915
to the Germans' proclamation of a North Atlantic "war zone."
While Woodrow Wilson at once threatened to hold the
Germans to "strict accountability," the *New Republic* wanted
the inevitable protest to be matched with one against the
British *Lusitania*'s illegal use of the American flag. So accommodating were the editors, in fact, that with the *Lusitania*
sinking still two months away, they declared that "American
citizens who sail under the British flag after the German warning do so at their own risk."

Meanwhile the editors continued their strong protests
against the ever-tightening British blockade, so much so as to
bring the caution from Straight to "deal gently with the
British in this crisis." Straight's worries may have been les-
sened, however, by a new theme that crept into the magazine's
columns early in 1915. Even at the height of the blockade
controversy, Croly, Weyl, and Lippmann argued that "a
victory on the part of Germany or Austria would be dangerous
to the security of the United States." More, they began to hint
at a certain "community of interest" between America and
Great Britain. Only in contrast to the deep emotional involve-

ment of Straight and many others could the *New Republic* make any pretense of real neutrality.

In fact, though Croly, Weyl, and Lippmann certainly tried to seem fair (and may even have tried to *be* so), quite a bit of propaganda found its way into their magazine's pages. Articles by George Santayana, John Dewey, Rebecca West, and many others seemed clearly designed to rouse American sympathies for the Allies. The editors' own tendency to use such terms as "militarism" and "human decency" when speaking of Germany suggested the feelings they themselves were suppressing.

The editors, nevertheless, resisted the "preparedness" agitation with which Roosevelt and others soon began to stir the country. Rather surprisingly for such advocates of power politics, their only early stand on the matter was to advise the Democrats to provide quickly for defense so as to steal the militarists' thunder and get the issue out of the way. Good pragmatists as always, Croly, Weyl, and Lippmann spent the rest of their time flailing at more absolute positions on either side. They ridiculed pacifist claims that arms were a cause of war, while at the same time challenging the militarists to define the purposes of their armament schemes. "Preparedness for What?" became the editors' slogan, as they drove home the thesis that power politics was too complex a game to be won through a mere maximization of power. Soon they were happily boasting that their stand on preparedness had been attacked both by Crystal Eastman of the Women's Peace Party and by the then very warlike Chicago *Tribune*.

For the time being the *New Republic* men could see only a very limited use for American power. Their first gambit in the process of making their nationalism internationalist was a "league of neutrals." They hoped such an organization might both help protect neutral rights and lay a base for a later league of all nations. But its pressure on the belligerents was to be moral rather than military.

The *New Republic* nationalists, therefore, were remarkably skeptical of the rather militant League to Enforce Peace that

Lodge, Taft, and Hamilton Holt of the rival *Independent* began to advocate early in 1915. Noting that the Central Powers were excluded from the proposed league, the *New Republic* condemned the idea as "nothing better than an alliance to assure the victors in the perpetual possession of the fruits of victory."

There was an ominous contradition, however, between the editors' belief in power politics and their mild proposal of a "league of neutrals." Croly, Weyl, and Lippmann seemed to see it themselves when, in their second issue, they scoffed at people who dreamt that America would have "a guiding influence in the settlement of the war." Even if the peace congress should be "held under the presidency of the United States," the board's editorial declared, "the decisions will be determined by the balance of power in which the war results." If the United States entered "the congress with nothing but a record of comfortable neutrality," its "voice ... [might] well be disregarded." While for the moment a league of neutrals seemed all the *New Republic* men could hope for, their own nationalistic faith in a politics of power beckoned ever onwards. The difficulty was one that would bedevil not only the editors but eventually Woodrow Wilson and many other Americans.

3. A New Kind of War

A friend happened to meet Walter Lippmann on the street the day in May 1915 when the news of the *Lusitania* torpedoing reached America. The friend was startled by the *New Republic* editor's violent reaction to the news. "The enormity of the event was felt by ... [Lippmann]," he wrote, "not any more as a human disaster than as an outrage committed by Germany on the United States." He was saddened that a mind like Lippmann's, generally so calm and dispassionate, was not "able to stop at such a moment and reflect that it would be an evil thing to add to the tide of warlike passion."

However shocked Lippmann may have been by the *Lusitania* slaughter, neither he nor the other editors were totally unprepared for the event. They had condemned a much less dramatic torpedoing in March as "an outrage," an act of "murder and piracy" that, if repeated, might bring a crisis "in which the use of force would be justified." The sinking of a neutral ship a month later led them to warn—in the issue that reached the stands the day the *Lusitania* went down—that "if more neutral ships . . . [were] torpedoed and innocent people killed, if, for example, a passenger ship should be sunk, Germany would have to deal with an anger all the more terrible because it had been so long suppressed."

New Republic readers of pacific bent must have expected the worst, but there were less volatile men on the magazine than Lippmann. After several days of reflection, the editors' reaction to the *Lusitania* disaster was surprisingly moderate. Croly, Weyl, and Lippmann merely used the event to justify notions of Anglo-American unity they had only dared hint at earlier. The loss of so many British and American lives on the *Lusitania*, their opening editorial declared, "emphasizes above all the existing commercial and political dependence of the United States on Great Britain." The United States, they contended, had the choice of either ending such dependence by expensive armament or of frankly admitting it and moving toward "some kind of understanding." The sinking of the *Lusitania*, concluded the *New Republic*, "has united Englishmen and Americans in a common grief and a common indignation, and . . . may unite them in a common war and conceivably a common destiny."

Evidently Croly, Weyl, and Lippmann had forgotten their own warning of two months before that Americans who sailed on British ships did so "at their own risk." They ignored the fact that a ban on such travel might have avoided so bloody a demonstration of Anglo-American unity. That the issue was a live one was to be shown even a year later by the bitter struggle in Congress over the Gore-McLemore Resolutions, which among other things would have restricted American passengers to neutral shipping. Yet any questioning of the right of Americans to travel on a munitions-carrying British liner would have lost the editors their newly won leverage toward a British alliance. Such an alliance, of course, had been Croly's dream at least as far back as *The Promise of American Life*.

As for Germany, the *New Republic* mixed bellicose words with moderate tactics. They spoke of Germany as the "world's outlaw" and railed against "Teutonic frightfulness"; they wanted strong pressure to be brought to bear, even if it meant a break in diplomatic relations. But the upshot of all the drum beating was a caution to the Administration "to proceed slowly . . . [and] if at all possible [to] avoid war, or steps which make war inevitable."

To justify such restraint the *New Republic* men turned to the very nationalism that might have made them more militant. War with Germany would be a national disaster, they argued, for it would mean "internal strain" and "the undoing of Americanization." Not only German-Americans, but all of America's foreign-born, were "hostages to peace" who made unwise any "over-hasty belligerent action." The editors, on the other hand, thought the very same diversity of population would make the United States an ideal "go-between for peace."

Those far removed from the moods of the progressive era might be suspicious of the new twist the editors had given their nationalism. Was it anything more than a slick journalistic effort to avoid the logical results of their power politics? In all probability, Croly, Weyl, and Lippmann were sincere, for they wrote in a day when the foreign-born were numerous and when the question of the "new immigrants" was still important to the middle-class mind. Within a year presidential candidates would be tossing the unpleasant word "hyphenate" back and forth without apology. Croly, too, had always been obsessed by the need for "national cohesion." The need now placed the same restraints on his foreign policy that it had on his domestic.

Within the limits of such restraint, however, the *Lusitania* crisis meant the end of any *New Republic* pretense to neutrality. In their attacks on Germany the editors became full-fledged pragmatists in a way they had never quite dared before. Croly, Weyl, and Lippmann wanted America to force Germany to abandon submarine warfare, not because such warfare violated neutral rights or abstract morality but because its end would harm Germany and benefit the Allies.

The editors called their new policy "differential neutrality." Tactically it meant insisting to the world at large on the strict letter of neutral rights, but pressing the case against Germany while deferring it against Great Britain until after the war. Whether the *New Republic* men knew it or not, they were merely calling publicly for what privately Lansing, Page, and to some extent Wilson were already doing.

Such notions of "differential neutrality" allowed Croly, Weyl, and Lippmann to seem to keep their eyes firmly on the "national interest." They still, at least in print, refused to blame Germany for causing the war. At worst the Teutonic power was merely the "immediate aggressor." The "national interest" also allowed the *New Republic* pragmatists to ask that Germany not be pressed too strongly. The continuing stalemate in Europe let them argue, for the moment at least, that Germany could no longer threaten American security by "imposing her own terms" on the Allies. On the contrary, the Allies were now trying to gain advantage by making secret territorial bargains with Italy and Rumania "for which the American democracy ... [would not] want to make itself responsible." The American national interest required a balance of power in Europe, not excessive advantage to either side.

Croly, Weyl, and Lippmann, therefore, met the submarine crisis with nothing much more aggressive than a Wilson-like "watchful waiting." While they now could be openly hostile toward Germany, they had not really resolved the central dilemma of their power politics. Only a sacrifice of American blood would give the United States any decisive say in peace-making. At the same time the editors had to admit that the people seemed not to have any "present intention of paying so great a price for so doubtful a privilege." The *New Republic* men were left with the half-hearted comfort that the world would be better if "one great Power . . . [remained] dis-interested." "The United States," they declared, "ought to be that power."

Merely saying, however, that the United States was the ideal disinterested power did not make it so. For example, the very diversity of population the editors saw as keeping America from war also made their cooly reasoned "differential neutral-ity" politically impossible. The great furor in the election of 1916 over the German-American vote was to make that evident enough. The connection between minority groups and iso-lationist sentiment, furthermore, made it very doubtful that America's nationalistic diversity made the country very suit-able as a "go-between for peace."

Obviously, too, the editors' belief that American security depended upon Great Britain lived uneasily with their in-creasingly realistic estimate of British designs in Europe. If the United States were not to support the deals the Allies found necessary for victory, then the force of the *New Republic*'s own logic—as well as of its nationalism—required an end to so extreme a dependence.

Probably only a candid review of the editors' assumptions could have resolved such contradictions, but for Croly, Weyl, and Lippmann, as for most other men, assumptions are re-examined, if at all, only under the brute coercion of events. Such events were to come, inexorably.

Full-scale war with Germany, of course, might have resolved the contradictions, if only by making them academic. Croly, Weyl, and Lippmann, however, shared much of that dislike of war that was more natural to their Jeffersonian opponents. "War," they declared early in 1915, "may well be described as murderous, damned nonsense,"—which was blunt enough for men who generally spoke in the measured accents of Harvard gentility. Not all wars, of course, but the editors made clear enough their dread of the hatreds and hysteria that most wars aroused.

The doughty *New Republic* nationalists continued to have little sympathy for such militant outfits as the Plattsburg training camp. Though Willard Straight was one of the strongest supporters of that upper-middle-class exercise in military parades and patriotism, the editors would have nothing to do with it. Similarly, in spite of their liking for national cohesion and discipline, they were hostile toward the proposals of Roosevelt, Straight, and others for universal military training. Nor were they attracted by the "socializing" tendencies of war. "Such socialism . . .," they wrote early in 1915, "is as different as night and day from the collectivism established in stages by a free people."

Unwilling to face the hazards and miseries of all-out war, yet feeling as the *Lusitania* wrangle dragged on that massive pressure had to be brought against Germany, Croly, Weyl, and Lippmann resolved their dilemma by making over war in their own liberal image. Norman Angell, invited to the United States in the spring of 1915 by the Carnegie Endowment for World Peace, showed them the way. What the Carnegie people thought of their rather militant "pacifist" is unknown, but the *New Republic* men had a ready ear for all the Englishman's notions of how world peace might be helped by an aggressive American policy.

Angell brought the editors a vision of "a new kind of war." Spelling out the Englishman's ideas in an editorial after his own lengthy article, the editors argued that his proposals might well be the "next step" for the United States. They agreed with Angell that Wilson's recent use of the words "deliberately unfriendly" toward Germany made a diplomatic break sooner or later highly probable. Yet they also agreed that all-out war would "fail to protect American lives upon the seas"; it would, in fact, remove the last restraints from Germany, force the United States to acquiesce in Allied policies, and end any chance for America "to be the champion of neutral rights."

On the other hand, Croly, Weyl, and Lippmann found Angell's "new kind of war" wonderfully attuned to their desires. By resorting merely to convoys, confiscations of German assets, and the use of interned German shipping, it met the challenge of the German submarine directly. Such limited warfare, furthermore, would not allow the Allies to "crush Germany" and thus would serve the American desire to preserve the balance of power in Europe. It would permit the United States to condemn Germany "as unfit for the society of nations" while at the same time declining "responsibility for Russian, Japanese and Italian policy." In sum, a limited warfare of naval convoying and commercial retaliation "would make the United States a real champion of neutral rights and a leader in the placing of civilized sanctions behind international law."

In the summer of 1915, therefore, Croly, Weyl, and Lippmann turned away from "the old fashioned kind of war" to a type of "limited war" not unknown—whether in the North Atlantic in 1940 or in Korea in 1950—to American liberals since. Angell's proposals, at least in theory, ended most of the contradictions that had bedeviled the editors' foreign policy. The "new kind of war," the *New Republic* men believed, would be more acceptable than the old kind to those Americans still bound by birth to the Central Powers. It recognized American dependence on Great Britain without tying the country to British plans in Europe and Asia. It would help defeat Germany while at the same time giving the United States leverage against a punitive peace. Best of all, it would spare America the illiberal and hysterical frenzy of an all-out war. The editors wanted war, when it came, to be a *New Republic* kind of war.

Such tactics, of course, were avowedly unneutral and pro-Allied. Yet they were hardly more so than those of forcing mediation on Germany, with American intervention as an alternative, that Colonel House and Wilson were discussing at the time. Nor did the *New Republic*'s tactics differ much from those Franklin Roosevelt followed from 1939 to 1941. The editors, unlike Roosevelt, however, wanted their program to be publicly avowed.

Even more striking is the almost item-by-item correspondence between *New Republic* policies and those the power-politics theorist, George Kennan, has held recently that the United States should have followed before World War I. Yet the difficulties Croly, Weyl, and Lippmann actually faced in 1915 appear clearly in the qualifications Kennan attaches even to his second guesses. He concedes that a militant policy against Germany, no matter how desirable, would have been "totally impossible from the standpoint of public opinion." Americans of the time, writes Kennan, "would never have dreamed of spending real money for armaments in time of peace . . .[and] would never have gone into war deliberately, as a result of a cold calculation upon the balance of power elsewhere." Instead, Americans "would have made war only upon direct provocation . . . [and] could never have been brought . . . to refrain from pressing such a war to its final conclusion." Kennan, writing thirty-six years later, felt that the limited capacity of Americans to wage limited war resulted from "domestic predilections and habits of thought," from "democracy as practiced in this country." The *New Republic* prophets of a new liberalism would only have agreed.

4. A MOTHLIKE GYRATION

When in January 1916 it seemed to most people that Wilson had wrested real concessions from Germany on the submarine issue, Croly was not impressed. He wrote Learned Hand that, whatever Wilson's limited triumphs, Roosevelt "might have succeeded better and more quickly by the use of different methods." Though Croly conceded immediately that some other President than Wilson "might not have succeeded at all," he and the other editors actually had Roosevelt much on their minds. Angell's new kind of war seemed a natural for the master of "big stick" diplomacy. Men of theory who hovered always just on the edge of practical power, Croly, Weyl, and Lippmann could hardly avoid their mothlike destiny.

During the crisis with Germany the editors often veered wildly from hostility to moderation, but nothing permanently dampened their heroic mood. Through they pretended to base their policies on the "national interest," they did nothing to follow up the startling admission in one issue that a German victory in Europe might bring no harm to the United States. For the most part, the editors demanded maximum pressure against Germany. Under the circumstances, they were justly amazed at finding themselves attacked as pro-German both by the Boston *Evening Transcript* and the Harvard philosopher Ralph Barton Perry.

By the end of 1915, in fact, the *New Republic* men wanted war. Late in December they demanded an immediate break with the Central Powers and preparation for "more drastic measures." In their last issue of the year, they published an all-out attack on Wilson for the weakness of his leadership. "Perhaps only a great genius among statesmen could have risen to the opportunity," argued the editors. It was clear enough that it was not Wilson they had in mind.

All the talk of war had brought the hero of San Juan Hill back to the *New Republic*'s pages. "He alone," said the editors of Roosevelt in September, "has had the courage to associate his own personality . . . with a policy . . . for increasing American international responsibilities." Even Wilson's conversion to preparedness in November brought from the *New Republic* only bitter ridicule. When the editors praised Wilson's December message to Congress, they did so only to hold Wilson up to the Roosevelt image. "The Democratic party . . . under Mr. Wilson's leadership," declared the *New Republic*, "is coming to resemble the more eager, vigilant and formative spirit which was described some years ago by Mr. Roosevelt as the 'New Nationalism.' "

By the end of the year, Croly, Weyl, and Lippmann were ready to come out openly for their hero. They were not at all surprised to find a Roosevelt presidential boom under way, when, as they said "other 'leaders' remain[ed] wrapped in the gloom of their prudence." In January 1916 an editorial called "The Roosevelt Method" argued that Wilson, in spite of all his firmness, had failed with Germany because he refused to back his protests with effective force. Roosevelt, on the other hand, said the editors at great length, would have dealt with the Germans bluntly and aggressively. Such a method, far from increasing "the real risk of war," opened the way to peace and was "likely to prove the method of genuine internationalism."

Unfortunately for their plans, the *New Republic* men were intellectuals. Even worse, they were honest intellectuals, and complete honesty is rarely welcome to politicians. When the editors turned to Roosevelt's domestic policy in another later editorial, "The Newer Nationalism," they had to record a few blemishes. They found the Colonel's concept of a "newer nationalism" a little vague. After citing a long list of questions on which Roosevelt had taken no position, they admitted that the chief feature of his nationalism seemed to be universal military training. The editorial ended valiantly but weakly by praising the former President's search for some "system of national moral education."

The *New Republic* men, however, were being more honest with their readers in their qualifications about Roosevelt than with themselves. Again and again they had justified their nationalistic ideas on foreign policy on the grounds that nationalism alone could lead to an effective internationalism. But such a theory could work, if at all, only if nationalism were kept very firmly the servant of internationalism. The "national interest" had to be identified inflexibly with the cause of world peace, not with the selfish interests of the United States nor with those of any group of world powers. Roosevelt, it is true, had always insisted on the need for "fighting for peace" in a way that Wilson did not yet understand. But the Colonel's fierce nationalism had by 1915 destroyed any chance that he could stand for a responsible internationalism. Both a violent jingo and a rabid partisan of the Allies, Roosevelt would never have followed the *New Republic's* cool and deliberate notions of "limited war." Nor, as the editors conceded themselves, was he any longer interested in the domestic reforms that alone gave human content to the *New Republic's* nationalism. The editors' renewed pursuit of Roosevelt violated every canon of their new liberalism. It is the nature of moths to be blinded by the light that will destroy them.

Armed with the first unequivocal editorial, Willard Straight led the flight of the intellectuals back to the heroic leader. More militantly patriotic than the others and always closer to Roosevelt, Straight had remained a friend despite the quarrel in 1915. Upon receiving "The Roosevelt Method," the Colonel admitted to having been "generally impressed." He had found the piece "very understanding" and descriptive of "just the kind of action . . . [he] would have taken, if President." He still resented, however, the harping on his "intemperance." "I have got to be emphatic to attract attention," Roosevelt declared. "We are not in a rose-water, pink tea crisis at present."

For all this, Straight evidently had real hope. A few weeks later he sent off the editors' effort on "The Newer Nationalism." Roosevelt replied that he was still "interested," but he was hardly pleased. He resented any implication that what he stood for had even "partly" been anticipated by Wilson; he resented more the editors' claim that he had given "only 'very vague hints' about foreign and domestic policy." Such statements, he wrote sarcastically, made him "feel more amiable"

toward the *New Republic* men than he had "for a long time."
"I have felt they were sinning against the light," he fulminated. "But really I think I have been mistaken. I think they
are nice well-meaning geese—early Victorian geese." Clearly
the Colonel was in no mood for an alliance with "the nice
old ladies of the *New Republic*."

So ended the editors' last gyration around their Bull Moose
hero. Frustrated as moths, Croly, Weyl, and Lippmann once
again became gadflies. By March 1916 they had discovered that
at the war's outbreak Roosevelt actually had wanted none of
the heroic things they had imagined. In an editorial, "Mr.
Roosevelt's Afterthought," they apologized to Wilson for the
unfairness of their earlier criticism. Thereafter they again and
again attacked the Colonel for failing to present alternatives
to Wilson's policies. When the Republicans did not nominate
Roosevelt for President in June, the best Croly, Weyl, and
Lippmann had for their former leader was a rather patron-
izing suggestion that he run for Senator in New York.

Roosevelt, for his part, responded with contempt. The *New
Republic*, he wrote a friend in September 1916, had "played
a cur's part." "I feel a genuine indignation," he said, his anger
so strong that he forgot both his grammar and the names of
his former supporters. "For Albert Croly is sinning against the
light like Walter Weil and Lippman, and know me well, and
when they deliberately misrepresent the facts, they are guilty
of grave misconduct." Croly and his colleagues may have come
upon heroic days, but they were not to have their hero.

5. DEFENSE AND THE NEW LIBERALISM

In the more forthright days when the new liberalism was
first stirring, defense was called "preparedness." Croly, Weyl,
and Lippmann had pounced on this vulnerable term with
their repeated challenge: "Preparedness for What?" By the
end of 1915, they had answered their own question when they

decided that the time had come for Norman Angell's "limited war." Without a hint of irony, the editors called their policy "Aggressive Pacifism." They wanted the United States to break relations with Germany and enter the war under conditions that would keep for the President control of both the war effort and the peace to follow.

Unknown probably to the *New Republic* men and certainly to the rest of the country, the Wilson Administration early in 1916 shared many of the magazine's aims. With Wilson's approval Colonel House had matured his scheme to force mediation on Germany or intervene for the Allies. In January, he was carrying on his delicate negotiations in Berlin. Wilson himself, facing the submarine crises that winter and spring, repeatedly foresaw the break with Germany for which the editors were calling. He also hoped that the seemingly inevitable rupture would lead only to a limited war.

Yet, while Croly, Weyl, and Lippmann were sure in their aims, Wilson was not. Facing the actual complexities of power, the President vacillated through each crisis from bellicosity to relief when the Germans made concessions. Wilson saw real hope for peace in the Germans' *Sussex* pledge, by which they bound themselves conditionally to restrict the submarine. The editors, on the other hand, were convinced that Germany would resort to the submarine again as soon as it became militarily profitable. "Then," they declared, "we shall probably drift into war . . . without the guidance of a constructive policy calculated to promote our own security and well-being or that of other nations."

In spite of their many disappointments, the *New Republic* intellectuals still had their hearts set on a "constructive policy." Wilsonian liberalism was not their own new liberalism, and the President's gingerly approach to preparedness brought the differences into focus. Croly, in February 1916, continued to see the Democratic party under Wilson as an "Unregenerate Democracy." All the accomplishments of the New Freedom, argued the *New Republic's* editor, had essentially come to nothing, because of the conservative and inefficient men who administered the new laws. The spur of preparedness might have given new life to the New Freedom, but the President's Jeffersonian creed was unable to meet the challenge. Though Wilson, wrote Croly, had recently joined the preparedness agitation by "stumping the country after the manner of Roosevelt," his propaganda was but a "pale and fluttering candle . . . contrived out of Republican and Progressive materials."

By 1916 it was obvious that Croly, Weyl, and Lippmann were suffering badly from the frustration of their new liberalism that had begun as early as their first issue. In June, Walter Lippmann defined the real issues facing the country with all the old accents of Bull Moose nationalism. Preparedness for the young publicist meant not only armaments but a willingness "to unify and socialize the railroads and the means of communication, to regulate rigorously [the] basic industries . . . to control the food supply and shipping and credit . . . [and to recognize] labor as a national institution."

The program of the new liberalism was clear, but its tactics still presented problems. Lippmann by 1916 had turned from the mass of progressive consumers to the elite. For him the real question was where "the minority which has some sense of the problem . . . [would] come to the top." Croly and Weyl had flirted with the idea of obtaining reform leverage from farm and labor groups on the left, but farmers and workers were unlikely as supporters of an aggressive policy of power diplomacy. The two older editors joined Lippmann therefore in following the fatal bent of their nationalism to find new life for liberalism in the preparedness campaign.

Croly, with his usual prescience, had foreseen as much in *The Promise of American Life.* He had little difficulty, therefore, in seeing the crisis with Germany as just the thing to arouse the people for a new liberalism. "The American nation needs the tonic of a serious moral adventure," wrote Croly in July, in words that echoed those of the militarist Roosevelt.

Preparedness together with a foreign policy of "aggressive pacifism" were to be the tonic's ingredients. Though the *New Republic* men had resisted the preparedness agitation for almost a year, they now saw it as the last fond hope of their new liberalism.

In joining the preparedness crusade, the *New Republic* men were putting considerable strain on the vaunted flexibility of their pragmatism. Randolph Bourne spoke for the others when late in 1915 in an unsigned editorial he called the war "the first real test of their pragmatism." "To be immutable," he wrote in words that were soon to have tragic echoes, "is really to be false to our whole American pragmatic philosophy." For Bourne, as for the other *New Republic* men, "the war . . . [presented an] incomparable opportunity of laying that foundation of stern realism on which to build our new ideals." In the summer of 1916, "stern realism" meant for Croly, Weyl, and Lippmann, if not for Bourne, joining the defense campaign in the interests of liberalism. Such an escape into war preparation has not been unknown to other American reform movements, particularly when their principles have been either nationalistic or vague.

Over and over again during 1916 the *New Republic* insisted that "the issue of military preparedness makes progressivism more urgent than ever." They continued to be sensitive to the boom-and-bust instability of capitalism, but now quite prophetically accented their point by showing how much the prosperity of 1916 depended on arms orders. The real problems would come, warned the editors, when the war ended and dragged the economy "down to depression." Arguing that "a time of world crisis . . . [was] a time for collective action," they made the hazards of both war and peace the sanction for all the demands of their new liberalism. The need for workers' loyalty in war became the justification for their old program of "industrial democracy." Wartime business efficiency was made the reason for the strict regulation and ultimate nationalization of large industry. And the desire to make the government flexible and powerful in war was brought forth to justify a thoroughgoing program of constitutional, fiscal, and administrative reorganization. All the old slogans of the editors' new liberalism—"constructive individualism," "constructive nationalism," "constructive radicalism"—were now merged in a call for "constructive patriotism." Forgotten, apparently, was their charge of only a year before that the "solidarity of war is the worst of all solidarities." The philosophers of a new liberalism were following in the end the logic of their nationalism.

The preparedness drive carried much further the long-term progression of Croly's nationalism from the cultural to the political. Though neither he nor the others could yet completely swallow the unabashed militarism of Roosevelt, even so their generally militant air soon made the Wilbur Littletons of their company restless. Randolph Bourne became the bellwether of the change.

By 1916 the young cultural nationalist was disturbed both by the editors' forceful policies and by their growing constraint toward "the more fervent things" he submitted. In September he noted that they were "getting restive under the burden of paying . . . a hundred dollars a month—mere living wage—for work they can't find space for." Others among the young intellectuals also found the *New Republic* increasingly uncongenial. Perhaps many of them, like Bourne, had their pieces on art and literature pushed aside for the political and military speculations that now filled the journal. Some of them may have shared Bourne's feelings that the needs of the magazine kept them from "any really honest work." The *New Republic*, in any case, seemed to have lost its bold aesthetic promise of 1914, and symptomatic of the change was the founding of the *Seven Arts* on the *New Republic*'s second anniversary in November 1916. The new magazine was put together by James Oppenheim, Waldo Frank, Van Wyck Brooks, and others of the cultural nationalists of the day. The *Seven Arts*' founders proclaimed that they were "living in the first days of a renas-

cent period." They were sure that America had come upon a
time when art would be "not only the expression of the
national life, but a means to its enhancement." Dedicated to
such a dream, the new magazine soon attracted such earlier
New Republic enthusiasts as Brooks, Bourne, Lee Simonson,
Robert Frost, Amy Lowell, and Paul Rosenfeld.

For the moment, however, the dissatisfaction of the *Seven
Arts* group meant no more than a weakening of those strands of
nationalism and art Croly had woven together so long before.
Bourne, Brooks, Rosenfeld, and Simonson kept writing for the
New Republic as well as their new magazine. And Croly, Weyl,
and Lippmann seemed little disturbed by the restlessness of the
younger intellectuals. The editors themselves after all had
rejected Bourne's "more fervent pieces." They had given their
magazine the ever more militant cast that troubled the young
cultural nationalists. Riding the whirlwind of preparedness
with pragmatic assurance, the editors were willing to suspend
their dreams of a cultural revival for the "duration."

6. LIBERALS AND A LEADER

The single-minded focus of the new liberalism upon foreign
policy and preparedness was only the start of the collapse of
many old dreams. With Roosevelt lost as a leader and the old
Bull Moose party virtually extinct, somehow, somewhere
Croly, Weyl, and Lippmann had to find a way to swing the
nation to their "aggressive pacifism."

Defense issues allowed the editors to face the election of
1916 with their usual air of bland impartiality. The catastro-
phic convention of the Progressive party in June left them
unmoved. They merely took a swipe at Roosevelt for his "unnecessary and inhuman treatment" of his followers and, for the
last of many times, tendered the party extreme unction. They
were even less impressed by the Socialists. That party, said the
editors, had stupidly seen preparedness as "nothing but a
capitalist conspiracy against the working classes."

When the major parties came forth in June with Wilson and Hughes as their candidates, Croly, Weyl, and Lippmann declared themselves to be "on the fence." People who knew them well, however, must have been astonished when a few weeks later they confessed that if the election were merely a choice between the two parties there were "plausible reasons for preferring the Democracy." The *New Republic* men regained their lofty balance at once, however, by declaring that between the two major party candidates there were "plausible reasons for preferring Mr. Hughes." The remark was hardly an endorsement, but it reflected the fact that privately the editors began the campaign strongly disposed toward the Republican candidate.

Croly, Weyl, and Lippmann were initially for Hughes and against Wilson largely because of foreign policy. Their complaints against the President boiled down to three major points. First, with all the vehemence of their pragmatic, anti-Jeffersonian hearts, they objected to Wilson's extreme emphasis upon abstract rights in diplomacy. "We can be legal," stormed the editors, "we can be utterly legal; we can be nothing but legal."

Second, the *New Republic* continued to argue that Wilson used the wrong methods to uphold world law and order. The President hoped to reform the world with legal principles and moral suasion rather than by the effective exercise of force. He had protested violations of neutral rights strongly only against the Central Powers, and then had tried to justify the discriminatory treatment on the moral grounds that the Germans were taking American lives. But such a stand, said the *New Republic*, merely made Americans want to go to war out of hate for the Germans rather than out of calm calculation of the "national interest."

The *New Republic*'s third charge against Wilson was probably, in the minds of the editors, the most serious. Anticipating the complaints of the Kennan-Morgenthau power politics school a half century later, the editors claimed that Wilson had failed most grievously in his role as a democratic leader. Through all the submarine crises, they wrote, the President had never given the American people "the faintest idea how near the government . . . [was] to a break with Germany." He had never made the people "fully aware of the overwhelming importance for the future of social democracy of a triumph of the principles for which . . . [he was] contending." Croly, Weyl, and Lippmann wanted Wilson to prepare Americans for a war to end war, a war to make the world safe for democracy. When the President, even in his preparedness campaign, showed no such inclination, the editors declared bluntly that he "was not up to his job."

In domestic affairs, the theorists of a new liberalism could at least credit the President with realizing the failure of his reliance on abstract rights and morality. "Oblivion," in fact, had "descended on the New Freedom." Wilson, said Croly in February 1916, was "associating with preparedness many different plans for domestic reorganization which only yesterday would have been dismissed as centralized paternalism." Yet Wilson's actions, unleavened by a conscious nationalism, were pure "opportunism." And his shift to nationalism, rather than "resurrecting" the Democratic party, had "ripped [it] to pieces."

Both a partisan and a philosophical bias influenced the editors' judgment, but they were not alone early in 1916 in their feeling that Wilson had failed to provide "concrete and constructive leadership." Even so ardent a Wilsonian as Ray Stannard Baker had concluded that "if Wilson . . . [did] not furnish . . . [leadership] for higher ends, Roosevelt . . . [was] on hand to furnish it for lower ends." Colonel House, Wilson's astute political adviser, sensed the general lack of enthusiasm for the President. To him the situation was serious, for Wilson's only chance seemed to lie in "getting the progressive forces in line." He resolved in his diary to concentrate on getting enough "of the independent and Progressive vote to overcome the normal Republican majority."

A magazine like the *New Republic* which could claim only 24,000 subscribers by 1916 might well have been beneath House's notice. Such, however, was not the case. A paper that had the support of Croly, Weyl, Lippmann, Frankfurter, Beard, Dewey, Hand, and so many others might just help swing the old Bull Moose vote. Furthermore, as the campaign unfolded, the editors showed they meant it when they put themselves "on the fence." Critical though they were of Wilson, they were unable to develop much enthusiasm for Hughes.

Immediately after the conventions they began to question the Republican candidate's mildness and tendency to temporize. "The Republican party," they argued, "will never be reunited by an olive branch." The Roosevelt image could cut both ways, for soon they were predicting that Hughes would "fail . . . unless he . . . [could] take over some of Mr. Roosevelt's aggressive and contagious energy." Hughes's German-American support made them wonder whether the Republican any better than Wilson could practice their "differential neutrality." They condemned, too, Hughes's failure to make social reform a part of preparedness and charged that his campaign speeches sounded "distressingly like Mark Hanna Republicanism."

Meanwhile, House and the other Wilson leaders might have found encouragement in the *New Republic*'s changed attitude toward their candidate. The change, in fact, marked a corresponding one in Wilson, for House was not alone among Administration leaders in seeing the need to attract old progressive voters. From the first of the year onwards the Administration's policies began to shift to the left. Wilson's biographer, Arthur Link, finds "the first public sign of the new departure" to have been the nomination in January of Louis D. Brandeis to the Supreme Court. The *New Republic* men were delighted. Speaking through Felix Frankfurter in an unsigned editorial, they hailed the move as a dramatic expiation of Wilson's previous sins on appointments. Engrossed by the crisis of a coming war, they were so happy to have a man of the Brandeis stamp in government that they refused to quibble over his former enthusiasm for the New Freedom.

Croly, Weyl, and Lippmann also became less skeptical about Wilson's attitude toward preparedness. When, in February, Lippmann went along with Wilson as a reporter on a preparedness tour, he interpreted the warm response of the crowds as a sign of the Democrat's growth as a popular leader. Really heartfelt praise for Wilson did not come, however, until May when the President took up the idea of a league of nations. Unknown to them, their own "An Appeal to the President" of the month before had been carefully read by Wilson as he prepared his speech. Though the President, of course, drew his ideas from many sources, his notions of a league were so close to the *New Republic*'s that the editors gave way to unprecedented enthusiasm. Wilson had shown "vision" and "courage." The President's speech, declared the editors, might well "mark a decisive point in the history of the world."

So enthusiastic were the editors that they saw things in Wilson's address that were not really there. They were right in claiming that the President had "broken with the tradition of American isolation," but their own militance rather than Wilson's came forth in the statement that he had "broken with the pernicious doctrine of American neutrality." Nor had the President said anything strong enough to justify the magazine's paraphrase that in the future the United States would "not be neutral between the aggressor and the victim." The editors ignored, too, the detailed parallel Wilson drew between individual rights and the rights of nations. To praise the Democratic leader so strongly, in fact, Croly, Weyl, and Lippmann had to make him over in their own nationalistic image.

Even more exciting things, however, seemed to be happening to Wilson's domestic policies. His support early in 1916 of a farm credits bill met a demand the editors had been making since late 1914. Equally pleasing was his strong pressure on Congress for child-labor regulation, a tariff commission, and a suspension of anti-trust laws in the export business.

Such things, the editors thought, marked a miraculous change. "In Mr. Wilson's present program," they declared late in June, "there is hardly a shred left of the fabric of his Jeffersonian revival. With every development of his policy he has been approximating to the spirit and creed of a Hamiltonian nationalist."

Deep prejudices, however, die slowly. After Wilson's nomination for re-election, the *New Republic* men still felt "certain misgivings." "What liberals need to obtain from Mr. Wilson," they declared, "is some assurance . . . that his later preference for a governing government will not prove to be as fugitive as his earlier preference for doctrinaire freedom." The moths had caught a flicker of light once again, but they were not quite certain about its color.

Croly, Weyl, and Lippmann, however, had betrayed a subtle shift in their own thought even as they recited their misgivings. They were talking now about "liberals," not as always before, "progressives." The shift in terms showed the strength of the lure of Wilson's power, but, to the subsequent confusion of American political thought, it also marked the piracy of a word that belonged rightfully to the Jeffersonians. By August, when Hughes made his acceptance speech, the editors could without a blush complain that the Republican had "not yet justified the faith of liberals."

"Liberals" now suited the *New Republic* men better than "progressives," because the old name was redolent enough of the Bull Moose to embarrass any rally around a new leader. The editors themselves, moreover, were suddenly undergoing some remarkable changes. Their comments on Hughes's acceptance speech, for instance, revealed them as somewhat bored by the "administrative efficiency" that had always been so important in their new liberalism. Even more startling, they contradicted many of their earlier attacks on Wilson by admitting that patronage concessions had been the necessary price of his remarkable legislative record.

Meanwhile, the Wilson leaders were doing all they could to

captivate former Progressives. Norman Hapgood, whose *Harper's Weekly* had recently reduced the number of *New Republic* competitors by merging with the *Independent*, became the leader of the drive. One after another during the summer such former Roosevelt supporters as Frederic C. Howe, Bainbridge Colby, John Dewey, Amos Pinchot, Jane Addams, and Lincoln Steffens declared for Wilson. Even William English Walling, Weyl's Socialist friend, joined the parade behind the Democratic candidate.

Of the *New Republic* men, Walter Lippmann, always the most mothlike, was the first to succumb. By July he was having Newton D. Baker, Wilson's Secretary of War, forward suggestions to the President for the campaign. "You can tell Mr. Lippmann," wrote Wilson early in August in reply to one such suggestion, "that . . . I hope sincerely that as his ideas clarify he will let me have the benefit of them, either directly or in an editorial expression."

The President clearly enough was willing to provide light for the circling moths. One man close to the editors that summer, however, realized that the light was not quite bright enough. Harold Laski, at work in the *New Republic* offices, probably had his colleagues in mind when he urged Hapgood to make Wilson "come out strong" in the campaign. Laski believed, Hapgood told Wilson, that many of the independents would be much affected by some kind of an expression of liberal doctrine, especially one that included a "program for the future." Laski was merely echoing the demands of the *New Republic* intellectuals that Wilson come out explicitly for their new liberalism.

Wilson got the point. He replied at once that undoubtedly at some place in his campaign he would have a chance to let his "underlying philosophy come out plainly enough." Lippmann, more flexible on points of doctrine than Croly and Weyl, was satisfied by the promise. On August 28, Hapgood wrote the President: "Lippmann is the ablest of the *New Republic* editors and the one who is working to swing the paper openly to you."

The Democratic candidate soon provided the candle power to help Lippmann with his more reluctant colleagues. The way the President handled the threatened railroad strike in late summer enormously impressed the editors. They saw his imposition of an eight-hour day through the Adamson Act as a long step toward the nationalization of the railways. Soon, too, they began to change their ideas on Wilson's leadership. His actions in the railroad crisis, they claimed, had made him "in a very real and accurate sense . . . the spokesman of the whole people." By October they were calling the President's settlement between the railroads and the unions an act "of reckless daring." Clearly they were finding in the scholar President the outlines of a more heroic figure.

Other actions by Wilson made the glare of presidential power all the more alluring. The President's fight to keep Croly's and Weyl's friend, George Rublee, on the Federal Trade Commission removed their last doubts about administrative efficiency. Wilson's courageous, albeit intolerant, disavowal of German-American support seemed to promise the forceful diplomacy the editors had long demanded. By contrast, they greeted with fury Hughes's promise to enforce American rights against the British as well as the Germans. Lippmann had a decade of prejudice to overcome in bringing his older colleagues around to Wilson, but the obstacles were not insuperable.

Once he had made up his own mind, Lippmann plunged wholeheartedly into the campaign. He bombarded the Democratic managers with suggestions. By the end of September the President was reporting to Hapgood that he had spent "something over an hour and a half with . . . [Lippmann], and enjoyed it greatly." To Lippmann himself Wilson wrote promising to be guided by the young editor's suggestions in a coming speech.

All this evidently was too much for Walter Weyl, who was

not immune to the lure of power. He had resigned from the magazine in August to write a book on foreign policy, but as always he found it hard to labor in his study when excitement was afoot. In October he made a pilgrimage to the President's summer home and numbered himself among the "independents . . . pledged . . . to aid the Wilson campaign." Together with Lippmann, he offered advice on the campaign that resounded with all the virility of the *New Republic*'s nationalism. Lippmann had advised, Hapgood wrote House the next day, that Wilson somehow "live down 'too proud to fight.' " Weyl in turn suggested that Wilson take the presidency less seriously. "What the people like Roosevelt for," Weyl told Hapgood, "is because he thought the presidency lots of fun."

Three weeks before the voting, Lippmann in the *New Republic* announced his vote for a President who had grown "from a laissez-faire Democrat into a constructive nationalist." Laski had understood rightly how much the abstractions of the new liberalism meant to his friends. Lippmann insisted that his vote was going to a man who was "evolving under experience and . . . remaking his philosophy in the light of it." Yet more than philosophy was now at stake for Lippmann. His mind was filled with the notion of the role America might play in an impending showdown with Germany. The United States should not change leaders, he argued, in a period "likely to be the most crucial . . . of our time."

Croly, always more deliberate than the other two, waited until the next to last issue before the election to declare his vote. All the tortured integrity that gave his leadership its peculiar strength came forth in his confession that he would vote for Wilson for a reason that had it "been predicted a few years ago would have seemed . . . incredible." Referring specifically to his attacks on Wilson of only a few months before, Croly confessed that the President, contrary to all expectations, had actually given the Democratic party "a chance of becoming the embodiment of a genuinely national democracy."

For Croly, however, more than the new liberalism was at

stake. Though he detailed the changes in Wilson's philosophy ponderously and at length, his last and strongest argument for the President had tragic significance for the future. He still believed that Wilson in foreign policy had missed many chances "for liberating and fusing national feeling." But he was now willing to admit that the leader might have been justified in "going slow." The people, said Croly, "are listening to him and have confidence in his leadership." "Such confidence," wrote the *New Republic*'s editor with intimations of impending crisis as strong as Lippmann's, "may be salutary in the not distant future."

The *New Republic*'s own declaration for Wilson the last issue before the vote came as an anti-climax. Speaking together for their board, the editors made it even clearer that they had turned to Wilson because he seemed the best man to lead America toward an heroic role in world affairs. Living and writing in the pro-Allied East, the *New Republic* men were able to ignore the less than heroic implications of the Democrats' slogan, "He kept us out of war." The doughty nationalists of the metropolis had yet to hear from the vast isolationist hinterland west of the Hudson.

The editors, moreover, had but to look within their own ranks to find reason enough for hesitation. Most of the men around the magazine supported Wilson, but their reasons were as varied as the President's policy was ambiguous. Even within the dominant trio, Walter Weyl shared few of the belligerent notions of his two colleagues. The book, *American World Policies*, that he had left the *New Republic* in August to write showed that he expected America to stay neutral. Published early in 1917, it argued neither for "aggressive pacifism" nor a "new kind of war," but instead it pictured the United States as a benevolent mediator in the peace that would follow the exhaustion of the European belligerents. Weyl supported Wilson as the pacific and cautious leader the President actually was, not as the heroic figure Croly and Lippmann had wrought out of their own ambitions.

The young cultural nationalists—Bourne, Stearns, and Hackett—also supported Wilson as a peacemaker rather than as a forceful diplomat. Strongly opposed to American intervention in the war, they thought Wilson the best man for keeping the country out. "I fell for the 'He kept us out of war' stuff," bitterly explained Stearns later.

The more politically oriented supporters of the magazine, such as Felix Frankfurter, John Dewey, and Harold Laski, were closer to the militant position of Croly and Lippmann. They backed the Democrat for his revamped liberalism and for his campaigns for preparedness and the League. So did Ralph Barton Perry, who not long before had attacked the *New Republic* as pro-German. And Alvin Johnson later claimed that he as well as the other editors had supported Wilson as a leader who would take the country to war to avert a German victory.

Significantly, however, the most nationalistic—and the least progressive—of the *New Republic* men went for Hughes. Henry L. Stimson, for example, argued in the magazine in October that the candidates should be judged "on the preparedness issue alone." Hughes, he felt, would support all-out armament and universal military training in the interests of "national efficiency and discipline." Most significant of all was the dissent of Willard Straight. Long an advocate of universal military training and an open alliance with Great Britain, never as liberal as Croly and the others, Straight, while leaving his editors completely free, could not swallow Wilson. In a letter to the *New Republic*, he declared that he much preferred "Mr. Hughes's record and promise to Mr. Wilson's performance."

The divisions of the *New Republic* group in the election showed how dangerously ambiguous a focus nationalism was for the new liberalism. To such supporters of Wilson as Weyl, Hackett, Stearns, and Bourne, nationalism meant continued emphasis on domestic reform and a pacific foreign policy. To Croly, Lippmann, Frankfurter, Johnson, and the other supporters of the Democratic candidate, nationalism required as much reform but a much more militant foreign policy. Meanwhile, such really ardent nationalists as Straight and Stimson were willing to abandon reform in the interests of following Hughes toward total military preparedness. The determined advocates of peace, of a dispassionate weighing of the "national interest," were in a distinct minority. And the strong reliance of the new liberalism upon leadership left all the nationalists prey to the calculated ambiguities of Wilson's campaign. Though a socialist like William English Walling had also come out for Wilson and would soon beat the drums for war, it was at least clear that in doing so he was violating cherished principles. The ambiguities that cloaked the differences among Croly's followers promised serious trouble in the future.

As the election came to a climax, however, most of the *New Republic* men had nothing but high hopes for Wilson's leadership. On October 30, Lippmann thrust himself in the forefront of the campaign by sending Wilson a friendly telegram asking him to refute Senator Lodge's charge that a conciliatory "postscript" had been secretly added to the second *Lusitania* note. With Wilson's widely publicized reply to Lippmann in hand, the editors joyously in the last issue before the vote chastised Lodge for "credulity . . . [of] colossal size." Against Hughes they leveled their full editorial guns. The Republican now embodied all the evils that only a few months before they had ascribed to Wilson. Hughes's promise to assert American "rights" everywhere against everyone brought forth their full ire as pragmatists. Even worse, far worse than anything the editors had held against Wilson's leadership, was Hughes's statement that he regarded "the President as the administrative head of the government . . . [not] the political leader and lawmaker of the nation."

Inevitably, in the climactic moment of their new allegiance, the editors' thoughts turned to their old hero, Roosevelt. An editorial entitled "Wilson and Roosevelt" argued that the

Democratic President had more than fulfilled their long held image of a leader. Wilson's work had been "a continuation of the work begun by President Roosevelt." Wilson now was held to have done "more in four years to incorporate progressive principles into the national economic system than his predecessors had accomplished in twelve." The New Freedom had died of its own impracticality, while Wilson had become the embodiment of the new liberalism.

In actual fact the intellectuals had moved as far toward Wilson's philosophy as they claimed he had moved toward theirs. The alignment with Wilson much strengthened the democracy that went with their nationalism. The editors admitted just before the election that Wilson had "remained faithful to one progressive principle which Mr. Roosevelt . . . [had] entirely thrown overboard." Wilson had "sought to make the foreign policy of the country expressive . . . of the consensus of popular opinion." Wilson's tactics had been the slow ones of Fabius, but, said the *New Republic*, "a wholesome democratic method should almost always be Fabian."

The moths had charred more than a wing or two in their new flight toward power. Yet, while the editors' new awareness of the necessary slowness of democratic change was a step toward realism, it was more an accommodation to a new leader than a real conviction. Croly's and Lippmann's tones of impending crisis as they cast their lot with the President suggested that they expected nationalistic deeds rather than Wilsonian words to rouse America to its responsibilities.

The *New Republic* intellectuals had violated fewer of their principles by supporting Wilson than they would have had they continued their drive for the now definitely conservative and blatantly militarist Roosevelt. Their willingness to accommodate themselves so flexibly to both leaders, however, suggested that the bright light of power held more allure for them than firm principle. For a decade or more Herbert Croly had been searching for that man "something of a saint and something of a hero" to lead the way toward America's promise. Roosevelt, the prototype of the hero, had failed. For better or worse, the *New Republic* men had aligned themselves and their hopes for America with Wilson, with the democratic saint not the nationalistic hero.

7. "Peace Without Victory"

How well a democratic saint would fare in a world at war was another question. For the moment Weyl was off writing his book, but Croly and Lippmann remained to face that old tension in their new liberalism between nationalism and democracy. In supporting Wilson, Croly and Lippmann seemed to be accepting in foreign policy the gradualist, democratic tactics of the absent Weyl. They had indicated a willingness to wait with Wilson for the slow conversion of America to internationalism.

But would the world crisis wait? With more than half their minds Croly and Lippmann knew it would not. Even with their new loyalty to the President, they still believed that Wilson's diplomacy had placed the choice of peace or war with Germany. They stressed the conditions calling for pressure on Great Britain that Germany had attached to its *Sussex* promises. They warned that should submarine warfare be revived Germany would "not be violating any pledge." They called attention to the struggle that was going on in Germany between liberals and militarists, arguing that "on the outcome . . . [depended] the question of whether von Tirpitz will succeed in renewing an absolute submarine campaign which would draw . . . [America] into the war."

The editors late in 1916, in fact, were embracing a contradiction. They saw war as probably imminent. At the same time they sensed the unwarlike mood of the isolationist American public. They had compounded the contradiction by continuing to advocate a "new kind of war" against Germany that the people plainly did not want. Some new resolution was badly needed if the *New Republic*'s politics of power was to be aligned with support for Wilson.

The editors found a way out by abandoning their nationalistic internationalism for democratic internationalism; that is, they substituted for their politics of power a diplomacy based on persuasion and appeals to world liberal opinion. The week after the election, the *New Republic* argued that victory for either side in Europe would mean security for no one. Even if the Allies, with American help, won, they would merely write "a treaty of peace [that], like all past treaties of peace . . . would become the instigator of future wars." It was better by far to demand a "peace without victory." Their ideas of the last two years came full circle in the hope that a neutral America through a league could bring "the neutral world into the balance." The intellectuals had given up the Rooseveltian sword for the Wilsonian word.

Late in November the editors welcomed rumors that the President intended "shortly to take some positive action in favor of peace." They called on him to obtain a clear statement of national aims from both the belligerents and the major neutrals. Such a move would give liberals the world over a chance to campaign for a just peace.

Meanwhile, Wilson's thinking had followed along the editors' line. He had decided before the election (and thus before the *New Republic*'s suggestions) to launch a peace campaign if re-elected. But he hung back during the early part of December largely because pro-Allied advisers like House and Lansing advised against American interference while the Germans were winning. While working out a tentative draft of a note to the belligerents, however, the President "studied with especial care" the November 28 *New Republic* editorial that had called on him to act for peace. The draft shows how much the editors and their new leader were moving in the same direction late in 1916.

On December 18 Wilson finally sent off a much-watered-down version of his original draft. It was sufficiently strong and impartial enough to bring from the *New Republic*'s English collaborator, Harold Laski, a "hearty damn." But the other men on the magazine were exultant. They hailed Wilson's action as "a move in the direction of a positive national policy"—from them, of course, the words of highest praise. Wilson, they thought, had made himself a leader around whom liberals everywhere could rally.

Behind the scenes Wilson's peace drive brought Croly and Lippmann closer to the Administration. "Both Mr. Lippmann and I," Croly wrote to House December 26, "are more interested in doing what little we can to back up the President in his work than in anything else we have ever tried to do through the New Republic." Specifically, Croly wanted House to let them "know whether or not . . . [they were] misinterpreting what the President . . . [was] trying to do, or whether . . . [they were] under-stating or overstating the real motives of his policy."

By January 1917 Croly and Lippmann were going each week to House's apartment in New York for conferences. "I gave them food for thought to keep them on the right road," wrote House in his diary after the first conference. Gradually, too, the magazine became known as a semi-official Wilson organ. The editors never claimed as much, but the marked parallelism of the President's policy with theirs made the impression fairly general. At one point, according to Oswald Garrison Villard, the New York stock market plummeted when a *New Republic* editorial was held to forecast Administration policy.

Lippmann has since denied, however, that the magazine was ever "the organ of the Wilson administration." "We never knew any secrets," he wrote, "we never had a request to publish or not to publish anything, and we were not in a confidential relationship." Lippmann dismissed the weekly conferences with House on the ground that the President's friend "made it his business to see all kinds of people, and we were among the people he saw." He denied also any particular influence of the magazine on Wilson. "Occasionally," said Lippmann, "the

President and Colonel House took an idea from the NR as they took it from many other sources."

Lippmann, writing more than a decade later, probably forgot the details of the magazine's relation to the Administration. House, for instance, stated at one point in his diary that during a conference with Lippmann he had "outlined one or two articles for him," thus contradicting at least Lippmann's claim that the *New Republic* "never had a request to publish . . . anything." Yet, in general, Lippmann's account seems true. Very probably the impact of the editors on Wilson was slight, certainly much less than the impact of the President on them. The similar courses followed by the intellectuals and the leader early in 1917 resulted mostly, as Lippmann said, from "coincidence . . . [and] a certain parallelism of reasoning."

Yet, fortunately for intellectuals, reputation for influence rarely depends on actuality. Croly must have known in 1917 how his work with Wilson resembled the happy charade with Roosevelt of eight years before. Once again the publicist's reputed sway over a leader hung heavily upon a single phrase. Just as his incidental use of the "new nationalism" in 1909 had made him seem the prophet of the Colonel's Bull Moose revival, so now the *New Republic*'s use of "peace without victory" made him and his colleagues seem the real brains behind Wilson's new world mission. They first used the phrase in December 1916 as the title of an editorial on the German peace campaign. They used it again later in the month to describe Wilson's peace note to the belligerents. When the President himself made "Peace without Victory" the keynote of his famous address to the Senate on January 22, 1917, Croly's and Lippmann's reputation as men of influence was made.

Perhaps Wilson did get the phrase from the *New Republic*, but it was so patly descriptive of his program as to need no independent source. Yet again, like Roosevelt so many years before, the politician was generously willing to flatter the intellectuals. Two days after the speech, Wilson wrote Croly: "I was interested and encouraged when preparing my recent address to the Senate to find an editorial in the New Republic which not only was written along the same lines but which served to clarify and strengthen my thought not a little. In that as in many other matters, I am your debtor."

What particular article struck Wilson is not known, but in the weeks before several had sounded the themes of the "peace without victory" address. Wilson, speaking to the world as much as the Senate, asserted the vital stake of the United States in the post-war settlement. He stressed that the peace would have to establish "not a balance of power, but a community of power; not organized rivalries, but an organized common peace." Conceding that the United States could have "no voice" in the peace terms, Wilson was all the same sure that America would have "a voice in determining whether . . . [the terms] shall be made lasting or not by the guarantees of a universal covenant."

For the *New Republic* men the speech was a new and ecstatic culmination. "Croly told me he felt it was the greatest event of his own life," House reported to Wilson the night of the address. Lippmann also, continued House, had characterized Wilson's words "in unmeasured terms of praise." "In that address," Croly wrote the President the next day, "you have marshalled with great lucidity and eloquence every important fact which has been brought by the two and a half years of world warfare, and every important principle which the experience of that two and a half years has made authoritative and real." In the magazine the two men were equally lyric. They questioned only one point where Wilson's call for freedom of the seas seemed to conflict with the principles of their new liberalism. An absolute freedom, they argued, which would preclude blockades of an aggressor by a future league, seemed to "imply a kind of Manchester laissez-faire of the seas." Except for this, however, they had nothing but praise. Wilson's address was sufficient answer to any charge "that the sources of American idealism . . . [had] run dry."

"Idealism" might seem a strange word coming from the *New*

Republic pragmatists. In less elated moments, however, they spoke of American ideals *and* interests, the parallels in foreign policy of the democracy and nationalism of their new liberalism. The "national interest" involved the ideal insofar as it required making the world safe for democracy.

The *New Republic* men also managed to keep their new campaign for peaceful persuasion in line with their pragmatism. As pragmatists they would strive for ideals, but not allow the ideals any absolute control over the means of such striving. An editorial called "The Will to Believe" two weeks before Wilson's speech had re-evoked the spirit of William James for guidance in the world crisis. Croly and Lippmann condemned the unpragmatic souls whose "patent-leather certainties" made them demand total victory over Germany. Equally contemptible, the editors thought, were those who wanted peace at any price. The world's problems could be solved neither by absolute war nor by absolute peace. What was needed was the will and courage to face the perplexities of the pragmatic in-between.

The campaign for "peace without victory" of early 1917 brought the new liberalism to another and, in some respects, a final climax. Now the editors had a leader who was trying to use American influence to promote peace and democracy the world over. No longer were they merely appealing to liberals at home for domestic reform. Instead they dreamed that liberals in Germany, in Great Britain, "liberals everywhere," might unite behind Wilson for a new world order. Wilson's note to the powers had "sounded a call which . . . [would] restore the morale of liberalism."

The nationalism of the new liberalism had reached its apogee in internationalism. For the moment the editors regained that feeling of power and influence that had marked their days with Roosevelt. Their closeness to Wilson and House gave them the hope that in no matter how small a way they had some hold on the destiny of the world as well as of America. By late December of 1916, for instance, Francis

Hackett was convinced that Lippmann had been "at the bottom of" Wilson's peace note to the powers. Striving manfully in the stream of events, Croly and Lippmann were riding the crest just before it broke and plunged uncontrollably into war and the dissolution of all their dreams.

The "peace without victory" campaign meant that Croly and Lippmann had given up the conversion of a reluctant America to "a new kind of war" for an effort to bring a warring world to compromise peace. The editors seemed at last to have sensed the fatal flaw in their ideas about "a new kind of war." It was very improbable that such a war could in fact be kept "limited." As rumors of a return to submarine war by Germany reached the editors late in 1916, they had decided to seek peace rather than pursue a policy that might lead to holocaust.

The *New Republic*'s policy of "aggressive pacifism," moreover, had faced other serious contradictions. Perhaps their "new kind of war" against Germany was not really necessary to protect American interests. They speculated now, as they had done only in weak moments earlier, that the Allies might have to accept German hegemony in central Europe. In January 1917 they denied that Germany would use such hegemony "as [a] basis for the domination of all Europe and the world."

Yet the editors' abandonment of their "new kind of war" merely revived the critical contradiction that had bedeviled them before Norman Angell sauntered into their offices in the spring of 1915. How was a neutral nation, a nation that had not paid for its claims in blood, really to influence nations and peoples that had made the bloody sacrifices of Great Britain, France, Germany, and Austria-Hungary? Moving now themselves on the warm fringes of power, the editors were able to believe that Wilson's leadership, his hold on the liberals of the world, could actually make the influence of a neutral America count.

The return to neutrality, with its attendant emphasis upon moral suasion and world liberal opinion, was quite a change.

It meant recanting the lusty faith in power politics that had been the distinctive contribution to foreign policy of the new liberalism. While some of the change may have arisen from the practical and theoretical difficulties of the earlier policy, Wilson's influence had been the basic cause. Nothing in the world picture had altered sufficiently to bring so quick a transformation. Even the danger of war with Germany over the submarine was a thing the editors had long lived with. The intellectuals were once again responding to events, but the most relevant event seems to have been their new acceptance of Wilson's leadership.

Croly and Lippmann, of course, could not believe that they had accommodated their ideas to the leader's. Instead, as they had so often done earlier with Roosevelt, they made Wilson's ideas over into their own. In January 1917, for instance, they attacked those who claimed that Wilson believed only in a non-coercive league of verbal protests. "He has repeatedly counselled," declared the *New Republic*, "the use by the United States of physical force against an unauthorized disturber of the world's peace. . . . He is certainly to be classed among the militant pacifists who seek to place organized international force behind the institutes of the international community."

In so arguing, however, the editors were giving an explicit and almost certainly unwarranted content to a point Wilson seemed purposely to have left vague. The President's "Peace without Victory" address had called for a "peace made secure by the organized major force of mankind," but he did not make clear whether that "major force" was to be military or merely moral. That the latter was closer to his actual thought seems probable from the passage in the speech where he declared: "There must be, not a balance of power, but a community of power; not organized rivalries, but an organized common peace." Whether they saw it or not, Croly and Lippmann in following Wilson were turning from their diplomacy of power to a new strategy where "world opinion" would be the guarantee of peace. They almost admitted as much when they entitled one of their editorials in praise of Wilson "The Power of the Pen."

Wilson, furthermore, was much more sincerely neutral in his peace efforts than the *New Republic* men had any intention of being. The President by late 1916 had come to dread war far more than the intellectuals did. He also was much more disturbed than they were by the ruthlessness of Great Britain's blockade and the selfishness of the Allied war aims.

Symptomatic of the difference was a plea Croly made to Colonel House at the time for a secret mission to allay British fears. While Wilson early in 1917 seemed sincerely to want to bring about "a peace without victory for either side," Croly and Lippmann came closer to wanting merely "a peace without a *German* victory." They were generally hostile to the German peace overtures. Even though the submarine crisis seemed likely to start anew at any moment, they consistently counseled against negotiations until "after the German army had tasted defeat." When the German reply to Wilson turned out to be "unsatisfactory," they did not join the President in his feelings of disappointment. After all, they declared complacently, Wilson's peace campaign had enabled him "to enhance in the eyes of all liberals the strength of the Allied position." The great enthusiasm of Croly and Lippmann for Wilson's efforts arose far less from a desire for peace than from the exhilaration of supporting a great leader in an "aggressive American policy."

Nor was the editors' militant pro-Allied bias without significance. The very delay they and many others pressed on the President helped deprive his mediation of what very small chance for success it may ever have had. When in early December strong elements in Germany were interested in a negotiated peace, Wilson hesitated. Later in the month, when he did move, the scale of war had shifted in favor of the Central Powers and von Tirpitz was winning his fight to stake everything on the submarine. Ironically Wilson's great "peace without victory" appeal of January 22, 1917, came far too late. The speech, which had so excited Croly and Lippmann, no longer had any meaning for the German leaders on whom the question of American peace or war depended. The Germans had already decided irrevocably to unleash the submarine against neutral as well as Allied commerce. That decision, when announced at the end of the month, made continued American neutrality impossible. The prophets of the new liberalism were to have not a liberal peace without victory, but an illiberal war and a punitive peace.

EIGHT

The New Liberalism Found Wanting

1917-1925

1. A LIBERAL WAR

The *New Republic* men betrayed no dismay whatever when Wilson's leadership brought not "peace without victory" but a break in relations with Germany and eventually war. The news about the German submarine warfare in February 1917 found them with their magazine already on the presses. The editors rushed to have a new cover printed together with a special supplement that called immediately for limited hostilities and discussion of "the terms and conditions of our entry into war."

Neither plea meant much to the *New Republic*'s chosen leader in the White House. Wilson spent the two months before the actual declaration of war belatedly longing for peace. Even so, when war was actually declared in April, the *New Republic* men remained unabashed. They boasted in an editorial that they and liberals like them had been largely responsible for America's intervention. Intellectuals, they insisted, "the college professors ... physicians, lawyers, clergymen ... writers on magazines and newspapers are the numerically insignificant class whose influence has been successfully exerted in favor of American participation." Nowhere in the editorial did the editors show any awareness of how formidable was the responsibility they had assumed for the intellectuals of the country.

In the period before the declaration of war President Wilson revealed a deeper sensitivity. Closer to the actual problems, he deeply regretted Germany's action and sensed his own helplessness. Uncertain as to what was needed and what was possible, the President settled back for a period of "watchful waiting" after the break in relations. There was no sign that the great liberal leader had absorbed any of the *New Republic*'s oft-repeated lessons in power politics.

The *New Republic*'s boast of influence in bringing on the war was at best inane. Products of the progressive era, when the liberal middle class seemed actually to run the nation, the publicists did not yet realize how much the World War had changed everything. They had placed all their hopes on the effectiveness of liberals under Wilson's leadership. Even after the failure of the "peace without victory" campaign, they remained convinced that Wilson, supported by liberals at home and abroad, could mold not only the destiny of America but of the world.

What the *New Republic* men failed to see was how little actually liberals had to say about problems of diplomacy and war. Both the preparedness and league issues had first been agitated by conservatives, and the President had taken them over only at the risk of losing many of his liberal supporters in the South and West. The submarine controversy had produced similar ambiguities. The old progressive Bryan, who saw clearly where Wilson's policies would lead, had been forced out almost at once. Congress, where the old propertied middle class still ruled, had tried to resolve the submarine crisis early in 1916 by prohibiting American travel on Allied ships. The effort, however, had been beaten back by massive pressures from the Administration. Foreign policy remained firmly in the hands of Wilson and his advisors and of men in similar positions in Germany.

Nor when the editors and the President made their appeal for "peace without victory," had world liberal sentiment seemed any more effective. Von Bethmann-Hollweg had lost out to von Tirpitz in Germany, and liberals everywhere were left to make the best of a submarine war of total ferocity. Though Croly and Lippmann spoke for the ideals and interests of the great liberal middle class, that class no longer had much power in a world ruled by the hard and secret decisions of admirals and generals, diplomats and heads of state.

Unaware of the changes in the distribution of power, the *New Republic* men continued to hope that the world might be reformed by an American policy of "aggressive pacifism" under liberal tutelage. As Floyd Dell put it, Croly and Lippmann thought "a war patronized by the *New Republic* could not but turn out to be a better war than anyone had hoped."

During their campaign to bend Wilson and other Americans toward a more aggressive policy, the editors turned once again to Norman Angell for aid. Croly cabled and Lippmann wrote him in England, where the publicist was marooned by his government's refusal of a visa, for an article that could be used "immediately." "Ever since the Germans proclaimed their new submarine warfare," said Lippmann, "we have had an exceedingly hard time with the pacifists who simply want to avoid trouble." Lippmann thought America's "opportunity might almost be decisive in the history of the world," for the country at war would have a chance "to crystallize and make real the whole league of peace propaganda."

The editors had difficulty restraining their impatience with Wilson. "I am finding it hard to keep them in line because of the Pres's slowness," House confessed in his diary after one of the weekly conferences. More than impatience, however, moved Croly and Lippmann. They were convinced that Wilson's wait for actual attacks by submarines put exactly the wrong emphasis on the reasons for American intervention.

The editors had long insisted that war should be made not for the negative cause of defending American rights but rather for the positive purposes of curbing Germany's power and creating a league. Almost desperately, in 1917, they asked Wilson to avow openly that American "neutrality" had purposely discriminated against Germany. Lippmann corresponded and conferred with House and rushed to Washington to try to submit a long memorandum personally to Wilson. He argued strongly that only a frank admission of "differential neutrality" would make Americans and Europeans understand that the United States was going to war not just against the submarine but in order to secure a league and a just peace. Invoking their earlier "limited war" ideas, the editors begged the President to make the size of the American war effort depend on Allied peace terms.

Right as Croly and Lippmann may have been in terms of the results they desired, they lived in a fool's paradise. After two and a half years of supposed "strict neutrality" Wilson would have risked both his political life and popular support for war had he confessed a long-term partiality for the Allies. When the war came in April 1917 it came in the way and for the reasons the *New Republic* men had all along feared. Their private pleas to Wilson went unheeded. Publicly they had little choice but to support an all-out war that ill conformed to their liberal illusions.

2. WAR AND NATIONALISM

"You will be surprised to hear that there is not a copy of the New Republic to be purchased," wrote the young music critic Paul Rosenfeld to Randolph Bourne from an army camp in 1918. "One would imagine that the gospel of polite liberalism without tears would be circulated here extensively.... [But] those war-like conversions to the principles of pragmatism and a democratic peace are rarer than one should be led to suppose." Rare they were to be indeed, as Croly, Lippmann, and the other nationalists who had agitated for a liberal war were soon to find.

The prophets of a new liberalism plunged into the war with sublime optimism. Their joyous claim that intellectuals like themselves had brought about American intervention conveniently obscured the fact that the intervention had occurred under none of the terms and conditions they had so long demanded. A war fought by the United States for the highest ideals of peace and democracy, they thought, could not help but be a good thing. Croly and Lippmann were certain that America would not "be possessed by the usual war psychology."

Croly still believed the sentiment of nationalism in the United States to be somehow different from patriotism elsewhere. He still saw no conflict between his nationalism and the internationalism he and the others now used to justify the war. "The spirit of nationalism," he wrote early in 1917, "does not necessarily stand in the path of the organization of . . . a league."

Yet Croly had changed his position somewhat from that of 1909. The "mountain of dead bodies" he had foreseen as preceding any real progress toward international understanding had come. Wilsonian idealism seemed to be stirring the hearts of multitudes of men as well as his own. The publicist had some hope that the naked power politics of his earlier theory might be outmoded. He rightly saw that permanent peace could not be had by a mere return to the old balance of power. Real international order would now depend upon a Wilsonian "concert" of powers. The nations of the world united in a league might be willing to be "aggressive and even belligerent on behalf of the common security."

The change from "balance" to "concert" was a fruitful step, however much lost upon many advocates of power politics even today. But it robbed the nationalism of the new liberalism of much of its meaning. A strong, active, nationalized state was much more vital to the virile diplomacy of Theodore Roosevelt than to the more pacific, democratic tactics of Woodrow Wilson. Yet Croly could still argue that peace depended upon a sense of "national responsibility," upon the "knowledge and conscience . . . of the more powerful nations." The nationalists of the *New Republic* still hoped to be the brains and conscience of an America at war.

For a time the hope seemed justified. During the war the circulation of Croly's magazine soared, from about 16,000 in 1917 to a peak of around 43,000 in the early part of 1919. So widespread became its reputation as an Administration organ that in wartime Washington, according to Oswald Garrison Villard, "it was considered bad form in some official circles to be seen without it."

Amid such triumphs, however, the loyal band of writers Croly had gathered around him began to disperse. Walter Weyl, who during the months before American intervention had taken a trip to the Far East, kept away from the magazine upon his return and began writing another book on the conditions of peace. Not until a year later, when service with the War Department showed him the American drift toward war hysteria, did he return to his editorial post. Walter Lippmann volunteered for government service as soon as war was declared and became an aide to Secretary of War Baker, serving ultimately as the opposite number to young Franklin Roosevelt on an Army-Navy labor relations committee. In October 1917 he won an influential position as secretary to Colonel House's "Inquiry," a group of intellectuals assigned to explore the problems of peace-making. The next year found him a captain in military intelligence in France, where he waged a propaganda campaign against Germany so vigorously that both Lansing and Wilson began to fear for their prerogatives. Only Croly of the dominant trio stayed with the *New Republic*, confident as always that no other work was of equal importance.

Others who had once been close to Croly's venture went in various directions under the pressure of war. Theodore Roosevelt was hardly reconciled by the *New Republic*'s militancy. He could speak only of the "degenerates" of a "pestilential" magazine that rivaled even the pacifist New York *Evening Post* "from the standpoint of infamy." The patriotic Englishman, Harold Laski, also was "angered at the New Republic and its war attitude." "A 'white peace'," he wrote, "sounds like a methodist tract on the 'cruciality of the cross.' " Yet Laski, far less hysterical than Roosevelt, was willing to work for the magazine through the rest of the war with some slight hope that he was influencing "the formation of American policy." Felix Frankfurter also stayed close to the editors. He plunged into war work so vigorously, however, that Laski began to suspect that beyond Wilson's control of foreign policy Frankfurter "sponser [ed] the rest of the government."

There were other men, however, who saw the *New Republic*'s boasts about war and liberalism from a different perspective. Even before all-out war had been declared, the magazine had become a major forum where in paid advertisements and correspondence pro-war and anti-war groups battled over intervention. Young cultural nationalists like Bourne, Brooks, and Stearns came out openly against the magazine's peculiar brand of pacifism. Bull Moose progressives, socialists, liberals of all kinds split and realigned themselves on both sides of the intervention issue.

Once the war began, the opposition of the cultural nationalists to it became increasingly strong. Francis Hackett insisted later that he had never been consulted on Croly's and Lippmann's decision to advocate intervention. Though he remained as literary editor during the war, his relationship to the others, particularly Lippmann, had little of its old camaraderie. The staff contributors Bourne and Stearns were aghast at the magazine's claim that liberal intellectuals had willed the war. Stearns, in need of money, continued to write reviews, but only on the explicit understanding that he would be given only "books *not* concerned immediately with the war." Bourne turned his talents to the *Dial* and the *Seven Arts*, where his brilliantly savage editorials made him a leader among the anti-war intellectuals.

Hackett's unhappiness and the dissents of Bourne and Stearns meant the final disintegration of Croly's synthesis between political and cultural nationalism. Randolph Bourne was angry to the depths of his being at what he saw as the smug folly of the *New Republic* men. He struck directly at Croly and Lippmann and their liberal justifications of war. In an article, "The War and the Intellectuals," published in the June 1917 *Seven Arts,* he blasted the "Socialists, college professors, publicists, new republicans, and practitioners of literature" who had supported American intervention. "A war," exploded Bourne with bitter sarcasm, "made deliberately by the intellectuals!"

Bourne's attack was particularly significant because, though violently opposed to intervention, he still shared with the *New Republic* men most of the underlying principles of the new liberalism. He was still a nationalist. He pleaded for "a true Americanism" rather than the "intense colonialism" that he thought had made most intellectuals the dupes of the British. The war, he said, had "reduced to rubbish most of the . . . democratic nationalism which had been the thread of our intellectuals' life." Like most of the *New Republic* writers he still hovered somewhere between socialism and orthodox middle-class liberalism. He was still a pragmatist, but argued that the war had driven the intellectuals from their real "pragmatic work into an emotional bath of . . . old ideals." He was an internationalist, too, but he wanted not the "political internationalism" of a league of victors but rather a league that would provide "for dynamic national growth . . . [and] international economic justice."

Bourne's sharing of the *New Republic*'s liberal assumptions made him strong on the attack but less so when it came to alternatives. He argued quite rightly that the "peace without victory" campaign had been "little more than a polite play." He agreed with the *New Republic* men that specific and just peace terms should have been made the price of American intervention, but noted that no real protest was made when Wilson failed to try for as much. He was most telling when he attacked the editors' basic claim that they were merely being realistic in accepting war as an instrument for peace and democracy. The *New Republic*'s realism, Bourne contended, had not been "a stern and intelligent grappling with realities." The intellectuals had merely put themselves in the predicament of a "child on the back of a mad elephant." Bourne's indictment made sense, but nowhere did he suggest how his absolute opposition to war was to be made politically effective.

Bourne's essay created a stir among the intellectuals. The pacifist Jane Addams, for instance, asked permission to have the Woman's Peace Party reprint it and expressed gratitude that "the preposterous editorial which appeared in The New Republic . . . [had been] replied to in such a masterly manner." But, for the time being, the *New Republic* men continued undaunted in their belief in the realism of their support for the war and the Wilson Administration.

The progress of the war soon suggested that Bourne had had the firmer grip on "reality." When Great Britain finally allowed Norman Angell to revisit the United States in mid-1917, the Englishman was surprised to find that "the mob mind in the United States often outdid that of Britain in violence and silliness." By October, Croly was writing Wilson in strong protest against the Administration campaign to suppress the socialist press. "The attitude of the government in respect to the censorship," and the government's handling of propaganda "in such a way that militarists like Mr. Roosevelt are allowed to appropriate it," wrote Croly, gave the editors the "utmost difficulty writing from week to week without making an appearance of opposing what your government is trying to do." Even the militantly patriotic Willard Straight wrote back from Europe to his wife toward the end of 1917: "As I have been writing Herbert today, this war appeals to me less and less. . . . I hate unfairness and greed and stupidity—and war is all that. . . . It must in the end brutalize." So spoke the most warlike of the *New Republic* militants.

The frightening drift of the country toward hysteria led Croly, now alone at his editorial post, to a long overdue reexamination of his nationalism. In an article called "The

Future of the State" published in September 1917, he took up once again the questions of the relation between the individual and the state, and between democracy and nationalism. Much that he had to say was merely the new liberalism as before. He was still a pragmatist, and a nationalist. He remained an internationalist, too, though he denied that the problems of man would be solved "by substituting for the many petty sovereigns of today one all-embracing sovereign." But he questioned with more rigor than ever before the state's claim to "moral sovereignty." The war, he argued, was weakening rather than strengthening the sentiment of nationalism. "A formidable reaction will set in," predicted the one-time prophet of a new nationalism, "against the arrogance of the idol which demanded so many sacrifices." Croly's new doubts, however, led at first only to vague demands for greater power to workers and for strong "corporate bodies" within the state to ensure its "earning rather than conscripting the allegiance of its citizens." Rather ironically Croly was turning to the very "corporatism" to control the state that the Fascists would later use to enhance it.

By December 1917 the excesses of the war had brought about a real change in Croly's thinking. He pressed a "Counsel of Humility" upon those liberals who talked too easily to fighting men about a league or a "war for democracy." If wars were to be prevented, Croly now speculated, "the agency of prevention will not be leagues of peace and political democracy, but a chastening of the human spirit, a profound conviction of the inability of governments . . . to heal the spiritual distempers of mankind." Amidst the horrors of war, Croly, like many men, was finding solace in the ideals of his childhood.

The year 1918 brought enough evidence of how serious the "spiritual distempers" of mankind were. In America, the mass indictment of I.W.W. leaders, the trial of the editors of the *Masses*, the suppression of an issue of Oswald Garrison Villard's *Nation*, firings or resignations in protest of academic friends like Simon N. Patten and Charles A. Beard, all helped bring home to Croly and the others the dangers of rampant nationalism. Walter Weyl, now back on the masthead, found his *The End of the War* widely attacked. Its call for a just peace brought charges of "Teutonic internationalism," "Bolshevik," and "*New Republic* type of thinking." Norman Angell was accosted by plain-clothes men in New York and questioned about his knowledge of "such subversive characters as the editors of the *New Republic*." The magazine itself came under surveillance by government agents until George Creel of Wilson's Committee of Public Information identified it as a supporter of the administration.

At the same time that socialists and syndicalists were being silenced by jail sentences, anti-war liberals like Bourne were free but hardly more effective. Toward the end of 1917, the *Seven Arts* collapsed, its end hastened, many thought, by such Bourne editorials as "The War and the Intellectuals." At about the same time the *New Republic* stopped paying Bourne its regular hundred dollars a month as a staff contributor. But the young writer could easily reconcile himself to being cut off from what he now called the "NR's priggishness." "The New Republic's sense of leadership," Bourne wrote Van Wyck Brooks early in 1918, "is obnoxious because it comes not from youthful violence, but from middle-aged dignity." Bourne charged that the magazine had presented "no clear program of values," but instead had chosen "for its first large enterprise a hateful and futile war, with its fatal backwash and backfire upon creative and democratic values at home." "Instead of politics taking its place in the many-sided interests of a modern mind, it had the dominant position which it occupies in the pages of the 'New Republic.' "

During the war Bourne clung firmly to his vision of an organic national culture, a culture that would find its leadership in the "youthful violence" of a few. The vision doubtless had moral grandeur. It had the flavor of the "Democratic Vistas" with which Walt Whitman had reacted to the bleakness that accompanied and followed the Civil War. Whitman also had transcended his despair with the dream of an American cultural revival to be led by some "democratic poet" of the future. Like Bourne, Whitman had rejected politics in favor of the delights of artistic anarchism. But Bourne, like the Whitman of a half-century before, did not indicate what the world was to do while waiting for poets and other artists to save it. At best, Bourne's cultural values sharpened his capacity for criticism and resistance without giving him much grasp of the practical alternatives.

Meanwhile, the *New Republic* men were sufficiently aware that their world was not to be saved by Bourne's "youthful violence." They knew that whatever the long-range influence of inspired thinkers the solutions for immediate problems lay in politics. Even though chastened by their experiences during the war, Croly and the others continued to rely heavily upon their closeness to the Wilson administration. Walter Weyl in time joined Lippmann as an "expert" in peace planning for the House "Inquiry." Felix Frankfurter, George Rublee, and other friends continued to be prominent in the war-time government. When Wilson sent Ray Stannard Baker on a secret mission to Europe early in 1918, accreditation to the *New Republic* was used as a cover. The politically astute William Allen White, wanting a position on Wilson's peace commission late in 1918, thought it best to work on the President through Walter Lippmann. And Lippmann himself, together with Frank Cobb of the New York *World*, became at the end of the war author of an official interpretation of the Fourteen Points Wilson submitted to the Allies.

Even so, the editors were not entirely happy in their moth-like role. As the war wore on they became increasingly skeptical of Wilson's leadership. "Wilson does not energetically enough strive to maintain liberalism," wrote Weyl in his diary in July 1918. "He allows liberalism to go by default . . . [while] the liberals . . . do nothing to embarrass him." By the end of the war Willard Straight was more convinced than ever that Wilson was "not a leader." "He's no more ready for peace than he was for war," wrote Straight. "We stand in fair way of having fought the war, lost thousands of lives and millions of dollars, upsetting everything, and of not getting the peace we started for."

Such doubts multiplied as the war rushed toward a conclusion in the latter part of 1918. The prophets of a new liberalism had learned something about the workings of nationalism even in America. They also began to worry about the effects of nationalism on the peace—the normally optimistic Weyl being the most dubious. He thought that even the *New Republic*'s relatively moderate peace terms would "be so unacceptable to Germany that she . . . [would] fight to the very last." In one editorial conference before the Armistice he argued his case so violently as almost to produce a rift. "Herbert afterwards," wrote Weyl in his diary, "wondered whether I would be able to write effectively & with enthusiasm for the N. R. in view of my own pessimism, but he explained that he *wanted* me to write."

Privately Croly was almost as pessimistic, whatever the mask he wore before his editors and the public. "The indications are increasing day by day that our friends abroad have not the slightest intention of writing anything but a punitive peace," wrote the editor to Learned Hand twelve days before the Armistice. Croly was virtually certain that "any League of Nations formed as a result of the war would merely be an organization . . . for the future domination of a French, English, and American alliance." "If this anticipation proves correct," he continued, in a sentence of great significance, "our attitude will necessarily become one of agitation against the League then existing and in favor for the time being of a resumption of our isolation in foreign affairs."

Only Walter Lippmann managed to reach the end of the war as optimistic as he had been at the start. "Frankly," he wrote House of efforts to get the Allies to accept the Fourteen Points, "I did not believe it was humanly feasible . . . to win so glorious a victory." He thought Wilson's success in getting the Allies to agree to be "a climax of a course . . . as wise as it . . .

[had been] brilliant, and as shrewd as it . . . [had been] prophetic." "The President and you have more than justified," concluded Lippmann, "the faith of those who insisted that your leadership was a turning point in modern history."

Yet if Croly and Weyl at their editorial desks could not share the optimism of Lippmann in the antechambers of power, they continued valiantly to support Wilson in the hope that such backing might somehow help. Where the editors' pessimism seeped into their columns, it was expressed "constructively" in tones of caution rather than of despair. However illiberal nationalism in the United States had turned out to be, they could still pin their hopes on a liberal peace. Their last editorials before the Armistice continued to express their confidence that "one supreme statesman . . . [was] forging out of a people's war a people's victory and a people's peace."

3. APOCALYPSE IN PEACE

Walter Weyl, who had teetered for many years between liberalism and socialism, was by November 1918 much concerned about the future of liberalism. Outlining in his diary still another version of "The Class War," he said of Wilson's peace policy: "It was a capitalistic, legalistic, middle-class conception; it was an appeal to an international class interest . . . but it failed to exert any kind of moderating influence upon rival nationalistic greeds." Weyl earlier the same year had published his *The End of the War*, which contained many of the ideas that John Maynard Keynes was later to express to a wider audience in *The Economic Consequences of the Peace*. Even before the peace negotiations had begun at Versailles, Weyl had begun to suspect that only socialism within nations and an economic internationalism between nations could save the world. For Weyl, as for Keynes, middle-class liberalism was on trial.

Weyl's views were not unusual. Even Woodrow Wilson in

private conversation was willing to speculate that "the only really internationally minded people are the labor people." "The world is going to change radically," Wilson told a friend several months before the end of the war. "I am satisfied for instance that . . . all the water power, all the coal mines, all the oil fields . . . will have to be government-owned." The president admitted that such views if expressed "outside" would lead people to call him a socialist. While denying any liking for socialism, he could not see how anything less could "prevent communism." But, if the friend's report fairly reflects Wilson's private views, the President was in no position to express them publicly. As a politician in power, Wilson realized how much a leader who would lead must remain a follower.

No such political restraints bound the *New Republic* men. Yet they had already compromised their independence so badly that they could not easily present alternatives to Wilson's public plans. Public criticism might mean both a reduction of Wilson's support among liberals and an end to the editors' confidential and hopefully influential relations with the Administration. Though the President had rarely, either before the war or during it, followed the editors' ideas, his leadership seemed to offer the only hope for a decent peace. Walter Weyl in his book had hazarded an independent line in the hope of "influencing the Peace Conference." But he found that the "authorities" (presumably Colonel House) only looked on his book "stupidly, as an aggravation." As a *New Republic* editor he had no choice but to hew to Croly's line of strong support for Wilson.

As they faced the issues of peace-making after the war, nationalism, in spite of rising doubts, continued to beguile the editors. "The whole meaning and promise of Americanism is involved in the question of the League of Nations," they declared a few weeks after the Armistice. To their credit, however, the *New Republic* nationalists wanted the same peace late in 1918 as they had when war was declared. Failure to get a League or the winning of only a punitive peace, they declared, would mean that the United States had "destroyed Prussia only to emulate Prussianism."

Though the *New Republic* men maintained for a time their strong support of Wilson, they did risk some criticism of past errors. They suggested that during the fighting Wilson had become if anything too virile a nationalist. The President might have to pay for the way he had run the country during the war. His methods had been "autocratic and coercive." His appeals to patriotism and enforced unity had failed to win for him a "loyal following among the people whose support he most needed."

The *New Republic* men meant people like themselves. As the war came to an end, a great deal of strain had developed between the Administration and the editors. Only Walter Lippmann of the dominant trio soared for a time ever higher in power and influence. Croly's weekly conferences with House had ended under the pressures of the war. Weyl had written one massive report for the House "Inquiry" but after that had done little further work with the peace-making group. Even Felix Frankfurter lost much of his influence after a rift with Secretary of War Baker. Under the circumstances, Croly's insistence on loyal support almost drove Weyl to revolt. "Liberalism in America is crumbling about our ears," he wrote in his diary, "& we are doing little or nothing." The *New Republic* was "supposed to be pro-Wilson" and thus "never . . . [came] out with a statement of Wilson's failures." Weyl wanted the magazine to be "more of a fighting organ."

The Versailles conference widened the gap between the publicists and Wilson. Weyl tried but failed to get a place on the peace delegation. When he went to Paris anyway, he merely watched from the sidelines, though he knew many important members of the commission. When Willard Straight was invited to help in Paris, he soon found that what was wanted was for himself and his wife to give "little parties." He was not at all sure that he wanted "to be used in just that way." And, though Lippmann plunged into the work of the peace conference with great enthusiasm, he quickly found himself "shunted aside" by men closer to Wilson. In February 1919 he returned to New York, "going," as Harold Laski reported, "straight for the paper."

For Lippmann as well as the others the *New Republic* was about all they had left. The negotiations at Versailles soon justified all their premonitions of doom. Walter Weyl now believed that the war had brought "to the surface a new group, the proletariat." Watching the Versailles meetings in April 1919, he concluded that even Karl Marx could not have foreseen "conditions so abnormal." The peace conference was marking the "suicide of capitalism."

At home Croly and Lippmann were equally despairing. Their loyal support of the President gave way in March to a suggestion that even friends of the league had to help save Wilson by criticizing the conference. The Versailles Treaty's Article Ten became the initial point of controversy. Though it was ostensibly designed to guarantee the "territorial integrity" of members of the league, the editors saw it as a guarantee to the Allies of the spoils of victory. In late March the *New Republic* called for the defeat of the article, and thereafter became more and more critical of developments at Versailles.

A month later, Croly also decided the conference was the apocalypse of liberalism. Like Weyl, he read the struggle at Versailles as one between classes. He, too, was convinced that capitalism was "on trial," that the middle class hovered on the brink of a great and final disaster. "The conferees at Paris and most of their class associates at home," he wrote, "are vindicating Marxian socialist fatalism. . . . By their blindness . . . they are tending to bring on the revolutionary catastrophe . . . they most desire to avoid." The leaders at Versailles could escape, Croly argued, "only by . . . accepting industrial democracy as the desirable alternative to the tyranny of Bolshevism or the anarchy of unredeemed capitalism."

Publication of the terms of the completed Versailles Treaty

in May brought Croly, Weyl, and Lippmann face to face with
the worst crisis of their publicist careers. When the editors had
pondered all the details of the treaty, they decided they could
follow Wilson no longer. Robert Morss Lovett had dinner with
the editors "on the evening of the day they decided to oppose
ratification." He came away from the meeting much impressed
by "Lippmann's vigorous denunciation of the treaty as a breaking of faith with Germany and a violation of moral obligations
to the world."

Walter Weyl, who had returned from Europe just in time to
join the crucial conference, probably felt if anything more opposed to Wilson's work than the others. In the next issue the
editors denounced the Versailles Treaty as a "punic peace of
annihilation." "The immediate task for Americans," they
declared, "is to decide just how they will limit their obligations
under the Covenant." As Croly had predicted, the alternative
to a liberal peace was a return to American isolation.

Battered as the editors' nationalism had been by the events
of the war, it still became their excuse for attacking the treaty.
They wanted no part of a peace that sought "to disintegrate the
German nation." The settlement, they wrote, "was expected
to cast imperialism out of Germany and substitute a nationalism with which other nationalisms could live in peace." While
war "had brought the system of nationalism to the verge of
ruin," the peace had been "expected to vindicate nationalism
as a form of organization under which mankind could live."
Actually the Versailles conferences had merely substituted the
perverted nationalism of the victors for the rabid nationalism
of the vanquished. As such, no democratic nationalist could
support it. In the midst of their abrupt switch on peace-making,
the editors could not be expected to admit that the only force
left to nationalism came from the inertia of their own minds.

The decision to reject the Versailles Treaty took real courage. Prophets of internationalism, ardent advocates of American intervention to secure a liberal peace, Croly, Weyl, and
Lippmann in repudiating Wilson also faced the humiliation of

repudiating all they themselves had stood for. It meant the final end of their closeness to men in power. It meant standing rigidly on principle rather than pragmatically doing the best with the materials at hand. And it meant the loss of thousands of *New Republic* subscribers just when the chance for real influence seemed closest.

The editors themselves saw their sacrifices as the only way to preserve the things they most valued. In subsequent weeks they showed that liberalism, the new liberalism, was their most vital concern. In so far as liberalism had been on trial at Versailles, so now the survival of liberalism depended upon the rejection of the Versailles Treaty. "In our opinion," said Croly, Weyl, and Lippmann in May 1919, "the Treaty of Versailles subjects all liberalism . . . to a decisive test." Liberalism depended on "the ability of the modern national state to avoid . . . irreconcilable class conflict." Wilson's treaty, however, "merely . . . [wrote] the future specifications for revolution and war." Only rejection of the peace and its coercive league offered any hope of a just peace and a league that liberals could support. Otherwise, the new liberalism would be left to be crushed "between the upper and lower millstones of reaction and revolution."

4. THE DEAD AND THE DISILLUSIONED

"I have had a rather forlorn feeling of recent years," wrote Croly to Learned Hand in 1922, "that the N. R. was making a difference between me & the friendship of some of the people I most loved, and it made me wish to give up the *New Republic*. But I hope those years are over." To Hand and many others, in fact, the *New Republic*'s bitter turn on Wilson and the Versailles Treaty had seemed inexplicable. Though consistent with the editors' long campaign against an imperialist peace, the abandonment of Wilson actually ended their internationalist dreams. Croly, Weyl, and Lippmann, of course, hoped that

American repudiation of the treaty would force a revision. But with Germany prostrate, and France and Great Britain ascendant, revision could hardly be expected. The drive for revision would come, but only many years later and by a German nationalist quite different from the *New Republic* men. "If I had it to do over again," confessed Lippmann a decade later, "I would take the other side. . . . We supplied the Battalion of Death with too much ammunition."

As it was, the liberals of the *New Republic* found themselves marching shoulder to shoulder with the isolationist battalion. Their hope that liberals the world over might yet secure a liberal peace quickly vanished in the bitter wrangling over the treaty. Even the liberals began to desert them. They soon lost over 10,000 subscribers. At the same time the rival *Nation*, which had been revitalized by Oswald Garrison Villard in 1918, soared from some 10,000 to over 38,000 by 1920. Good friends like Hand turned cool. The issues continued to come forth each week, but the old air of confidence was gone. The editors could only moodily rehash past triumphs and past failures. By 1921 only Croly of the original founders remained. Death, political dissent, and the feeling that a liberal journal lacked realism had removed the others.

Willard Straight died late in 1918 deeply skeptical that anything good could come of the war whose virtues he had once celebrated. His widow, following both her own inclinations and Straight's will, continued the subsidy that kept Croly and his magazine going.

Randolph Bourne also died the same year. Though he succumbed to a disease, just as the well-fed, healthy Straight had done, a legend quickly arose that made him a hungry, neglected martyr to war resistance. But Bourne's martyrdom was spiritual, not physical. Nor were his spiritual sufferings during the war any worse than Croly's. The young writer left behind him an unfinished article called "The State," which bitterly condemned war as "the health of the state." Yet, oddly enough, Bourne with his loathing of rabid patriotism and the omnivorous state did not much differ from the post-war Croly. Both men continued to call for a humane, democratic nationalism, for a proper pragmatic balance between realism and idealism, and for new "corporate bodies" to chasten the power of the state. Both of them ended up by seeing the working masses as the group that would force the state to "earn . . . rather than conscript . . . the allegiance of its citizens."

There were, of course, significant differences, but, with respect to these, Croly's position seems the more plausible. The very realism with which Bourne had viewed the causes and consequences of the war drove him to an unrealistic anarchism. To Bourne the state had become totally evil, while for Croly it remained a necessary "agency of coordination" for labor unions, corporations, and other elements within the nation. Bourne put much more emphasis upon the state as the tool of the "privileged classes" than Croly was yet willing to do. Bourne also saw *all* wars as wicked and illiberal, while Croly continued to argue that some wars might serve a liberal purpose. Though neither Bourne nor Croly would ever have to face the question of war against the rabid nationalism of Nazism, Croly would have been better equipped for the challenge.

Bourne's leading role among the young intellectuals was taken over after the war by Harold Stearns. In 1919 Stearns wrote *Liberalism in America*, a primer for the middle-class intellectual much like those of Croly, Weyl, and Lippmann a decade earlier. In it he tried to rescue as much as possible from liberalism's post-war debacle. Stearns's liberalism, however, was very different from that of Croly, Weyl, and Lippmann. Much of his criticism of wartime liberals focused, in fact, on the *New Republic* men. Again and again he used the magazine's editorials to show just where liberalism had gone wrong.

The alternatives that Stearns presented to the *New Republic*'s liberalism combined clear insight and muddle-headedness. He was right when he denied that liberalism, whether new or old, could any longer be a viable political creed. He showed sense in his redefinition of liberalism as merely a "tolerant and rationalistic temper" that might characterize anyone from a socialist to a conservative. Equally reasonable was Stearns's rejection of the nationalism of the new liberalism. Like the *New Republic* men, he was appalled by the excesses of the recent nationalistic war. He went too far, however, when he held the national government to be useless in the future as an instrument of liberal reform.

Stearns came to grips with one of the major failures of the *New Republic* men with his criticism of the leadership emphasis of the new liberalism. With the sympathy of one who had not been totally immune to the temptation himself, he showed how the editors and others had been seduced by hopes for prestige and power into supporting a leader like Wilson. Stearns saw clearly how little the President had been influenced by the intellectuals. He argued rightly that there was an inherent incompatibility between the intellectuals and the prima donnas of politics. Publicists would keep more of their independence and accomplish more if they worked on the "great man" by proselytizing lesser leaders and their followings.

Equally impressive was the way Stearns handled the relationship between pragmatism and reform. Striking directly at the *New Republic* men, he showed how again and again they had condoned Wilson's mistakes and hypocrisies because they hoped by working in the stream of events to control the situation. Yet Stearns did not reject pragmatism as a philosophy for reformers. He was right in his claim that pragmatism could justify staunch resistance as well as compromise, firmly articulated ideals as well as accommodations to "utility."

Stearns's *Liberalism in America* was but one sign among many of the collapse of most of Croly's dreams. The post-war years saw the rapid dispersal of the *New Republic*'s band of editors. Robert Hallowell and Francis Hackett brought an ironic denouement to Croly's cultural nationalism by joining the post-war tide of American expatriates. Charles Merz went to work for the New York *World*; Alvin Johnson became director of New York's New School for Social Research; while Croly's close friend, Philip Littell, was taken by death. For the diffident but warm-hearted Croly each departure, as well as Littell's death, meant a wrenching loss.

Walter Weyl had also died, of cancer, in November 1919, at the age of forty-six. In the months before his fatal illness Weyl had turned once again to "The Class War," that major revision of his political philosophy that he had begun seven years earlier. The war, he admitted in his diary, "has rudely shattered my optimism concerning the progress of humanity." He began to speculate on alternative titles for his book. Perhaps it should be "The Crisis of Capitalism," he mused, or should it be "The Collapse of Capitalism"? Noting the poverty and bankruptcy that followed the fighting, Weyl felt that the war had made "a clean sweep of the Bourgeoisie."

Yet Weyl did not abandon his middle-class liberalism easily. The confirmation by the peace conference of many of Marx's predictions did not make the economist jump on the dialectical bandwagon. Class war still had for him no iron inevitability. He thought it perfectly possible that recovery in Europe might be won "by a new and more capable bourgeois class."

The survival of Bolshevism in Russia against tremendous odds shook Weyl's faith in liberalism even further, however. He concluded that, despite the intervention of the Allies, the communist experiment could not "be easily crushed." He faced the challenge of Communism to his own philosophy squarely. "Here we have," he noted, "an institution which is flatly opposed to our ordinary conceptions of Democracy and yet gains the adherence of millions of supporters. What does this mean? Is it a criticism of democracy as it has hitherto developed . . .?" Weyl marked a major shift in his thinking when he decided that the issue was "not one of political forms but of class supremacy within a nation."

For the United States, however, Weyl was still "not in favor of Bolshevism." The great steel strike of 1919 convinced him that America was "approaching ignorantly and blindly the most disastrous (or the reverse) labor crisis in . . . history." But, he added, "we do not need or want—as I see it at present—a dictatorship of the proletariat." He thought there was still a chance that the United States would progress much as before, "but more rapidly in the future." But such progress would come not through the efforts of middle-class liberals but "by the unfolding power of the wage-earning class."

Though something less than a wild-eyed radical in his final months, Weyl did decide to abandon "bourgeois reform movements" altogether. He became more and more impatient with what he saw as "the increasing conservatism of the NR." The magazine turned down an article called "Tired Radicals," in which he satirized onetime liberals who had given up the fight and retired to prosperous disillusionment. Weyl decided to break with Croly and Lippmann entirely, convinced that Oswald Garrison Villard's *Nation* provided a better outlet.

In the end Weyl abandoned most of the ideas he had contributed to the new liberalism. Gone was the great mass of embattled consumers who once were to have brought the liberal millennium. Gone, too, was his hope that America's "social surplus" would bring progress without a class struggle. The success of the Soviets completed the disintegration. In August 1919, in the last political entry in his diary before his death three months later, Weyl raised once again the central question of his still unfinished "Class War." "What," he asked, "is the issue presented by this Bolshevik denial of democracy? . . . Are our own skirts clean? . . . Is our democratic government adaptable & can it be made adaptable . . . to a real Industrial Democratization such as the people want?" "The ultimate test," said Weyl, answering a lifelong question for the last time, "is survival."

Walter Lippmann, who had kept Weyl's "Tired Radicals" out of the *New Republic* because he thought it was directed at him, left the magazine in 1920 to become an editorial writer for, and ultimately editor of, the New York *World*. The debacle at Versailles had driven him, like Weyl, to revert to the central question of his publicist life—the relationship between public opinion and political action. He had seen the record of Wilson both in war and peace as largely a matter of the president's "Jeffersonian Democracy," of his "naïve confidence in the character of popular support." By the end of 1919 Lippmann was proclaiming in the *Atlantic Monthly* that the ignorance of the public was "the basic problem of democracy."

Lippmann's profound disillusionment with most of the assumptions that had sustained the new liberalism came forth most clearly in his *Public Opinion* of 1922. He wrote with his customary brilliance, but also showed a mature penetration that had been lacking in his earlier books. His major aim was to tear to shreds the notion of a democracy based upon an informed, rational, and intelligent public. Lippmann argued that modern man reacted not to reality but to "pictures in his head," pictures grotesquely and inevitably distorted by modern communications. For Lippmann the essential problem was how to work out some successful relationship between the misguided or apathetic "outsiders" and the knowledgeable "insiders." Lippmann did not feel that the masses would help much. "Political decision," he wrote, "is inevitably the concern of comparatively few people." Nor would reliance upon a clash of "interests" work. In the modern world men could rarely clearly see their interests or pursue them rationally. "No electoral device, no manipulation of areas, no change in the system of property," wrote Lippmann, "goes to the root of the problem." The problem for Lippmann was how to bring fact, understanding, and action into some kind of viable relationship. His solution, for the moment, was the organization of impartial and independent "intelligence bureaus" co-ordinated by a "central agency" that could go to the facts and provide some basis for judgment between warring partisans.

Though Lippmann's post-war views were part of a conservative trend in his thought that had begun as early as 1912, the war had not so much driven him to the right in politics as above it. In his work for the *World* and later for the conservative New York *Herald Tribune*, he saw himself providing the rational, dispassionate commentary he had hoped organized "intelligence bureaus" might provide. Thus he remained the middle-class, liberal intellectual, but instead of turning to labor and farm groups after the fashion of Stearns and Weyl, he spoke to the elite, to the "insiders" he saw as really running things. During the 1920's he continued under the liberal banner, partly because Harding and Coolidge were hardly the men to stir the enthusiasm of the "enlightened conservative" he had become at heart. More and more he turned away from politics to philosophy and morals. He wanted to find some rational basis for that "virtuous populace" without which the "philosopher kings" he had appealed to in *Public Opinion* could not rule. His matured speculations appeared in 1929 as *A Preface to Morals*, wherein he sought some non-religious "principle of order" by which rational men might live.

When Herbert Croly took up Lippmann's *A Preface to Morals* as "the first bit of serious reading" he attempted during what turned out to be his final illness, he was not impressed. "He treats . . . [the subject]," Croly wrote Hand, "with just as much clearness and even more versatility than he ordinarily gives to his work, but the journalistic method tends to make him pursue the obvious relation of ideas one to another rather than dig into the meaning of any particular idea." Croly had wondered many years before when he hired Lippmann for the *New Republic* whether the younger man would develop from a "political journalist" into a "political philosopher." For Croly, at least, the final answer was negative.

Croly did not live to see what happened to Lippmann a few years later when another progressive movement stirred the country. The New Deal found Lippmann in opposition. So staunch was his conservatism that he voted for Alfred Landon in 1936. The next year found him publishing *The Good Society*, in which he condemned almost everything the New

Deal stood for. Lippmann now reverted to the old liberalism of natural laws and individual rights that once he had so effectively satirized. He condemned all those who called for a "planned new social order." He rumbled against "bureaucrats" and against leaders who forgot that they were "only men," who could "know only a little" and could "do only a few things." He called for a decentralized society that would respond to the dictates of the "common law" rather than to "overhead administrative commands." Thus spoke one of the early prophets of the new liberalism when the philosophy seemed once again to have some force in the land.

As for Croly, about all he had left of his pre-war dreams was the *New Republic*, and that more a specter than a thing of shining promise. Only George Soule and Felix Frankfurter remained of the early editors and supporters. New men such as Robert Morss Lovett, Edmund Wilson, Eduard Lindeman, T. S. Matthews, and Robert Littell joined the paper, but, with the exception perhaps of Wilson, they lacked the buoyancy and brilliance of the original staff. Villard's *Nation* remained a serious rival, as did Albert J. Nock's *Freeman*, which attracted such old friends as Harold Stearns, Charles A. Beard, and Van Wyck Brooks.

Briefly early in 1920 the magazine recaptured something of its old fervor. Once again Croly succumbed to his obsessive search for a leader. The new hero was none other than Herbert Hoover, the efficient and humanitarian leader of war relief. The *New Republic* helped start a presidential boom, which was given real impetus by the New York *World*. But, though Hoover began by calling himself an "independent progressive," he soon joined the regular Republicans and declared himself for Harding. Croly had had his last flirtation with a hero. "When Mr. Hoover rallied to a candidate such as Harding," said the editor sourly later in the year, "middle of the road liberalism skidded ... until it reached the declivity of the far right."

With Hoover ironically the last best hope for a positive

liberalism, Croly and his magazine went on the defensive. In the grim post-war days, however, even a negative stance had a semblance of vigor. Though Weyl in his last days thought the magazine was "trimming," Lippmann remembered its resistance to the "Red Scare" as his "most exhilarating experience" while an editor. In truth, Croly's stand was strong and courageous. The magazine was equally bold in its opposition to the Allied intervention against the Bolsheviks in Russia. And with even more bravery, considering that most of its readers probably still supported Wilson, it remained inveterately hostile to the Versailles settlement.

Yet Croly, too, like Weyl and Lippmann in their different ways, had abandoned most of his dreams of a new liberalism. The war ended his hope for a cultural renaissance that had once been the starting point and inspiration of his nationalism. He continued to write about architecture for the *Architectural Record*, but his mind no longer focused on that union of art and life that had once so enthralled him. Croly had long since sacrificed the cultural aspects of his nationalism to the political. He ended up by losing both.

In the 1920's few of the young men who had once worked with Croly tried any longer to beat the drums for a cultural revival. Van Wyck Brooks quoted extensively from Croly in *The Ordeal of Mark Twain* while trying to show the cultural values that Twain had betrayed. But Brooks's voice was a lonely one. More typical was Harold Stearns, who in *Liberalism in America* thought "the prospect of the artist in America . . . not a particularly fortunate one." Like Croly ten years earlier, Stearns believed a real "native growth" of art in the United States would have to await the solution of political and social problems. Others of the oncoming generation rejected entirely that fusion of art and politics that had once seemed so promising. "How tired I am of the perpetual ferment of the New Rep[ublic]," wrote the young poet Hart Crane in 1921, speaking for his generation. "These gentlemen are merely clever at earning their livelihood in clean cuffs." In the debacle of the once proud dream of a vibrant culture, Croly's mind turned from the ghost of Wilbur Littleton to the ghosts of Flanders fields.

The war with its dead finally led Croly to abandon political nationalism as well as cultural nationalism. More and more his mind turned to the speculations he had begun during the war about how rival loyalties might be created to restrain the excesses of nationalism. It was a much chastened nationalist who complained, as Croly now did again and again, that "the most vital religion of the present day consists in the worship of the state." It was Croly's greatest misfortune that such a thought had not occurred to him a decade earlier.

Croly was still not willing to admit, however, that his nationalistic ideas in foreign policy had been a mistake. When the *Nation* attacked him in 1920 for having helped destroy liberalism by favoring war, Croly demurred. The intervention, he argued, had been inevitable. American participation had been the only alternative to a German victory and the only chance for a just and enduring peace. At worst the pro-war liberals had been guilty of one "serious miscalculation." Croly admitted that he had had false notions "of what the psychology of the American people would be under the strain of fighting a world war." The American people, in fact, had turned out to be malevolently nationalistic. They had fought the war for vengeance and victory, not for the just and enduring peace Croly wanted. Croly's candor was admirable, but his studies of both American and European history before the war might well have warned him of the malevolence that crouched always just beneath the surface of nationalism.

Yet the war did make Croly see how dangerous had been his attempt to center a reform movement upon the idea of nationalism. In the post-war years the word disappeared from his vocabulary as he sought other means of giving force and direction to liberalism. By the latter part of 1922 he was preaching against the pressures for conformity and centralization in American life. He advised liberals in search of "worthy political activity" to turn to their local communities. Local consumer and producer co-operatives, local schools, and local churches, he thought, might stem the trend toward "national aggrandizement." Such became the final way toward "surely good Americanism" for the onetime prophet of the New Nationalism.

Croly's retreat to the community also meant the abandonment of his "metropolitanism," of that once grand vision he had had of New York as the wellspring and focus of national culture. The idea no longer appeared in his writing, and he left the field to a new group of "regionalists" who stressed the need for local variety in American culture.

During the 1920's Croly recovered from the almost neurotic preoccupation with leadership that had seemed to flow by some process of inversion from his own exaggerated diffidence. The flurry for Hoover in 1920 showed with what difficulty the obsession subsided, but in the end Croly achieved an intelligent skepticism about the performance of great leaders. Roosevelt's once brave Bull Moose crusade now moved Croly only to cynicism. Roosevelt's party, Croly declared, had "included not only every shade of liberalism but almost every degree of conservatism." For all the Colonel's magnetism, "too often he [had] beguiled rather than convinced his converts."

Wilson's assumption of liberal leadership had led only to worse catastrophes. Domestic reform, argued Croly, had been hamstrung by the persistence of a vacuous Jeffersonianism in the President's thought. Even more destructive had been Wilson's leadership in war and peace. Wilson's suppression of all dissent during the war and his abandonment of all principle at Versailles had "shattered what was left of American progressivism as a coherent body of conviction." From his new perspective Croly during the 1920's no longer sought that great leader, "something of a saint and something of a hero," who might rally the reforming hosts.

Yet Croly's post-war writings dwelt on the mistakes of past leaders rather than upon any "miscalculation" of his own in making so much of the principle of leadership. He did not generalize his experiences with Roosevelt and Wilson into a realization that national reform leaders by the very circumstances of their rise to power must act more as a restraint upon than an inspiration for their reformist supporters. Croly never quite realized how badly he had been seduced away from his own most cherished ideals by the glamour of the men of power.

If the war led Croly largely to abandon the ideas of nationalism, metropolitanism, and leadership, it did not make him less the internationalist. Though disillusioned with Wilson and Versailles, he was still sure that the ideal of a world community would in the future "become increasingly articulate and aggressive." But no longer was Croly the theorist of power politics and the balance of power. Instead Croly and his magazine now stressed the common economic problems that might become the basis of peace between nations. In the same vein, Croly insisted over and over again that only the rise of strong labor parties would give countries enough "moral self-possession . . . to invalidate the moral and political pretexts for wars between nations." But here, too, Croly was belatedly reaching conclusions that had occurred long before to thinkers of socialist persuasion.

What then remained of Croly's new liberalism? In truth, not much. He realized that liberalism could no longer hope to be a coherent set of doctrines and tactics for middle-class reformers. Instead he agreed with Stearns that liberalism was at best a tolerant, pluralistic, experimental attitude that might characterize many groups. Pre-war liberals like himself, Croly rightly argued, had failed to see how much their ideas kept "economic and social power predominantly in the hands of one class." What was needed now was for "American labor . . . [to] obtain the candid, discriminating yet loyal support of a sufficiently numerous group of liberals who belong to other classes." But neither the liberals nor the middle class could any longer hope to be the real force behind reform. That force, concluded the onetime prophet of a new liberalism, would come by "strengthening wage-earners to resist capitalist domination."

In practical politics Croly's abandonment of liberalism brought a sharp swing to the left. The shift was open and uncompromising. In 1920, he identified himself as "an American who [had] called himself a reformer from 1890 to 1908, a Republican insurgent from 1908 to 1912, and since 1912 a progressive." Admitting that he had "shared most of the mistakes and illusions of the reformers, insurgents, and progressives," he now flatly declared his support "for the Farmer-Labor candidate for the presidency." Four years later he still supported the farmer-labor cause as it merged with the Progressive-party candidacy of Senator La Follette. In 1928, just before the paralytic stroke that ended his work, he was still convinced that real reform would depend upon "a combination of conscious and discontented economic classes." Croly's disillusionment with the new liberalism was deep and enduring.

The leftward bent of Croly's post-war thought, however, did not mean the rejection of all his earlier ideas. He continued, for instance, to be a pragmatist. He also stuck to his role as a middle-class liberal intellectual. He wanted as much as ever to preserve democracy, to prevent economic exploitation, and to avoid class warfare. "In so far as liberals are pragmatists," he wrote in 1921, "they are bound to attach importance to continuity of results." Continuity meant achieving reforms "without the shock of revolutionary dislocation." Though his turn from nationalism had left Croly a quasi-socialist, it did not make him a revolutionary. In espousing the farmer-labor cause he had merely chosen a new means for gaining the ends of the new liberalism.

Croly's shift to the left in politics was matched by what might be termed a move to the right in philosophy. The agony of the post-war disillusionments brought him full circle in his religious beliefs. He turned once more to the faith of his father, to that "religion of humanity" that had made his youth a mystic orgy. The Versailles conference started him brooding about how the reform and revival of religion might avoid the ultimate "choice between capitalism and revolutionary social-ism," on how once again "the peremptory gospel of human brotherhood" might be made meaningful in the lives of men. Soon he came to believe that the main failure of liberalism had been its encouragement of "an increasing divorce between science and religion." Liberals, he argued, had concentrated too much "on the exercise of political and economic power," and not enough on the way that the insights of experimental science, combined with the force of religion, might bring a real "regeneration" of mankind. In 1920, he gathered his ideas together in a book. But, though the book was announced for publication and already in type, Croly decided that his ideas were at best "journalistic" and withdrew it.

Croly spent most of the seven years of active life left to him trying to achieve that reconciliation of religion and science that had been his childhood dream. He met frequently with various religious groups. He plunged deeply into "behavior-ism," and published in the *New Republic* his speculations on the way religion and science might work together to "illumi-nate human nature." The collapse of the farmer-labor move-ment in 1924 drove him more and more within himself. He tried to find a personal discipline that would bring him the peace he had once sought for all society. In 1925, he came under the influence of Alfred Richard Orage, the former editor of the *New Age* in London, who was himself a disciple of the Russian mystic, Gustave Gurdjieff. In time Gurdjieff himself arrived on a visit to America, and Croly went deeper and deeper into the discipline of the cult. Whether he found an answer there remains appropriately shrouded in mystery.

In the end Croly had suffered the fate of Wilbur Littleton. The publicist had tried to work in throne room and market place while searching for the truths sacred to intellectuals. A paralytic stroke cut him down two years before his death in 1930. Littleton's effort to build both mansions and churches had ended in frustration and self-destruction. So too with Croly, though the disintegration of body and spirit came more slowly. The brilliant and original stand for the truth as he saw it in *The Promise of American Life* had given way to the half truths and rationalizations of his later books and the *New Republic*.

Croly himself had been half hero and half saint. He had rarely been able to bring the two parts of his being into working harmony. While in the realm of theory he had been able to combine the harsh truths of *Realpolitik* with warm dreams of a religion of humanity, the real world was less malleable. Croly could not find a resolution for his own inner tensions in either the heroic Roosevelt or the saintly Wilson. Both associations ended in frustration and bitter recrimination. Croly himself worked best neither as saint nor as hero, but as prophet. Both early and late he would have fared better had he left power to the politicians and mysticism to the theologians.

What has endured of Croly's work is the creed he set forth in *The Promise of American Life*. The new liberalism was to have its fullest realization in practice during the era that dawned just as Croly died. Yet, Croly reached his greatest stature as prophet when he realized early in the 1920's how inadequate the new liberalism was even for his own relatively uncomplicated time.

5. The Future of Liberalism

Although only a few men like Croly and Weyl realized it then (and too few realize it now), the years during and following World War I marked the crossroads of liberalism. After the war in Great Britain and elsewhere liberal parties gave way to labor or social democratic groups. In the United States, on the other hand, the socialists during the 'twenties virtually disappeared while liberals were reduced to an ineffectual few. The absence of a real left in America allowed liberalism—the new liberalism—to revive during the depression 'thirties in a way that was impossible in Europe. But the new liberalism proved as inadequate during the New Deal era as it had been during the early days of the *New Republic*.

Croly and Weyl were spared having to watch the failure of their new liberalism in the later reformist era. The nationalistic reforms of the New Deal did not cure the economic depression. As in 1914, only a rearmament program did that. Nor did Franklin Roosevelt's seemingly skillful playing of power politics help either to prevent World War II or bring about America's necessary participation under auspicious circumstances. Had Croly and Weyl lived, they would probably like Lippmann have been critics of the New Deal—but from the left, not the right. Chastened by their experiences with Theodore Roosevelt and Woodrow Wilson, they might even have resisted the lure of the second Roosevelt's personality. In their proper role as independent intellectuals, they might have provided the balanced and informed criticism from the left that the New Deal so badly needed.

There were, of course, men in the 'thirties who essayed such a role. John Chamberlain put the case succinctly in his *Farewell to Reform*. Bruce Bliven, when he took over Croly's editorial post on the *New Republic*, sniped at the New Deal from a quasi-Marxist perspective. But men like Chamberlain and Bliven had reacted to the disillusionments of the progressive era far more violently than Croly and Weyl. They had been driven to a Marxist metaphysic that had as little hope of changing America as the New Deal's patchwork measures. Bliven and Chamberlain (and Lippmann for that matter) had been too young to see the progressive era from the Croly-Weyl perspective of McKinley conservatism. Consequently, the younger men had not felt the full sweep of the great burst of democratic enthusiasm that had been the progressive movement's most tangible element. They did not share the faith in the democratic pursuit of essentially socialist ends that Croly and Weyl kept even amidst post-war disillusionments.

Enthralled by Marxist absolutes, most of the leftist intellectuals in the 'thirties could not see the revived new liberalism as a step, however inadequate, in the right direction. Rather than seeking popular leverage for real reform they bade farewell to all reform. Though they rightly attacked the New Deal for its feckless incoherence, they were equally disdainful of the disciplined pragmatism that was another of America's legacies from the progressive era. They were as absolutist in their belief in the dialectic as was the rightist Lippmann in his search for absolute moral values to reform the body politic.

As a result, the Marxist intellectuals, while rightly condemning the New Deal for not doing even the possible, themselves asked the impossible. The depression brought no revolutionary proletariat to the forefront in the United States. Though the "inherent contradictions" of capitalism became clear enough, the New Deal with its revamped liberalism proved that the system could be at least patched and kept running. Franklin Roosevelt's flexible response to labor and agrarian pressures (particularly after 1935) was enough to prevent the revolutionary cataclysm to which the extreme leftists looked forward. Most intellectuals of democratic and liberal persuasion become partisans of Roosevelt and the Democrats. Most of the moderate left abjectly defended the New Deal's ineffective measures against the conservative Jeffersonian Liberty League, instead of subjecting those measures to constructive criticism. Frustrated members of the extreme left like Chamberlain had only the questionable satisfaction of swinging from the absolutes of the left to those of the right.

The experience of intellectuals during the progressive and New Deal eras remains strikingly relevant. The evidence is strong that the 1960's will mark for the United States another progressive decade. A reaction has long been brewing against Eisenhower's attempt to turn the country as far back as possible toward McKinley Republicanism. In the cities and states, where the first progressive movement had its start, reform mayors and governors have become remarkably prevalent. Each election has increased the number of liberals in Congress, politicians as talented and aggressive as any that challenged the Old Guard during Theodore Roosevelt's years as president. Rising prices, a new wave of corporate consolidations, increased unrest about the "labor problem," a stronger concern for civil liberties, all are signs that history is not ungiven to approximate repetitions.

Intellectuals like David Riesman, C. Wright Mills, and John Kenneth Galbraith have had a part in the new ferment. But such critics of society have, like the muckrakers, been more apt at description than prescription. The negative picture of conformity and corruption in the midst of aimless affluence has been made clear enough. The reluctance of farm groups and unions to pursue anything but their special interests and the rear-guard apathy of the huge new white-collar class have been demonstrated with an enervating repetitiousness. What is missing is men who are willing to trace out new lines of thought and action as Croly, Weyl, and Lippmann did in their early books. Just as they demolished the old individualistic liberalism in favor of democratic nationalism, so new writers are needed to bring forth the social-democratic alternatives to the new liberalism. Yet, for all the rich experience of a half century, the new age of reform finds American intellectuals as yet woefully unprepared.

In part the unpreparedness results from the surprising ideological sterility of the New Deal era. Except for the rather special works of Thurman Arnold and Adolf A. Berle, Jr., little in the way of new thought emerged despite an enormous ferment. Yet, in view of the circumstances that evoke new patterns of thought from intellectuals, the philosophical poverty of the period is not surprising. Except for the depression, the circumstances and problems of men in the New Deal period were much like those of the progressive era. What changes had taken place were masked, furthermore, by the depression itself with its pressing problems. Rather than provoking new insights from the intellectuals the depression seems to have left them in a state of shock.

When the experiences of Croly, Weyl, and Lippmann are taken in this perspective, they are quite revealing. As intellectuals the three men were lucky. They lived in one of those periods that occur from time to time when great events demand a new ordering of thought. While the mind of the intellectual like that of the ordinary man responds chiefly to events, his response has a special precociousness. Croly, Weyl, and Lippmann had the genius to see the bent of their time long before most other men, and to work out in response to it a new liberal philosophy.

The great changes that have taken place in the world since World War II may in similar fashion bring a thorough revision of the new liberalism. Automation, the trend to corporate consolidations, vast shifts of population both geographically and occupationally, a new militancy among minority groups are but a few of the massive domestic changes. On the foreign scene the polarization of the world power conflict, the great weight of the United States in the world's economy, a technological revolution in warfare, and the awakening of Asia, Africa, and Latin America have created a world unlike anything known to either progressives or New Dealers. With the experience of two reform movements to build upon, the time is ripe for a rethinking of the new liberalism.

The experiences of the *New Republic* intellectuals with Roosevelt and Wilson, for instance, raise serious questions about the leadership emphasis of the new liberalism. There is a need for a proper definition of the relationship between intellectuals and great popular leaders. The careers of Croly, Weyl, and Lippmann suggest that intellectuals can at best hope to have but a slight and tangential influence on the politicians. In the cases of Roosevelt, Wilson, and the *New Republic* men the flow of influence ran mostly the other way, from the politicians to the publicists. On occasion the influence of the practical politician added an extra note of realism to the intellectuals' speculations. More often it led to rationalizations and half truths that much diminished the publicists' effectiveness before their wider audience. Intellectuals should maintain a proper skepticism about their chances of influencing men of power. Only such skepticism can breed the independence necessary for their best work.

When viewed with sophistication the relationship of publicist and politician can be of mutual benefit. Much of the attention and prestige that Croly and his later *New Republic* colleagues won arose from their reputation, however unwarranted, of being highly influential first with Roosevelt and then with Wilson. The relationships had that delightful circularity whereby the publicists' repute for closeness to the politicians gave them prominence and a following. The politicians were then inclined to cultivate the publicists because of the following, thus strengthening the appearance of influence—and so the spiral continued. Yet, while largely self-generating, the spiral of reputed influence and enhanced prestige has its natural limits. Intellectuals work with principles, while politicians must practice. The abrupt and rancorous conclusions of the relationship of the *New Republic* men to both Roosevelt and Wilson suggest how strong are the inherent tensions. Even so, no harm need come to either politician or publicist from exploiting the spiral. The harm is done when a lack of sophistication in viewing the relationship leads to a rift that damages a common cause.

The naïveté of the *New Republic* men's dreams of reforming the country through their influence on Roosevelt and Wilson does not mean that the leadership emphasis of the new liberalism was totally misguided. No one can deny the need for strong executives in a country where reformers are often hamstrung by constitutional restrictions and political anachronisms. But the limitations of such leadership must be far more clearly recognized than they were by Croly, Weyl, and Lippmann. Liberals today, still mesmerized by the personality of the second Roosevelt, are as much obsessed as was Croly with the hope of finding some great leader to galvanize the reforming hosts. But the disillusionment in which the dreams of

Croly, Weyl, and Lippmann ended has its moral. Studies of the careers of Wilson and the two Roosevelts suggest that such politicians have been more led than leading. Liberals ignore even today the countless instances when F. D. R., like Roosevelt and Wilson, agreed to press reforms only reluctantly, in watered-down versions, when political pressures left little choice. In Franklin Roosevelt, liberals found a leader who was neither saint nor hero and far more fox than lion. The New Deal's leader had an uncommon amount of the genius by which politicians dramatize their acquiescence into the appearance of dramatic assertiveness.

The publicist careers of Croly, Weyl, and Lippmann also raise the question of the utility of pragmatism as a philosophy for reformers. Significantly the philosophy was the one important part of the new liberalism that Croly did not abandon during his post-war years of disillusionment. Even Randolph Bourne during his wartime attacks on the *New Republic* intellectuals condemned not pragmatism itself but the lack of realism with which such liberals had made their pragmatic calculations. For Bourne, Croly, and many others, pragmatism survived as the most consequential relic of liberalism's wartime debacle.

The *New Republic* men, of course, were not alone in making pragmatism a part of the American liberal tradition. Virtually all of the progressive intellectuals of the time, whether in politics, law, economics, philosophy, or the arts, took a similar line. In this respect the intellectuals differed from both the leaders and the rank and file of reformers who clung to their absolutes as of old. Yet while the pragmatism of the leading thinkers helped prepare the way for the later thorough-going experimentalism of the New Deal, the upshot was rather different from anything Croly, Weyl, and Lippmann would have liked. The three intellectuals always insisted that their experimentalism be directed toward some "formative purpose." With remarkable rigor they tried to make their reformist ideas cohere to, and serve as a test of, their theme of democratic nationalism. The experiment for experiment's sake without over-all plan that characterized the New Deal would hardly have satisfied them. Men who devoted so much of their lives to a revision of liberal theory would hardly have liked a liberalism that gloried in its absence of theory.

Finally, therefore, it is in terms of their theory of democratic nationalism that Croly, Weyl, and Lippmann must be judged. In the domestic realm nationalism meant accepting and attempting to manipulate such huge modern concentrations of power as corporations, unions, and the state. In the international realm it meant accepting the great nation-state system and the power relations that seemed to govern it. As such the new liberalism was an improvement upon the old Jeffersonian liberalism, which preferred either hopeless assaults upon such concentrations of power or the pretense that they did not exist.

The effort of the *New Republic* men to infuse nationalism into the American liberal tradition, however, shows how intellectuals in their precocious response to events frequently over-respond. Certainly in 1909 the idea of democratic nationalism seemed, as Croly said, one "of some promise." In the half-century before Croly wrote, nationalism had been exploited with great and sometimes revolutionary consequences by such men as Napoleon III, Cavour, Disraeli, and Bismarck. Even more impressive to Croly's precocious mind was the liberal direction nationalism seemed to have taken in the United States under Theodore Roosevelt. What Croly failed to see until too late, however, was how coincidental the conjunction of nationalism and reform had been in Roosevelt. Roosevelt from first to last was a nationalist. He was a reformer only when the swelling tide of progressivism made it expedient. The outbreak of World War I was enough to reveal how thin was the liberal veneer over Roosevelt's nationalism. When the United States itself became involved in the war, the national mood showed the universal illiberalism of modern nationalism. Once again, and in the most fundamental of their assumptions, the publicists had been misled by a politician.

The core of the new liberalism lay in its dream of exploiting the sentiment of nationalism for social-democratic ends. The N.R.A.'s Blue Eagle during the New Deal reflected a similar aspiration. Similarly in foreign relations the new liberalism hoped to develop from the play of power among nations a democratic and peaceable international system. Had Croly, Weyl, and Lippmann merely noted the existence of such forces in the modern world, they would have contributed greatly to the realism of American liberal thought. But their proselytizing for nationalism transmuted the acceptance of a necessary evil into its glorification. World War I taught the *New Republic* men the inherent madness of nationalism within nations and of militant power struggles among them. The ravages of nationalism under a Mussolini, a Hitler, or a Stalin, plus another world war, should have brought the lesson home to most other men.

In the end Croly, Weyl, and Lippmann provided as good a measure as any of their own mistakes. The questions raised by Lippmann in *Public Opinion*'s withering dissection of modern democratic practice are still much with us. The answer does not lie in the virtual abandonment of democracy of his recent *The Public Philosophy*, if only because of the past and present horrors perpetrated by the elitist leaders with whom Lippmann has cast his lot. But Americans who see democracy as a thing of value in itself have yet to make it more than sporadically real in the twentieth century.

On the other hand, Croly and Weyl sought to escape from their earlier delusions about a new liberalism through a candid avowal of democratic socialism. Like most liberals in other democracies of the time, they abandoned the middle class as a source for reform and sought leverage among the farming and laboring masses. In America, however, the great majority of liberals have failed to see what Croly and Weyl saw so clearly, and, as a result, the United States alone among the democratic nations has no viable socialist movement.

In foreign affairs Croly and Weyl also admitted the folly of their earlier confidence in power politics and the balance of power. While realistically conceding the durability of the struggle for power among nations, they knew that only some move beyond that struggle held out any hope for permanent peace. They continued to dream that some form of democratic internationalism might yet save the world from the hopeless maelstrom of naked power conflicts. Versailles also taught them that the danger of war arose not so much from politics as from economics. The solution of world economic problems became for them another major way to peace, an idea that has acquired increasing meaning since World War II.

There was one further lesson that Croly and Weyl took away from the Versailles debacle. When they pictured the peace conference as the suicide of the middle class, they acknowledged how much a nation's foreign policy reflects its domestic organization. For them, therefore, the democratic internationalism between nations that seemed to be the world's only hope depended upon democratic socialism within nations. But even after the passage of four decades most Americans have yet to learn how democracy can be made the source not only of liberty but of creative social change.

NOTES ON SOURCES

This book was written with detailed documentation for all statements of fact and, in so far as possible, for all interpretations. To my mind the much-maligned footnote provides an essential discipline for the writer of history—particularly of intellectual history. But this discipline is less necessary for the reader. The notes that follow, therefore, have been distilled from my manuscript's documentation to indicate only those sources that are not self-evident in the text and those that involve particularly controversial or difficult points. Specialists who want fuller documentation can find some of it in an earlier version of the manuscript called "Intellectuals in Crisis: Croly, Weyl, Lippmann, and the *New Republic*, 1900-1919," a Ph.D. dissertation held by the Library of the University of Wisconsin, or by directing an inquiry to me.

My major source of material has been, of course, the books and magazine articles of Croly, Weyl, and Lippmann. Lists of these can be compiled from the standard bibliographical sources. Where I have been able to establish the definite authorship of an unsigned *New Republic* article from manuscripts or other references it will be indicated in the following source notes. In order to place the *New Republic* in some sort of perspective, I have also read extensively in such magazines of the progressive era as the *Outlook*, the *Independent*, the *Nation, Harper's Weekly*, the *Masses*, the *Dial*, and the *Seven Arts*. A large number of newspaper references to the *New Republic* or its editors has also been consulted. A clipping file maintained by the School of Journalism of Columbia University proved particularly useful in this respect.

Manuscript sources have been of incalculable value. They alone have made it possible for me to try to get behind the abstractions, in which Croly, Weyl, and Lippmann very properly delighted, to the men themselves and the complex web of events and human associations out of which their ideas grew. According to Bruce Bliven, who followed Croly as the *New Republic's* editor, Croly's private papers were destroyed soon after his death. Several years ago, however, Judge Learned Hand during an interview most generously pulled from his safe a bulging file of his correspondence with Croly between 1909 and 1930. Croly's letters to Hand are the most revealing that I have been able to find; my only regret is that the focus of the study has kept me from quoting at length from Judge Hand's own part in the correspondence. Some important Croly letters can also be found among the papers of Randolph S. Bourne in the Columbia University Library, of Eduard Lindeman (lent to me through the generosity of Dr. Jacob E. Cooke) , of Willard Straight in the Cornell University Library, and in the Theodore Roosevelt, Woodrow Wilson, Edward M. House, and Henry Cabot Lodge collections at the Library of Congress and elsewhere. I am greatly indebted to the generosity of the late Professor Howard K. Beale for allowing me to consult his extensive notes on the Roosevelt and Lodge papers, and similarly to Professor Arthur S. Link for his notes on the Wilson and House papers. Without the aid of these men the widely scattered references in these collections to Croly, his colleagues, and his magazine would have been virtually impossible to obtain.

The most valuable and extensive single collection of manuscripts for the purposes of my book, however, is the private diaries and other papers of Walter Weyl in the possession of his widow, Bertha Poole Weyl, at Woodstock, New York. I have expressed elsewhere my very deep gratitude to Mrs. Weyl for letting me use (without restrictions) her husband's papers. Weyl used his day-to-day diary partly as a workbook for formulating his ideas and partly as a running commentary on his life. In both respects it is fascinating. Very little of Weyl's correspondence has been kept, though fortunately he frequently wrote first drafts of important letters in his diary. An unexplained break in the diary between October 1913 and February 1917 deprived me of Weyl's comments and reflections during a period when they would have been especially valuable. A considerable number of letters to and from Weyl are to be found in the aforementioned collections of the Roosevelt and Wilson papers.

Walter Lippmann's papers have been deposited in the Library of Yale University, but are not presently available. Many letters are to be found, however, among the Roosevelt and Wilson papers as well as those of Lincoln Steffens in the Columbia University Library.

The *New Republic* has followed a policy of destroying its files after three years. The Willard Straight papers now at Cornell University hold disappointingly little on the magazine or its editors, but what references there are are of exceptional interest. I am deeply indebted to Professor Charles Vevier for keeping an eye out for material relevant to my study while going through the Straight papers in preparation for his own book, *The United States and China, 1906-1913* (Rutgers University Press, 1955). Numerous volumes of printed correspondence were consulted; these are listed below at the places where they proved most useful.

It is difficult to think of a prominent progressive who did not either write his own autobigraphy or have a collection of intimate memorials devoted to him. Recently one of the latter was published (Marquis Childs and James Reston, eds., *Walter Lippmann and His Times* [Harcourt, Brace, 1959]), which, if available when this book was begun, would have saved me many arduous and delightful months of scholarly detective work. The autobiographies, biographies, and collections of memoirs that I have used are listed at appropriate places below.

Finally, one of the great joys of writing this book has been the experience of meeting and talking with people who knew Croly, Weyl, and Lippmann. There are, of course, many other people with whom I would also like to have talked but failed to reach because of problems raised by time and geography or my own diffidence. In the case of the following, however, I was able to find plausible excuses for imposing, and I am enormously grateful to them for their helpfulness and courtesy: Justice Felix Frankfurter, Judge Learned Hand,

Mr. Ralph Reinhold, Mr. James T. Shotwell, and Mrs. Walter E. Weyl. An effort to interview Mr. Walter Lippmann several years ago failed, to my great regret, because of a conflict of schedules and the absence of any suggestion that I might try again.

In the detailed references that follow I have listed the names of the publishers rather than the places of publication, since this seems more useful than place designations for sources most of which were published in New York. Complete citations are given only for the first listing of a source in each chapter.

BOOK ONE. IDEAS IN THE MAKING

CHAPTER ONE

HERBERT CROLY: NATIONALIST LIBERAL, 1900-1909

1. Three Intellectuals and a Politician. The account of the meeting at Sagamore Hill is based on accounts given by Lippmann in his essay in *Walter Weyl: An Appreciation* (privately printed, 1922) , 89, and in a letter to Mabel Dodge printed in Mabel Dodge Luhan, *Movers and Shakers* (Harcourt, Brace, 1936) , 164. Letters concerning arrangements for the meeting can be found in the Roosevelt papers. The best accounts of the *New Republic*'s relationship to Roosevelt in the first few weeks of publication can be found in the Lippmann essay on Weyl mentioned above and in another on Croly, "Notes for a Biography," *New Republic*, LXIII (July 16, 1930) , 250. For further material on the quarrel between Roosevelt and the editors, see Chapter Six, Section 4, below.

2. Portrait of a Publicist. Some of the material in this section and in those sections on Croly that follow was previously published in my "Croly and Nationalism," *New Republic*, CXXXI (Nov. 22, 1954), 17-22. The items of praise listed for Croly can be found in: *American Magazine*, LXXV (Nov. 1912), 23; articles by Lippmann, Felix Frankfurter, and Waldo Frank in the very important collection of memorial essays on Croly in *New Republic*, LXIII (July 16, 1930), 250, 262; and Alvin Johnson, *Pioneer's Progress: An Autobiography* (Viking, 1952), 240-41. Photographs of Croly can be found in the *American Magazine* as cited immediately above and in the New York *World*, May 18, 1930. Justice Felix Frankfurter corrected several of my earlier mistaken notions about Croly's general appearance. The description of Croly's shyness when confronted with strangers is drawn from Edmund Wilson's contribution to the *New Republic* memorial edition mentioned above and is confirmed by an almost identical experience recounted in T. S. Matthews, *Name and Address* (Simon and Schuster, 1960) , 186. The remaining material on Croly's personality and habits is drawn from further essays in the *New Republic*'s memorial issue by John Chamberlain, T. S. Matthews, and Philip Littell. Laski's comment can be found in Mark DeWolfe Howe, ed., *Holmes-Laski Letters* (Harvard University Press, 1953) , I, 43, while other relevant material appears in: Robert Morss Lovett, *All Our Years* (Viking, 1948) , 178, and Francis Hackett, *I Chose Denmark* (Doubleday, Doran, 1940) , 15.

3. **A Man and a Movement.** The description of the progressive movement in 1909 is drawn from Henry F. Pringle's invaluable *Theodore Roosevelt* (Harcourt, Brace, 1931), 508-24; his useful *Life and Times of William Howard Taft* (Farrar and Rinehart, 1939), I, 418-69; George E. Mowry, *Theodore Roosevelt and the Progressive Movement* (University of Wisconsin Press, 1947), 36-49; Belle Case and Fola La Follette, *Robert M. La Follette* (Macmillan, 1953), I, 266-78; and Alpheus T. Mason, *Bureaucracy Convicts Itself: The Ballinger-Pinchot Controversy of 1910* (Viking, 1941), 73-98. Evidence for the spate of soul-searching among progressives in 1909 can be found in George Norris, *Fighting Liberal* (Macmillan, 1945), 104, 107-19; William Allen White, *Autobiography* (Macmillan, 1946), 422-3; Lincoln Steffens, *Autobiography* (Harcourt, Brace, 1931), 581; Ida M. Tarbell, *All in a Day's Work* (Macmillan, 1939), 280; and Ray Stannard Baker, *American Chronicle* (Scribner, 1945), 255-60. Croly's predictions about the future of progressivism occur on page 154 of his *Promise of American Life* (Macmillan, 1909), while the equally prophetic *Outlook* editorial was "At the Parting of the Ways," *Outlook*, CXIV (April 16, 1910), 830-31.

4. **Middle-Class Intellectual in the Making.** Material on the relationship of Croly and his father to the *Architectural Record* can be found in *Architectural Record, I* (July 1891), frontispiece; IX (Feb. 1900), iii; and XCIV (Aug. 1930), 138. See also, New York *Real Estate Record and Builder's Guide*, XX (May 4, 1889), 613; and Thomas S. Holden and Frederic H. Glade, Jr., "The House That Dodge Built: Story of a Business Service Organization" (unpublished business history, F. W. Dodge Corporation, 1954), 28-30, 53-4. Croly books on architecture are William Herbert (pseud.), *Houses for Town and Country* (Duffield, 1907); and, with Harry W. Desmond, *Stately Homes in America from Colonial Times to the Present Day* (Appleton, 1903). The most recent and best discussion of the general characteristics of progressive reformers is to be found in George E. Mowry, *Era of Theodore Roosevelt, 1900-1912* (Harper, 1958), ch. 5. The discussions of Croly's mother are based on: *Memories of Jane Cunningham Croly, "Jenny June"* (Putnam, 1904); Philadelphia *Press*, Dec. 25, 1901; *Dictionary of American Biography*, IV, 560; New York *Times*, Dec. 24, 1901; Phebe A. Hanneford, *Daughters of America or Women of the Century* (True, 1883), 667; New York *Sun*, Dec. 7, 1902; New York *Daily Tribune*, Dec. 24, 1901; Haryot Holt Day, "Jennie June Croly, the Mother of Clubs," New York *Post*, May 10, 1916; Ralph G. Martin, "In Defense of Women's Clubs," *Tomorrow*, IX (March 1950), 5-6; T. C. Evans, "Jane Cunningham Croly," New York *Times*, Dec. 28, 1901; as well as upon her own voluminous writings. Material on Croly's father can be found in many of the above sources as well as in: New York *Real Estate Record and Builder's Guide*, XXXII (May 4, 1889), 613; *D.A.B.*, IV, 560; New York *Times*, April 30, 1889. The elder Croly's most revealing work is David Goodman Croly, *Glimpses of the Future* (Putnam, 1888), but see also his *Seymour and Blair, Their Lives and Services* (Richardson, 1868), and his anonymous *Miscegenation: The Theory of the Blending of the Race Applied to White Man and Negro* (H. Dexter Hamilton, 1864). Sidney Kaplan, "The Miscegenation Issue in the Election of 1864," *Journal of Negro History*,

XXIV (July 1949), 274-343, credits David Croly with coining "miscegenation." Croly's relations with his parents are revealed in Robert Morss Lovett, *All Our Years*, 173; Lovett's obituary of Croly in Harvard College, Class of 1890, *Fiftieth Annual Report*, 113; Edmund Wilson, "H. C.," *New Republic*, LXIII (July 16, 1930), 268; and Herbert Croly, "Testimonial to His Father . . ., May, 1889," *Memories of Jane Cunningham Croly*, 61-2. The Crolys' work for Positivism is discussed in many places in the memorial volume just cited.

5. **From Positivism to Pragmatism.** Descriptions of Harvard while Croly was there can be found in R. M. Lovett, *All Our Years*, 33; Hutchins Hapgood, *Victorian in the Modern World* (Harcourt, Brace, 1939), 43-50; and W. E. Burghart DuBois, *Dusk at Dawn: An Essay Toward an Autobiography of a Race Concept* (Harcourt, Brace, 1940), 34-7. Material on the philosophy department at Harvard and Croly's work in it can be found in Ralph Barton Perry, *Thought and Character of William James* (Harvard, 1948), 161-4; 233; George Santayana, *Middle Span* (Scribner, 1954), 152-3; New York *Times*, May 18, 1913; and Transcript of the record of Herbert D. Croly (1910), Harvard University Archives. Croly's conflict with his father at college is discussed in his memorial to the elder Croly in *Memories of Jane Cunningham Croly*, 62-5; A. Johnson, *Pioneer's Progress*, 241; R. M. Lovett, "Herbert Croly," Harvard College, Class of 1890, *Fiftieth Annual Report*, 113; and R. M. Lovett, *All Our Years*, 173. For passages showing Croly's care in avoiding the dialectical absolutes of Hegel despite his courses with Royce, see: Herbert Croly, *Promise of American Life* (Macmillan, 1909), 32, 195, 211. David W. Noble, "Herbert Croly and American Progressive Thought," *Western Political Quarterly*, VII (Dec. 1954), 537-53, describes Croly as a Hegelian, but I find his argument unconvincing. The quotation with which Croly closes *The Promise of American Life* is from George Santayana, *Reason in Society* (Scribner, 1905), 136. For the full measure of Croly's indebtedness to Santayana compare ibid. 128-36, to *Promise of American Life*, 399-421, 427-54. The possibilities of William James's influence are illuminated by Croly's transcript at Harvard; *Harvard University Catalogue, 1886-1887*; and R. B. Perry, *Thought and Character of William James*, 128-9, 153, 278, 296-9. For the testimonials of Croly's friends to his dedication to pragmatism, see A. Johnson, *Pioneer's Progress*, 240; the memorial issue to Croly, *New Republic*, LXIII (July 16, 1930), 262, 263; and John Chamberlain, "Herbert Croly and America's Future," ibid. CI (Nov. 8, 1939), 34. For instances beyond the article by D. W. Noble mentioned above where the pragmatic content of Croly's thought has been misconstrued, see Louis Filler, "The Dilemma, So-Called, of the American Liberal," *Antioch Review*, VIII (June 1948), 138-43, and R. H. Gabriel, *Course of American Democratic Thought*, 365. The passages cited illustrating Croly's pragmatism occur in his *Progressive Democracy*, 122, and *Promise of American Life*, 280, and for others, see ibid. 3, 7, 12, 13, 17, 21, 25, 177, 178, 213, 265-73, 286, 310-14, 405, 407, 425-6, 452. The editorial cited from his magazine is "Mental Unpreparedness," *New Republic*, IV (Sept. 11, 1915), 144.

6. **The Ghost of Wilbur Littleton.** Descriptions of Croly's house at Cornish and of the life of the summer colony there can be found in *Architectural*

Record, XV (March 1904) , 194-5; R. M. Lovett, *All Our Years*, 204; and Edith Bolling Wilson, *My Memoir* (Bobbs-Merrill, 1938) , 69-74. Robert Grant, who wrote several other novels besides *Unleavened Bread* (Scribner, 1900) , was a friend of Theodore Roosevelt, and, as a judge of the Probate Court of Suffolk County, Massachusetts (1893-1923) , later became a member of the famous committee that approved the death sentence against Sacco and Vanzetti. Croly's comments on his intentions in *Promise of American Life* in this section are drawn from H. Croly, "Why I Wrote My Latest Book: My Aim in 'The Promise of American Life,' " *World's Work*, XX (May 1910) , 13086; and Herbert Croly to Learned Hand, Dec. [5], 1909, Hand Papers. Croly's concern for the plight of Wilbur Littleton is revealed not only in the *World's Work* piece cited above but also in the following articles: "American Artists and Their Public," *Architectural Record*, X (Jan. 1901) , 256-62; "New York as the American Metropolis," ibid. XIII (March 1903) , 200; and "The Architect in Recent Fiction," ibid. XVII (Feb. 1905) , 139. Carlton J. H. Hayes, *Historical Evolution of Modern Nationalism* (Macmillan, 1931), shows that European intellectuals of the early nineteenth century went through a transformation similar to Croly's from cultural nationalism to other varieties. None of Hayes's categories fits Croly satisfactorily. "Cultural nationalism" and "political nationalism" seem the best phrases, therefore, to describe Croly's early and later phases.

   7. *The Promise of American Life.* Documentation for points in *Promise of American Life* in this section is provided only for those that cannot easily be found by consulting the table of contents or index. Hand's letters to Croly on the book are dated Nov. 5, Dec. 3, 1909. Examples of Croly's tone of crisis can be found in *Promise of American Life* [hereafter cited as *Promise*], 22-3, 25-6, 128-9, 131, 137, 142, 147, 151-2, 165, 166-7, 171, 269, 389-90, 419, 423-4. For evidence of Croly's concern with the problem of poverty, see *Promise*, 138-9, 196, 205, 209, 406, 409, 417, 426, 430, 442, 449. Particularly relevant passages where Croly attacks the Jeffersonian tradition occur in ibid. 23, 44, 46, 118, 127, 144, 147, 148-54, 359, 386. The fundamentally democratic orientation of Croly's thought becomes clear from statements in ibid. 41, 51, 77, 169, 178, 179, 194, 197, 198, 200, 212, 234, 280, 405. The picture of Croly as "an amoral genie of Realpolitik" occurs in Louis Filler, "The Dilemma, So-Called, of the American Liberal," *Antioch Review*, VIII (June 1948) , 140-41. See also, E. F. Goldman, *Rendezvous With Destiny* (Knopf, 1952), 244-5. Passages illustrating Croly's concern for peace can be found in *Promise*, 293, 295, 300-309, 313. See ibid. 32, for Croly's key passage on his book's being "nationalistic" rather than "socialistic."

   The charges that Croly exhibited totalitarian or Fascist tendencies can be found in the article by Louis Filler cited above; a quotation from Alvin Johnson in William H. Attwood, "Pathfinders of American Liberalism" (unpublished bachelor's essay, Princeton University Library, 1941) , 25-6. Critics of Croly have often been misled by his inveterate habit of citing at length opinions he disapproved before presenting his own. See, for instance, Arthur E. Ekirch, Jr., *Decline of American Liberalism* (Longmans, Green, 1955) , 188, where he ascribes to Croly a desire for "a Federal commission to regulate business." Croly faced directly the problem of how to keep his élite democratic. See particularly passages in ibid. 196, 441, 449. Croly's semi-religious calls for leadership occur in ibid. 175, 453, but see ibid. 87-99, and "The Paradox of Lincoln," *New Republic*, XXI (Feb. 18, 1920) , 350-53, for his views on Lincoln as the ideal leader. Croly's ideas on the "national life" being the "national school" are to be found in *Promise*, 175, 286, 407, 465.

8. Nationalism and Democracy. William Allen White's racism becomes evident in *Old Order Changeth* (Macmillan, 1910) , 197-200, 252. Croly's attacks on socialism occur in *Promise*, 210-11, 241, 315. Croly emphasized the need for a thoroughgoing redistribution of wealth in the United States in ibid. 22, 23, 116-17, 139, 181, 202-6, 209-10, 239, 380, 381-5, 409, 413, 417. For Croly's early development of the theme of "metropolitanism" see his "New York as the American Metropolis," *Architectural Record*, XIII (March 1903) , 193-206. Croly's hopes for the converts that his book might win are expressed in a letter to Learned Hand, Dec. [5], 1909, Hand Papers.

CHAPTER TWO

WALTER WEYL: DEMOCRATIC LIBERAL, 1900-1912

1. A Magazine and a Maverick. Weyl's relationship to Roosevelt and the Progressive party is revealed in Walter Weyl to Theodore Roosevelt, Aug. 8, 1912, Roosevelt Papers; the articles on Weyl by Walter Lippmann and Howard Brubaker in Howard Brubaker (ed.) , *Walter Weyl: An Appreciation* (privately printed, 1922) [hereafter cited as *Weyl, Appreciation*], 86, 122; Theodore Roosevelt, *Autobiography* (Macmillan, 1913), 25; and an entry in Walter Weyl, MS. Diary, Dec. 15, 1912. The picture of Weyl as a person is largely based on entries in his diary, but see also *Weyl, Appreciation, passim*. The essays by Francis Hackett and Walter Lippmann in the memorial volume are particularly revealing about Weyl's relationship to the *New Republic* and its editors. My conversations with Mrs. Weyl were very helpful on this score, as were many entries in the diary. See also Robert Morss Lovett, *All Our Years* (Viking, 1948) , 172, and Alvin Johnson, *Pioneer's Progress* (Viking, 1952) , 234.

2. A German-American Francophile. Essays by Martin Schutze and Maurice Weyl in *Weyl, Appreciation* give much information on his early years, though Mrs. Weyl has suggested that the material on the family's financial circumstances should be handled with caution. The jottings Weyl made for an autobiographical novel are in Weyl, MS. Diary, April 11, 1913. A few surviving fragments of Weyl's allegorical novel on Christ remain among his miscellaneous papers. Weyl's record at the Wharton School is revealed in his University of Pennsylvania Transcript. His precocious prize essay can be found in Walter Weyl, et al., *Equitable Taxation: Six Essays . . .* (Crowell, 1892) . Simon Nelson Patten's early struggles with the law, his economic theories, and his love for the culture of Germany are discussed in: *D.A.B.*, XIV, 299; Roswell C. McCrea,

"A Biographical Sketch . . .," *Annals of the Academy of Political and Social Science*, XXXVII (May 1923) , supplement; Henry R. Seeger, "Introduction" to Simon Nelson Patten, *Essays in Economic Theory* (Knopf, 1924) ; Rexford Guy Tugwell, "Notes on the Life and Work of Simon Nelson Patten," *Journal of Political Economy*, LXXXVI (April 1923) , 198-9; Emory R. Johnson, *Life of a University Professor* (Ruttle, Shaw & Wetherill, 1943) . The last work cited, by Emory R. Johnson, who supervised Weyl's Ph.D. thesis, is generally useful on life at Halle, Germany, and at the Wharton School. Croly's views on Germany can be found in *Promise of American Life* (Macmillan, 1909) , 246-54; Weyl's in *New Democracy: An Essay Concerning Certain Political and Economic Conditions in the United States* (Macmillan, 1912), 223, and W. Weyl, MS. Diary, March 28, 1915, Sept. 28, 1918. See Walter Weyl, "Depopulation in France," *North American Review*, CXCV (March 1912) , 343-55, for his views on France.

3. The Dismal Science Unfolds a Promise. Martin Schutze's recollections of Weyl's conservatism at the University of Pennsylvania can be found in *Weyl, Appreciation*, 56-7. Weyl's acknowledgments of his indebtedness to Simon Patten occur in *New Democracy*, 191 n., and in a letter to Patten drafted in Weyl's MS. Diary, March 18, 1912. Other references to Patten in the diary are to be found in the entries for Sept. 4, Dec. 18, 1911, Feb. 10, 1912, April 19, 1913, June 28, 1918, and June 12, 1919. The theories of Patten discussed can be found in Simon Nelson Patten, *Essays in Economic Theory*, 31-2, 78-9, 148, 181, 207-18, 219, 287, 288, and the parallel ideas from Weyl are in *New Democracy*, 249-53, 330-33, 260, 276, 355-6.

4. A Scholar Adrift. The essays by Martin Schutze and Maurice Weyl in *Weyl, Appreciation* are particularly informative on Weyl's early career. His MS. Diary for Jan. 20, March 20, 1912, and April 11, 1913, also contains musings on his earlier life adrift. The reports of Weyl's investigations for Carroll D. Wright can be found in *United States Bureau of Labor Bulletin*, VII (Jan. 1902) , 1-94; ibid. X (March 1905) , 540-64; ibid. XI (Nov. 1905) , 723-856; ibid. XII (May 1906) , 699-848. The important article on workers in France is "Labor Conditions in France," *Annals of the American Academy of Political and Social Science*, XII (Sept. 1898) , 250-58. Ernest Poole's article in *Weyl, Appreciation*, 34-47, and his *Bridge: My Own Story* (Macmillan, 1940) , 68-72, throw light on Weyl's life at the University Settlement. The Coal Strike of 1902 and Weyl's part in it are illuminated by Elsie Glück, *John Mitchell, Miner: Labor's Bargain with the Gilded Age* (John Day, 1929) , 66-74, 101, 104, 114, 133-51, 173, 250; Maurice Weyl's and Ernest Poole's articles in *Weyl, Appreciation*; Samuel Gompers, *Seventy Years of Life and Labor* (Dutton, 1925) , 123-26. Weyl's articles on the Coal Strike were: "John Mitchell: The Man the Miners Trust," *Outlook*, LXXXII (March 24, 1906), 657-62; "Mine Discipline and Unionism," ibid. LXXI (July 19, 1902) , 734-7; "The Relief System of the Mine Workers," *Charities*, IX (Sept. 6, 1902) , 242-4; "The Award of the Anthracite Coal Strike Commission," *Review of Reviews*, XXVII (April 1904) , 460-4. For Ray Stannard Baker's reaction to the strike see his *American Chronicle* (Scribner, 1945), 167. Mitchell's *Organized Labor* (American Book and Bible House, 1903) acknowledged Weyl's aid in "the compilation of data and preparation . . ."; Elsie Glück in the work cited above speaks of Weyl's "very substantial collaboration." Mrs. Weyl, however, believes her husband wrote the entire book. The latter judgment seems to me the most likely.

5. A Scholar Becomes Publicist. The picture of Weyl's wife, Bertha Poole Weyl, has been put together from the essays by Francis Hackett, Robert W. Bruere, and Ernest Poole in *Weyl, Appreciation*; E. Poole's *Bridge*, 67-73, 177-8; Francis Hackett, *I Chose Denmark* (Doubleday, Doran, 1940), 61-2; Louis Levine, *Women's Garment Workers* (Huebsch, 1924), 156, 594; Bertha Poole, "An Incident in the Sweat Shop," *Independent*, LX (May 31, 1906), 1276-7; Bertha Poole, "The Human Side of the Sweat Shop," *Charities*, XVII (Feb. 2, 1907), 610-11; as well as from numerous entries in Weyl, MS. Diary and from my conversations with Mrs. Weyl. Weyl's success as a magazine writer and his dissatisfaction with his "merely popular" pieces are fully revealed by numerous diary entries from 1911 to 1913. The same source gives an unusually detailed account of his financial circumstances. The information on the Socialist convention of 1912 is derived from Ernest Poole's essay in *Weyl, Appreciation*; Weyl, MS. Diary, April-May 1912; and David A. Shannon, *Socialist Party of America* (Macmillan, 1955), 71-3. For Weyl's important article on France, see "An Experiment in Population," *Atlantic Monthly*, CIII (Feb. 1909), 261-7.

6. The Publicist and Progressivism. Weyl's MS. Diary is the best source on his purposes in *The New Democracy* and his relationship to the Progressive movement. The entry quoted on his book's being "an argument for an American point of view" is, in fact, the earliest entry that has been found in the bound notebooks of his diary. It may be that the writing of his book and his hopes for its success led him to start the diary. Weyl's indebtedness to other progressives can be judged by consulting *New Democracy*'s fairly accurate index, as can his opposition to the doctrines of various Socialists. For the pragmatic tenor of his thought see Ernest Poole's essay in *Weyl, Appreciation*, 37; and Weyl, *New Democracy*, 162-3, 183, 255, 264, 270. Weyl has been labeled a Jeffersonian in Walter Lippmann, "Notes for a Biography," *New Republic*, LXIII (July 16, 1930), 251; Granville Hicks, *John Reed: The Making of a Revolutionary* (Macmillan, 1937), 171; Eric F. Goldman, *Rendezvous With Destiny* (Knopf, 1952), 231; and Harry J. Carman and Harold C. Syrett, *History of the American People* (Knopf, 1952), II, 345; but, for his repudiation of Jeffersonianism, see *New Democracy*, 16, 57, 161-2, 320-42.

7. *The New Democracy*. Because of its detailed table of contents and adequate index only a few points from *The New Democracy* need special mention here. Passages in ibid. 7-22, indicate that Weyl, like Croly, shared with many progressives the view that the Constitution was in its inception undemocratic. Weyl's very important reservations about the nature of the impact of the frontier on American life can be found in ibid. 23-36. For a more recent evaluation of the importance of consumer protest in the progressive movement

see Richard Hofstadter, *Age of Reform: From Bryan to F.D.R.* (Knopf, 1955),
170-72. Although Weyl did not make a major point of the matter, his opinions
on immigration restriction are of interest in view of his closeness both to immigration and the labor movement. Influenced by his population theories as
well as by his concern for labor, Weyl advocated immediate restrictive
legislation to cut immigration to about "5 or 10 millions" for the next fifty
years. Ibid. 346-7. For Weyl's many mentions of the theme of population and
democracy, see ibid. 26, 68, 91, 146, 194, 199, 320-21, 356-7.

CHAPTER THREE

WALTER LIPPMANN: VOLUNTARIST LIBERAL, 1909-1913

1. **The Triumvirate's Prodigy.** Theodore Roosevelt's flattering estimate of
Lippmann can be found in Elting E. Morison (ed.), *Letters of Theodore Roosevelt* (Harvard, 1951-54), VIII, 872. William J. Ghent's less happy view comes
from a letter to Morris Hillquit, April 15 [1915], Hillquit Papers. Reed's poem
is quoted in Granville Hicks, *John Reed: The Making of a Revolutionary* (Macmillan, 1937), 77. Mabel Dodge's remark is given in Mabel Dodge Luhan,
Movers and Shakers (Harcourt, Brace, 1936), 118. Other estimates of Lippmann
by his contemporaries (usually unflattering) can be found in ibid. 92, 257,
301-2, 321, 438, 485-7; Conrad Aiken, *Ushant* (Little, Brown, 1952), 201;
Hutchins Hapgood, *Victorian in the Modern World* (Harcourt, Brace, 1939),
352-3; Van Wyck Brooks, *Confident Years* (Dutton, 1952), 478; and Van Wyck
Brooks, *Scenes and Portraits* (Dutton, 1954), 219. Croly's judgments can be
found in two letters to Judge Learned Hand in the Hand Papers dated Jan. 5,
1914, and Jan. 27, 1930. The evaluations quoted of other men close to the *New
Republic* come from Harold Stearns, *Street I Know* (Furman, 1935), 137;
Robert Morss Lovett, *All Our Years* (Viking, 1948), 172; A. S. Johnson,
Pioneer's Progress, 241; Mark DeWolfe Howe (ed.), *Holmes-Laski Letters*
(Harvard, 1953), I, 242.

2. **Conservative Genesis.** As mentioned earlier, the best source now available
for Lippmann's early years is Marquis Childs and James Reston (eds.), *Walter
Lippmann and His Times* (Harcourt, Brace, 1959). This collection of essays
in honor of Lippmann, however, added nothing to what I had been able to
learn from such sources as Amos Pinchot, "The Great Obfuscator," *Nation*,
CXXXVII (July 19, 1933), 69; David Eliot Weingast, *Walter Lippmann: A
Study in Personal Journalism* (Rutgers, 1949); John Mason Brown, *Through
These Men: Some Aspects of Our Passing History* (Harper, 1956); and Beverly
Smith, "Man with a Flashlight Mind," *American Magazine*, CXIV (Sept. 1932),
17. The last mentioned essays by Brown and Smith are particularly interesting
since both are based on interviews with Lippmann. Lippmann's early books
are filled with very interesting autobiographical passages. Of use in this section
have been *A Preface to Politics* (Kennerley, 1913), 225, 231, 301; and *Drift and
Mastery* (Kennerley, 1914), xx, 155, 171, 204-5, 234, 240-42, 244, 346. Lippmann's
views on the problems of Jews can be found in "For Christian-Jewish Friend-

ship," *Literary Digest*, LXXIII (May 20, 1922) , 34; and *Time*, XXXII (Dec. 5, 1938) , 19.

3. Middle-Class Intellectual at Harvard. In addition to the biographical sources cited in the last section, the following are useful on Lippmann's career at Harvard: Louis Untermeyer, *From Another World* (Harcourt, Brace, 1939), 57-8; G. Hicks, *John Reed*, 38, 48; H. V. Kaltenborn, *Fifty Fabulous Years, 1900-1950* (Putnam, 1950) , 43; C. Aiken, *Ushant*, 201; V. W. Brooks, *Scenes and Portraits*, 97-122, 217; H. Stearns, *Street I Know*, 72, 78; R. M. Lovett, *All Our Years*, 49; and John Reed, "Almost Thirty," *New Republic Book* (Republic, 1916) , 65-7. Lippmann himself is revealing on his years at Harvard in *Preface to Politics*, 203, 205; *A Preface to Morals* (Macmillan, 1929) , 331; and Harvard College, Class of 1910, *Twenty-fifth Annual Report* (1935) , 446. Especially interesting on Lippmann's espousal of socialism at Harvard is his own "Socialism at Harvard," *Harvard Illustrated Magazine*, X (March 1909) , 137-9; and Thomas Nixon Carver to the editor, *Atlantic Monthly*, CXCV (March 1955) , 23. Lippmann's relationship to William James is illuminated by quoted interview material in the essays by Beverly Smith and John Mason Brown mentioned above, but see also Walter Lippmann, "An Open Mind — William James," *Everybody's Magazine*, XXXII (Dec. 1910), 800-801; *Preface to Politics*, 11, 40, 47, 48, 113, 114, 119, 225, 233, 236; and *Drift and Mastery*, 202, 261-3, 295-7. These books were not indexed. John Mason Brown's article also has directly quoted material on Lippmann's relationship to Santayana, but Brown incorrectly credits the latter with having kept Lippmann "from becoming a pragmatist." For Lippmann's pragmatism see not only the passages in *Preface to Politics* and *Drift and Mastery* cited above, but Walter Lippmann, et al., " 'Traffic in Absolutes,' An extract from John Dewey, with a Review and a Footnote," *New Republic*, III (July 17, 1915) , 281-5. Lippmann's indebtedness to Santayana is evident, however, in *Preface to Politics*, vi, 168, 209, 216, 233, 285; *Drift and Mastery*, 284, 289. On occasion Lippmann in quoting Santayana gave the philosopher's words a completely different meaning from that intended. Compare *Drift and Mastery*, 298-9, with George Santayana, *Life of Reason* (Scribner, 1905) , V, 12-13. Since I wrote the passage on "essence" and ballot-box stuffing, Lippmann has attempted the seemingly impossible. See his use of the concept of "essence" in *Public Philosophy* (Little, Brown, 1955) , 141-2, 161-6. For Lippmann's relationship to Graham Wallas, see H. Stearns, *Street I Know*, 115-16; *Drift and Mastery*, 36; Graham Wallas, *Great Society: A Psychological Analysis* (Macmillan, 1914) , v; *Preface to Politics*, 76-7.

4. Muckraking and Socialism. General accounts of Lippmann's relationship to Lincoln Steffens can be found in Lincoln Steffens, *Autobiography* (Harcourt, Brace, 1931) , 592-7; Harvard College, Class of 1910, *Twenty-fifth Annual Report* (1935) , 446; and *Preface to Politics*, 19-20, 218-20, 314; but letters between the two men among the Steffens Papers (some of which are quoted in the text) considerably alter both the chronology and substance of these accounts based on memory. For *Everybody's Magazine* and Lippmann's work as a muckraker, see Louis Filler, *Crusaders for American Liberalism* (Harcourt, Brace, 1939) , 171-

89, 362; Harvard College, Class of 1910, *Twenty-fifth Annual Report* (1935), 446; *Preface to Politics*, 196; and *Drift and Mastery*, 7. The references to Lippmann's post-college Socialist phase in the John Mason Brown and Beverly Smith articles, as well as in Lippmann's own report to his Harvard class, are highly inaccurate. See Robert William Iverson, "Morris Hillquit: American Social Democrat" (unpublished Ph.D. dissertation, State University of Iowa Library, 1951), 148-52; Walter Lippmann, "Two Months in Schenectady," *Masses*, III (April 1912), 13; and Ernest Sutherland Bates, "Walter Lippmann: The Career of Comrade Fool," *Modern Monthly*, VII (June 1933), 266-74; Hutchins Hapgood, *Victorian in the Modern World*, 292, 352; and *Preface to Politics*, 54-5, 182-3.

5. **Socialism and Progressivism.** Lippmann's new strictures against Socialism can be found in *Preface to Politics*, 16, 54, 56, 282, 287, and his attitudes toward the presidential candidates of 1912 in ibid. 23-4, 55, 258-9.

6. *A Preface to Politics.* For information on Lippmann's fortuitous discovery of Freud I am indebted to Professor Frederick J. Hoffman of the University of Wisconsin, who has corresponded with Lippmann on the subject. See also, Fred Rodell, "Walter Lippmann," *American Mercury*, LX (March 1945), 271; A. A. Brill, "The Introduction and Development of Freud's Work in the United States," *American Journal of Sociology*, XLV (Nov. 1935), 318-25; and *Preface to Politics*, 34-52, 83, 106. Theodore Roosevelt's letter on Lippmann's book was dated May 22, 1913, but has not been included in the various printed collections of Roosevelt's letters. The *Nation's* review of *A Preface to Politics* can be found in the issue of Sept. 11, 1913, and Lippmann's own humorous reference to the book occurs in the previously cited *Twenty-fifth Annual Report* of his Harvard class. Lippmann's references to the Sherman Act as "repressive" legislation can be found in *Preface to Politics*, 21, 23, 28, 36, 61. The theme of the "new businessman" is developed in ibid. 57, and in *Drift and Mastery*, 32-65. Lippmann's references to Nietzsche occur in *Preface to Politics*, 51-2, 233-6, 238, 245, 310. Lippmann himself has since come to agree with the argument for at least vaguely defined principles as a necessary basis for democratic government. But in his recent *Public Philosophy* he makes the agreement among men on such principles the sanction of authoritarian but "responsible" leadership. See Charles Forcey, "Leadership and 'Misrule by the People,'" *New Republic*, CXXXII (Feb. 21, 1955), 13-16. For a discussion of the significance of Bergson, Nietzsche, and Sorel as forerunners of Fascism, see George Sabine, *History of Political Theory* (Holt, 1937), 755-8.

BOOK II: THE NEW LIBERALISM IN PRACTICE

CHAPTER FOUR

BULL MOOSE NATIONALISM, 1909-1912

1. **"You Certainly Hit the Game."** Several efforts to obtain the sales figures on Croly's and Weyl's books from the Macmillan Company have been unsuccess-

ful. The 7500 estimate cited is from Felix Frankfurter's memorial essay on Croly in *New Republic*, LXIII (July 16, 1930), 247. Frankfurter's estimate may not have included a French edition of the book, *Les promesses de la vie américaine*, translated by M. Firmin Roz (Paris, F. Alcon, 1913) . The perceptive English review of Croly's book can be found in *Saturday Review*, CIX (April 2, 1910) , 433-44. Evidence for the appeal of *The Promise of American Life* to the young men around Roosevelt can be found in the Croly-Hand correspondence in the Hand Papers; Henry L. Stimson and McGeorge Bundy, *On Active Service in Peace and War* (Harper, 1948) , 59-60; Frankfurter's memorial essay on Croly previously cited; and Herbert Croly, *Willard Straight* (Macmillan, 1924) , 288-402, 472. The account of the stalking of Roosevelt is drawn almost entirely from correspondence between Croly and Judge Hand early in 1910, but also relevant are Henry Cabot Lodge to Theodore Roosevelt, April 19, 1910, Lodge Papers; Roosevelt's reply in *Selections from the Correspondence of Theodore Roosevelt and Henry Cabot Lodge* (Scribner, 1925), II, 378. The Croly-Hand correspondence has forced me to dissent from the accounts of how Croly's book reached Roosevelt in Matthew Josephson, *President-Makers, 1896-1916* (Harcourt, Brace, 1940) , 369; Alvin Johnson, *Pioneer's Progress* (Viking, 1952) , 233; and Eric F. Goldman, *Rendezvous With Destiny* (Knopf, 1952), 189. No copy of Roosevelt's extremely important letter to Croly praising *The Promise of American Life* and promising to use Croly's "ideas freely in speeches" has been found by the numerous scholars who have examined the Roosevelt Papers. The version quoted is taken from a copy of the Roosevelt letter that Croly incorporated in a letter to Judge Hand, Aug. 1, 1910, Hand Papers. The views of Theodore Roosevelt and Henry Cabot Lodge that are compared with Croly's are drawn from Elting E. Morison (ed.) , *Letters of Theodore Roosevelt* (Harvard, 1951-54) , VI, 370; Henry Cabot Lodge, *Early Memories* (Scribner, 1913) , 209, 211; and Henry F. Pringle, *Theodore Roosevelt* (Harcourt, Brace, 1931) , 297, 318.

2. **A Question of Influence.** Among the scholars who have, with varying degrees of emphasis, credited Croly with inspiring Roosevelt's New Nationalism are: H. F. Pringle, *Theodore Roosevelt*, 540-41 (but see Pringle's somewhat more circumspect account in *Life and Times of William Howard Taft* [Farrar & Rinehart, 1939], II, 569) ; John Chamberlain, "Herbert Croly and America's Future," *New Republic*, CI (Nov. 8, 1939) , 33; John Chamberlain, *Farewell to Reform* (Liveright, 1932) , 199-224; Felix Frankfurter, "Herbert Croly and American Political Opinion," *New Republic*, LXIII (July 16, 1930) , 247; George E. Mowry, *Theodore Roosevelt and the Progressive Movement* (Wisconsin, 1947) , 146; E. F. Goldman, *Rendezvous With Destiny*, 189, 209; Walter Lippmann, "Notes for a Biography," *New Republic*, LXIII (July 16, 1930) , 250-51; Russel B. Nye, *Midwestern Progressive Politics* (Michigan State, 1951) , 274-8; Ralph Henry Gabriel, *Course of American Democratic Thought* (Ronald, 1956) , 364; Daniel Aaron, *Men of Good Hope: A Story of American Progressives* (Oxford, 1951) , 250-51; Byron Dexter, "Herbert Croly and the Promise of American Life," *Political Science Quarterly*, LXX (June 1955) , 197-218; John A. Garraty, *Henry Cabot Lodge: A Biography* (Knopf, 1953) , 285.

Lippmann in his essay in *Weyl, Appreciation* predicted that when Theodore Roosevelt's letters were published by impartial scholars the real importance of Croly (as well as Weyl) would become clear. Elting E. Morison in his edition of *The Letters of Theodore Roosevelt*, VII, 77 n., concludes, however, that ". . . Roosevelt, as some have believed, did not derive his progressivism from Croly. The two simply agreed." The passages from Roosevelt's letters quoted to illustrate his prior commitment to ideas similar to Croly's can be found in ibid. V, 351, 352, 802-3, VI, 1372, 1527, VII, 228-9; H. F. Pringle, *Theodore Roosevelt*, 368; and John Morton Blum, *Republican Roosevelt* (Harvard, 1954), 30. For other passages illustrating the parallelism of Roosevelt's and Croly's thought see E. E. Morison (ed.), *Letters of Theodore Roosevelt*, V, 347, 349, 368, 407, 410, 469. Croly's single reference to the "new Nationalism" occurs in *Promise of American Life*, 272. He did at other points in the book refer to "The New National Democracy" or "the new national movement," but in both cases only as a means of describing Jacksonian democracy, which Croly, of course, abhorred.

3. **The New Nationalism.** The political dilemmas Roosevelt faced on his return to the United States in June 1910 are fully revealed in E. E. Morison (ed.), *Letters of Theodore Roosevelt*, VII, 45-170; H. F. Pringle, *Theodore Roosevelt*, 523-39; G. E. Mowry, *Theodore Roosevelt and the Progressive Movement*, 120-41. Roosevelt's Osawatomie, Kansas, address can be found in Hermann Hagedorn (ed.), *Works of Theodore Roosevelt* (Scribner, 1926), XVII, 5-22. Roosevelt's qualifications of the address are drawn from E. E. Morison (ed.), *Letters of Theodore Roosevelt*, VII, 122, 124, 134, 170.

4. **A Measure of Influence.** Virtually every issue of the *Outlook* from Jan. 1909 on contains some expression of its "New Federalism." Roosevelt's remarks on his "imperialist democracy" or "Democratic Imperialism" can be found in E. E. Morison (ed.), *Letters of Theodore Roosevelt*, VII, 104, 112. The similarity of Croly's and Roosevelt's reasoning in calling for a "revision of the rules of the game" can be seen in H. Croly, *Promise of American Life*, 172-3, and H. Hagedorn (ed.), *Works of Theodore Roosevelt*, XVII, 5-22. Roosevelt's belief, contrary to Croly's, in regulating the trusts through a commission is revealed in E. E. Morison (ed.), *Letters of Theodore Roosevelt*, VII, 277 n.; G. E. Mowry, *Theodore Roosevelt and the Progressive Movement*, 192, 266; Theodore Roosevelt, "The Trusts, the People and the Square Deal," *Outlook*, XCIX (Nov. 18, 1911), 649-56. George W. Perkins's revealing statement on the kind of regulatory commission he desired is quoted in Edwin C. Rozwenc (ed.), *Roosevelt, Wilson and the Trusts* (Heath, 1950), 72-9. John A. Garraty's *Right-Hand Man: The Life of George W. Perkins* (Harper, 1960), though very useful, does not discuss this aspect of Perkins's views on the trusts. The references to Roosevelt's views on the trust question are drawn from E. E. Morison (ed.), *Letters of Theodore Roosevelt*, VII, 230-31, 231 n.; Theodore Roosevelt, "Nationalism and Special Privilege," *Outlook*, XCVII (Jan. 28, 1911), 145-8; E. F. Goldman, *Rendezvous With Destiny*, 210; Theodore Roosevelt, *Autobiography* (Scribner, 1913), 579.

5. An Influential Publicist. The various indications of Croly's closeness to Roosevelt in the public records can be found in New York *Herald*, Oct. 10, 1910; E. E. Morison (ed.) , *Letters of Theodore Roosevelt*, VIII, 1471, 1477, 1486: Theodore Roosevelt, "Nationalism and Popular Rule," *Outlook*, XCVII (Jan. 21, 1911) , 96-101; Theodore Roosevelt, *Autobiography*, 25, 77; and *American Magazine*, LXXV (Nov. 1912) , 23. Numerous letters from Croly to Judge Learned Hand in the Hand Papers, however, give a truer picture of the actual relationship. Evidence for the rapid expansion of Croly's political activities after 1910 is drawn from these letters as well as from the articles in the *North American Review* and *World's Work* as cited, and from Theodore Roosevelt to Herbert Croly, Oct. 6, Nov. 21, Dec. 29, 1911, Roosevelt Papers. Croly's views on the western insurgents are revealed in his letters to Learned Hand. The circumstances surrounding Croly's writing of *Marcus Alonzo Hanna: His Life and Work* (Macmillan, 1912) , are revealed in its preface, as well as in James Ford Rhodes, *McKinley and Roosevelt Administrations* (Macmillan, 1922), 8-9; E. E. Morison (ed.), *Letters of Theodore Roosevelt*, VII, 446 n.; and Herbert Croly to Learned Hand, May 21, 1910, Feb. 24, 1911, [Oct.?] 1911, Hand Papers; Herbert Croly to Theodore Roosevelt, Oct. 5, Dec. 4, 1911, Theodore Roosevelt to Herbert Croly, Oct. 6, Nov. 21, Dec. 29, 1911, Roosevelt Papers; and E. E. Morison (ed.) , *Letters of Theodore Roosevelt*, VII, 513. The various comments on Croly's biography of Hanna that are cited can be found in *Nation*, XCIV (May 30, 1912) , 540-41; Walter Weyl, MS. Diary, May 5, 1912; *Review of Reviews*, XXV (May 1912) , 638; *Athenaeum* (London) , I (May 25, 1912) , 592; *Dial*, LIII (July 16, 1912) , 54; *Outlook*, CI (July 27, 1912) , 786; *Literary Digest*, XLV (July 6, 1912) , 25-6; and Thomas Beer, *Hanna, Crane, and the Mauve Decade* (Knopf, 1941) , 396.

6. Ideas, Intellectuals, and a Movement. Croly's attitude toward Roosevelt in the early stages of the campaign of 1912 is revealed in Croly to Learned Hand, June 9, [Dec. 10?], 1911, Jan. [12?], 1912, Hand Papers; and Herbert Croly to Theodore Roosevelt, Feb. 28, 1912, Theodore Roosevelt to Herbert Croly, Feb. 29, 1912, Roosevelt Papers. Weyl's work for La Follette and his relationship to the Senator are revealed in Weyl, MS. Diary, Sept. 14, 1911-Feb. 7, 1912. Weyl wrote his diary in bound notebooks that allow excisions to be detected. A page is missing after the incomplete entry on La Follette for Dec. 17, 1912, and two pages that also, from the fragmentary context, obviously dealt with La Follette have been removed by hand unknown after the entry for Feb. 7, 1912. Only one other such excision occurs anywhere in the diary. The contrast of Weyl's views on foreign policy and population problems with Roosevelt's can best be seen by comparing Howard K. Beale, *Theodore Roosevelt and the Rise of America to World Power* (Johns Hopkins, 1956) , 23-41, 181-2. For Weyl's endorsement of Roosevelt and the Progressive party, see Walter Weyl to Theodore Roosevelt, Aug. 8, 1912, Roosevelt Papers. Croly's public stand in the electoral campaign is revealed in "A Test of Faith in Democracy," *American Magazine*, LXXV (Nov. 1912) , 21-3, but, as indicated by quotations in the text, this public statement is considerably modified by statements in his correspondence with Learned Hand. See especially letters from Croly to Hand, June 17,

July 13, [July or August], 1912. His misunderstanding with Roosevelt about becoming the ex-President's biographer is revealed in Herbert Croly to Theodore Roosevelt, July 26, 1912, and Theodore Roosevelt to Herbert Croly, July 30, 1912, Roosevelt Papers. Weyl's intensive campaign activity is described in H. Brubaker (ed.), *Weyl, Appreciation*, 46-7, 86, 122; and Weyl, MS. Diary, Nov. 11, 1912. Lippmann's reactions to Roosevelt and the campaign are indicated in Lippmann, *A Tribute to Theodore Roosevelt, October 27, 1858-1935* (Women's Roosevelt Memorial Association, 1935), 3; and Lippmann, "Notes for a Biography," *New Republic*, LXIII (July 16, 1930), 250.

CHAPTER FIVE

TOWARD A NEW REPUBLIC, 1912-1914

1. A Loyal Bull Moose Trio. Roosevelt's post-campaign attitudes are examined in Henry F. Pringle, *Theodore Roosevelt* (Harcourt, Brace, 1931), 571; and George E. Mowry, *Theodore Roosevelt and the Progressive Movement* (Wisconsin, 1947), 284-91. Weyl's continued loyalty to the Bull Moose cause is revealed in Walter Weyl to Roosevelt, Nov. 6, 1912, Roosevelt Papers; and Weyl, MS. Diary, Nov. 15, 16, Dec. 4, 1912. The latter source for Dec. 15, 1912, also suggests Croly's continued role in the movement, together with Croly to Learned Hand, [Jan. 28], Feb. 4, [Feb. ?], [Feb. 20], March [4-10], 1913, Hand Papers; and Herbert Croly, *Progressive Democracy* (Macmillan, 1914), 333-6. For Lippmann's attitudes see Walter Lippmann to Theodore Roosevelt, May 30, 1913, June 1, 1914, Roosevelt Papers.

2. Croly and Democracy. Much of the evidence for this section is drawn from Croly's *Progressive Democracy* and, in view of the book's detailed table of contents and reliable index, requires no elaborate documentation. For evidence of the impact of John Dewey and Albion Small on Croly's thought, however, see ibid. 267-83, 423, 426. Croly's substitutions of "social democratic ideal" for "national ideal" can be found in ibid. 173, 176, 177, 183, 184, 199, 208, 230, 240, 241, 243. Suggestions as to the impact on eastern intellectuals of the I.W.W.'s leadership of the Lawrence and Paterson strikes can be found in Mary Heaton Vorse, *Footnote to Folly* (Farrar & Rinehart, 1935), 17, 52-4; Walter Weyl, MS. Diary, Jan. 24, Feb. 1, March 6, 11, 16, 18, 20, 1912; Hutchins Hapgood, *Victorian in the Modern World* (Harcourt, Brace, 1939), 360; Mabel Dodge Luhan, *Movers and Shakers* (Harcourt, Brace, 1936),186-211; Granville Hicks, *John Reed: The Making of a Revolutionary* (Macmillan, 1937), 100-101. Croly's optimistic response to the outbreak of World War I can be found in a letter to Learned Hand, Aug. 17, 1914, Hand Papers.

3. Weyl and the Class War. Weyl's struggles to revise his political philosophy in the "Class War" book are revealed in numerous entries in his MS. Diary from Dec. 1911 through Aug. 30, 1913. A fuller description of his efforts, with documentation, can be found in Charles Forcey, "Walter Weyl and the Class

War" in Harvey Goldberg (ed.) , *American Radicals: Some Problems and Personalities* (Monthly Review Press, 1957) , 265-76. Also helpful are Walter Weyl, "The Strikers at Lawrence," *Outlook*, C (Feb. 10, 1912) , 309-12; and Weyl, "It is Time to Know," *Survey*, XXVIII (April 6, 1912), 65-7.

4. **Lippmann and Mastery.** Walter Lippmann, *Drift and Mastery: An Attempt to Diagnose the Current Unrest* (Mitchell Kennerley, 1914) , is not indexed. Documentation of some of the more important of the new departures in Lippmann's thinking, therefore, is in order. For his reiterated use of the theme of the "new, responsible businessmen," see ibid. xix, 23, 24, 27, 37, 45-6, 48, 50, 63, 67, 103, 117, 118, 125, 136, 144, 166, 206, 244, 269, 315. The less happy view of Louis Brandeis on businessmen is revealed in Alpheus T. Mason, *Brandeis: A Free Man's Life* (Viking, 1946) , 350-59. Lippmann's development of the theme of consumers as a new political force occurs in *Drift and Mastery*, 65, 76, 101, 144, 145, 168, 224, 254. Lippmann's new cautions against voluntaristic leadership can be found in ibid. 168-9, 285-6, while references to Bill Haywood, the I.W.W., and the idea of "industrial democracy" occur in ibid. 87-91, 95, 173, 174, 183, 190, 191, 244, 314. For the impact of the Lawrence and Paterson strikes see the references cited in Section 2 above, and Walter Lippmann, "A National Diagnosis," *Everybody's Magazine*, XXVIII (Feb. 1913) , 247-8. Graham Wallas' important letter cautioning Lippmann against anti-intellectualism is printed in the Englishman's *Great Society: A Psychological Analysis* (Macmillan, 1914) , v, and Wallas's influence is acknowledged by Lippmann in *Drift and Mastery*, 36. Lippmann's revised views on pragmatism and science are particularly evident in passages in ibid. 260-3, 275-6, 282-6, 306, 309, 317, 327. See ibid. 310-11, for his explicit rejection of socialism for middle-class liberalism.

5. **A Meeting of Minds and Money.** The best source on Willard Straight for the purposes of this section is Herbert Croly, *Willard Straight* (Macmillan, 1924) , but see also Charles Vevier, *United States and China, 1906-1913: A Study of Finance and Diplomacy* (Rutgers, 1955) . Straight's attitude toward the Wilson administration in its early days is further revealed in Willard Straight to Edward V. Morgan, Oct. 17, 1912, to J. A. Thomas, Feb. 28, 1913, to J. O. P. Bland, March 26, 1913, to Theodore Roosevelt, May 26, 1914, Straight Papers. For the discussions between Croly and the Straights that led to the founding of the *New Republic*, see Bruce Bliven, "Herbert Croly and Journalism," *New Republic*, LXIII (July 16, 1930) , 259; H. Croly, *Willard Straight*, 474; Robert Morss Lovett, *All Our Years* (Viking, 1948) , 160; Alvin Johnson, *Pioneer's Progress* (Viking, 1952) , 233-4. The story of Norman Hapgood's effort to revamp *Harper's Weekly* into an organ for Wilson's New Freedom is revealed in Louis Filler, *Crusaders for American Liberalism* (Harcourt, Brace, 1939) , 363; Norman Angell, *After All* (Farrar, Straus & Young, 1951) , 315-16; M. D. Luhan, *Movers and Shakers*, 46-7; Philip Littell, "Norman Hapgood," *New Republic*, I (Dec. 16, 1914) , 13-15; and A. Johnson, *Pioneer's Progress*, 232. Croly expressed his reactions to Hapgood's venture in letters to Learned Hand, Jan. 5, 8, 1914, Hand Papers. The materials on the general condition of American magazines at the time of the *New Republic*'s founding are drawn

from L. Filler, *Crusaders for American Liberalism*, 361-71; Lincoln Steffens, *Autobiography* (Harcourt, Brace, 1931) , 535-6; G. Hicks, *John Reed*, 65, 92-9, 112; Ida M. Tarbell, *All in a Day's Work: An Autobiography* (Macmillan, 1939) , 296-8; M. D. Luhan, *Movers and Shakers*, 84; Louis Untermeyer, *From Another World* (Harcourt, Brace, 1939) , 39-49; H. Hapgood, *Victorian in the Modern World* (Harcourt, Brace, 1939) , 312; Floyd Dell, *Homecoming: An Autobiography* (Farrar & Rinehart, 1933) , 248-9; John E. Drewry, *Some Magazines and Magazine Makers* (Stratford, 1924) , 40-44; Oswald Garrison Villard, *Fighting Years: Memoirs of a Liberal Editor* (Harcourt, Brace, 1939) , 349; and from readings in contemporary issues of *Pearson's, Metropolitan, American Magazine, Masses, Outlook,* and *Nation.* The experiences of Lippmann, Weyl, Hackett, and Hallowell on the muckraking magazines are revealed in W. Lippmann, *Preface to Politics,* 196; W. Weyl, MS. Diary, Jan. 10, Feb. 6, 1913; and L. Filler, *Crusaders for American Liberalism,* 366. The size of the Straight fortune is not known, but it was large enough to support the *New Republic* and several other magazines, plus numerous other philanthropies, until 1935, when the magazines were put under a permanent trust arrangement. B. Amiden, "The Nation and the New Republic," *Survey Graphic,* XXIX (Jan. 1940) , 24. The Straight family support of the *New Republic* continued until April 1953, and a request for public subscriptions at that time declared that the Straight subsidy had averaged $95,000 a year, or approximately $3,662,500 for the thirty-eight and a half years of support. The story of the editors' negotiations with the Straights over control of the *New Republic* emerges from H. Brubaker (ed.) , *Weyl, Appreciation,* 96; H. Croly, *Willard Straight,* 473-4, 566; W. Lippmann, "Notes for a Biography," *New Republic,* LXIII (July 16, 1930) , 250; Herbert Croly to Learned Hand, March 17, June 29, 1914, Hand Papers; Willard Straight to Theodore Roosevelt, June 9, 1917, Straight Papers. For William J. Ghent's disparaging comment see his letter to Morris Hillquit, April 15 [1915], Hillquit Papers. Edmund Wilson reveals that after Croly's death Dorothy Straight's forbearance did not hold up when his successor, Bruce Bliven, held the *New Republic* to an anti-British, isolationist line before World War II. Her second husband, an Englishman, took charge, according to Wilson, fired several editors, and forced a reversal of policy. See Edmund Wilson, *A Piece of My Mind* (Doubleday Anchor, 1958) , 39-41.

CHAPTER SIX

NATIONALISM AND THE NEW FREEDOM, 1914-1916

1. **Ideas and Men.** Herbert Croly's initial aims in founding the *New Republic* are revealed in letters to Learned Hand, Jan. 5, 1914, Hand Papers, and to Randolph S. Bourne, June 3, 1914, Bourne Papers, as well as in Herbert Croly, *Willard Straight* (Macmillan, 1924) , 472-3. Walter Lippmann's slightly divergent views are quoted in Van Wyck Brooks, *Scenes and Portraits: Memories of Childhood and Youth* (Dutton, 1954) , 218. Croly's straitened financial circumstances when he assumed the editorship of the *New Republic* are revealed in letters to Learned Hand in the Hand Papers dated [Spring?], June [?], Oct.

13, 17, 1913, March 18, 21, 1914. Weyl's flush financial condition is clear from numerous entries in his diary for the period, but the frustrations that beset him are revealed not only in the diary but in Louis Levine, *Women's Garment Workers* (Huebsch, 1924) , 202, 283; Robert William Iversen, "Morris Hillquit, American Social Democrat: A Study of the American Left from Haymarket to the New Deal" (unpublished Ph.D. dissertation, State University of Iowa, 1951), 99-111; and Alpheus T. Mason, *Brandeis: A Free Man's Life* (Viking, 1946) , 308-9. Information on Lippmann's life at the time he joined the *New Republic* can be found in Granville Hicks, *John Reed: The Making of a Revolutionary* (Macmillan, 1937) , 77, 176, 225; Lincoln Steffens, *Autobiography* (Harcourt, Brace, 1931) , 655-6; and Mabel Dodge Luhan, *Movers and Shakers* (Harcourt, Brace, 1936) , 118, 303, 324-5. For relevant information on Francis Hackett, see Hackett's *I Chose Denmark* (Doubleday, Doran, 1940) , 61-3, 78-80; Floyd Dell, *Homecoming: An Autobiography* (Farrar & Rinehart, 1933) , 195-6, 206; V. W. Brooks, *Scenes and Portraits*, 153. On Philip Littell, see "Concerning F. M. Colby," *Bookman*, LXVIII (June 1928) , 175-6; Malcolm Cowley, "Books and People," *New Republic*, CIX (Nov. 13, 1943) , 689; Hutchins Hapgood, *Victorian in the Modern World* (Harcourt, Brace, 1939) , 323; *New Republic*, XXI (Dec. 21, 1919) , 144; Oswald Garrison Villard, *Disappearing Daily* (Knopf, 1944) , 70-77. On Charlotte Rudyard, see W. Lippmann, "Notes for a Biography," *New Republic*, LXIII (July 16, 1930) , 250; *Who's Who in America*, XII (1922-1923), 2679; A. Johnson, *Pioneer's Progress*, 234; and Randolph S. Bourne to Elizabeth Shepley Sergeant, June 25, 1915, Bourne Papers. Material on Robert Hallowell can be found in the books and articles by Walter Lippmann, Mabel Dodge Luhan, and Granville Hicks already cited, as well as in *Who's Who in America*, XII (1922-23) , 1379-80; Harold Stearns, *Street I Know* (Furman, 1936) , 253-4; and *New Republic*, CXXVIII (March 30, 1953) , 32. My interviews with Judge Learned Hand and Justice Felix Frankfurter have been very useful for defining their relationship to the magazine, as has Croly's correspondence with Judge Hand, but further information is available in Randolph S. Bourne, MS. Pocket Diary, Sept. 11, Nov. 9, 15, 1916; Norman Angell, *After All* (Straus & Young, 1951) , 203; "Statement of Ownership, Management, Etc., . . . for April 1, 1915," *New Republic*, II (April 10, 1915), 268. For George Soule's relationship to the magazine, see *New Republic*, IX (Jan. 6, 1917) , 260. For Alvin Johnson's, see his *Pioneer's Progress*, 241; and *New Republic*, IV (Sept. 4, 1915), 116. George Rublee's closeness to the editors is revealed in H. Croly to L. Hand, Jan. 8, 1914, Hand Papers; R. S. Bourne, MS. Pocket Diary, July 5, 1916; H. Croly to R. S. Bourne, Sept. 15, 1914, Bourne Papers. The maneuvers of Ellery Sedgwick and Charles A. Beard to secure Randolph Bourne a position on the *New Republic*, as well as the upshot, are revealed in Ellery Sedgwick to R. S. Bourne, May 9, Aug. 27, Sept. 16, 1914; C. A. Beard to R. S. Bourne, May 15, 1914; H. Croly to R. S. Bourne, June 3, Aug. 27, Sept. 8, 15, 24, Oct. 5, 16, 1914, Bourne Papers.

2. **Plans and Politics.** Descriptions of the *New Republic*'s offices can be found in Robert Morss Lovett, *All Our Years* (Viking, 1948) , 174; E. Wilson, "H. C.," *New Republic*, LXIII (July 16, 1930) , 267; N. Angell, *After All*, 203; and T. S.

Matthews, *Name and Address: An Autobiography* (Simon & Schuster, 1960),
186-90. For the *New Republic's* editorial procedures, see H. Croly to R. S.
Bourne, Oct. 5, 1914, Bourne Papers; H. Croly, *Willard Straight*, 472-4; and the
sources cited in Section 5 of Chapter Five on the Straights' role in editorial
policy. The early publicity for the *New Republic* cited appeared in New York
Times, April 20, 1914, and Croly's admission of his cautious policy in a letter to
Learned Hand, Aug. 17, 1914, Hand Papers. For the lull in the progressive
ferment in the months before the *New Republic's* first appearance, see Arthur
S. Link, *Woodrow Wilson and the Progressive Era, 1910-1917* (Harper, 1954),
78-80; Henry F. Pringle, *Theodore Roosevelt* (Harcourt, Brace, 1931), 575;
George F. Mowry, *Theodore Roosevelt and the Progressive Movement* (Wis-
consin, 1947), 296-308; Willard Straight to Henry P. Fletcher, April 6, 1914,
Straight Papers. The work of the *New Republic* men with Roosevelt during the
spring and summer of 1914 is revealed in letters from Weyl, Lippmann, and
Straight to Roosevelt, together with his responses, in the Roosevelt and Straight
Papers.

3. The First Firecrackers. Hereafter in this essay the *New Republic* will be
cited merely as *NR*, followed by the date of the issue in abbreviated form and
the page number of the reference. The editors' determination to keep the focus
of their magazine on the domestic scene rather than the war is revealed in H.
Croly to L. Hand, Aug. 17, 1914, Hand Papers. Croly's leader on the war in *NR*,
11/7/14, 9-10, while unsigned is identified as his by Lippmann, *NR*, 7/16/30, 251.
The figures on the *New Republic's* pre-publication subscriptions are from
Frederick L. Paxson, *American Democracy and the World War* (Houghton
Mifflin, 1936), I, 189. Freda Kirchwey gives her account of the New Haven
newsstand survey in "Anniversaries," *Nation*, CXLIX (Nov. 11, 1939), 513-14.
The reactions of young intellectuals to the new magazine are revealed in R. S.
Bourne to Alyse Gregory, Sept. 28, [Dec. ?], 1914, Bourne Papers; S. Foster
Damon, *Amy Lowell: A Chronicle, With Extracts from Her Correspondence*
(Houghton Mifflin, 1935), 283; Edmund Wilson, *A Piece of My Mind: Re-
flections at Sixty* (Doubleday Anchor, 1958), 38; V. W. Brooks, *Scenes and
Portraits*, 219; M. D. Luhan, *Movers and Shakers*, 303; John Reed, "Almost
Thirty," *New Republic Book* (Republic, 1916), 65-6; G. Hicks, *John Reed*,
49; and Mary Hurlbutt to R. S. Bourne, Nov. 24, 1914, Bourne Papers. The
figures for the *New Republic's* circulation are from C. Wright Mills, "A Soci-
ological Account of Some Aspects of Pragmatism" (unpublished Ph.D. dissertation, University of Wisconsin, 1942), 281; *NR*, 10/24/24, ii; and N. W. Ayer
and Sons, *Newspaper Annual and Directory* (1917-25).

4. The Light That Failed. The *New Republic's* praise of Roosevelt's vigorous
stand on Belgium appears in *NR*, 11/14/14, 7-8, but was retracted in *NR*,
3/26/16, 204, when the editors discovered that his position had not been what
they imagined. The editors' night at Oyster Bay was described in Section 1 of
Chapter One, and Roosevelt's review of Croly and Lippmann appeared as "Two
Noteworthy Books on Democracy," *Outlook*, CVIII (Nov. 18, 1914), 648-51.
Roosevelt's controversial piece on Mexico was "Our Responsibilities in Mexico,"

New York Times Magazine, LXIV (Dec. 6, 1914) , 1. The editors' response appears in *NR*, 12/12/14, 5, while the subsequent controversy is revealed in ibid. 7/16/30, 250; H. Croly to T. Roosevelt, Jan. 11, 1915, Roosevelt Papers; and H. Brubaker (ed.) , *Weyl, Appreciation*, 89. For Lippmann's confession of bias see his *A Tribute to Theodore Roosevelt* (Women's Roosevelt Memorial Association of New York, 1935) , 2.

5. Liberalism and Leadership. The editors' comments on the leadership of Roosevelt and Wilson are drawn from *NR*, 12/5/14, 11; 2/10/15, 81; 4/24/15, 289; 5/1/15, 313; 5/8/15, 4-6; 5/29/15, 78-9; 11/21/14, 3-5, 7, 11/28/14, 3; 12/26/14, 3-4; 1/2/15, 5; 1/16/15, 9-10; and 3/27/15, 194-5. The best expressions of the editors' attacks on the two-party system can be found in *NR*, 11/14/14, 10-11; 7/15/16, 264; while the confusions that resulted are fully revealed in *NR*, 11/14/14, 4-5; 12/5/14, 11; 12/19/14, 3-4; 12/26/14, 3-4; 1/9/15, 45; 1/30/15, 5; 2/6/15, 2-3; 3/13/15, 140-42; 12/4/15, 105, 111-12.

6. A National Renaissance. The general picture of the "little renaissance" with which this section opens has been put together from information in Russell Lynes, "Whirlwind on Twenty-sixth Street," *Harper's Magazine*, CCVIII (June 1954), 62-9; L. Untermeyer, *From Another World*, 106-12; V. W. Brooks, *Confident Years* (Dutton, 1952) , 479, 513, 539; V. W. Brooks, *New England: Indian Summer* (World, 1946) , 526; Maxwell Geismar, *Rebels and Ancestors: The American Novel, 1890-1915* (Houghton Mifflin, 1953) , *passim*; Alfred Kazin, *On Native Grounds: An Interpretation of Modern American Prose Literature* (Doubleday, 1956) , 1-68, 140-45; F. Dell, *Homecoming*, 190-96; F. Hackett, *I Chose Denmark*, 61-80; L. Untermeyer, *From Another World*, 185-7. Evidence for nationalism's being a major theme of the "little renaissance" was found in F. Dell, *Homecoming*, 218; V. W. Brooks, *Confident Years*, 497, 513; A. Kazin, *On Native Grounds*, 133; V. W. Brooks, *America's Coming-of-Age* (Doubleday Anchor, 1958) , *passim*. On the political radicalism of the young cultural nationalists, see F. Dell, *Homecoming*, 248-89; L. Untermeyer, *From Another World*, 39-49; M. D. Luhan, *Movers and Shakers*, 186-211; H. Hapgood, *Victorian in the Modern World*, 293, 350-52; V. W. Brooks, *Scenes and Portraits*, 156-7, 202-3; Mary Heaton Vorse, *Footnote to Folly* (Farrar & Rinehart, 1935), 52-5. The contributions of the young cultural nationalists to the *New Republic* that are mentioned can be found by consulting the indexes of the magazine's bound volumes in its early years, but see also H. Croly to R. S. Bourne, Sept. 15, 1914, Bourne Papers, and "Our Literary Poverty," *NR*, 11/21/14, 10-11. George Santayana's remarks on nationalism and his feelings about the United States can be found in *Winds of Doctrine* (Scribner, 1913) , 5-6, and *Middle Span* (Scribner, 1946) , 178. The Santayana article discussed is his "Liberalism and Culture," *NR*, 9/4/15, 123-5, but this is only one among a dozen that he published in the magazine from 1914 to 1916. On Randolph Bourne at the time he began writing for the *New Republic*, see V. W. Brooks, *Confident Years*, 494-7; Carl Van Doren, *Three Worlds* (Harper, 1936) , 167-8; Louis Filler, *Randolph Bourne* (American Council on Public Affairs, 1943) , 45-95; Max Lerner, *Ideas for the Ice Age* (Viking, 1941) , 122-9; and F. Dell, *Homecoming*,

310-13. Bourne's correspondence is filled with his strong belief in cultural nationalism, but see particularly R. S. Bourne to Prudence Winterowd, March 11, 1914; to H. W. Elsasser, Nov. 27 [1913]; and to Carl [Zigrosser], Feb. 16, 1914. The article by Bourne discussed is "Continental Cultures," *NR*, 1/16/15, 14-16, but see also his "American Use for German Ideals," *NR*, 9/4/15, 117-19, for an equally fascinating development of similar themes. The material on Ezra Pound, T. S. Eliot, and Alan Seeger has been drawn from several of the autobiographies and memoirs listed above, but see also Louise Bogan, *Achievement in American Poetry* (Gateway, 1951) , 34, 63; H. Croly, "Henry James and His Countrymen," *Lamp*, XXVIII (Feb. 1904) , 47-53; Alan Seeger, *Letters and Diary* (Scribner, 1917) , 184-5; and Seeger's "As a Soldier Thinks of War," *NR*, 5/22/15, 66-8.

7. **Progressives and the New Liberalism.** The evidence that the *New Republic*'s editors considered their journal nationalistic not only in its policy but also in its contributions and coverage can be found in *NR*, 11/11/16, 56; A. Johnson, *Pioneer's Progress*, 234-5; and Edward A. Fitzpatrick, *McCarthy of Wisconsin* (Chicago, 1944) , 233-4. My conclusions on the geographical distribution of *New Republic* writers are based on a survey of the residences of all contributors during the first year of publication. In only eight cases was it impossible to determine residence. Of the American contributors, 32 were from New York, Boston, Philadelphia, Washington, or their vicinities, while only 6 came from the Middle West, and only 2 from the South and Far West. More than half (17) of the Northeastern contributors were from New York City. To break the data down in terms of contributions, there were 89 individual contributions to the *New Republic* that did not come from writers intimately associated with the magazine or serving as salaried contributors. Of these, 33 came from metropolitan New York, 58 in all from the Northeast. If the salaried or regular contributors, most of whom lived near the magazine, were included, the figures would, of course, be even more heavily weighted toward New York and the Northeast. The negative statement on the failure of most prominent progressives outside the Northeast to work with the *New Republic* would probably not be acceptable in a court of law, but history fortunately deals only in probabilities. The statement is based on a careful (even laborious) card file that has been kept of names in all the diaries, letters, memoirs, and other sources relevant to the *New Republic* consulted. For a fuller discussion of the evidence see Chapter VIII, Sections 2-3, of my Ph.D. dissertation. On the matter of the *New Republic*'s coverage of reform movements outside New York, the following figures will illustrate the point made. During the first year, of 10 articles or editorials referring to developments in specific cities, 7 referred to New York, 2 to Chicago, 1 to Paterson, New Jersey; of 16 articles or editorials referring to specific states, 13 dealt with New York, 2 with Wisconsin, and 1 with Massachusetts. My point about the Jeffersonian cast of the liberalism of reformers from the West and South is, of course, basic to this study, and is confirmed by Russel B. Nye, *Midwestern Progressive Politics* (Michigan State College, 1951) , 274-309; George E. Mowry, *California Progressives* (California, 1951) , 97-104; G. E. Mowry, *Theodore Roosevelt and the Progressive Movement*, 269-83; and Richard Hofstadter, *Age of Reform: From Bryan to F.D.R.*

(Knopf, 1955), 242-54. The conclusions about the friends of Croly, Weyl, and Lippmann who supported the *New Republic* are based on the card file of names mentioned above. In a few cases a contributor or supporter was a friend of one or more of the leading editors; in many others, even those of such prominent men as John Dewey and Charles A. Beard, no probable relationship with any one of the editors could be determined; and in still others, the magazine's growing reputation or the writer's friendship with other members of the group such as Hackett or Frankfurter probably established the connection. Even so, the over-all pattern of assent to the *New Republic* by those close to Croly and Lippmann and dissent from it by those close to Weyl emerges strikingly from the record.

8. **Liberalism and Nationalism.** Justice Holmes's letters to Harold Laski provide a running commentary on the *New Republic* in its early years. For the two examples cited, see Mark DeWolfe Howe (ed.), *Holmes-Laski Letters* (Harvard, 1953), I, 17, 99. The editors' fears about the future of the progressive movement early in 1915 are expressed in "The Tide of Reaction," *NR*, 1/16/15, 6-8. The attacks on Wilson's legislative record mentioned can be found in ibid. 11|/7/14, 4, 8; 12/5/14, 4; [Learned Hand], 1/9/15, 7-8; 12/9/16, 136-7. Arthur S. Link, who has now written three volumes of what should long remain the most definitive biography of Wilson, agrees with the *New Republic's* judgment of the President's early trust measures in *Wilson: The New Freedom* (Princeton, 1956), 417-44. Link, in fact, uses quotations from Croly or the *New Republic* on Wilson's domestic and foreign policies so frequently as to identify himself with the magazine's generally critical position. The materials for the editors' efforts to distinguish their position on the control of business from Wilson's are drawn from *NR*, 11/21/14, 11-12; 12/19/14, 4, 8-9; 12/26/14, 10-11; 1/9/15, 12; 3/27/15, 192; 12/23/16, 200-201; 12/27/15, 80; 10/7/16, 233; 1/9/15, 6-7; 1/23/15, 10-11; 6/17/16, 161-2; 12/9/16, 140-41; and 5/8/15, 2-3. The magazine's position on "industrial democracy" can be understood from ibid. 11/7/14, 11-12; 12/26/14, 5-6; 1/9/15, 3; 9/18/15, 170-71; 10/9/15, 249-50; 5/20/16, 55-7; 1/9/15, 6-7; 1/30/15, 6-7; 2/6/15, 5-7; 3/27/15, 196-7; 5/8/15, 7-8, but see especially "A Substitute for Violence," ibid. 12/12/14, 9-10. The editors' demands for strong and expert administration together with various devices for direct democracy are expressed in ibid. 1/9/15, 5; [Randolph Bourne], 7/8/16, 240-41; 8/26/16, 78; 2/5/16, 18; 1/21/14, 4; 12/5/14, 6; 1/16/15, 4; 1/23/15, 8-9; 1/13/15, 30; 4/10/15, 246; 6/26/15, 186-7; 7/10/15, 240; 1/23/15, 3-4; 11/6/15, 4-6; 1/30/15, 4; 4/3/15, 222-3; 6/5/15, 105; 10/9/15, 246; 12/11/15, 132; 7/22/16, 287; 11/28/14, 7-8; 10/21/15, 58-9; 12/16/16, 170-72. The continuing faith of Croly, Weyl, and Lippmann in the massed pressure of middle-class progressivism becomes evident in ibid. 1/9/15, 4; 1/30/15, 5; 7/14/15, 29-30; 5/27/16, 74-5; 7/15/16, 264. For a discussion of Wilson's feelings about the substantial completeness of his New Freedom program in 1914, see Arthur S. Link, *Woodrow Wilson and the Progressive Era* (Harper, 1954), 78-80, and for the editors' response, see "Presidential Complacency," *NR*, 11/21/14, 7. Evidence of the editors' awareness of the instability of capitalism and of their anticipation of New Deal measures will be found in ibid. 12/5/14, 2; 12/12/14, 9-10; 12/19/14, 4; 1/30/15, 6-7; 2/20/15, 56; 5/8/15,

7-8; 11/20/15, 66-8; 8/12/16, 124-6. *New Republic* articles that foreshadow the "technocrat" movement of the 'thirties will be found in ibid. 12/5/14, 5; [Randolph Bourne], 6/26/15, 191-2; 10/2/15, 221-3; 10/7/16, 237-8; 12/23/16, 204-5; 1/20/17, 315-17. Bourne's unsigned editorials for the *New Republic* are identified in his MS. Pocket Diary. For Wilson's record on civil liberties, see A. S. Link, *Wilson: The New Freedom*, 243-54, 274-6, and for the record of progressives generally, Eric F. Goldman, *Rendezvous With Destiny* (Knopf, 1952), 77-9, 176-85. The *New Republic's* record, on the other hand, can be traced in *NR*, 4/24/15, 290; 6/26/15, 186; 7/24/15, 300; 8/21/15, 56; 9/4/15, 112-14; 1/9/15, 45; 5/22/15, 56-7; 6/26/15, 185; 7/3/15, 214-15; [Randolph Bourne], 7/17/15, 269-70; 10/9/15, 245-6; 10/16/15, 274-5; 1/30/15, 3; 5/8/15, 1-2; 5/22/15, 52; 9/18/15, 164; 11/6/15, 4; 11/27/15, 81; 12/4/15, 106-7; 11/21/14, 5; 4/10/15, 245; 4/24/15, 291; 5/8/15, 3; 6/5/15, 105; 6/26/15, 186; 11/13/15, 28; 11/20/15, 54-5, 60-61; 11/24/14, 10. Evidence for the editors' increasing discouragement about the popular basis for their new liberalism by the latter part of 1915 can be found in "Popular Discussion," *NR*, 8/7/15, 35-6; W. Weyl, "The Average Voter," *Century*, XC (Oct. 1915), 901-7; and W. Lippmann, "Insiders and Outsiders," *NR*, 11/13/15, 35-6. For a discussion of Lippmann's lifelong elaboration of his distrust of popular democracy, see my "Leadership and 'Misrule by the People,' " ibid. 2/21/55, 13-16. The *New Republic* editors' chastened views of the business elite can be found in ibid. 12/26/14, 5-6; 1/9/15, 3; 1/30/15, 12-13; 2/6/15, 7-8; 4/3/15, 217; 6/5/15, 106-7; 7/3/15, 221-3; 7/17/15, 266-7; 10/2/15, 218-19; 12/4/15, 112; [Randolph Bourne], 7/15/16, 267-8; 7/22/16, 301-2. The *New Republic's* essential case against the Socialist party was presented in "Socialist Degeneration," ibid. 12/12/14, 10-11, but, see also ibid. 12/16/15, 10, 24; 12/23/15, 6; 1/15/15, 10-12; 2/13/15, 50. Sharp replies to the magazine's charges can be found in William J. Ghent to *New Republic*, ibid. 1/9/15, 23-4, and Max Eastman, "Knowledge and Revolution, Negative Pacifism," *Masses*, VI (Feb. 1915), 14, but, for modern scholarly support for the *New Republic's* case, see David A. Shannon, *Socialist Party of America: A History* (Macmillan, 1955), 1-42. The *New Republic's* editorial that praises Elihu Root appears in *NR*, 9/18/15, 163-4. For the magazine's role in the presidential boomlet for Root that fall, see Richard W. Leopold, *Elihu Root and the Conservative Tradition* (Little, Brown, 1954), 109-12. The editors' important leader in which they expressed discouragement with middle-class reform and looked, very tentatively, toward a farm-labor movement was "Homeless Radicals," *NR*, 7/1/16, 211-13.

BOOK THREE: THE DECLINE OF THE NEW LIBERALISM

CHAPTER SEVEN

NATIONALISM AND INTERNATIONALISM, 1914-1917

1. **Nationalists and a War.** For this chapter and the final one that follows, space does not permit the extensive documentation of *New Republic* policies that has been given thus far. Such documentation can be obtained for many

of the points in my Ph.D. dissertation or, as suggested earlier, by correspondence with me. Documentation will be given here only on points of particular interest or possible controversy. Randolph Bourne made the confession of innocence for the editors in an unsigned editorial, "Mental Unpreparedness," *NR*, 9/11/15, 143-4. Croly's ideas on foreign policy have been discussed in Chapter One, Section 7, above, but for the ideas mentioned here, see *Promise of American Life* (Macmillan, 1909), 256-7, 290, 310-14. His initial response to the outbreak of war in Europe is revealed in H. Croly to Learned Hand, Aug. 17, 1914, Hand Papers. Walter Weyl's response is discussed in Howard Brubaker (ed.), *Walter Weyl, An Appreciation* (privately printed, 1922), 72, 91, 106, 126; while his prewar views on foreign policy can be found in Walter Weyl, "An Experiment in Population," *Atlantic Monthly*, CIII (Feb. 1909), 261-7; and Walter Weyl, *New Democracy* (Macmillan, 1912), 260-61, 356-7. Lippmann's admission of his disinterest in diplomatic matters was quoted in *Time*, XLI (June 14, 1943), 100, and for his views, see *Preface to Politics* (Kennerley, 1913), 46-9, 105; *Drift and Mastery* (Kennerley, 1914), 43, 163-4, 311. For Lippmann's reactions to the war's outbreak and his friends' reactions to his reactions, see W. Lippmann, *Stakes of Diplomacy* (Holt, 1915), 5; Harold Stearns, *Street I Know* (Furman, 1935), 122-3; and Mabel Dodge Luhan, *Movers and Shakers* (Harcourt, Brace, 1936), 301.

2. **Nationalism and Neutrality.** Charles A. Beard's changing views on isolation are discussed in Howard K. Beale (ed.), *Charles A. Beard: An Appraisal* (Kentucky, 1954), 168-74, 242, and see also Charles A. Beard, *Open Door at Home: A Trial Philosophy of National Interest* (Macmillan, 1934), *passim*. For the editors' linkage of pacifism and isolation with the old Jeffersonian liberalism, see "Pacifism vs. Passivism," *NR*, 11/14/14, 7-8. Randolph Bourne's remarkable celebration of the bloody conflict of cultures taking place in Europe occurs in his "Contented Cultures," ibid. 1/16/15, 14-16. The story of the early effort of a British publisher to bribe the editors comes from W. Lippmann, "Notes for a Biography," ibid. 7/16/30, 251. Croly's pro-Allied cast of mind is discussed in the article by Lippmann just cited, in another by Edmund Wilson in the same issue of the *New Republic*; in Robert Morss Lovett, *All Our Years* (Viking, 1948), 192; and is revealed in his own "The Meaning of It," *NR*, 8/7/15, 10-11. Weyl's more neutral but essentially similar views are revealed in his MS. Diary, March 28, 1915, Sept. 28, 1918, and in H. Brubaker (ed.), *Weyl, Appreciation*, 75. For Lippmann's boast about his own lack of neutrality see ibid. 88-9. Willard Straight's strongly pro-Allied views are revealed in H. Croly, *Willard Straight* (Macmillan, 1924), 476; and Willard Straight to J. O. P. Bland, [Sept. 1914], Straight Papers. The attitudes of Frankfurter, Hand, Johnson, and Hackett toward the war become clear from Hermann Hagedorn, *Roosevelt Family of Sagamore Hill* (Macmillan, 1954), 340-43; Elting E. Morison (ed.), *Letters of Theodore Roosevelt* (Harvard, 1951-1954), VIII, 826; H. Croly to L. Hand, Feb. 25, 1915, Hand Papers; Alvin Johnson, *Pioneer's Progress* (Viking, 1952), 241; R. M. Lovett, *All Our Years*, 173; Francis Hackett, *I Chose Denmark* (Doubleday, Doran, 1940), 12-13, 20. For the rather different views of Bourne and Stearns see R. S. Bourne to E. G., Aug. 30, 1915, Bourne Papers;

and H. Stearns, *Street I Know*, 140-44. For the relationship of the Englishmen Norman Angell and Harold Laski to the *New Republic* and for their views on the war, see Norman Angell, *After All* (Farrar, Straus & Young, 1951) , 201-15; A. Johnson, *Pioneer's Progress*, 243; R. S. Bourne to Alyse Gregory, Nov. 10, [1916], Bourne Papers; Mark DeWolfe Howe (ed.) , *Holmes-Laski Letters* (Harvard, 1953) , I, 11, 91, 97, 101, 155. The relationship of the other Britons mentioned to the magazine is revealed first of all by their contributions, but in the cases of Ratcliffe, Zimmern, West, Wallas, Morgan, and Brailsford also in Van Wyck Brooks, *Scenes and Portraits: Memories of Childhood and Youth* (Dutton, 1954) , 218; New York *Times*, March 24, 1958; A. Johnson, *Pioneer's Progress*, 243; and R. S. Bourne, MS. Pocket Diary, Dec. 18, 1916, Bourne Papers. Places where the *New Republic* denied Germany's war guilt are *NR*, 11/14/14, 25-6; 12/12/14, 6-7; 1/23/15, 7-8; 7/24/15, 297-8; 8/7/15, 10-11. See ibid. 12/19/14, 6; 11/27/15, 86-7; 10/14/16, 273-4, for the magazine's unusual skepticism on German atrocities in Belgium, and *Literary Digest*, L (Jan. 23, 1915) , 133, for that magazine's evaluation of the *New Republic*'s neutrality. Willard Straight's caution about dealing gently with the British was in a letter to Croly, March 3, 1915, Straight Papers, and the revealing remarks on the dangers of a German victory and on an Anglo-American "community of interest" were in *NR*, 3/20/15, 163-4; 4/3/15, 219-20. For the organization of the League to Enforce Peace, see Henry F. Pringle, *Life and Times of William Howard Taft* (Farrar & Rinehart, 1939) , II, 928; and John A. Garraty, *Henry Cabot Lodge* (Knopf, 1953) , 343-5; and for the magazine's reaction, see *NR*, 3/20/15, 167-9; 6/26/15, 190-91.

3. A New Kind of War. Walter Lippmann's reaction to the sinking of the *Lusitania* is related in Hutchins Hapgood, *Victorian in the Modern World* (Harcourt, Brace, 1939) , 402-3, while the magazine's pre-crisis fulminations can be found in *NR*, 4/3/15, 216; 5/8/15, 1. The magazine's policy of "differential neutrality" can be followed in ibid. 5/22/15, 54-5; 7/3/15, 212-13; 7/10/15, 238-9; 8/28/15, 82-3, but see especially "Not Our War," ibid. 6/5/15, 108-10. For the policies of the Wilson administration, see Arthur S. Link, *Woodrow Wilson and the Progressive Era, 1910-1917* (Harper, 1954) , 197-222. For Willard Straight's connection with the "Plattsburg Idea," see p. 478 of Croly's biography of him, and for the magazine's disapproval of the camp, see *NR*, 10/9/15, 247-9; 7/17/15, 267. Sir Norman Angell describes his mission to America in 1915 with admirable candor in his autobiography, *After All*, 201-14. The important articles outlining his ideas are Norman Angell, "A New Kind of War," *NR*, 7/31/15, 327-9; and the editors' "The Next Step," ibid. 322-3. The second guessing by George F. Kennan that so strongly resembles *New Republic* policy of the time can be found in his *American Diplomacy* (Mentor, 1952) , 56-73.

4. A Mothlike Gyration. Croly's private reflections on the leadership of Roosevelt and Wilson can be found in his letter of Jan. 21, 1916, in the Hand Papers. The editors' startling admission about the inconsequence of a German victory occurs in *NR*, 9/11/15, 141-2, while the attacks on them can be found in Ralph Barton Perry to *NR*, 12/18/15; and Boston *Evening Transcript*, Nov. 23,

1915. Willard Straight's continuing cordiality with Theodore Roosevelt, his efforts to bring about a rapprochement between the editors and the leader, and Roosevelt's reactions are all revealed in E. E. Morison (ed.), *Letters of Theodore Roosevelt*, VIII, 964, 999-1000, 1004-5, 1019-21. Morison did not print, however, Roosevelt's vehement attack on his former supporters, which can be found in Theodore Roosevelt to Dan Wister, Sept. 28, 1916, Roosevelt Papers.

5. **Defense and the New Liberalism.** The *New Republic's* call for limited war early in 1916 is best expressed in "Aggressive Pacifism," *NR*, 1/22/16, while the Wilson administration's rather parallel militant policies can be followed in A. S. Link, *Woodrow Wilson and the Progressive Era*, 168-9, 197-206, 215-17. Croly's call for a "serious moral adventure," which struck a more warlike note than was customary yet even for the *New Republic*, appeared as "The Effect on American Institutions of a Powerful Military and Naval Establishment," *Annals of the American Academy of Political and Social Science*, LXVI (July 1916), 157-72. Randolph Bourne's important article on the war and pragmatism appeared unsigned (identified in his pocket diary) as "Mental Unpreparedness," *NR*, 9/11/15, 143-4. Other direct expressions of the same relationship can be found in ibid. 12/26/14, 6-7; 8/7/15, 11; and 9/18/15, 171-2. Randolph Bourne's difficulties with the *New Republic* are revealed in his letters to Elizabeth Shepley Sergeant, Nov. 15, 1915, Aug. 16, Sept. 20, Dec. 6, 21, 1916, Bourne Papers. For the founding of the *Seven Arts*, see Louis Untermeyer, *From Another World* (Harcourt, Brace, 1939), 80-87.

6. **Liberals and a Leader.** The opinion expressed as to the editors' early private support of Hughes in the campaign of 1916 is based on a comment by Justice Felix Frankfurter on an earlier draft of this book. The *New Republic's* columns for this period are, of course, filled with iterations and reiterations of the editors' dissatisfaction with Wilson, but for the three main points of their criticism, see *NR*, 5/13/16, 28-9; 5/13/16, 25; 12/18/15, 156-7; 2/19/16, 53. Croly's lack of conviction as to the meaningfulness of the administration's shift to nationalism in its domestic policies is expressed in his "Unregenerate Democracy," *NR*, 2/5/16, 17-19. For the dismay of other reformers about Wilson's leadership early in 1916, see Ray Stannard Baker, *American Chronicle* (Scribner, 1945), 280; Walter Johnson (ed.), *Selected Letters of William Allen White* (Holt, 1947), 167; Charles Seymour (ed.), *Intimate Papers of Colonel House* (Houghton Mifflin, 1926), II, 338-47. For Wilson's reading of the *New Republic's* "Appeal to the President," *NR*, 4/22/16, 303-4, see Ray Stannard Baker, *Woodrow Wilson, Life and Letters* (Doubleday, Doran, 1935-1939), VI, 203 n. The same source, VI, 222-3, reveals that the *New Republic's* praise of Wilson's stand on the League found its way to the President. For the editors' misconstructions of Wilson's meaning, compare "Mr. Wilson's Great Utterance," *NR*, 6/3/16, 102-4, and Albert Shaw (ed.), *Messages and Papers of Woodrow Wilson* (Review of Reviews, 1924), I, 271-5. Norman Hapgood's drive to rally former Progressives to Wilson and its results are revealed in Preston William Slosson, *Great Crusade and After* (Macmillan, 1930), 369; Frederic C. Howe to W. Wilson, June 9, 1916, Norman Hapgood to W. Wilson, June 28, 29, Aug.

3, 28, 1916, Wilson to N. Hapgood, Aug. 5, 1916, Wilson Papers; New York *Times*, Oct. 14, 15, 20, 1916. The maneuvers of Hapgood, Harold Laski, Lippmann, and Wilson to bring the *New Republic* over to the President's side in the campaign can be followed in W. Wilson to Newton D. Baker, Aug. 7, 1916; N. Hapgood to W. Wilson, Aug. 10, 28, 1916; and W. Wilson to N. Hapgood, Aug. 12, 1916, Wilson Papers. For Lippmann's and Weyl's roles in the Wilson campaign, see W. Wilson to N. Hapgood, Sept. 27, 1916, W. Wilson to W. Lippmann, Sept. 29, 1916, Wilson Papers; New York *Times*, Oct. 16, 1916; N. Hapgood to E. M. House, Oct. 17, 1916, House Papers. The great variety of sentiments that inspired the *New Republic* supporters of Wilson can be traced in Walter Weyl, *American World Policies* (Macmillan, 1917), *passim*; H. Stearns, *Street I Know*, 81-2, 137; R. S. Bourne, MS. Pocket Diary, Sept. 2, 1916; Nov. 7, 1916; L. Filler, *Randolph Bourne*, 92-102; R. M. Lovett, *All Our Years*, 172; M. DeW. Howe (ed.), *Holmes-Laski Letters*, I, 32; John Dewey, "The Hughes Campaign," *NR*, 10/28/16, 319-21; Archibald MacLeish (ed.), *Law and Politics: Occasional Papers of Felix Frankfurter, 1913-1938* (Harcourt, Brace, 1939), xxi-xxii; Ralph Barton Perry, "On Changing One's Mind," *NR*, 11/4/16, 9-11; A. Johnson, *Pioneer's Progress*, 245; while the sentiments of the dissenters appear in Henry L. Stimson, "Why I Shall Vote for Hughes," *NR*, 10/28/16, 317-19; and "A Letter from Mr. Straight," ibid. 313.

7. "Peace Without Victory." For the parallelism of Wilson's thinking with that of the *New Republic* editors late in 1916, see A. S. Link, *Woodrow Wilson and the Progressive Era*, 352-61. Link argues that the draft note to the powers discussed here represented Wilson's "most secret thoughts on the war and America's relation to it." The draft itself is reprinted in R. S. Baker, *Woodrow Wilson*, VI, 381-5, where Baker also discusses the President's scrutiny of the magazine's "Moving Toward Peace," *NR*, 11/25/16, 81-3. The reactions of the *New Republic* men to Wilson's first peace moves can be found in M. DeW. Howe (ed.), *Holmes-Laski Letters*, I, 44-5; *NR*, 12/30/16, 228-31, 231-2; H. Croly to E. M. House, Dec. 26, 1916, House Papers. The editors' close relationship to Colonel House and Villard's and Lippmann's comments thereon can be found in E. M. House, MS. Diary, Jan. 15, 22, 30, Feb. 5, 27, March 9, 26, 1917; O. G. Villard, *Fighting Years*, 261; W. Lippmann, "Notes for a Biography," *NR*, 7/16/30, 251-2; and W. Lippmann, *U. S. Foreign Policy: Shield of the Republic* (Little, Brown, 1943), 33-4. Further evidence of the magazine's reputation as an administration organ can be found in N. Angell, *After All*, 203-4; *Nation*, CIII (May 28, 1930), 613; Frederick L. Paxson, *American Democracy and the World War* (Houghton Mifflin, 1936), I, 189. Other discussions of the source of Wilson's "peace without victory" can be found in R. S. Baker, *Woodrow Wilson*, VI, 425, and A. S. Link, *Woodrow Wilson and the Progressive Era*, 264-5, while Wilson's expression of gratitude is in W. Wilson to H. Croly, Jan. 25, 1917, Wilson Papers. The lyric response of Croly and Lippmann to Wilson's "Peace Without Victory" speech is fully revealed in E. M. House to W. Wilson, H. Croly to W. Wilson, Jan. 23, 1917, W. Wilson to H. Croly, Jan. 25, 1917, Wilson Papers; and "America Speaks," *NR*, 1/27/17, 340-42. The actual tenor of Wilson's address and the *New Republic*'s interpretations thereof can be compared in A. Shaw (ed.), *Messages and Papers of Woodrow Wilson*, I, 348-56; "The Opposition Gathers," *NR*, 1/13/17, 283-5; and "The Power of the Pen," ibid. 1/20/17, 313-15. Though Edward H. Buehrig's *Woodrow Wilson and the Balance of Power* (Indiana, 1955), is about many of the themes mentioned here, it is not very helpful in defining Wilson's actual position. For Wilson's dread of war and distrust of the British at this time, see A. S. Link, *Wilson the Diplomatist: A Look at His Major Foreign Policies* (Johns Hopkins, 1957), 67-9.

CHAPTER EIGHT

THE NEW LIBERALISM FOUND WANTING, 1917-1925

1. **A Liberal War.** Wilson's actions on the brink of war can best be followed in A. S. Link, *Wilson the Diplomatist* (Johns Hopkins, 1957), 80-90. The editors' boastful editorial on the intellectuals and the war was "Who Willed American Participation?" *NR*, 4/14/17, 308-10. Floyd Dell's remark is quoted in Granville Hicks, *John Reed: The Making of a Revolutionary* (Macmillan, 1937), 231. The editors' campaign through Norman Angell and others to promote American intervention in the interests of power politics can be traced in Norman Angell, *After All* (Farrar, Straus & Young, 1951), 217-20; Edward M. House, MS. Diary, March 9, 1917; W. Lippmann to E. M. House, March 10, 1917, House Papers; W. Lippmann to W. Wilson, March 11, 1917, Wilson Papers.

2. **War and Nationalism.** Paul Rosenfeld's remarks on the dearth of *New Republics* in training camps and Oswald Garrison Villard's on their prevalence in wartime Washington can be found in P. Rosenfeld to Randolph S. Bourne, July 7, 1918, Bourne Papers; and O. G. Villard, *Fighting Years: Memoirs of a Liberal Editor* (Harcourt, Brace, 1939), 361. Walter Weyl's wartime activities can be followed in his MS. Diary, which he began to keep regularly again in 1917, perhaps because he was no longer following the hectic routines of weekly journalism. Lippmann's war work can be followed in New York *Times*, May 30, Aug. 11, 1917, Nov. 1, 1918; Frank Freidel, *Franklin D. Roosevelt* (Little, Brown, 1952), I, 328-9; Joseph Dorfman, *Thorstein Veblen and His America* (Viking, 1935), 373-4; Charles Seymour (ed.), *Intimate Papers of Colonel House* (Houghton Mifflin, 1926), III, 170; Ray Stannard Baker, *Woodrow Wilson: Life and Letters* (Doubleday, Doran, 1935-39), VII, 275; James R. Mock and Cedric Larson, *Words That Won the War* (Princeton, 1939), 165, 245, 258-9. For the attitudes of Roosevelt and Laski toward the *New Republic* at war, see Elting E. Morison (ed.), *Letters of Theodore Roosevelt* (Harvard, 1951-54), VIII, 1156-7, 1198; Donald R. Richberg, *My Hero: The Indiscreet Memoirs of an Eventful but Unheroic Life* (Putnam, 1954), 94; Mark DeWolfe Howe (ed.), *Holmes-Laski Letters* (Harvard, 1953), I, 43. The reactions of Hackett, Bourne, and Stearns to the magazine's war policies are evident in Robert Morss Lovett, *All Our Years* (Viking, 1948), 172; Francis Hackett, *I Chose Denmark* (Doubleday, Doran, 1940), 12-13, 19-22, 168-9; Louis Filler, *Randolph Bourne* (American Council on Public Affairs, 1943), 98, 104-6, 111; Harold Stearns, *Street I*

Know (Furman, 1935), 143, 162. For the stir raised by Bourne's blast at the *New Republic*, see Jane Addams to R. S. Bourne, June 13, 1917, Prestonia Mann Martin to R. S. Bourne, June 11, 1917, and Herbert Elsworth Cory to R. S. Bourne, June 9, 1917, Bourne Papers. The reactions of Angell, Croly, and Straight to America's war hysteria can be found in N. Angell, *After All*, 200; R. S. Baker, *Woodrow Wilson*, VII, 318; and Herbert Croly, *Willard Straight* (Macmillan, 1924), 481. The wartime attacks on Weyl are evident from his diary and a clipping file he kept, while Norman Angell's experience and the surveillance of the *New Republic* are related in N. Angell, *After All*, 204-5; J. R. Mock and C. Larson, *Words That Won the War*, 88-9; and W. Lippmann, "Notes for a Biography," *NR*, 7/16/30, 251-2. The account of Randolph Bourne during the war is derived from R. M. Lovett, *All Our Years*, 151; Floyd Dell, *Homecoming: An Autobiography* (Farrar & Rinehart, 1933), 310-13; R. S. Bourne to Everett Benjamin, Nov. 26, 1917, to his mother, Nov. 4, 1918, to Van Wyck Brooks, March 27, 1918, Bourne Papers; Louis Untermeyer, *From Another World* (Harcourt, Brace, 1939), 95-6. Evidence for the continued closeness of the *New Republic* to the Wilson administration can be found in Weyl's MS. Diary, Sept. 3, Oct. 5, 10, 1917; M. DeW. Howe (ed.), *Holmes-Laski Letters*, I, 97-8; Ray Stannard Baker, *American Chronicle* (Scribner, 1945), 305; R. S. Baker, *Woodrow Wilson*, VII, 527, 546; William Allen White, *Autobiography* (Macmillan, 1946), 540; and C. Seymour (ed.), *Intimate Papers of Colonel House*, IV, 152-3. The attitudes of Weyl, Straight, and Lippmann at the end of the war are taken from W. Weyl, MS. Diary, July 28, Aug. 10, 1918; H. Croly, *Willard Straight*, 525-6; and C. Seymour (ed.), *Intimate Papers of Colonel House*, IV, 188-90.

3. Apocalypse in Peace. The remarkable account of Woodrow Wilson's views at the end of the war is drawn from Richard Hofstadter, *American Political Tradition and the Men Who Made It* (Knopf, 1949), 273-4. The cooling of relations between the *New Republic* men and the Wilson administration as peacemaking got under way can be traced in numerous entries in Weyl's MS. Diary, as well as in M. DeW. Howe (ed.), *Holmes-Laski Letters*, I, 132-3, 184; H. Croly, *Willard Straight*, 535; W. Lippmann, "Notes for a Biography," *NR*, 7/16/30, 252; R. S. Baker, *American Chronicle*, 391. Croly's despairing views on the Versailles conference appear in his "The Obstacle to Peace," *NR*, 4/26/19, 406. For a picture of the editors at the moment they decided to turn against Wilson and the Versailles Treaty, see R. M. Lovett, *All Our Years*, 172. Lovett's account disagrees markedly with Lippmann's in "Notes for a Biography," *NR*, 7/16/30, 252, wherein Lippmann claims to have followed Croly very reluctantly in opposing the League, but for Lippmann's attitudes at the time, see R. S. Baker, *American Chronicle*, 440; and W. Lippmann, "The Peace Conference," *Yale Review*, VIII (July 1919), 710-21.

4. The Dead and the Disillusioned. Lippmann's change of heart about the Versailles Treaty is recounted in his "Notes for a Biography," *NR*, 7/16/30, 252, while the *Nation* and *New Republic* circulation figures are drawn from N. W. Ayer and Sons, *Newspaper Annual and Directory* (1918-21). For Straight's feelings at the time of his death, see H. Croly, *Willard Straight*, 533-46. While my personal sympathies tend to be very much with Randolph Bourne's position during World War I, I have found, in his correspondence and elsewhere, little to justify, and much to contradict, the legend of his wartime martyrdom. For his income and publications in the last year of his life, see R. S. Bourne, MS. Pocket Diary. For comparison with Bourne's "The State," consult H. Croly, "The Future of the State," *NR*, 9/15/17, 179-83; and H. Croly, "The Counsel of Humility," ibid. 12/13/17, 173-6. For Harold Stearns's activities after the war, see his *Street I Know*, 170-89; and his *Liberalism in America: Its Origin, Its Temporary Collapse, Its Future* (Boni & Liveright, 1919), *passim*. The postwar dispersal of the *New Republic* group can be traced in F. Hackett, *I Chose Denmark*, 38; H. Stearns, *Street I Know*, 253-4; *NR*, 8/30/22, 27; A. Johnson, *Pioneer's Progress*, 268-81. A fuller, documented account of Walter Weyl's views after the war can be found in my "Walter Weyl and the Class War," Harvey Goldberg (ed.), *American Radicals: Some Problems and Personalities* (Monthly Review Press, 1957), 265-76. Weyl's essay, "Tired Radicals," that led to controversy with Lippmann was printed as the title piece of a collection of his essays, W. Weyl, *Tired Radicals and Other Papers* (Huebsch, 1921). Walter Lippmann's postwar views can be traced in W. Lippmann, "The Peace Conference," *Yale Review*, VIII (July 1919), 710-21; W. Lippmann, "The Basic Problem of Democracy," *Atlantic Monthly*, CXXIV (Nov. 1919), 625; W. Lippmann, *Public Opinion* (Macmillan, 1922), *passim*; W. Lippmann, *Men of Destiny* (Macmillan, 1927), *passim*; W. Lippmann, *Preface to Morals* (Macmillan, 1929), *passim*; and W. Lippmann, *An Inquiry into the Principles of the Good Society* (Little, Brown, 1937), *passim*. Croly's views on Lippmann's *Preface to Morals* can be found in H. Croly to L. Hand, Jan. 27, 1930, Hand Papers. For the *New Republic*, the *Nation*, and the *Freeman* in the postwar years, see William H. Attwood, "Pathfinders of American Liberalism" (unpublished bachelor's thesis, Princeton University, 1941), 102; H. Stearns, *Street I Know*, 191; Carl Van Doren, *Three Worlds* (Harper, 1936), 136-9; O. G. Villard, *Fighting Years*, 348-51. Material on the *New Republic*'s role in the presidential boom for Herbert Hoover in 1920 can be found in Walter W. Liggett, *Rise of Herbert Hoover* (Fly, 1932), 295-310; W. Lippmann, "Notes for a Biography," *NR*, 7/16/30, 252; R. S. Baker, *American Chronicle*, 476; R. M. Lovett, *All Our Years*, 176-7; and H. Croly, "The Eclipse of Progressivism," *NR*, 10/27/20, 210-11. Numerous entries in W. Weyl, MS. Diary, relate to the *New Republic*'s role in the postwar "red scare" and its attitude toward Soviet Russia, but see also Lippmann's biographical article cited immediately above; W. H. Attwood, "Pathfinders of American Liberalism," 92; and R. M. Lovett, *All Our Years*, 176. For the postwar thoughts of the cultural nationalists of the "little renaissance," see Van Wyck Brooks, *Ordeal of Mark Twain* (Dutton, 1920, Meridian, 1955), 54-5, 70-71, 83, 132, 145; H. Stearns, *Liberalism in America*, 228-32; and Brom Weber (ed.), *Letters of Hart Crane, 1916-1932* (Hermitage, 1952), 58-9. Croly's postwar views can be traced in his major *New Republic* editorials, the most useful of which are his "The Eclipse of Progressivism," *NR*, 10/27/20, 210-11; "Liberalism vs. War," ibid. 12/8/20, 37-8; "Surely Good Americanism," ibid. 11/15/22, 294-6; "American Withdrawal from Europe," ibid. 9/12/23, 65-6; "Why I Shall Vote for La Follette," ibid. 10/27/24, 222-4; and "The Progressive Voter, He Wants to Know," ibid. 7/25/28, 242. The last two articles listed give his positions in the campaigns of 1924 and 1928, but see also R. M. Lovett, *All Our Years*, 181-3, and numerous letters to Eduard R. Lindeman during the period, Lindeman Papers. One chapter of the book in which Croly tried to reformulate his liberalism after the war was published as "Regeneration," *NR*, 6/9/20, 40-47, with a note indicating publication of the book "early in the fall by the Macmillan Company." Croly, himself, however, withdrew the book from publication, as indicated in a letter he wrote to Learned Hand, Jan. 27, 1930, Hand Papers, and by Justice Felix Frankfurter in my interview with him, Dec. 29, 1955. The galley proofs of the book, which was to be entitled "The Breach in Civilization," have been deposited in the Harvard College Library. Croly's religious experiments during the 'twenties are revealed in his correspondence with Eduard Lindeman mentioned above, as well as in such of his articles as "Behaviorism in Religion," *NR*, 2/22/22, 367-70; "Reconstruction of Religion," ibid. 6/21/22, 100-102; and "Nationalism and Christianity," ibid. 2/28/23, 9-11. For descriptions of the cult of Gustave Gurdjieff, see R. M. Lovett, *All Our Years*, 192; Margaret Anderson, *Fiery Fountains* (Hermitage, 1951), 103-62; Malcolm Cowley, *Exile's Return: A Literary Odyssey of the 1920's* (Viking, 1934), 61; Waldo Frank, *Rediscovery of America and Chart for Rough Waters* (Duell, Sloan & Pearce, 1929, 1940), 300; and T. S. Matthews, *Name and Address* (Simon & Schuster, 1960), 65, 204-7, 305.

5. **The Future of Liberalism.** This section of conclusions, based as it is upon all of the above, was written without documentation.

INDEX